RESEARCH DESIGN
in the
SOCIAL SCIENCES

DECLARATION, DIAGNOSIS, AND REDESIGN

Graeme Blair
Alexander Coppock
Macartan Humphreys

Princeton University Press
Princeton and Oxford

Copyright © 2023 by Princeton University Press

Princeton University Press is committed to the protection of copyright and the intellectual property our authors entrust to us. Copyright promotes the progress and integrity of knowledge. Thank you for supporting free speech and the global exchange of ideas by purchasing an authorized edition of this book. If you wish to reproduce or distribute any part of it in any form, please obtain permission.

Requests for permission to reproduce material from this work should be sent to permissions@press.princeton.edu

Published by Princeton University Press
41 William Street, Princeton, New Jersey 08540
99 Banbury Road, Oxford OX2 6JX

press.princeton.edu

All Rights Reserved

ISBN 9780691199566
ISBN (pbk.) 9780691199573
ISBN (e-book) 9780691199580

British Library Cataloging-in-Publication Data is available

Editorial: Bridget Flannery-McCoy and Alena Chekanov
Production Editorial: Mark Bellis
Cover Design: Wanda España
Production: Erin Suydam
Publicity: William Pagdatoon
Copyeditor: Bhisham Bherwani

Cover Credit: Burin Suporntawesuk / Alamy Stock Vector

This book has been composed in Minion Pro and Gotham

Printed on acid-free paper. ∞

Printed in the United States of America

10 9 8 7 6 5 4 3 2 1

RESEARCH DESIGN
in the
SOCIAL SCIENCES

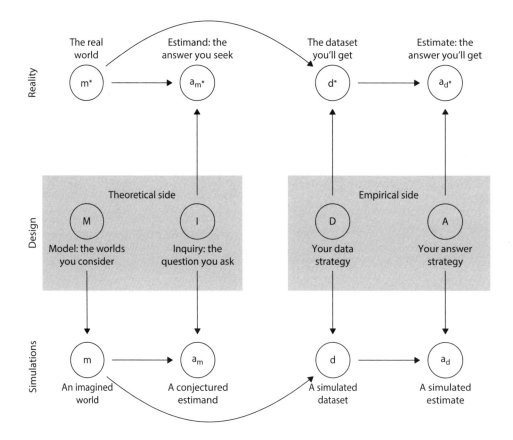

Contents

Acknowledgements xi

I Introduction   1

1 Preamble **3**
    1.1   How to Read This Book 3
    1.2   How to Work This Book 5
    1.3   What This Book Will Not Do 5

2 What Is a Research Design? **6**
    2.1   MIDA: The Four Elements of a Research Design 6
    2.2   Declaration, Diagnosis, Redesign 14
    2.3   Example: A Decision Problem 17
    2.4   Putting Designs to Use 22

3 Research Design Principles **24**

4 Getting Started **28**
    4.1   Installing R 28
    4.2   Declaration 29
    4.3   Diagnosis 30
    4.4   Redesign 31

v

	4.5	Library of Designs	32
	4.6	Long-Term Code Usability..	32

II Declaration, Diagnosis, Redesign 33

5 Declaring Designs 35
5.1	Definition of Research Designs..	35
5.2	Declaration in Code	38

6 Specifying the Model 41
6.1	Elements of Models...	42
6.2	Types of Variables in Models	46
6.3	How to Specify Models..	48
6.4	Summary...	51

7 Defining the Inquiry 52
7.1	Elements of Inquiries	53
7.2	Types of Inquiries	58
7.3	How to Define Inquiries..	61
7.4	Summary...	64

8 Crafting a Data Strategy 65
8.1	Elements of Data Strategies	67
8.2	Challenges to Data Strategies	87
8.3	Summary...	91

9 Choosing an Answer Strategy.................................... 92
9.1	Elements of Answer Strategies...	92
9.2	Types of Answer Strategies...	97
9.3	How to Choose an Answer Strategy	107
9.4	Summary...	115

10 Diagnosing Designs 116

- 10.1 Elements of Diagnoses 118
- 10.2 Types of Diagnosands 122
- 10.3 Estimation of Diagnosands 124
- 10.4 How to Diagnose Designs 131
- 10.5 Summary 136

11 Redesigning 137

- 11.1 Redesigning over Data Strategies 137
- 11.2 Redesigning over Answer Strategies 143
- 11.3 Summary 146

12 Design Example 148

- 12.1 Declaration in Words 148
- 12.2 Declaration in Code 149
- 12.3 Diagnosis 151
- 12.4 Redesign 152

13 Designing in Code 154

- 13.1 Model 154
- 13.2 Inquiry 164
- 13.3 Data Strategy 166
- 13.4 Answer Strategy 169
- 13.5 Declaration 173
- 13.6 Diagnosis 175
- 13.7 Redesign 179

III Research Design Library — 181

14 Research Design Library 183

15 Observational : Descriptive ... 185
- 15.1 Simple Random Sampling ... 185
- 15.2 Cluster Random Sampling ... 190
- 15.3 Multilevel Regression and Poststratification ... 193
- 15.4 Index Creation ... 198

16 Observational : Causal ... 203
- 16.1 Process Tracing ... 203
- 16.2 Selection-on-Observables ... 208
- 16.3 Difference-in-Differences ... 211
- 16.4 Instrumental Variables ... 216
- 16.5 Regression Discontinuity Designs ... 221

17 Experimental : Descriptive ... 227
- 17.1 Audit Experiments ... 228
- 17.2 List Experiments ... 232
- 17.3 Conjoint Experiments ... 236
- 17.4 Behavioral Games ... 242

18 Experimental : Causal ... 249
- 18.1 Two-Arm Randomized Experiments ... 250
- 18.2 Block-Randomized Experiments ... 257
- 18.3 Cluster-Randomized Experiments ... 260
- 18.4 Subgroup Designs ... 263
- 18.5 Factorial Experiments ... 266
- 18.6 Encouragement Designs ... 271
- 18.7 Placebo-Controlled Experiments ... 279
- 18.8 Stepped-Wedge Experiments ... 283
- 18.9 Randomized Saturation Experiments ... 288
- 18.10 Experiments over Networks ... 292

19 Complex Designs 299

- 19.1 Discovery Using Causal Forests 299
- 19.2 Structural Estimation 305
- 19.3 Meta-analysis 310
- 19.4 Multi-site Studies 313

IV Research Design Lifecycle 319

20 Research Design Lifecycle 321

21 Planning 322

- 21.1 Ethics 322
- 21.2 Partners 326
- 21.3 Funding 329
- 21.4 Piloting 330
- 21.5 Criticism 333
- 21.6 Preanalysis Plan 334

22 Realization 338

- 22.1 Pivoting 338
- 22.2 Populated Preanalysis Plan 340
- 22.3 Reconciliation 341
- 22.4 Writing 344

23 Integration 347

- 23.1 Communicating 348
- 23.2 Archiving 349
- 23.3 Reanalysis 351
- 23.4 Replication 356
- 23.5 Meta-analysis 358

V Epilogue　　361

24　Epilogue **363**

VI References　　365

Bibliography 367
Index 377

Acknowledgements

We are grateful to have worked with Jasper Cooper for six years on the ideas and tools introduced in this book. His words, ideas, and voice echo throughout the entire project.

Each of us inflicted early versions of `DeclareDesign` and our ideas about research design on our students and colleagues at UCLA, Yale, Columbia, and WZB Berlin, and at many summer schools and workshops. We thank our students for their patience and feedback on the tools and approach, which deeply shaped what you find in this book.

We held a book conference over Zoom and are grateful for the incisive feedback of Dorothy Bishop, Don Green, Nahomi Ichino, Kosuke Imai, Gary King, Andy Gelman, Felix Elwert, Molly Roberts, Cyrus Samii, and Rocio Titiunik. For feedback at our EGAP feedback session on Part I and Part IV, we thank Adam Berinsky, Jake Bowers, David Broockman, Cesi Cruz, Ryan Enos, Alex Hartman, Morgan Holmes, Ryan Moore, Pia Raffler, Dan Rubenson, and Rebecca Wolfe. We thank Abigail Pena-Alejos for her wonderful work constructing the index, Elayne Stecher for work on design examples, Phoenix Dalto for checking code in the book, and Cristian-Liviu Nicolescu and Santiago Sordo Ruz for wonderful last lap support. We also thank the three anonymous reviewers of the manuscript for generous and helpful feedback.

A core part of the `DeclareDesign` project is its software implementation in R. We were lucky to work with a big group of talented graduate students and programmers on nearly every aspect of it. We are grateful to Neal Fultz who moved the software from prototype to professional software product and who made many big contributions to how the tools work now. Luke Sonnet is responsible for the speed and technical workings of estimatr; Aaron Rudkin for many ideas in fabricatr; Clara Bicalho, Markus Konrad, and Sisi Huang for `DeclareDesignWizard`; and Clara Bicalho and Lily Medina for `DesignLibrary`.

We are grateful to the many people who have intensively used the software in its early versions for their generous feedback, Tom Leavitt, Daniel Rubenson, Vartika

Savarna, Tara Slough, Georgiy Syunyaev, Anna Wilke, and Linan Yao. Special thanks also to Dorothy Bishop, Jake Bowers, and Erin Hartman for so many thoughts and suggestions.

We are grateful to the Laura and John Arnold Foundation, and especially Stuart Buck, for seeing the virtues of our approach and providing early funding of the project. We also thank EGAP for seed funding that got us started. We thank Lynn Vavreck for offering Alex a Hoffenberg Visiting Fellowship at UCLA to work on the software and an early version of the manuscript.

We thank Bridget Flannery-McCoy for shepherding this book to fruition and for her willingness to engage with us about offering a free online version of the book. We are also grateful to Eric Crahan for our early conversations about the idea for the book and to Alena Chekanov for guidance in the production phase.

Finally, Graeme and Alex thank Alex's spouse Penelope Van Grinsven for warmly putting up with us for a semester in Los Angeles and a year in New Haven and for many coworking sessions in the pottery studio.

PART I

Introduction

CHAPTER 1

Preamble

This book introduces a new way of thinking about research designs in the social sciences. Our hope is that this approach will make it easier to develop and to share strong research designs.

At the heart of our approach is the *MIDA* framework, in which a research design is characterized by four elements: a model, an inquiry, a data strategy, and an answer strategy. We have to understand each of the four on their own and also how they interrelate. The design encodes your beliefs about the world, it describes your questions, and it lays out how you go about answering those questions, in terms of both what data you collect and how you analyze it. In strong designs, choices made in the model and inquiry are reflected in the data and answer strategies, and vice versa.

We think of designs as objects that can be interrogated. Each of the four design elements can be "declared" in computer code and—if done right—the information provided is enough to "diagnose" the quality of the design through computer simulation. Researchers can then select the best design for their purposes by "redesigning" over alternative, feasible designs.

This way of thinking pays dividends at multiple points in the research design lifecycle: planning the design, implementing it, and integrating the results into the broader research literature. The declaration, diagnosis, and redesign process informs choices made from the beginning to the end of a research project.

1.1 How to Read This Book

We had multiple audiences in mind when writing this book. First, we were thinking of people looking for a high-level introduction to these ideas. If we only had 30 minutes with a person to try and communicate the core ideas, we would give them Part I. We were thinking of people who are new to the practice of research design and who are embarking on their first empirical projects. The *MIDA* framework introduced in Part I accommodates many different empirical approaches: qualitative and quantitative, descriptive and causal, observational and experimental. Beginners starting out in any of these traditions can use our framework to consider how the design elements in those approaches fit together. We were also thinking of researchers-in-training: graduate students in seminar courses where the main purpose is to read papers and discuss the credibility of research findings. Such discussions can sometimes feel like a laundry list of complaints, but we hope our framework can focus attention on the most relevant issues. What, exactly, is the inquiry? Is it the right one to be posing? Are the data and answer strategies suited to the inquiry? We were also thinking of funders and decision-makers, who often wish to assess research in terms not of its results but of its design. Our approach provides a way of defining the design and diagnosing its quality.

Part II is more involved. We provide the formal foundations of the *MIDA* framework. We walk through each component of a research design in detail, describe the finer points of design diagnosis, and explain how to carry out a "redesign." We hope Part II will resonate with several audiences of applied researchers both inside and outside of academia. We imagine it could be assigned early in a graduate course on research design in any of the social sciences. We hope data scientists and monitoring and evaluation professionals will find value in our framework for learning about research designs. Scholars will find value in declaring, diagnosing, and redesigning designs whether they are implementing randomized trials or multi-method archival studies, or calibrating structural theories with data.

In Part III, we apply the general framework to specific research designs. The result is a library of common designs. Many empirical research designs are included in the library, but not all. The set of entries covers a large portion of what we see in current empirical practice across social sciences, but it is not meant to be exhaustive.

We are thinking of three kinds of uses for entries in the design library. Collectively, the design entries serve to illustrate the fundamental principles of design. The entries clarify the variety of ways in which models, inquiries, data strategies, and answer strategies can be connected and show how high-level principles operate in common ways across very different designs. The second use is pedagogical. The library entries provide hands-on illustrations of designs in action. A researcher interested in understanding the "regression discontinuity design," for example, can quickly see a complete implementation and learn under what conditions the standard design performs well or poorly. They can also compare the suitability of one type of design against another for a given problem. We emphasize that these descriptions of different designs provide entry points but they are not exhaustive, so we refer readers to recent methodological treatments of the different topics. The third use is as a starter kit to help readers get going on designs of their own. Each entry includes code for a basic design that can be fine-tuned to capture the specificities of particular research settings.

The last section of the book describes how our framework can help at different stages of the research process. Each of these sections should be readable for anyone who has read Part I. The entry on preanalysis plans, for example, can be assigned in an experiments course as guidance for students filing their first preanalysis plan. The entry on research ethics could be discussed among coauthors at the start of a project. The entry on writing a research paper could be assigned to college seniors writing their first original research papers.

1.2 How to Work This Book

We will often describe research designs not just in words, but in computer code. If you want to work through the code and exercises, fantastic. This path requires investment in R, the `tidyverse`, and the `DeclareDesign` software package. Chapter 4 helps get you started. We think working through the code is very rewarding, but we understand that there is a learning curve. You could tackle the declaration, diagnosis, and redesign processes using any computer language you like,[1] but it is easier in `DeclareDesign` because the software guides you to articulate each of the four design elements.

If you want nothing to do with the code, you can skip it and just focus on the text. We have written the book so that understanding of the code is not required in order to understand research design concepts.

1.3 What This Book Will Not Do

This is a research design book, not a statistics textbook, or a cookbook with recipes applicable to all situations. We will not derive estimators, we will provide no guarantees of the general optimality of designs, and we will present no mathematical proofs. Nor will we provide all the answers to all the practical questions you might have about your design.

What we do offer is a language to express research designs. We can help you learn that language so you can describe your own design in it. When you can declare your design in this language, then you can diagnose it, figure out if it works the way you think it should, and then improve it through redesign.

---

[1] On our Web site, we provide examples in R, Python, Stata, and Excel.

CHAPTER 2

What Is a Research Design?

At its heart, a research design is a procedure for generating answers to questions. Strong designs yield answers that are close to their targets, but weak designs can produce answers that are misleading, imprecise, or just irrelevant. Assessing whether a design is strong requires having a clear sense of what the question to be answered is and understanding how the empirical information generated or collected by the design will lead to reliable answers. This book offers a language for describing research designs and an algorithm for selecting among them. In other words, it provides a set of tools for characterizing and evaluating the dozens of choices we make in our research activities that together determine the strength of our designs. Throughout, we keep our focus on empirical research designs—designs that seek to answer questions that are answerable with data—and we use the term "research design" as a shorthand for these.

We show that the same basic language can be used to represent research designs whether they target causal or descriptive questions, whether they are focused on theory testing or inductive learning, and whether they use quantitative, qualitative, or a mix of methods. We can select a strong design by applying a simple algorithm: declare-diagnose-redesign. Once a design is declared in simple enough language that a computer can understand it, its properties can be diagnosed through simulation. We can then engage in redesign, or the exploration of a range of neighboring designs. The same language we use to talk to the computer can be used to talk to others. Reviewers, advisers, students, funders, journalists, and the public need to know four basic things to understand a design.

2.1 MIDA: The Four Elements of a Research Design

Research designs share in common that they all have an inquiry I, a data strategy D, and an answer strategy A. Less obviously, perhaps, these three elements presuppose a model M of how the world works. We refer to the four together as *MIDA*.

We think of *MIDA* as having two sides. M and I form the theoretical half, comprising your beliefs about the world and your target of inference. D and A form the

2.1 MIDA: The Four Elements of a Research Design

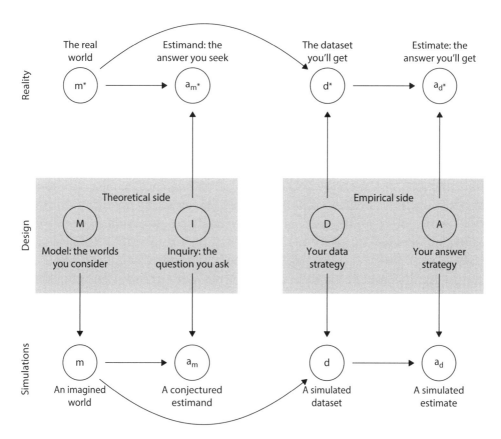

Figure 2.1: The *MIDA* framework. An arrow between two points means that the point at the end of an arrow depends in some way on the one at the start of the arrow. For instance, 'the answer you'll get' depends on the dataset you'll get and the answer strategy you specify.

empirical half, comprising your strategies for collecting and summarizing information. The theoretical side sets the research challenges for you to overcome and the empirical side captures your responses to those challenges.[1]

Figure 2.1 shows how these four elements of a design relate to one another, how they relate to real-world quantities, and how they relate to simulated quantities. We will unpack this figure in the remainder of this chapter, highlighting two especially important parallelisms, first between the upper and lower halves representing actual processes and simulated processes, and second between the left (*M, I*) and right (*D, A*) halves representing the theoretical and empirical sides of research designs.

---

[1] We call *M* and *I* the theoretical half because specifying them requires conceptualizing contexts, imagining processes, and posing questions. We call *D* and *A* the empirical half because they describe the empirical strategies. We recognize of course that the theories on the *MI* side may sometimes be very thin and that strategies on the *DA* side should be theoretically motivated.

2.1.1 Model

The set of models in M comprises speculations about what causes what and how. It includes guesses about how important variables are generated, how they are correlated, and the sequences of events.

The M in *MIDA* does not necessarily represent our beliefs about how the world actually works. Instead, it describes a set of possible worlds in enough detail that we can assess how our design would perform *if* the real world worked like those in M. For this reason we sometimes refer to M as a set of "reference" models. Assessment of the quality of a design is carried out with reference to the models of the world that we provide in M. In other contexts, we might see M described as the "data generating process." We prefer to describe M as the (imagined) "event generating process" to honor the fact that data are produced or gathered via a data strategy— and the resulting data are measurements taken of the events generated by the world.

We are conscious that the term "model" is used in many different ways by researchers and so a little disambiguation is helpful. Our use of the term when discussing M—as a representation of how the world works for the purposes of posing questions and assessing strategies—contrasts with two other usages. First, in some usages, the model is the object of inquiry: our goal in research is to *select* a model of the world that provides a useful representation of the world. We might refer to this as an "inquiry model," to distinguish it from a reference model. We will discuss such approaches and when we do so we will make clear how such models serve a function distinct from M. Second, researchers commonly use "model" to describe a representation of event generating processes used specifically for the purpose of generating estimates. For instance, researchers might use a "a linear probability model" or an "ordered probit model." Such "statistical models" might be justified on the grounds that they reflect beliefs about how the world works, but they might also be used simply because they are helpful in generating answers to questions. We think it clearer to think of these models as part of A. They are part of the *method* used to answer questions given data. We can then assess, for a given research question, whether the answer strategy provides good answers, whether or not the model assumed by the statistical procedure is consistent with M.

2.1.1.1 What's in a model?

The model has two responsibilities. First, the model provides a setting within which a question can be answered. The inquiry I should be answerable *under the model*. If the inquiry is the average difference between two possible outcomes, those two outcomes should be described in the model. Second, the model governs what data can be produced by any given data strategy D. The data that might be produced by a data strategy D should be foreseeable under the model. For example, if the data strategy includes random sampling of units from a population and measurement of an outcome, the model should describe the outcome variable for all units in that population.

These responsibilities in turn determine what needs to be in the model. In general, the model defines a set of units that we wish to study. Often, this set of units is larger than the set of units that we will actually study empirically, but we can nevertheless define this larger set about which we seek to make inferences. The units might be all of the citizens in Lagos, Nigeria, or every police beat in New Delhi. The set may be restricted to the mayors of cities in California or the catchment areas of schools in rural Poland. The model also includes information about characteristics of those units: how many of each kind of unit there are and how features of the units may be correlated.

For descriptive and causal questions alike, we usually imagine *causal* models. Even if questions are fundamentally descriptive, they can be usefully posed in the context of a causal model, because causal models can explain the level of variables and not simply the nature of effects.

Causal models (see, for instance, Pearl and Mackenzie, 2018) include a set of exogenous and endogenous variables as well as functions that describe the values endogenous variables take depending on the values of other variables. If we think of one variable influencing another, we think of the first as a treatment variable that specifies a condition and the second as an outcome variable. Treatments might be delivered naturally by the world or may be assigned by researchers. The values that an outcome variable would take depending on the level of a treatment are called *potential* outcomes. In the simplest case of a binary treatment, the treated potential outcome is what would arise if the unit were treated, the untreated potential outcome if it were not. Both potential outcomes are part of the model.

Summarizing, we can think of three functions of a model that characterize *units*, *conditions*, and *outcomes*: an identification of a population; a conjecture of values of exogenous variables—conditions; and a description of the values of endogenous variables—outcomes—given the values of other variables on which they depend.

2.1.1.2 M as a set

In Figure 2.1, we describe M as the "the worlds you'll consider." The reason for this is that we are uncertain about how the world works. As scientists, we are skeptical of easy assertions about what the right model is and we freely admit we don't know the "true model" of the world. Of course the term 'true model' is an oxymoron of sorts, we use it here to highlight the formal similarity between the models in M and the true processes we care about. When conducting empirical research into the true model, we have to think through how our design would play out under different possible models, including ones we think more likely and those we think less likely. For instance, the correlation between two variables might be large and positive, but it could just as well be zero. We might believe that, conditional on some background variables, a treatment has been *as if* randomly assigned by the world—but we might be wrong about that too. In the figure we use m^* to denote the true model, or the actual, unknown, event generating process. We do not have access to m^*, but our hope is that m^* is sufficiently well represented in M so that we can reasonably imagine what will happen when our design is applied in the real world.

How can we construct a sufficiently varied set of models of the world? For this we can draw on existing data from past studies or on new information gathered from pilot studies. Getting a reasonable characterization of the set of plausible models is a core purpose of theoretical reflection, literature review, meta-analysis, and formative research. If there are important known features about your context it generally makes sense to include them in M.

Examples of models

1. Contact theory: When two members of different groups come into contact under specific conditions, they learn more about each other, which reduces prejudice, which in turn reduces discrimination.

2. Prisoner's dilemma. When facing a collective action problem, each of two people will choose noncooperative actions independent of what the other will do.

3. Health intervention with externalities. When individuals receive deworming medication, school attendance rates increase for them and for their neighbors, leading to improved labor market outcomes in the long run.

2.1.2 Inquiry

The inquiry is a research question stated in terms of the model. For example, the inquiry might be the average causal effect of one variable on another, the descriptive distribution of a third variable, or a prediction about the value of a variable in the future. We refer to "the" inquiry when talking about the main research question, but in practice we may seek to learn about many inquiries in a single research study.

Many people use the word "estimand" to refer to an inquiry, and we do too when casually talking about research. When we are formally describing research designs, however, we distinguish between inquiries and estimands, and Figure 2.1 shows why. The inquiry I is the function that operates on the events generated (or conjectured to be generated) by the real world m^* or a simulated world m. The estimand is the value of that function: a_{m^*} or a_m. In other words, we use "inquiry" to refer to the question and "estimand" to refer to the answer to the question.

As with models, inquiries are also defined with respect to *units*, *conditions*, and *outcomes*: they are summaries of outcomes of units in or across conditions. Inquiries may be causal, as in the sample average treatment effect (SATE). The SATE is the average difference in treated and untreated potential outcomes among units in a sample. Inquiries may also be descriptive, as in a population average of an outcome. While it may seem that descriptive inquiries do not involve conditions, they always do, since the realization of outcomes must take place under a particular set of circumstances, often set by the world and not the researcher.

Figure 2.1 shows that when I is applied to a model m, it produces an answer a^m. This set of relationships forces discipline on both M and I: I needs to be able to return an answer using information available from M and in turn M needs to provide enough information so that I can do its job.

Examples of inquiries

1. What proportion of voters lives with limited exposure to voters from another party in its neighborhood?
2. Does gaining political office make divorce more likely?
3. What types of people will benefit most from a vaccine?

2.1.3 Data strategy

The data strategy is the full set of procedures we use to gather information from the world. The three basic elements of data strategies parallel the three features of inquiries: *units* are selected, *conditions* are assigned, and *outcomes* are measured.

All data strategies require an identification of units. Many involve sampling, gathering data on a subset of units specified by a model or by an inquiry.

Data strategies also involve conditions. Most obviously, experimental interventions are used to produce controlled variation in conditions. If we present some subjects with one piece of information and other subjects with a different piece of information, we've generated variation on the basis of an assignment procedure. Observational approaches often seek to do something similar, selecting units so that natural variation can be exploited. In such cases, units are often selected for study because of the conditions that they are in.

Measurement procedures are the ways in which researchers reduce the complex and multidimensional social world into a parsimonious set of empirical data. These data need not be quantitative data in the sense of being numbers or values on a predefined scale; qualitative data are data too. Measurement is the vexing but necessary reduction of reality to a few choice representations.

Figure 2.1 shows how the data strategy is applied to both the imagined worlds in M and to the real world. When D is applied to the real world (m^*), we obtain the realized dataset d^*. When D is applied to the worlds we imagine in M, we obtain *simulated* datasets, which may or may not be like the dataset d^* we would really get. When our models M more accurately represent the real world, our simulated datasets will look more like the real data we will eventually collect.

> **Examples of data strategies**
>
> *Sampling procedures.*
>
> 1. Random digit dial sampling of 500 voters in the Netherlands
> 2. Respondent-driven sampling of people who are HIV positive, starting from a sample of HIV-positive individuals
> 3. "Mall intercept" convenience sampling of men and women present at the mall on a Saturday
>
> *Treatment assignment procedures.*
>
> 4. Random assignment of free legal assistance intervention for detainees held in pretrial detention
> 5. Nature's assignment of the sex of a child at birth
>
> *Measurement procedures.*
>
> 6. Voting behavior gathered from survey responses
> 7. Administrative data indicating voter registration
> 8. Measurement of stress using cortisol readings

2.1.4 Answer strategy

The answer strategy is what we use to summarize the data produced by the data strategy. Just like the inquiry summarizes a part of the model, the answer strategy summarizes a part of the data. We can't just "let the data speak" because complex, multidimensional datasets don't speak for themselves—they need to be summarized and explained. Answer strategies are the procedures we follow to do so.

Answer strategies are functions that take in data and return answers. For some research designs, this is a literal function like the R function `lm_robust` that implements an ordinary least squares (OLS) regression with robust standard errors. For some research designs, the function is embodied by the researchers themselves when they read documents and summarize their meanings in a case study.

The answer strategy is more than the choice of an estimator. It includes the full set of procedures that begins with cleaning the dataset and ends with answers in words, tables, and graphs. These activities include data cleaning, data transformation, estimation, plotting, and interpretation. Not only do we define our choice of OLS as the estimator, we also specify that we will focus attention on a particular coefficient estimate, assess uncertainty using a 95% confidence interval, and construct a coefficient plot to visualize the inference. The answer strategy also includes all of the if-then procedures that researchers implicitly or explicitly follow depending on initial results and features of the data. For example, in a stepwise regression procedure, the answer strategy is not the final regression specification that results from iterative model selection, but the whole procedure.

D and A impose a discipline on each other in the same way as we saw with M and I. Just as the model needs to provide the events that are summarized by the inquiry, the data strategy needs to provide the data that are summarized by the answer strategy. Declaring each of these parts in detail reveals the dependencies across the design elements.

A and I also enjoy a tight connection stemming from the more general parallelism between (M, I) and (D, A). We elaborate the principle of parallel inquiries and answer strategies in Section 9.3.

Figure 2.1 shows how the same answer strategy A is applied both to the realized data d^* and to the simulated data d. We know that in practice, however, the A applied to the real data differs somewhat from the A applied to the data we plan for via simulation. Designs sometimes drift in response to data, but too much drift and the inferences we draw can become misleading. The *MIDA* framework encourages researchers to think through what the real data will actually look like, and adjust A accordingly *before* data strategies are implemented.

Examples of answer strategies

1. Multilevel modeling and poststratification
2. Bayesian process tracing
3. Difference-in-means estimation

2.2 Declaration, Diagnosis, Redesign

With the core elements of a design described, we are now ready to lay out the declaration, diagnosis, and redesign workflow.

2.2.1 Declaration

Declaring a design entails figuring out which parts of your design belong in *M*, *I*, *D*, and *A*. The declaration process can be a challenge because mapping our ideas about a project into *MIDA* is not always straightforward, but it is rewarding. When we can express a research design in terms of these four components, we are newly able to think about its properties.

Designs can be declared in words, but declarations often become much more specific when carried out in code. You can declare a design in any statistical programming language: Stata, R, Python, Julia, SPSS, SAS, Mathematica, among many others. Design declaration is even possible—though somewhat awkward—in Excel. We wrote the companion software, `DeclareDesign`, in R because of the availability of other useful tools in R and because it is free, open-source, and high-quality. We have designed the book so that you can read it even if you do not use R, but you will have to translate the code into your own language of choice. On our Web site, we have pointers for how you might declare designs in Stata, Python, and Excel. In addition, we link to a "Design wizard" that lets you declare and diagnose variations of standard designs via a point-and-click Web interface. Chapter 4 provides an introduction to `DeclareDesign` in R.

2.2.2 Diagnosis

Once you've declared your design, you can diagnose it. Design diagnosis is the process of simulating a research design in order to understand the range of ways the study could turn out. Each run of the design comes out differently because different units are sampled, or the randomization allocates different units to treatment, or outcomes are measured with different errors. We let computers do the simulations for us because imagining the full set of possibilities is—to put it mildly—cognitively demanding.

Diagnosis is the process of assessing the properties of designs, and provides an opportunity to write down what would make the study a success. For a long time, researchers have classified studies as successful or not based on statistical significance (Chopra et al., 2022). If significant, the study "worked"; if not, it is a failed "null." Accordingly, statistical power (the probability of a statistically significant result) has been the most front-of-mind design property when researchers plan studies. As we learn more about the pathologies of relying on statistical significance, we learn that features beyond power are more important. For example, the "credibility revolution" throughout the social sciences has trained a laser-like focus on the biases that may result from omitted or "lurking" variables.

Design diagnosis relies on two new concepts: diagnostic statistics and diagnosands.

A "diagnostic statistic" is a summary statistic generated from a single "run" of a design. For example, the statistic *e* (error) refers to the difference between the estimate and the estimand. The statistic *s* (significance) refers to whether the estimate was deemed statistically significant at the 0.05 level (for instance).

A "diagnosand" is a summary of the distribution of a diagnostic statistic across many simulations of the design. The bias diagnosand is defined as the average value of the *e* statistic and the power diagnosand is defined as the average value of the *s* statistic. Other diagnosands include quantities like root-mean-squared error (RMSE), Type I and Type II error rates, how likely it is that subjects were harmed, and average cost. We describe these diagnosands in much more detail in Chapter 12.3.

One especially important diagnosand is the "success rate," which is the average value of the "success" diagnostic statistic. As the researcher, you get to decide what would make your study a success. What matters most in your research scenario? Is it statistical significance? If so, optimize your design with respect to power. Is what matters most whether the answer has the correct sign or not? Then diagnose how frequently your answer strategy yields an answer with the same sign as your estimand. Diagnosis involves articulating what would make your study a success and then figuring out, through simulation, how likely you are to obtain that success. Success is often a multidimensional aggregation of diagnosands, such as the joint achievement of high statistical power, manageable costs, and low ethical harms.

We diagnose studies over the range of possibilities in the model, since we want to learn the value of diagnosands under many possible scenarios. A clear example of this is the power diagnosand over many possible conjectures about the true effect size. For each effect size that we entertain in the model, we can calculate statistical power. The minimum detectable effect size is a summary of this power curve, usually defined as the smallest effect size at which the design reaches 80% statistical power. This idea, however, extends well beyond power. Whatever the set of important diagnosands, we want to ensure that our design performs well across many model possibilities.

Computer simulation is not the only way to do design diagnosis. Designs can be declared in writing or mathematical notation and then diagnosed using analytic formulas. Enormous theoretical progress in the study of research design has been made with this approach. Methodologists across the social sciences have described diagnosands such as bias, power, and root-mean-squared error for large classes of designs. Not only can this work provide closed-form mathematical expressions for many diagnosands, it can also yield insights about the pitfalls to watch out for when constructing similar designs. That said, pen-and-paper diagnosis is challenging for many social science research designs, first because many designs—as actually implemented—have idiosyncratic features that are hard to incorporate and, second, because the analytic formulas for many diagnosands have not yet been worked out by statisticians. For these reasons, when we do diagnosis in this book we will usually depend on simulation.

Even when using simulation, design diagnosis doesn't solve every problem and, like any tool, it can be misused. We outline two main concerns. The first is the worry that the diagnoses are plain wrong. Given that design declaration includes conjectures about the world, it is possible to choose inputs such that a design passes any diagnostic test set for it. For instance, a simulation-based claim of unbiasedness that incorporates all features of a design is still only good with respect to the precise conditions of the simulation. In contrast, analytic results, when available, may extend over general classes of designs. Still worse, simulation parameters might be chosen opportunistically. Power analysis is useless if implausible parameters are chosen to raise power artificially. While our framework may encourage more principled declarations, it does not guarantee good practice. As ever, garbage-in, garbage-out. The second concern is the risk that research may be evaluated on the basis of a narrow or inappropriate set of diagnosands. Statistical power is often invoked as a key design feature, but well-powered studies that are biased are of little use. The importance of particular diagnosands can depend on the values of others in complex ways, so researchers should take care to evaluate their studies along many dimensions.

2.2.3 Redesign

Once your design has been declared, and you have diagnosed it with respect to the most important diagnosands, the last step is redesign.

Redesign entails fine-tuning features of the data and answer strategies to understand how they change your diagnosands. Most diagnosands depend on features of the data strategy. We can redesign the study by varying the sample size to determine how big it needs to be to achieve a target diagnosand: 90% power, say, or an RMSE of 0.02. We could also vary an aspect of the answer strategy, such as the choice of covariates used to adjust a regression model. Sometimes the changes to the data and answer strategies interact. For example, if we want to use covariates that increase the precision of the estimates in the answer strategy, we have to collect that information as a part of the data strategy. The redesign question now becomes, is it better to collect pretreatment information from all subjects or is the money better spent on increasing the total number of subjects and only measuring post-treatment?

The redesign process is mainly about optimizing research designs given ethical, logistical, and financial constraints. If diagnosands such as total harm to subjects, total researcher hours, or total project cost exceed acceptable levels, the design is not feasible. We want to choose the best design we can among the feasible set. If the designs remaining in the feasible set are underpowered, biased, or are otherwise scientifically inadequate, the project may need to be abandoned.

In our experience, it's during the redesign process that designs become *simpler*. We learn that our experiment has too many arms or that the expected level of heterogeneity is too small to be detected by our design. We learn that in our theoretical excitement, we've built a design with too many bells and too many whistles. Some of the complexity needs to be cut, or the whole design will be a muddle. The upshot of many redesign sessions is that our designs pose fewer questions but obtain better answers.

2.3 Example: A Decision Problem

Imagine you want to study whether a new policy—implicit bias training—changes social norms of police officers or is merely window dressing. You have a research budget of $3,000 to run a randomized experiment to test the training program. You expect the police department will scale up the training program across the force if you find it shifts norms by at least 0.3 standard units, and otherwise it will not be implemented more widely. The department is also enamored by classical statistical testing so they will likely only go forward if your estimates are statistically significant.

Though we describe this particular setting to fix ideas, we think this example is relevant for many decision problems in which the results of a study will inform implementation.

You will consider the experiment to be a success if you conclude that the program is effective and indeed it is effective (which in this example we will take to mean that there is in fact an effect of at least 0.2). Otherwise you consider it a failure, whether because you reached the wrong conclusion or because resources were spent that could have been used on an effective intervention.

For the experiment itself, you're deciding between two designs. In one you run a study with 150 officers, randomly assign half to receive the training and half to not receive it, then compare outcomes in treatment and control using a survey about their perceived norms of reporting. In the second, you spend part of your funding gathering background information on the officers—whether they have been investigated in the past by internal affairs and were found to have discriminated against citizens—and use that information to improve both randomization and inference. Let's suppose the two designs cost exactly the same amount. Interviewing each officer at endline costs $20, so the total cost of the larger trial is $150 * 20 = 3,000$. The block-randomized design costs the same for endline measurement, but measurement of the history variable from police administrative records costs $10 per individual because you have to go through the department's archives, which are not digitized, so the total is the same: 100 * 20 + 100 * 10 = 3,000.

The two designs cost the same but differ on the empirical side. Which strategy should you use, given your goals?

2.3.1   Design 1: N = 150, complete random assignment

- *M*: We first define a model that stipulates a set of 18,000 units representing each officer and an unknown treatment effect of the training lying somewhere between 0 and 0.5. This range of possible effects implies that in 60% of the models we consider, the true effect is above our threshold for a program worth implementing, 0.2. Outcomes for each individual depend on their past infractions against citizens (their history). The importance of history is captured by the parameter **b**. We don't know how important the history variable is, so we will simulate over a plausible range for **b**. *M* here is a *set* of models as each "run" of the model will presuppose a different treatment effect for all subjects as well as distinct outcomes for all individuals.

- *I*: The inquiry is the difference between the average treated outcome and the average untreated outcome, which corresponds to the average treatment effect. We are writing it this way to highlight the similarity between the inquiry and the difference-in-means answer strategy that we will adopt.

- *D*: We imagine a data strategy with three components relating to units, conditions, and outcomes: we sample 100 deputies to participate in the experiment, assign exactly half to treatment and the remainder to control, and finally measure their outcomes through a survey.

- *A*: The answer strategy takes the difference-in-means between the treated and untreated units. Thus the answer strategy uses a function similar to the inquiry itself.

When we put these all together we have a design, Declaration 2.1.

Declaration 2.1 Two-arm trial design.

```
b <- 0
model <-
  declare_model(
    N = 1000,
    history = sample(c(0, 1), N, replace = TRUE),
    potential_outcomes(Y ~ b * history + runif(1, 0, 0.5) * Z + rnorm(N)))
```

2.3 Example: A Decision Problem

```
inquiry <-
  declare_inquiry(ATE = mean(Y_Z_1) - mean(Y_Z_0))

data_strategy <-
  declare_sampling(S = complete_rs(N = N, n = 150), filter = S == 1) +
  declare_assignment(Z = complete_ra(N)) +
  declare_measurement(Y = reveal_outcomes(Y ~ Z))

answer_strategy <-
  declare_estimator(Y ~ Z, .method = difference_in_means, inquiry = "ATE")

declaration_2.1 <- model + inquiry + data_strategy + answer_strategy
```

Table 2.1: Simulated data from two-arm trial design.

ID	history	Y_Z_0	Y_Z_1	S	Z	Y
0003	0	−2.01	1.30	1	1	1.30
0015	0	1.33	0.77	1	1	0.77
0017	1	−1.07	−0.86	1	1	−0.86
0021	0	−0.39	3.09	1	0	−0.39
0024	0	1.01	1.45	1	1	1.45
0034	1	−0.69	0.77	1	1	0.77

The design is now ready to be used, diagnosed, developed. We can generate simulated data directly from the design using `draw_data(declaration_2.1)`. We show a snapshot of such simulated data below.

To evaluate the design, we need to specify our criteria for what counts as a good design. We could assess the design in terms of its statistical power, whether estimation is unbiased, and so on. For now though we will focus on a specific design characteristic, its "success rate," which is the probability you will deem the research a success, using the criteria defined above.[2]

We specify the criteria for success in this call to `declare_diagnosands`:

```
program_diagnosands <-
  declare_diagnosands(
    success = mean(estimate > 0.3 & p.value < 0.05 & estimand > 0.2)
  )
```

---

[2] We could define more complex diagnosands that, for example, give correct decisions to implement a positive weight and incorrect decisions to implement a negative weight. The diagnosands you choose should reflect what you care about most in any given design setting.

2.3.2 Design 2: N = 100, baseline measurement, block random assignment

The alternative design differs on the empirical side in three ways. First, fewer subjects are sampled. Second, information about the subjects' background (their "history") is used to implement a block randomization that conditions assignment on history. Third, the subjects' history is taken into account in the analysis. This last choice is an instance of adjusting the answer strategy in light of a change to the data strategy.

In Declaration 2.2, we can leave the model and inquiry intact, but we have to work on the data and answer strategies.

Declaration 2.2 A design that exploits background information.

```
data_strategy_2 <-
  declare_sampling(S = complete_rs(N = N, n = 100),
                   filter = S == 1) +
  declare_assignment(Z = block_ra(blocks = history)) +
  declare_measurement(Y = reveal_outcomes(Y ~ Z))

answer_strategy_2 <-
  declare_estimator(Y ~ Z, .method = difference_in_means,
                    blocks = history, inquiry = "ATE")

declaration_2.2 <-
  model + inquiry + data_strategy_2 + answer_strategy_2
```

2.3.3 Diagnosis and comparison

We can then diagnose both designs over a series of conjectured values for the importance of history (b) and see how they perform on our specified criterion for success.

Diagnosis 2.1 Diagnosis of `declaration_2.1` and `declaration_2.2`.

```
declaration_2.1 |>
  redesign(b = seq(0,3,0.25)) |>
  diagnose_design(diagnosands = program_diagnosands)

declaration_2.2 |>
  redesign(b = seq(0,3,0.25)) |>
  diagnose_design(diagnosands = program_diagnosands)
```

The results are shown in Figure 2.2.

When background factors don't make much of a difference for the social norms outcome, the first design outperforms the second: after all, the first design has a sample size of 150 compared with the second design's 100. We're successful over

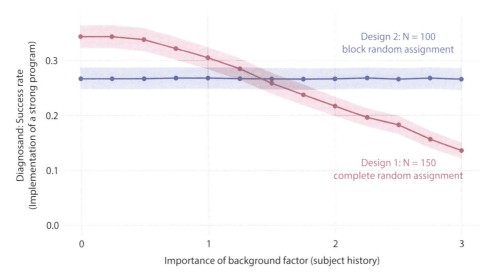

Figure 2.2: How success depends on choice of *D* and *A* given different possibilities for *M*.

30% of the time when using the first design, compared with about 25% when using the second. These rates seem low, but recall that the treatment effect variation we built into the model implies that the program is *worth* implementing only 60% of the time, because the other 40% of the time the true effects are smaller than 0.2.

As subject history has a bigger impact on the outcome variable, however, the first design does worse and worse. In essence, the additional variation due to background factors makes it more difficult to separate signal from noise, making it more likely that our estimates are not significant and therefore more likely that we decline to implement the program.

Here is where the smaller design that blocks on subject history shines: this variation is conditioned in two places, in the assignment strategy and in the estimator. The result is a more precise procedure that is better able to separate signal from noise. Ultimately, the blocked design has the same success rate regardless of the importance of the background factors.

The overall result of this declaration, diagnosis, and redesign process is that which design you choose depends on *beliefs* about the importance of background conditions for outcomes. Now the design question hinges on something you can go learn about: how much variation is explained by subject history?

2.3.4 Three principles

We see from this example the gains from entertaining a diverse model set rather than presupposing we already know *M*. We also see an example of design parts tailored to each other, most importantly the adjustment of answer strategies in light of data strategies. And we see that design choices are informed by a clear specification of a success criterion. In the next chapter we develop these three features as broader principles, referring to them as Principle 3.1: *Design holistically*, Principle 3.2: *Design agnostically*, and Principle 3.3: *Design for purpose*.

2.4 Putting Designs to Use

The two pillars of our approach are the language for describing research designs (*MIDA*) and the algorithm for selecting high-quality designs (declare, diagnose, redesign). Together, these two ideas can shape research design decisions throughout the lifecycle of a project. The full set of implications is drawn out in Part IV but we emphasize the most important ones here.

Broadly speaking, the lifecycle of an empirical research project has three phases: planning, realization, and integration. Having a clear characterization of your design in terms of *MIDA* is helpful in all three of these stages.

2.4.1 Planning, realization, integration

Planning entails some or all of the following steps, depending on the design: conducting an ethical review, seeking human subjects approval, gathering criticism from colleagues and mentors, running pilot studies, and preparing preanalysis documents. The design as encapsulated by *MIDA* will go through many iterations and refinements during this period, but the goal is simple: to assess whether your data strategy and answer strategy are capable of providing reliable answers to your inquiry given different models that you might entertain. Planning is the time when frequent reapplication of the declare, diagnose, redesign algorithm will pay the highest dividends. How should we investigate the ethics of a study? Consider casting the ethical costs and benefits as diagnosands. How should we respond to criticism, constructive or not? By reinterpreting the feedback in terms of M, I, D, and A. How can we convince funders and partners that our research project is worth investing in? By credibly communicating our study's diagnosands: its statistical power, its unbiasedness, and its high chance of success, however the partner or funder defines it. What belongs in a preanalysis plan? You guessed it—a specification of the model, inquiry, data strategy, and answer strategy.

Realization is the phase of research in which all those plans are executed. We implement the data strategy in order to gather information from the world. Once that's done, we follow the answer strategy in order to finally generate answers to the inquiry. Of course, that's only if things go exactly according to plan, which they never do. Survey questions don't work as we imagine, partner organizations lose interest in our study, subjects move or become otherwise unreachable. A critic or a reviewer may insist we change our answer strategy, or may think a different inquiry altogether is theoretically more appropriate. We may ourselves change how we think of the design as we embark on writing up the research project. It is likely that some features of *MIDA* will change during the realization phase, in which case you can again use diagnosis to assess whether changes to *MIDA* are for good or for bad. Some design changes have very bad properties, like sifting through the data ex-post, finding a statistically significant result, then backfitting a new *I* to match the new *A*. Indeed, if we declare and diagnose this actual answer strategy (sifting through data ex-post), we can show through design diagnosis that it yields misleading answers. Other changes made along the way may help the design quite a bit. If the planned design did not include covariate adjustment, but a friendly critic suggests adjusting for the pretreatment measure of the outcome, the "standard error" diagnosand might drop nicely. The point here is that design changes during the implementation process, whether necessitated by unforeseen logistical constraints or required by the review process, can be understood in terms of *M*, *I*, *D*, and *A* by reconciling the planned design with the design as implemented.

A happy realization phase concludes with the publication of results. But the research design lifecycle is not finished: the study and its results should be integrated into the broader community of scientists, decision-makers, and the public. Studies should be archived, along with design information, to prepare for reanalysis. Future scholars may well want to reanalyze your data in order to learn more than is represented in the published article or book. Good reanalysis of study data requires a full understanding of the design as implemented, so archiving design information along with code and data is critical. Not only may your design be reanalyzed, it may also be replicated with fresh data. Ensuring that replication studies answer the same theoretical questions as original studies requires explicit design information, without which replicators and original study authors may simply talk past one another. Indeed, as our studies are integrated into the scientific literature and beyond, we should anticipate disagreement over our claims. Resolving disputes is very difficult if parties do not share a common understanding of the research design. We might also anticipate that our results will be formally synthesized with others' work via meta-analysis. Meta-analysts need design information in order to be sure they aren't inappropriately mixing together studies that ask different questions or answer them too poorly to be of use. Finally, with luck your designs will be a model for others. Having an analytically complete representation of your design at hand will make it that much easier to use redesign to build on what you have done.

2.4.2   Three more principles

This discussion motivates three more principles: Principle 3.4: *Design early* to reap the benefits of clarity; Principle 3.5: *Design often* so that you can correct course; and Principle 3.6: *Design to share* so that you maximize transparency and contribute maximally to knowledge creation.

CHAPTER 3

Research Design Principles

With the *MIDA* framework and the declare, diagnose, redesign algorithm in hand, we can articulate a set of six principles for research design.

This section offers succinct discussions of each principle. We will expand on the implications of these principles for specific design choices throughout the book.

Design principles

1. Design holistically
2. Design agnostically
3. Design for purpose
4. Design early
5. Design often
6. Design to share

Principle 3.1 Design holistically

This is perhaps the most important of our principles. Designs are good not because they have good components but because the components work together to get a good result. Too often, researchers develop and evaluate parts of their designs in isolation: Is this a good question? Is this a good estimator? What's the best way to sample? But if you design with a view to diagnosis you are forced to focus on how each part of the design fits together. An estimator might be appropriate if you use one assignment scheme but not another. The evaluation of data and answer strategies depends on whether your model and inquiry call for descriptive inference, causal inference, or generalization inference (or perhaps, all three at once). If we ask, "What's your research design?" and you respond "It's a regression discontinuity design," we've learned something about what class your answer strategy might fall into, but we don't have enough information to decide whether it's a strong design until we learn about the model, inquiry, data strategy, and other parts of the answer strategy. Ultimately design evaluation comes not from assessment of the parts but from diagnosis of the full design.

When we consider whole designs rather than just thinking about one aspect at a time, we notice how designs that have "parallel" theoretical and empirical sides tend to be strong. We develop this idea in Section 9.3. If you want your estimate $a_{d^*} = A(d)$ to be close to the estimand $a_{m^*} = I(m^*)$, it's often best to choose data strategies that parallel models and answer strategies that parallel inquiries, i.e., to make sure that this rough analogy holds: *M:I::D:A*.

Principle 3.2 Design agnostically

When we design a research study, we have in mind a model of how the world works. But a good design should work, and work well, even when the world is different from what we expect. One implication is that we should entertain many models, not just seeking to ensure the design produces good results for models that we think likely but also trying to expand the set of possible models for which the design delivers good results. A second implication is that inquiries and answer strategies should still *work* when the world looks different from what we expect. Inquiries should have answers even when event generating processes are different from how you imagine them. In the same way, the ability to apply an answer strategy should depend as little as possible on strong expectations of how the data you will get will look.

A corollary to "Design agnostically" is that we should know for which models our design performs well and for which models it performs poorly. We want to diagnose over many models to find where designs break. All designs break under some models, so the fact that a design ever breaks is no criticism. As research designers, we just want to know which models pose problems and which do not.

Principle 3.3 Design for purpose

When we say a design is good we mean it is good for some specific purpose. That purpose should be captured by the diagnosands used to assess design quality and design decisions should then be taken with respect to the specified purpose. Too often, researchers focus on a narrow set of diagnosands, and consider them in isolation. Is the estimator unbiased? Do I have statistical power? The evaluation of a design nearly always requires balancing multiple criteria: scientific precision, logistical constraints, policy goals, as well as ethical considerations. And oftentimes these might come into conflict with each other. Thus one design might be best if the goal is to assess whether a treatment has any effect, another if the goal is to assess the size of an effect. One design might be optimal if the goal is to contribute to general knowledge about how processes work, but another if the goal is to make a decision about whether to move forward with a policy in a given context.

In the MIDA framework, the goals of a design are not formally a part of the design. They enter at the diagnosis stage, and, of course, a single design might be assessed for performance for different purposes.

Principle 3.4 Design early

Designing an empirical project entails declaring, diagnosing, and redesigning the components of a research design: its model, inquiry, data strategy, and answer strategy. The design phase yields the biggest gains when we design early. By frontloading design decisions, we can learn about the properties of a design while there is still time to improve them. Once data strategies are implemented—units sampled, treatments assigned, and outcomes measured—there's no going back. While applying the answer strategy to the revealed dataset, you might well wish you'd gathered data differently, or asked different questions. Post-hoc, we always wish our previous selves had planned ahead.

A reason deeper than regret for designing early is that the declaration, diagnosis, and redesign process inevitably changes designs, almost always for the better. Revealing how each of the four design elements are interconnected yields improvements to each. These choices are almost always better made before any data are collected or analyzed.

Principle 3.5 Design often

Designing early does not mean being inflexible. In practice, unforeseen circumstances may change the set of feasible data and answer strategies. Implementation failures due to nonresponse, noncompliance, spillovers, inability to link datasets, funding contractions, or logistical errors are common ways the set of feasible designs might contract. The set of feasible designs might expand if new data sources are discovered, additional funding is secured, or if you learn about a new piece of software. Whether the set expands or contracts, we benefit from declaring, diagnosing, and redesigning given the new realities.

In part IV on the research design lifecycle, we push this principle to the limit, encouraging you to keep on designing even after research is completed, arguing that *ex post* design can help you assess the robustness of your claims and help you decide how to respond to criticism of your work.

Principle 3.6 Design to share

The *MIDA* framework and the declaration, diagnosis, and redesign algorithm can improve the quality of your research designs. It can also help you communicate your work, justify your decisions, and contribute to the scientific enterprise. Formalizing design declaration makes this sharing easier. By coding up a design as an object that can be run, diagnosed, and redesigned, you help other researchers see, understand, and question the logic of your research.

We urge you to keep this sharing function in mind as you write code, explore alternatives, and optimize over designs. An answer strategy that is hard-coded to capture your final decisions might break when researchers try to modify parts. Alternatively, designs can be created specifically to make it easier to explore neighboring designs, let others see why you chose the design you chose, and give them a leg up in their own work. In our ideal world, when you create a design, you contribute it to a design library so others can check it out and build on your good work.

CHAPTER 4

Getting Started

This chapter serves as a quick start guide for the code used throughout this book, and in particular the `DeclareDesign` package for the R programming language. `DeclareDesign` is a software implementation of every step of the declare-diagnose-redesign process. While you can declare, diagnose, and redesign using nearly any programming language, `DeclareDesign` is structured to make it easy to mix and match design elements while handling the tedious simulation bookkeeping behind the scenes.

First, we provide instructions for getting started in R and RStudio. We then introduce the code structure for the three steps of the research planning process: declaration, diagnosis and redesign. After this introduction, readers should be able to *use* the code, but perhaps not write it themselves yet. We devote a longer section (Chapter 13) to getting started *writing* the code.

4.1 Installing R

You can download R for free from CRAN. We also recommend the free program RStudio, which provides a friendly interface to R. Both R and RStudio are available on Windows, Mac, and Linux.

Once you have R and RStudio installed, open up RStudio and install `DeclareDesign` and its related packages. These include three packages that enable specific steps in the research process: `fabricatr` for simulating social science data, `randomizr` for random sampling and random assignment, and `estimatr` for design-based estimators. You can also install `rdss`, which includes datasets and helper functions used in the book. To install them all, copy the following code into your R console:

```r
install.packages(c("DeclareDesign", "rdss"))
```

We also recommend that you install and get to know the `tidyverse` set of packages for data analysis, which we will use throughout:

```
install.packages("tidyverse")
```

For introductions to R and the `tidyverse` we especially recommend the free resource *R for Data Science* https://r4ds.had.co.nz/ (Wickham and Grolemund, 2016).

All of the code in this book assumes that the `DeclareDesign` family of packages, the `tidyverse` suite, and the companion package to the book `rdss` have been loaded. Once they have been installed on your computer, you can load them with the following code:

```
library(DeclareDesign)
library(tidyverse)
library(rdss)
```

4.2 Declaration

Designs are constructed from design elements: models, inquiries, data strategies, and answer strategies.

In `DeclareDesign`, each design element is made with a function that starts with the word `declare`. For example, we can declare an assignment procedure using `declare_assignment` as follows:

```
simple_random_assignment <-
  declare_assignment(Z = simple_ra(N = N, prob = 0.6))
```

Each element created by a `declare_*` function, perhaps surprisingly, is itself a function. The object `simple_random_assignment` is not a particular assignment—instead, it is a function that conducts assignment when called. Each time we call `simple_random_assignment` we get a different random assignment:

```
participants <- data.frame(ID = 1:100)

assignment_1 <- simple_random_assignment(participants)
assignment_2 <- simple_random_assignment(participants)
assignment_3 <- simple_random_assignment(participants)

bind_cols(assignment_1, assignment_2, assignment_3)
```

Table 4.1: Three random assignments from the same random assignment step.

ID 1	Z 1	ID 2	Z 2	ID 3	Z 3
1	0	1	1	1	0
2	0	2	0	2	0
3	0	3	1	3	1
4	1	4	0	4	1
5	0	5	1	5	0

Every step in a research design can be declared using one of the `declare_*` functions. Table 4.2 collects these according to the four elements of a research design. In Chapter 13, we detail how to build each kind of step.

Table 4.2: Declaration functions in `DeclareDesign`.

Design component	Function	Description
Model	`declare_model()`	background variables and potential outcomes
Inquiry	`declare_inquiry()`	research questions
Data strategy	`declare_sampling()`	sampling procedures
	`declare_assignment()`	assignment procedures
	`declare_measurement()`	measurement procedures
Answer strategy	`declare_estimator()`	estimation procedures
	`declare_test()`	testing procedures

We use the + operator to build from elements of a design to a design. Declaration 4.1 (see Figure 4.1) shows the format of most declarations throughout the book. This declaration represents a two-arm randomized experiment with 100 units from which we aim to estimate the average treatment effect.

4.3 Diagnosis

Diagnosis is the process of simulating the design many times and calculating summary statistics about the design that describe its properties, which we call diagnosands. Once a design is declared, diagnosis is as simple as using the `diagnose_design` function on it.

Declaration 4.1 Two-arm randomized experiment.

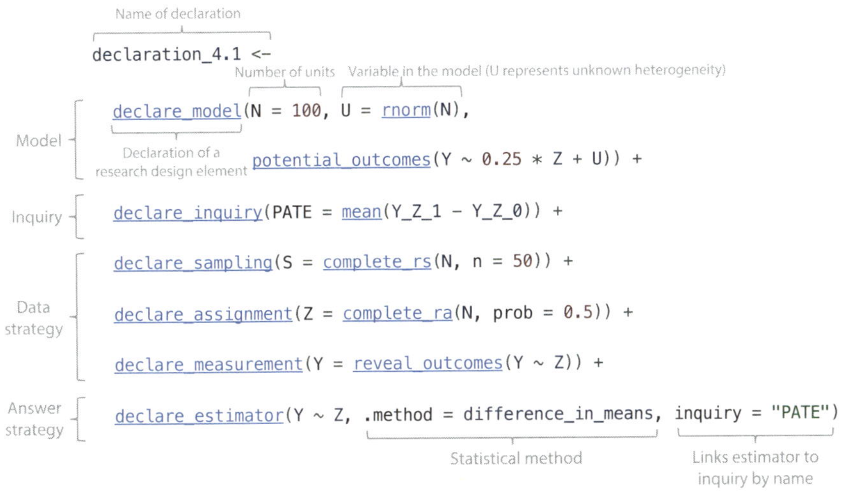
Name of declaration
declaration_4.1 <-
Number of units
Variable in the model (U represents unknown heterogeneity)
declare_model(N = 100, U = rnorm(N),
Model
Declaration of a research design element
potential_outcomes(Y ~ 0.25 * Z + U)) +
Inquiry
declare_inquiry(PATE = mean(Y_Z_1 - Y_Z_0)) +
declare_sampling(S = complete_rs(N, n = 50)) +
Data strategy
declare_assignment(Z = complete_ra(N, prob = 0.5)) +
declare_measurement(Y = reveal_outcomes(Y ~ Z)) +
Answer strategy
declare_estimator(Y ~ Z, .method = difference_in_means, inquiry = "PATE")
Statistical method
Links estimator to inquiry by name

Figure 4.1: Two-arm randomized experiment declaration.

Diagnosis 4.1 Example design diagnosis.

```
diagnose_design(declaration_4.1, sims = 100)
```

Table 4.3: Design diagnosis.

Bias	RMSE	Power
−0.02	0.31	0.11
(0.03)	(0.02)	(0.03)

The output of the diagnosis includes the diagnosand values (top row), such as bias of −0.02, and our uncertainty about the diagnosand value (bootstrapped standard error in parentheses in the bottom row). The uncertainty estimates tell us whether we have conducted enough simulations to precisely estimate the diagnosands. The fact that the estimate of bias is −0.02 and the standard error is 0.03 means that we cannot distinguish the amount of bias from no bias at all.

4.4 Redesign

We redesign to learn how the diagnosands change as design features change. We can do this using the `redesign` function over a range of sample sizes, which produces a list of designs.

```
designs <- redesign(declaration_4.1, N = c(100, 200, 300, 400, 500))
```

Our simulation and diagnosis tools can operate directly on this list of designs:

```
diagnose_design(designs)
```

4.5 Library of Designs

In our `DesignLibrary` package, we have created a set of common designs as "designers" (functions that create designs from just a few arguments), so you can get started quickly.

```
library(DesignLibrary)

block_cluster_design <-
  block_cluster_two_arm_designer(N = 1000, N_blocks = 10)
```

4.6 Long-Term Code Usability

We have written the code examples with `DeclareDesign` version 1.0.0, the package version we released along with the book. We are committed to the long-term maintenance of this software, but inevitably, the evolution of the R ecosystem and further package development will mean that some of the printed code will break in the future.

However, even if code eventually becomes obsolete, a virtue of writing out designs in code is that they are explicit: the entire design is encoded in the declarations we provide. Even if the code itself won't run, you can still use it to understand the design and to draw insights from the diagnosis.

PART

II

Declaration, Diagnosis, Redesign

CHAPTER 5

Declaring Designs

In Chapter 2, we gave a high-level overview of our framework for describing research designs in terms of their models, inquiries, data strategies, and answer strategies, our process for diagnosing their properties, and a general purpose approach for improving them to better fit research goals. Now in this chapter, we place our approach on a firmer formal footing. We employ elements from Pearl's (2009) approach to causal modeling, which provides a syntax for mapping design inputs to design outputs. We also use the potential outcomes framework as presented, for example, in Imbens and Rubin (2015), which many social scientists use to clarify their inferential targets.

Describing a research design in the *MIDA* framework allows us to see the fundamental symmetries across the theoretical (M and I) and empirical (D and A) halves of a research design. An aim of this chapter is to make these somewhat abstract relationships concrete.

5.1 Definition of Research Designs

Research designs are defined by four elements: a model M, an inquiry I, a data strategy D, and an answer strategy A. Describing a research design entails "declaring" each of these four elements.

M is a set of possible models of how the world works. Following Pearl's definition of a probabilistic causal model, a model in M contains three core elements. The first is the "signature" (Halpern, 2000), or the specification of the variables X about which research is being conducted, including the endogenous and exogenous variables (V and U respectively) and their ranges. The second element (F) is a specification of how each endogenous variable depends on other variables. These dependencies can be considered functional relations or, as in Imbens and Rubin (2015), potential outcomes because they describe what *would* happen under different possible conditions. The third and final element is a probability distribution over exogenous variables, written as $P(U)$. Sometimes it is useful to think of the draws from U as implying distinct models of their own, in which case we might think of M as a family of models that fully specifies what would happen under all conditions and a particular model m as an element of M that describes one of those conditions. We eschew the phrase "data generating process" when referring to M (since data are generated by the data strategy) and instead use the phrase "event generating process."

The inquiry I is a summary of the values that variables X will or could take on. All inquiries are either descriptive or causal. Descriptive inquiries are those that do not involve comparisons across counterfactual worlds, for example, the average value of an outcome Y over all N units in the population: $\frac{\sum_i^N Y_i}{N}$. Causal inquiries do involve comparisons across counterfactuals, as in the average treatment effect: $\frac{\sum_i^N Y_i(Z_i=1) - Y_i(Z_i=0)}{N}$.

We let a_m denote the answer to I *under the model*. Conditional on the model, a_m is the value of the estimand, the quantity that the researcher wants to learn about, or would want to learn about if the world were like the model. The connection of a_m to the model is given by: $a_m = I(m)$.

As the saying goes, models are wrong but some may be useful. We denote the *true* causal process as m^*: the process that generates events in the real world. The *right* answer, then, is $a_{m^*} = I(m^*)$. The answer under a reference model a_m may be close or far from the true value a_{m^*}, which is to say it could be wrong. If the model m is far from m^*, then of course a_m need not be correct. Moreover a_{m^*} might even be undefined, since inquiries can only be stated in terms of reference models. If the reference model is wrong enough—for instance it conditions on events that could not arise—then the inquiry might be nonsensical. For example, "what is the ideological slant of a speech that is not given" is an inquiry that is undefined.

A data strategy D generates data d. Data d arises under model M with probability $P_M(d|D)$. The data strategy includes sampling, assignment, and measurement strategies. Nearly all data strategies sample and measure, but not all assign treatments. Whether or not the data strategy includes assignment is the defining distinction between experimental and observational studies. When applied in the real world, the data strategy operates on m^* to produce the realized data: $D(m^*) = d^*$. When we simulate research designs, the data strategy operates on a simulated model draw m to produce fabricated data: $D(m) = d$.

Finally, the answer strategy A generates answers using data. When applied to realized data, the answer strategy returns the empirical answer: $A(d^*) = a_{d^*}$. When applied to simulated data, it returns a simulated answer: $A(d) = a_d$.

Table 5.1 provides a concise description of each element of a research design and relates them to some common terms. We flag here that the term estimand has

Table 5.1: Elements of research design.

Notation	Description	Related terms
M	a stipulated collection of causal models	
m	a single model in M, represented by events	a hypothetical data generating process
m^*	the true model	true data generating process
I	the inquiry	estimand, quantity of interest
$a_m = I(m)$	the answer under the model, an estimand	
$a_{m^*} = I(m^*)$	the true answer, the estimand	quantity of interest
D	the data strategy	
$d = D(m)$	fabricated data; simulated data	
$d^* = D(m^*)$	realized data	
A	the answer strategy	data analysis, estimator, method
$a_d = A(d)$	a simulated answer, an estimate	a hypothetical estimate
$a_{d^*} = A(d^*)$	the empirical answer, the estimate	the observed estimate

a slightly different meaning in our framework than elsewhere. We say that an estimand a_m is the value of an inquiry I, whereas in some traditions "estimand" can refer to the inquiry I or to an intermediate parameter that happens to be targeted by an estimator.

The full set of causal relationships between M, I, D, and A, with respect to m and m^*, a_m and a_{m^*}, d and d^*, and a_d and a_{d^*} can be seen in the schematic representation of a research design given in Figure 5.1. The figure illustrates how a research design involves a correspondence between $I(m) = a_m$ and $A(d) = a_d$. The theoretical half of a research design produces an answer to the inquiry *in theory*. The empirical half of a research design produces an *empirical estimate* of the answer to the inquiry. Neither answer is necessarily close to the truth a_{m^*}, of course. And, as shown in the figure, the truth is not directly accessible to us. Our gamble in empirical research, however, is that the truth is like the set of models we imagine and so data and answer strategies that perform well on the models we imagine will also perform well in actuality. If the models in M do not contain m^* or are too different from it, then even seemingly strong research designs could yield unreliable answers.

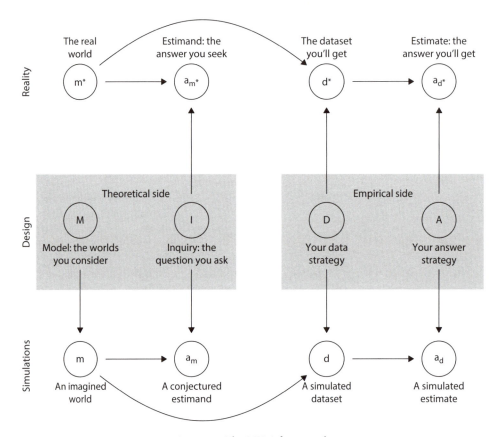

Figure 5.1: The *MIDA* framework.

Figure 5.1 reveals a striking analogy between the *M*, *I* relationship and the *D*, *A* relationship. The answer we aim for (the estimand) is obtained by applying *I* to a draw from *M*. The answer we have access to (the estimate) is obtained by applying *A* to a draw from *D*. Our hope, usually, is that these two answers are quite similar. In some cases, this parallelism suggests that the function *A* should be "like" the function *I*. For instance, if we are interested in the mean of a population and we have access to a random sample, the data available to us from *D* is like the ideal data we would have if we could observe the components of *M* directly.

Finally, in Figure 5.1 no arrows go into *M*, *I*, *D*, or *A*, since they are not caused by any of the other nodes. We could have included a node for the research designer, who deliberately sets the details of *M*, *I*, *D*, and *A*, but we omit it for clarity.

5.2 Declaration in Code

Table 5.2 illustrates these different quantities through `DeclareDesign`. We stipulate a model, *M*, in which *Y* depends on *X*. We define an inquiry, *I*: what is the average value of *Y* when $X = 1$? We calculate what the value of our inquiry (the estimand)

Table 5.2: Elements of research design in code.

Description	Draw

`M <- declare_model(N = 1000,`
`  U = rnorm(N),`
`  X = rbinom(N, 1, prob = pnorm(U)),`
`  Y = rbinom(N, 1, prob = pnorm(U + X)))`
`m <- M()`
	m: an imagined world
	
	| ID | U | X | Y |
	|---|---|---|---|
	| 0001 | -1.40 | 0 | 0 |
	| 0002 | 0.52 | 1 | 1 |
	| 0003 | 0.14 | 1 | 0 |
	| 0004 | -0.85 | 0 | 1 |
	| 0005 | -0.41 | 0 | 1 |

`I <- declare_inquiry(Ybar = mean(Y[X==1]))` `a_m <- I(m)`	a_m: a conjectured estimand | inquiry | estimand | |---|---| | Ybar | 0.90 |

`mstar <- fabricate(N = 1000,`
`  U = rnorm(N),`
`  X = rbinom(N, 1, prob = pnorm(U)),`
`  Y = rbinom(N, 1, prob = pnorm(U)))`
	m^*: the real world
	
	| ID | U | X | Y |
	|---|---|---|---|
	| 0001 | -0.11 | 0 | 0 |
	| 0002 | 1.20 | 0 | 1 |
	| 0003 | 0.71 | 1 | 1 |
	| 0004 | 1.65 | 1 | 1 |
	| 0005 | 0.74 | 0 | 0 |

`a_mstar <- I(mstar)`	a_{m^*}: the estimand | inquiry | estimand | |---|---| | Ybar | 0.68 |

`D <- declare_sampling(`
`  S = simple_rs(N, prob = 0.1))`
`dstar <- D(mstar)`
	d^*: the realized dataset
	
	| ID | X | Y |
	|---|---|---|
	| 0005 | 0 | 0 |
	| 0014 | 0 | 0 |
	| 0015 | 1 | 1 |
	| 0052 | 1 | 1 |
	| 0058 | 0 | 1 |

`A <- declare_estimator(`
`  Y ~ 1, .method = lm_robust,`
`  subset = X == 1, inquiry = "Ybar")`
`a_dstar <- A(dstar)`
	a_{d^*}: the realized estimate
	
	| estimate | std.error | conf.low | conf.high |
	|---|---|---|---|
	| 0.69 | 0.07 | 0.56 | 0.83 |

would be under one of our simulated models, $I(m)$. We also imagine we could describe how the world in fact is, m^*, and calculate what the right answer would be in that case, a_{m^*}. We then apply the data strategy D to produce realized data d^* and use an answer strategy A to calculate the answer a_d^* we would get given d^*.

For each of these steps we show `DeclareDesign` code in the first column. In the second column, we show the simulated m, m^*, and d^* datasets, along with the values of a_m, a_{m^*}, and a_{d^*} for one run of the simulation.

As described in the getting started guide in Chapter 4, we concatenate the design steps into a full design declaration using the + operator:

Declaration 5.1 Example declaration.

```
declaration_5.1 <-
  declare_model(
    N = 1000,
    U = rnorm(N),
    X = rbinom(N, 1, prob = pnorm(U)),
    Y = rbinom(N, 1, prob = pnorm(U + X))
  ) +
  declare_inquiry(Ybar = mean(Y[X == 1])) +
  declare_sampling(S = simple_rs(N, prob = 0.1)) +
  declare_estimator(Y ~ 1,
                    .method = lm_robust,
                    subset = X == 1,
                    inquiry = "Ybar")
```

This design declaration includes a specification of all four design elements: model, inquiry, data strategy, and answer strategy. The next four chapters will describe each of these four design elements in great detail. For now, notice that the declaration does not include a specification of m^* (the true causal model), and includes only M, a model we entertain for research planning purposes.

CHAPTER 6

Specifying the Model

Models are theoretical abstractions we use to make sense of the world and organize our understanding of it. They play many critical roles in research design. First and foremost, models describe the units, conditions, and outcomes that define inquiries. Without well-specified models, we cannot pose well-specified inquiries. Second, models provide a framework to evaluate the sampling, assignment, and measurement procedures that form the data strategy. Models encode our beliefs about the kinds of information that might result when we conduct empirical observations. Third, they guide the selection of answer strategies: what variables should we condition on, what variables should we *not* condition on, how flexible or rigid should our estimation procedure be? Whenever we rely on assumptions in the model—for example, normality of errors, conditional independencies, or latent scores—we are betting that the real causal model m^* has these properties.

We need to imagine models in order to declare and diagnose research designs. This need often generates discomfort among students and researchers who are new to thinking about research design this way. In order to compute the root-mean-squared error, bias, or statistical power of a design, we need to write down *more than we know for sure* in the model. We have to describe joint distributions of covariates, treatments, and outcomes, which entails making guesses about the very means, covariances, and effect sizes (among many other things) that the empirical research design is supposed to measure. "What do you mean, write down the potential outcomes—that's what I'm trying to learn about!"

The discomfort arises because we do not know the true causal model of the world—what we referred to as m^* in Figure 5.1. We are uncertain about which of the many plausible models of the world we entertain is the correct one. In fact we can be fairly certain that none of them is really correct.

The good news is that they do not have to be correct. The *M* in *MIDA* refers to these possible models, which we call "reference models." *M* is a set of reference models. Their role is to provide a stipulation of how the world works, which allows us to answer some questions about our research design. *If* the reference model were true, what *then* would the value of the inquiry be? Would the estimator generate unbiased estimates? How many units would we need to achieve an RMSE of 0.5? Critically, whether a design is good or bad depends on the reference models. A data and analysis strategy might fare very well under one model of the world but poorly under another. Thus to get to the point where we can assess a design we need to make the family of reference models explicit. Our hope is that when we apply A and I to the real event generating processes we will have a similar relation between the answer we seek and the answers we get as we have between conjectured estimands and simulated estimates. Beyond that, we don't have to actually believe any of the models in M.

6.1 Elements of Models

Models are characterized by three elements: the signature, the functional relationships, and a probability distribution over exogenous variables (Halpern, 2000). We'll describe each in turn.

6.1.1 Signature

The signature of the model describes the variables in the model and their ranges. The signature comprises two basic kinds of variables: exogenous variables and endogenous variables. Exogenous means "generated from without" and endogenous means "generated from within." Stated more plainly, exogenous variables are not caused by other variables in the model because they are randomly assigned by nature or by human intervention. Endogenous variables result as a consequence of exogenous variables; they are causally downstream from exogenous variables.

What kinds of variables are exogenous? Typically, we think of explicitly randomly assigned variables as exogenous: the treatment assignment variable in a randomized experiment is exogenous. We'll often use the variable letter Z to refer to assignments that were explicitly randomized. We also often characterize the set of unobserved causes of observed variables as exogenous. We summarize the set of unobserved causes of an observed variable with the letter U. These unobserved causes are exogenous in the sense that, whatever the causes of U may be, they do not cause other endogenous variables in a model.

What kinds of variables are endogenous? Everything else: covariates, mediators, moderators, and outcome variables. We'll often use the letter X when describing covariates or moderators, the letter M when describing mediators, and the letter Y when describing outcome variables. Each of these kinds of variables is the downstream consequence of exogenous variables, whether those exogenous variables are observed or not.

Critically the signature of a model *is itself a part of the design*: we as designers must choose the variables of interest. We do not, however, get to decide the functional relations between variables—those are set by m^*.

6.1.2 Functional relations

The second element of the model is the set of functions that produce endogenous variables. The outputs of these functions are always endogenous variables and the inputs can be either exogenous variables or other endogenous variables. We embrace two different, but ultimately compatible, ways of thinking about these functional relationships: structural causal models and the potential outcomes model.

The structural causal model account of causality is often associated with directed acyclic graphs or DAGs (Pearl, 2009). Each node on a graph is a variable and the edges that connect them represent possible causal effects. An arrow from a "parent" node to a "child" node indicates that the value of the parent sometimes influences the outcome of the child. More formally: the parent's value is an argument in a functional equation determining the child's outcome. DAGs emphasize a mechanistic notion of causality. When the exposure variable changes, the outcome variable changes as a result, possibly in different ways for different units.

DAGs represent nonparametric structural causal models. The qualifier "nonparametric" means that DAGs don't show *how* variables are related, just *that* they are related. This is no criticism of DAGs—they just don't encode all of our causal beliefs about a system. We illustrate these ideas using a DAG to describe a model for an abstract research design in which we will collect information about N units. We will assign a treatment Z at random, and collect an outcome Y. We know there are other determinants of the outcome beyond Z, but we don't know much about them. All we'll say about those other determinants U is that they are causally related to Y, but not to Z, since Z will be randomly assigned by us.

This nonparametric structural causal model can be written like this:

$$Y = f_Y(Z, U).$$

Here, the outcome Y is related to Z and U by some function f_Y, but the details of the function f_Y—whether Z has a positive or negative effect on Y, for example—are left unstated in this nonparametric model. The DAG in Figure 6.1 encodes this model in graphical form. We use a blue circle around the treatment assignment to indicate that Z is randomly assigned as part of the data strategy.

To assess many properties of a research design we often need to make the leap from nonparametric models to *parametric* structural causal models. We need to enumerate beliefs about effect sizes, correlations between variables, intra-cluster correlations (ICCs), specific functional forms, and so forth. Since any particular

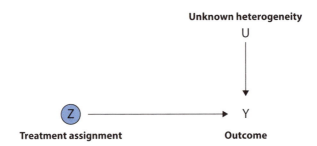

Figure 6.1: Directed acyclic graph of a randomized experiment.

choice for these parameters could be close to or far from the truth, we will typically consider a range of plausible values for each model parameter.

One possible parametric model is given by the following:

$$Y = 0.5 \times Z + U.$$

Here, we have specified the details of the function that relates Z and U to Y. In particular, it is a linear function in which Y is equal to the unobserved characteristic U in the control condition, but is 0.5 higher in the treatment condition. We could also consider a more complicated parametric model in which the relationship between Z and Y depends on an interaction with the unobservables in U:

$$Y = -0.25 \times Z - 0.05 \times Z \times U + U.$$

Both of these parameterizations are equally consistent with the DAG in Figure 6.1, which underlines the powerful simplicity of DAGs, but also their theoretical sparsity. The two parametric models are theoretically quite different from one another. In the first, the effects of the treatment Z are positive and the same for all units; in the second, the effects may be negative and quite different from unit to unit, depending on the value of U. If both of these reference models are plausible, we'll want to include them both in M, to ensure that our design is robust to both possibilities. Here we have a small instance of Principle 3.2: *Design agnostically*. We want to consider a wide range of plausible parameterizations since we are ignorant of the true causal model (m^*).

The potential outcomes formalization emphasizes a counterfactual notion of causality. $Y_i(Z_i = 0)$ is the outcome for unit i that would occur were the causal variable Z_i set to 0, and $Y_i(Z_i = 1)$ is the outcome that would occur if Z_i were set to 1. The difference between them defines the effect of the treatment on the outcome for unit i. Since at most only one potential outcome can ever be revealed, at least one of the two potential outcomes is necessarily counterfactual, meaning not observable. Usually, the potential outcomes notation $Y_i(Z_i)$ reports how outcomes depend on one feature, Z_i, ignoring all other determinants of outcomes. That's not to say those other causes don't matter—they might—they are just not the focus. In a sense, they are contained in the subscript i since the units carry with them all relevant features other than Z_i. We can generalize to settings where we want to consider more than one cause, in which case we use expressions of the form $Y_i(Z_i = 0, X_i = 0)$ or $Y_i(Z_i = 0, X_i = 1)$.

The potential outcomes version of the first structural causal model might be written for $i \in \{1, 2, \ldots, n\}$ as:

$$Y_i(0) = U_i$$
$$Y_i(1) = 0.5 + U_i.$$

The potential outcomes under the second model would be written:

$$Y_i(0) = U_i$$
$$Y_i(1) = -0.25 - 0.05 \times U_i + U_i.$$

Despite what might be inferred from the sometimes heated disagreements between scholars who prefer one formalization to the other, structural causal models and potential outcomes are compatible systems for thinking about causality. Potential outcome distributions can also be described using Pearl's do() operator: $\Pr(Y|do(Z=1))$ is the probability distribution of the treated potential outcome. We could use only the language of structural causal models or we could use only the language of potential outcomes, since a theorem in one is a theorem in the other (Pearl, 2009, p. 243). We choose to use both languages because they are useful for expressing different facets of research design. We use structural causal models to describe the web of causal interrelations in a concise way (writing out the potential outcomes for every relationship in the model is tedious). We use potential outcomes when the inquiry involves comparisons across conditions and to make fine distinctions between inquiries that apply to different sets of units.

6.1.3 Probability distributions over exogenous variables

The final element of a model is a description of the probability distribution of exogenous variables. For example, we might describe the distribution of the treatment assignment as Bernoulli with $p = 0.1$ for "coin flip" random assignment with a 10% chance of a unit being assigned to treatment. We might stipulate that the unobserved characteristics U are normally distributed with a mean of 1 and a standard deviation of 2. The distributions of the exogenous variables then ramify through to the distributions of the endogenous variables through the functional relations.

In general, multiple distributions can behave equivalently in a model. For instance, if we specify that u is distributed normally with mean 0 and standard deviation σ and that $Y = 1$ if and only if $U \geq 0$, then the distribution induced on Y will be the same regardless of the choice of σ. Indeed the same distribution on Y could be generated by countless other distributions on U. The focus then is not on getting these distributions "right," but on selecting distributions in light of their implications about the distributions of endogenous nodes.

6.2 Types of Variables in Models

Any particular causal model can be a complex web of exogenous and endogenous variables woven together via a set of functional relationships. Despite the heterogeneity across models, we can describe the roles variables play in a research design with reference to the roles they play in structural causal models. There are seven roles:

1. **Outcomes**: Variables whose level or responses we want to understand, generally referred to as Y, as in Figure 6.2. Variously described as "dependent variables," "endogenous variables," "left-hand side variables," or "response variables."

2. **Treatments**: Variables that affect outcomes. We will most often use D to refer to the main causal variable of interest in a particular study. Sometimes labeled as "independent variables," or "right-hand side variables."

3. **Moderators**: Variables that condition the effects of treatment variables on outcomes: depending on the level of a moderator, treatments might have stronger or weaker effects on outcomes. Nonparametric structural causal models (like those represented in DAGs) represent moderators as additional causes of Y. See, for example, $X2$ in Figure 6.2. Be warned however that the fact that moderators are represented as additional causes of an outcome does not imply that every additional cause of an outcome is necessarily a moderator.

4. **Mediators**: Variables "along the path" from treatment variables to outcomes. M is an example of a mediator in Figure 6.2. Mediators are often studied to assess "how" or "why" D causes Y.

5. **Confounders**: Variables that introduce a non-causal dependence between D and Y. In Figure 6.2, $X1$ is a confounder because it causes both D and Y and could introduce a dependence between them even if D did not cause Y.

6. **Instruments**: An instrumental variable is an exogenous variable that affects a treatment variable which itself causes an outcome variable. We give a much more detailed treatment of these variables in Section 16.4. We reserve the letter Z for instruments. Random assignments are instruments in the sense that the assignment is the instrument and the actual treatment received is the treatment variable.

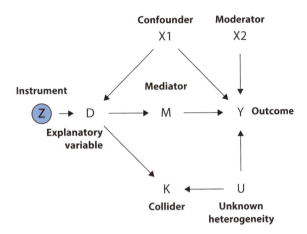

Figure 6.2: A directed acyclic graph with a treatment of interest (D), an outcome of interest (Y), a mediator (M), a confounder (X1), a moderator (X2), an instrument (Z), and a collider (K).

7. **Colliders**: Colliders are variables that are caused by two other variables. Colliders can be important because conditioning on a collider introduces a non-causal relationship between all parents of the collider. The intuition is that if you learn that a child is tall, then learning that one parent is small makes you more likely to believe that the other parent is tall. In Figure 6.2, K is a collider that can create a non-causal dependence between D and Y (via U) if conditioned upon.

These labels reflect the researcher's interest as much as their position in a model. Another researcher examining the same graph might, for instance, label M as their treatment variable or K as their outcome of interest.

6.2.1 What variables are needed?

Our models of the world can be more or less complex, or at least articulated at higher or lower levels of generality. How specific and detailed we need to be in our specification of possible models depends on the other features of the research design: the inquiry, the data strategy, and the answer strategy. At a minimum, we need to describe the variables required for each of these research design elements.

Inquiry: In order to reason about whether the model is sufficient to define the inquiry, we need to define the units, conditions, and outcomes used to construct our inquiry. If the inquiry is an average causal effect among a subgroup, we need to specify the relevant potential outcomes, the treatment, and the covariate that describes the subgroup.

Data strategy: If a sampling procedure involves stratification or clustering, then in the model, we need to define the variables that will be used to stratify and cluster. Similarly, treatment assignment might be blocked or clustered; correspondingly, the variables that are used to construct blocks or clusters must be defined in the model. Finally, all of the variables that will be measured should also be defined in the model. When we measure latent variables imperfectly, the model describes the latent trait and how measured responses may deviate from it. If you expect to encounter complexities in D that you need to take account of in A, such as missing data, noncompliance, or attrition, then possible drivers of these should also be included in M.

Answer strategy: Any measured variable that will be used in the answer strategy should be included in the model. This requirement clearly includes the observed outcomes and treatments, but also any covariates that are used to address confounding or to increase precision.

The variables required by the inquiry, data strategy, and answer strategy are necessary components of the model, but they are not always sufficient. For example, we might be worried about an unobserved confounder. Such a confounder would not be obviously included in any of the other research design elements, but is clearly important to include in the model. Ultimately, we need to specify all variables that are required for "diagnosand completeness" (see Chapter 10), which is achieved when research designs are described in sufficient detail that diagnosands can be calculated.

6.3 How to Specify Models

To this point, we have described formal considerations, but we have not described substantive considerations, for including particular variables or stipulating particular relations between them. The justification for the choice of reference models will depend on the purpose of the design. Broadly, we distinguish between two desiderata for selecting reference models: reality tracking and agnosticism.

6.3.1 Reality tracking

In stipulating reference models, we have incentives to focus on models that we think track reality (m^*) as well as possible. Why waste time and effort stipulating processes we don't think will happen?

The justification for a claim that a model is reality tracking typically comes from two places: past literature and qualitative research. Past theoretical work can guide the set of variables that are relevant and how they relate to one another. Past empirical work can provide further insight into the distributions and dependencies across variables. However, when past research is thin, there is no substitute for insights gained through qualitative data collection: focus groups and interviews with key informants who know aspects of the model that are hidden from the researcher, archival investigations to understand a causal process, or immersive participant observation to see with your own eyes how social actors behave. Fenno (1978) memorably describes this process as "soaking and poking." This mode of model development is separate from the qualitative research designs that provide answers to well-specified inquiries (see the process tracing entry, Section 16.1, for an example of such a design). Instead, qualitative insights such as this, which Lieberman (2005) labels "model-building" case studies, do not aim to answer a question, but rather yield a new theoretical model. Quantitative research is often seen as distinct from qualitative research, but the model building phase in both is itself qualitative.

The next step—selecting statistical distributions and their parameters to describe exogenous variables and the functional forms of endogenous variables—is often more uncomfortable. We do not know the magnitude of the effect of an intervention or the correlation between two outcomes before we do the research; that's why we are conducting the study. However, we are not fully in the dark in most cases and can make educated guesses about most parameters.

We can conduct meta-analyses of past relevant studies on the same topic to identify the range of plausible effect sizes, intra-cluster correlations, correlations between variables, and other model parameters. Conducting such a meta-analysis might be as simple as collecting the three papers that measured similar outcomes in the past and calculating the intra-cluster correlations in each of them. How informative past studies are for your research setting depends on the similarity of units, treatments, and outcomes. Except in the case of pure replication studies, we are typically studying a (possibly new) treatment in a new setting, with new participants, or with new outcomes, so there will not be perfect overlap. However, the variation in effects across contexts and these other dimensions will help structure the range of our guesses specified in the model.

When there are past studies that are especially close to our own, we may want our model to match the observed empirical distribution from that past study as closely as possible. To do so, we can resample or bootstrap from the past data in order to simulate realistic data. Where there are no past studies that are sufficiently similar in some dimensions, we can collect new data through pilot studies (see Section 21.4) or baseline surveys to serve a similar purpose.

It is also possible to use the distribution over quantities in a model to represent our *uncertainty* over some quantities and in this way let our diagnostics integrate over our uncertainty. We did this already in Declaration 2.1, where we let the treatment effect be a random draw from a stipulated distribution. In doing this, the success function represents expected success with respect to this distribution over treatment effects.

Since it excludes cases we deem improbable, a focus on reality tracking models seems to contradict Principle 3.2: *Design agnostically* (see also below, Section 6.3.2). However, by focusing on reality-tracking models, we aim to contain the smallest set of plausible models that are needed to capture the essentials of the true process. In practice, of course, we might never represent m^* accurately. For instance, we might contemplate a set of worlds in which an effect lies between 0 and 1 yet not include the true value of 2. This is not necessarily a cause for concern. The lessons learned from a diagnosis do not depend on the realized world m^* being among the set of possible draws of M; the relevant question is only whether the kinds of inferences one might draw given stipulated reference models would also hold reasonably well for the true event generating process. For instance, if our aim is to assess whether an analysis strategy generates an unbiased estimate of a treatment effect, we may go to pains to make sure to model treatment assignment carefully, but modeling the size of a treatment effect correctly may not be important. The idea is that what you learn from the models that you do study is *sufficient* for inferences about a broader class of models within which the true event generating process might lie.

6.3.2 Agnosticism

For some purposes, the reference model might be developed not to track reality, as you see it, but rather to reflect assumptions in a scholarly debate. For instance, the purpose might be to question whether a given conclusion is valid *under the assumptions maintained by some scholarly community*. Indeed, it is possible that a reference model is used specifically because the researcher thinks it is inaccurate, allowing them to show that even if they are wrong about some assumptions about the world in M, their analysis will produce useful answers.

One useful exercise is to return to and question the assumptions you have built into your model. Many of these can be read directly from a DAG, but some are more subtle. In a directed acyclic graph, every arrow indicates a possible relation between a cause and an outcome. The big assumptions in these models, however, are seen not in the arrows but in the absence of arrows: every missing arrow represents a claim that an outcome is not affected by a possible cause. Answer strategies often depend upon such assumptions. Even when arrows are included, functional relations might presuppose particular features that are important for inference. For instance, a researcher using instrumental variables analysis (see Section 16.4) will generally assume that Z causes Y through D but not through other paths. This "excludability" assumption is about absent arrows. The same analysis might also assume that Z never affects D negatively. That "monotonicity" assumption is about functional forms. An agnostic reference model might loosen these assumptions to allow for possible violations of the excludability or monotonicity assumptions.

When we are agnostic, we admit we don't know whether the truth is in the set of models we consider reasonable—so we entertain a wider set than we might think plausible. We suggest three guides for choosing these ranges: the logical minimum and maximum bounds of a parameter, a meta-analytic summary of past studies, or best- and worst-case bounds, based on the substantive interpretations of previous work. A design that performs well in terms of power and bias under many such ranges might be labeled "robust to multiple models."

A separate goal is assessing the performance of a research design under different models implied by alternative theories. A good design will provide probative evidence no matter the true event generating process. A poor design might provide reliable answers only for specific types of event generating processes.

An important example is the performance of a research design under a "null model," where the true effect size is zero. A good research design should report with a high probability that there is insufficient evidence to reject a null effect. That same research design, under an alternative model with a large effect size, should with a high probability return evidence rejecting the null hypothesis of zero effect. The example makes clear that in order to understand whether the research design is strong, we need to understand how it performs under different models.

6.4 Summary

If this section left you spinning from the array of choices we have to make in declaring a model, in some ways that was our goal. Inside every power calculator and bespoke design simulation code is an array of assumptions. Some crucially determine design quality and others are unimportant. The salve to the dizziness is in Principle 3.2: *Design agnostically*. Where you are uncertain, explore whether both options produce similar diagnosands. The goal is for our data and answer strategies to hold up under many models.

CHAPTER 7

Defining the Inquiry

An inquiry is a question we ask of the world, and in the same way, of our models of the world. If we stipulate a reference model, m, then our inquiry is a summary of m. Suppose in some reference model that X affects Y. One inquiry might be descriptive: what is the average level of Y when $X = 1$, under the model? A second might be causal: what is the average treatment effect of X on Y? A third is about counterfactuals: for what share of units would Y have been different if X were different? If a model involves more variables, many more questions open up, for instance, regarding how the effect of one variable passes through, or is modified by, another.

When designing research, we should have our inquiries front of mind. Amazingly, very many research projects do not specify the target of inference, focusing instead on the specification of estimation procedures. At some stages of research it is not possible to specify the inquiry with great precision. In early stages you may need to do model-building research in order to find out what the right question is. But once you are at the stage of thinking through inferential strategies you need an inquiry in mind in order to select among options. For the same reason readers need to know your inquiry in order to evaluate your choices.

Formally, an inquiry is a summary function I that operates on an instance of a model $m \in M$. When we summarize the model with the inquiry, we obtain an "answer under the model." We formalize this idea as $I(m) = a_m$, with the important special case a_{m^*} representing our estimand. The difference between I and a_m is the difference between a question and its answer: I is the question we ask about the model and a_m is the answer.

In this book when we talk about inquiries, we will usually be referring to single-number summaries of models. Some common inquiries are descriptive, such as the means, conditional means, correlations, partial correlations, quantiles, and truth statements about variables in the model. Others are causal, such as the average difference in one variable when a second variable is set to two different values. We can think of a single-number inquiry as the atom of a research question.

While most inquiries are "atomic" in this way, some inquiries are more complex than a single-number summary. For example, the best linear predictor of Y given X is a two-number summary: it is the pair of numbers (the slope and intercept) that minimizes the total squared distance between the line and each value of Y. No need to stop at two-number summaries though. We could imagine the best quadratic predictor of Y given X (a three-number summary), and so on. We could have an inquiry that is the full conditional expectation function of Y given X, no matter how wiggly, nonlinear, and nuanced the shape of that function. It could in principle be a 1,000-number summary of the model, or something still more complex.

The inquiry could be constituted by a series of interrelated questions about the model. Indeed the goal of the research may be to generate or to test a model of the world.[1] For instance, a researcher might articulate a handful of important questions about the model that all have to come out a certain way or the model itself should be rejected. These complex inquires are made up of a series of atomic inquiries. We're interested in the sub-inquiries only insofar as they help us understand the real inquiry—is this model of the world a good one or not?

7.1 Elements of Inquiries

Every inquiry operates on the events generated by the model. We can think of the events as the data set that describes the units, treatment conditions, and outcome variables over which inquiries can be defined. This definition is closely connected to the common UTOS (units, treatments, outcomes, and settings) framework (Shadish, Cook and Campbell, 2002). The units are from the set of units within the model that the inquiry refers to, either all or a subset. The treatment conditions represent the set chosen for study. A descriptive inquiry is a summary of a single condition (reality), whereas a causal inquiry is a summary of multiple conditions. The outcomes are the set of nodes in the model that the inquiry concerns. Finally, the inquiry operates on the model events via a summary function. For example, the "population average" inquiry summarizes the outcome for all units in the population with the mean function. We discuss each element of inquiries in turn.

7.1.1 Units

The units of an inquiry are the set of people, places, or things that we are interested in studying. They may refer to all the units in a study or just a subset of them. For example, we can distinguish between many different average causal effect inquiries on the basis of their units: the average treatment effect (ATE) refers to all units in the study, the average treatment effect on the treated (ATT) refers to the units who

---

[1] Here, we are referring to an "inquiry model" not a "reference model," as discussed in Section 2.2.1. We provide an example of this type of inquiry model in Section 19.2.

actually are treated, the average treatment effect on the untreated (ATU) refers to those who *actually are not* treated, and the complier average causal effect (CACE) refers to those who would take treatment if assigned to be treated but not otherwise.

The reason we need to specify the units of an inquiry is inquiry values (estimands) may differ across units. If the units that are included in the sample live in easier-to-reach areas and people who live in easier-to-reach areas are wealthier than others, the sample average will differ from the population average—and also from the average among those in hard-to-reach places.

The choice of which set of units to focus on depends on theoretical considerations. To whom does the theoretical expectation apply? As a general matter, seeking insights that apply across many individuals is the goal of many social scientists. We are not typically interested in the effect of a treatment or the average outcome in a random sample of 100 units because we care about those units in particular, but because we wish to understand the treatment effect or outcomes in a broader population. Our theories often have so-called scope conditions, which define the types of units for which our theory is operative. A mechanism might operate only for coethnics of a country's president, small to medium towns, blue collar workers, or the mothers of daughters. The units of an inquiry should be defined by these theoretical expectations, not by which inquiries our data and answer strategies can target easily.

Distinctions among inquiries often arise in debates over instrumental variables designs, which target local average treatment effects (LATEs), meaning the average treatment among a subset. The effect these designs estimate is the average treatment effect among those units that are "compliers." Compliers are the subset of units that take treatment if assigned and don't take treatment if not assigned. The effect among compliers may or may not be like the effect among the whole sample or the population from which the sample was drawn. The debate between Deaton (2010) and Imbens (2010) centers precisely on which inquiry is the appropriate one, the LATE among compliers or the ATE in the whole sample. In many settings, the LATE may be the only inquiry we can reliably estimate, so the question becomes—is the LATE a theoretically relevant inquiry?

If the inquiry is defined with respect to the units sampled by the data strategy, then we do not have to engage in generalization inference—we learn directly about the sample from the sample. But if the inquiry is defined at the population level, then we need to generalize from the sample to the population. We also need to engage in generalization inference when we want to generalize study results to *other* populations that we did not explicitly sample from. Whether an inquiry requires generalization inference depends on the data strategy in the following way. If the data strategy samples the units that define the inquiry, we do not need to generalize beyond the study. If the data strategy explicitly samples from a well-defined population, we can generalize from sample to population using canonical sampling theory. But if we want to generalize to an inquiry defined over some other set of units (for example, Brazilian citizens ten years in the future), we need to engage in generalization inference (see Egami and Hartman, 2022).

7.1.2 Outcomes

Every inquiry is also defined by what outcomes are considered for each of the units. The choice of outcome also draws on theory: what outcomes are to be described, or with which outcomes do we want to measure the effects of a treatment? An inquiry might be about a single outcome or multiple outcomes. The average belief that climate change is real would be a single-outcome inquiry, and the difference between that belief and support for government rebates for purchasing electric vehicles a multiple-outcome inquiry.

In some cases, an inquiry will be about a latent outcome that we cannot directly measure, such as preferences, attitudes, or emotions. We can construct data strategies that measure these latent outcomes by asking questions or observing behavior, but we cannot directly measure them. Even though these constructs may be difficult or impossible to measure well, it is often preferable to define the inquiry in terms of the latent outcome of interest rather than in terms of the measured outcome.

7.1.3 Treatment conditions

The final element of an inquiry is the treatment conditions under consideration and, in the case of more than one, compared.

Descriptive inquiries are defined with respect to one single treatment condition. That treatment condition is often the "unmanipulated" condition in which the researcher exposes units to no additional causal agents. Here the goal is to learn about the summaries of the distributions of outcomes as we observe them. Table 7.1 (top panel) enumerates some common descriptive inquiries. These inquiries have in common that you do not need any counterfactual quantities in order to define them. The covariance (similarly, the correlation) between X and Y enters as a descriptive inquiry; so too does the line of best fit for Y given X. For each descriptive inquiry, we list the units, treatment conditions, and outcomes that define them. We also provide R code snippets for each.

Causal inquiries involve a comparison of at least two possible treatment conditions. For example, an inquiry might be the causal effect of D on Y for a single unit. In order to infer that causal effect, we would need to know the value of Y in two worlds: one world in which D is set to 1 and one in which D is set to 0. Table 7.2 (middle panel) enumerates some common causal inquiries. These inquiries vary in the units they refer to. For instance, some are questions about samples (SATEs) and others about populations (PATEs). Inquiries can also be defined for units of a particular covariate class (CATEs). Finally, they may be summaries of more than one potential outcome. For instance, the interaction effect is defined here at the individual level as the effect of one treatment on the effect of another treatment.

Table 7.1: Examples of descriptive inquiries and their three elements: units, treatment conditions, and outcomes.

Inquiry	Units	Treatment conditions	Outcomes	Code
Average value of variable Y in a finite population	Units in the population	Unmanipulated	Y	`mean(Y)`
Average value of variable Y in a sample	Sampled units	Unmanipulated	Y	`mean(Y[S == 1])`
Conditional average value of Y given X = 1	Units for whom X = 1	Unmanipulated	Y	`mean(Y[X == 1])`
The variance of Y	Units in the population	Unmanipulated	Y	`pop.var(Y)`
The covariance of X and Y	Units in the population	Unmanipulated	X, Y	`pop.cov(X, Y)`
The best linear predictor of Y given X	Units in the population	Unmanipulated	Y	`cov(Y, X) / var(X)`
Conditional expectation function of Y given X	Units in the population	Unmanipulated	Y	`cef(Y, X)`

Generations of students have been told to excise words that connote causality from their empirical writing. "Affects" becomes "is associated with" and "impacts" becomes "moves with." Being careful about causal language is of course very important (it's really true that correlation does not imply causation!). But this change in language is not usually accompanied by a change in inquiry. Many times we are faced with drawing causal inferences from less than ideal data, but the deficiencies of the data strategy should not lead us too far away from our inferential targets. If the inquiry is a causal inquiry, then although the move from "causes" to "is correlated with" might involve more defensible claims about the data, we still need a strategy to get to an answer to the inquiry.

7.1.4 Summary functions

With the units, treatments, and outcomes specified, the last element of the inquiry is the summary function that is applied to them. For a great many inquiries, this function is the `mean` function: the ATE, the CATE, the LATE, the SATE, the

Table 7.2: Examples of causal inquiries and their three elements: units, treatment conditions, and outcomes.

Inquiry	Units	Treatment conditions	Outcomes	Code
Average treatment effect in a finite population (PATE)	Units in the population	D = 0, D = 1	Y	mean(Y_D_1 - Y_D_0)
Conditional average treatment effect (CATE) for X = 1	Units for whom X = 1	D = 0, D = 1	Y	mean(Y_D_1[X == 1] - Y_D_0[X == 1])
Complier average causal effect (CACE)	Complier units	D = 0, D = 1	Y	mean(Y_D_1[D_Z_1 > D_Z_0] - Y_D_0[D_Z_1 > D_Z_0])
Causal interactions of D1 and D2	Units in the population	D1 = 1, D1 = 0, D2 = 1, D2 = 0	Y	mean((Y_D1_1_D2_1 - Y_D1_0_D2_1) - (Y_D1_1_D2_0 - Y_D1_0_D2_0))

population mean—these are all averages. These and other inquiries are "decomposable" in the sense that you can think of an average effect for a large group as being the weighted average of a set of average effects of smaller groups.

However, not all inquiries are of this form. For example, the line of best fit is defined as the covariance of X and Y divided by the variance of X. This inquiry is a complex summary of all the units in the model.

The inquiry that the regression discontinuity design shoots at is also non-decomposable. In the RDD model (see Section 16.5), we imagine units with $Y_i(1)$, $Y_i(0)$. Each i also has a value on a "running variable," X_i, and units receive treatment if and only if $X_i > 0$. In this case the "effect at the point of discontinuity" might be written:

$$E_{i|X_i=0}(Y_i(Z_i=1) - Y_i(Z_i=0)).$$

Curiously, however, there may be no units for whom X_i equals exactly 0 (a candidate who wins exactly 50% of the vote happens, but it is rare), so we cannot easily think of the inquiry as being a summary of individual potential outcomes. Instead, we construct a conditional expectation function for both potential outcome functions with respect to X_i and evaluate the difference between these when $X_i = 0$. Though not an average of individual effects, this difference is nevertheless a summary of the potential outcomes.

Table 7.3: Examples of data-dependent inquiries and their three elements: units, treatment conditions, and outcomes.

Inquiry	Units	Treatment conditions	Outcomes	Code
Average treatment effect in a sample (SATE)	Sampled units	D = 0, D = 1	Y	`mean(Y_D_1[S == 1] - Y_D_0[S == 1])`
Average treatment effect on the treated (ATT)	Treated units	D = 0, D = 1	Y	`mean(Y_D_1[D == 1] - Y_D_0[D == 1])`
Average treatment effect on the untreated (ATU)	Untreated units	D = 0, D = 1	Y	`mean(Y_D_1[D == 0] - Y_D_0[D == 0])`

7.2 Types of Inquiries

The largest division in the typology of inquiries is between descriptive and causal inquiries. It is for this reason that Part III, the design library, is organized into descriptive and causal chapters, separated by whether the data strategy is observational or experimental. In this section, we describe other important ways inquiries vary and how to think about declaring them.

7.2.1 Data-dependent inquiries

Most of the inquiries we have introduced thus far depend on variables in the model, but not on features of the data and answer strategies. However, common inquiries do depend on realizations of the research design.

The first type depends on realizations of the data d: inquiries about units within a sample depend on which units enter the sample; inquiries about treated units depend on which are treated. For example, the average treatment effect on the treated (ATT) is a data-dependent inquiry in the sense that it is the average effect of treatment among the particular set of units that happened to be randomly assigned to treatment. The value of that *particular* ATT doesn't change depending on the data strategy, of course, but *which* ATT we end up estimating depends on the realization of the data strategy. Table 7.3 describes three data-dependent inquiries.

7.2.2 Causal attribution inquiries

A causal attribution inquiry is a different kind of data-dependent inquiry. A causal effect inquiry focuses on the change in an outcome that would be induced by a change in the causal variable, irrespective of the values that the outcome takes in the realized data. By contrast, causal attribution inquiries focus on inquiries that condition on realized outcomes, such as the "the absence of the outcome in the hypothetical absence of the treatment ($Y_i(0) = 0$) given the actual presence of both ($D_i = Y_i = 1$)" (Yamamoto, 2012, pp. 240–241). In other words, had this feature been different, would the outcome have been different? Goertz and Mahoney (2012) and others refer to causal attribution inquiries as cause-of-effects questions because they start with an outcome (an "effect") and seek to validate a hypothesis about its cause.

The dependence of these inquiries on actual outcomes makes them harder (though not impossible!) to answer with the tools of quantitative science, though they are often of central interest to scientific and policy agendas and have occupied a large number of qualitative studies. Questions like "Was economic crisis necessary for democratization in the Southern Cone of Latin America?" or "Were high levels of foreign investment in combination with soft authoritarianism and export-oriented policies sufficient for the economic miracles in South Korea and Taiwan?" are examples of such inquiries (Goertz and Mahoney, 2012). Though they bear a resemblance to causal effect inquiries that focus on observed subsets (such as the average treatment effect on the treated, or ATT),[2] it is important not to confuse the two kinds of inquiries.

While it is increasingly common to explicitly formalize causal effect inquiries, it is less common to formalize causal attribution inquiries. Doing so, however, can provide the specificity required to diagnose a design. Pearl (1999) provides formal definitions for these inquiries using the language of causal necessity and sufficiency, depicted in Table 7.4. To put these inquiries in the context of the democratic peace hypothesis (which states that no two democracies will go to war), for example, in a given country dyad-year, $Y_i = 1$ and $D_i = 1$ could represent "Peace" and "Both democracies" and $Y_i = 0$ and $D_i = 0$ could represent "War" and "Not both democracies."[3] Then $\Pr(Y_i(D_i = 0) = 0 \mid D_i = Y_i = 1)$ asks, among peaceful, fully democratic dyads, what is the proportion that would have had wars were they not both democracies—that is, in what proportion of dyad-years was democracy a necessary cause of peace? Similarly, $\Pr(Y_i(D_i = 1) = 1 \mid D_i = Y_i = 0)$ asks, among dyads that had a war and at least one non-democracy in a given year, what is the proportion that would have experienced peace if both countries were democracies—in other words, in what proportion of cases would democracy have been sufficient to cause peace? Yamamoto (2012) extends on this account to focus on causal attribution inquiries for particular subsets, such as compilers.

---

[2] Specifically, as Yamamoto (2012) points out, the causal attribution inquiry for binary variables can be written $\Pr(Y_i(0) = 0 \mid D_i = Y_i = 1)$, while the average treatment effect among those successfully treated can be written $E[Y_i(1) - Y_i(0) \mid D_i = Y_i = 1]$. Given binary outcomes and the additive property of expectations, the ATE among those successfully treated can be written $\Pr(Y_i(1) \mid D_i = Y_i = 1) - \Pr(Y_i(0) \mid D_i = Y_i = 1)$. The causal attribution inquiry can be written as 1 minus the second term of the ATE among the successfully treated.

[3] Note that we can think of the probability in this statement as implying a population level inquiry—the share with a given feature; or as a representation of a unit level Bayesian *answer* to the question. See, e.g., Dawid, Humphreys and Musio (2022).

Table 7.4: Examples of causal attribution inquiries and their three elements: units, treatment conditions, and outcomes.

Inquiry	Units	Treatment conditions	Outcomes	Code
Probability D necessary for Y	Units for whom $D = 1$ and $Y = 1$	$D = 0$	Y	mean(Y_D_0[D == 1 & Y == 1] == 0)
Probability D sufficient for Y	Units for whom $D = 0$ and $Y = 0$	$D = 1$	Y	mean(Y_D_1[D == 0 & Y == 0] == 1)
Complier probability D necessary for Y	Units for whom $D = 1$ and $Y = 1$ who are compliers	$D = 0, Z = 1, Z = 0$	Y	mean(Y_D_0[D == 1 & Y == 1 & D_Z_1 == 1 & D_Z_0 == 0] == 0)

7.2.3 Complex counterfactual inquiries

The causal inquiries we have considered thus far have involved comparisons of the counterfactual values an outcome could take, depending on the value of one or more treatment variables. These inquiries are mind-bending in that we have to imagine two counterfactual states at the same time. *Complex* counterfactual inquiries require more mind bending still.

An example of a complex counterfactual inquiry is the "natural direct effect." Suppose our model contains a treatment Z_i, a mediator M_i, and outcome Y_i. The natural direct effect of the treatment is defined as:

$$\text{NDE} = Y_i(Z_i = 1, M_i = M_i(Z_i = 1)) - Y_i(Z_i = 0, M_i = M_i(Z_i = 1))$$

In the second term of this expression, we have to hold in our minds the complex counterfactual: what is the level of Y_i, when Z_i equals 0, but M_i is at the (possibly different) value it would take if Z_i equaled one?

7.2.4 Inquiries with continuous causal variables

The forgoing causal inquiries have focused on contrasts between discrete levels of a treatment variable. We can also imagine many different types of inquiries defined in continuous treatment spaces. For example, we could think of the effects of any level of salary from 5 dollars an hour to 500 dollars an hour on workplace satisfaction. We could "discretize" these continuous treatments in bins, in which case we are back to defining inquiries with discrete treatment conditions. Another possibility is to describe the inquiry as the average of the slopes from many lines of best fit.

For each subject, we describe the line of best fit of the outcome with respect to the treatment. Our inquiry is then the average of the resulting slopes.

7.3 How to Define Inquiries

There are multiple criteria for choosing an inquiry. We want to pick one that is interesting in its own right or one that would facilitate a real-world decision. We want to pick research questions that we can learn the answer to someday, possibly with a lot of effort. We want to avoid unfeasible research questions. Among feasible research questions, we want to select ones that we are likely to obtain the most informative answers, in terms of moving our priors the most.

Sometimes, advisers tell students to follow a "theory-first" route to picking a research question. Read the literature, find an unsolved puzzle, then start choosing among the methodological approaches that might answer the problem. Others are more skeptical of starting with questions that might not be answerable and encourage students to first master tools that can answer particular types of questions and then find places to apply them. You don't have to subscribe to either of these positions but you do have to keep an eye simultaneously on the substantive importance of questions and the scope for generating informative answers.

The first criterion for a good inquiry is then the subjective importance of a question. The answer may be important for science (building a theoretical understanding of the world) or for decision-making (choosing which policies to implement). Even so, the scientific enterprise is designed around the idea that importance is in the eye of the beholder and is not some objective quantity. This is for two reasons. First, the scientific or practical importance of a discovery may not be understood until decades later, when other pieces of the causal model are put together or the world faces new problems. Moreover, "importance" differs for different segments of society, and scientists must be able to study questions not judged important by groups in power in order to discover new ways to solve problems faced by the left-out groups.

The second important criterion for a good inquiry is that it should be answerable, or at least *partially* answerable. The main way an inquiry might not be answerable is we can't find a feasible data or answer strategy. When for ethical, legal, logistical, or financial constraints, we simply can't conduct the study, the inquiry is not answerable.

There are subtler ways in which an inquiry might not be answerable. For example, it might be undefined. Inquiries are undefined when I returns $I(m) = a_m = \text{NA}$. For example, sometimes audit studies consider the effect of treatment on responding to an email and on the tone of the email. However, in conditions where the email is never sent, it has no tone. As a result, we can't learn about the average effect of treatment on tone, we can only learn about the effect in a subgroup: those units who always respond to email, regardless of condition. This new inquiry is well defined, but hard to estimate (see Coppock, 2019).

An inquiry is also not answerable if it is not, at least partially, identifiable. A question is at least partly answerable if there are at least two different sets of data you might observe that would lead you to make two different inferences. In the best case, one might imagine that you have lots of data and each possible data pattern you see is consistent with only one possible answer. You might then say that your model, or inquiry, is identified. Failing that, you might imagine that different data patterns at least let you rule out some answers even though you can't be sure of the right answer. In this case we have "partial identification." Some inquiries might not even be partially identifiable. For instance if we have a model that says an outcome Y is defined by the equation $Y = (a+b)X$, no amount of data can tell us the exact values of a and b. Indeed without limits on the values of a and b (such as $a \geq 0$), no amount of data can even narrow down the ranges of a and b. The basic problem is that for any value of a we can choose a b that keeps the sum of $a+b$ constant. In this setting, even though there is an answer to our inquiry (a) in theory, it is not one we can ever answer in practice. Many other types of inquiries, such as mediation inquiries, are not identifiable. There are some circumstances in which we can provide a partial answer to the inquiry, such as learning a range of values within which the parameter lives. At a minimum, we urge you to pose inquiries that are at least partially answerable with possible data.

One place in which a trade-off between substantive importance and answerability can come to a head is in selecting the population for which an inquiry is defined. One common approach is to define inferences with respect to a "finite population." For instance, all US states. You might then sample from this finite population in the data strategy in such a way that you can use the sample to draw inferences about the population. The probability distribution over the exogenous variables simply enumerates the values that these variables take on in the population. Any randomness in the design is generated by the sampling and, perhaps, by assignment procedures, not in the values of the exogenous variables.

A second, and closely related, approach is to define inferences for a finite *sample*. This is like population inference when you sample the whole population. In a sense the sample *is* the population. Finite sample inference is common in research designs that involve random assignment of treatments. The only source of randomness in the finite sample setting is the random assignment itself.

A third approach is to think in terms of "superpopulations," in which we imagine that any particular population is just a draw from an infinite superpopulation. In this case, we can conceive of the randomness in the design as being fundamental—every unit is a random draw from the superpopulation.

7.3 How to Define Inquiries

Implicitly, if you set up a simulation and draw data using some probability density function, you are drawing from a superpopulation. But you get to specify the type of target of inference when you specify the inquiry, as in Declaration 7.1.

Declaration 7.1 Super-population, population, and finite sample design.

```
declaration_7.1 <-
  declare_model(
    N = 20,
    U = rnorm(N),
    Y = 1 + U
  ) +
  declare_inquiry(
    superpopulation_mean = 1,
    population_mean = mean(Y)
  ) +
  declare_sampling(
    S = complete_rs(N, n = 10)
  ) +
  declare_inquiry(sample_mean = mean(Y))
```

Here is one draw on the estimands:

```
draw_estimands(declaration_7.1)
```

Table 7.5: Super-population, population, and finite sample inquiries.

inquiry	estimand
superpopulation_mean	1.00
population_mean	1.19
sample_mean	1.50

Which of these to choose? Researchers sometimes prefer superpopulation inquiries because they describe general processes on substantive grounds, seeing understanding general processes as the primary goal of social scientific interest. Some are skeptical, however, about speculating about general, unobservable, processes, preferring to make statements about cases that actually exist in the world. They prefer to select populations of substantive importance. Others seeking to avoid engaging in generalization inference prefer to focus on sample quantities. In some cases the statistics are more suited for finite populations: for instance, randomization inference is based on the randomness induced by assignment and not from sampling populations from superpopulations or samples from populations.[4] Critics worry that keeping the focus on the sample means having inquiries that are determined by the realizations of your data strategy rather than having data strategies developed to answer prespecified inquiries.

7.4 Summary

Inquiries define our targets of inference, stated in terms of a model of the world. We described how inquiries are defined with respect to specific outcomes expressed by specific units under specific conditions, which are summarized with a chosen function. Inquiries can be descriptive or causal, depending on the mix of conditions they depend on. They can be data-dependent or not and decomposable or not. They should be well defined and they should be answerable. When we lose track of our inquiries, research studies can end up estimating whatever the answer strategy ends up targeting. Researchers should choose their inquiries with intention so that they can select appropriate empirical strategies for them.

---

[4]For some purposes the statistics are easier for the superpopulation quantities: for instance, the Neyman variance estimate is exact in this case but conservative in the finite population case (for instance, Aronow, Green, and Lee, 2014).

CHAPTER 8

Crafting a Data Strategy

In order to collect information about the world, researchers must deploy a data strategy. Depending on the design, the data strategy could include decisions about any or all of the following: sampling, treatment assignment, and measurement. Sampling is the procedure for selecting which units will be measured; treatment assignment is the procedure for allocating treatments to sampled units; and measurement is the procedure for turning information about the sampled units into data. These three procedures parallel the three elements of an inquiry: the units, treatment conditions, and outcomes.

We think about data strategies in response to Principle 3.1: *Design holistically*—we make data strategy choices to respond to model features.

Sampling choices are used to justify generalization inferences: we want to make general claims, which often implies inferences about units *not* sampled. For this reason, we need to pay special attention to the procedure by which units are selected into the sample. We might use a random sampling procedure in order to generate a design-based justification for generalizing from samples to populations. Nonrandom sampling procedures are also possible: convenience sampling, respondent-driven sampling, and snowball sampling are examples of data strategies that do not include an explicitly randomized component.

Assignment choices are used to justify causal inferences: we want to make inferences about the conditions to which units were *not* assigned. For this reason, experimental design is focused on the assignment of treatments. Should the treatment be randomized? How many treatment conditions should there be? Should we use a simple coin flip to decide who receives treatment, or should we use a more complicated strategy like blocking?

Measurement choices are used to justify descriptive inferences: we want to make inferences about latent values *not* observed on the basis of measured values. The tools we use to measure are a critical part of the data strategy. For many social scientific studies, a prominent way we collect information is through surveys. A huge methodological literature on survey administration has been developed to help guide questionnaire development. Bad survey questions yield distorted or noisy responses due to large measurement error. A biased question systematically misses the true latent target it is designed to measure, in which case we say the question has low "validity." A question is high variance if (hypothetically) we would obtain different answers each time we ask, in which case we say the question has low "reliability." The concerns about validity and reliability do not disappear once we move out of the survey environment. For example, the information that shows up in an administrative database is itself the result of many human decisions, each of which has the possibility of increasing or decreasing the distance between the measurement and the latent measurement target.

Strong research design can help address these three inferential challenges, but we can never be sure that our sample generalizes, or that we know what would have happened in a counterfactual state of the world, or what the true latent value of the outcome is (or if it even exists). Researchers have to choose good sampling, treatment assignment, and measurement techniques that, when combined and applied to the world, will produce analysis-ready information.

More formally, the data strategy, D, is a set of procedures that result in a dataset d^*. It is important to keep these two concepts straight. If you apply data strategy D to the world m^*, it produces a dataset d^*. Similarly, application of D to model m produces d. We say d^* is "the" result of D, since when we apply the data strategy to the world, we only do so once and we obtain the data we obtain. But when we are crafting a data strategy, we have to think about the many datasets that the data strategy *could have* produced under all the models in M, since we don't know m^*. Some of the datasets might be really excellent (from the researcher's perspective). For example, in good datasets, we achieve good covariate balance across the treatment and control groups. Or we might draw a sample whose distribution of observable characteristics looks really similar to the population. But some of the datasets might be worse: because of the vagaries of randomization, the particular realizations of the random assignment or random sampling might be more or less balanced. We do not have to settle for data strategies that might produce weak datasets—we are in control of the procedures we choose. We want to choose a data strategy D that is likely to result in a high-quality dataset d^*.

In Figure 8.1, we illustrate these three elements of data strategies: sampling (S), treatment assignment (Z), and measurement (Q). These nodes are highlighted by blue boxes to emphasize that they are in the control of the researcher. No arrows go into the S, Z, or Q nodes; they are *set* by the researcher. In each case, the strategy selected by the researcher affects a corresponding endogenous variable. The sampling procedure causes changes in the endogenous response (R), which represents whether participants provide outcome data, for example responding to survey questions. R is not under the full control the researchers: it is affected by S, the sampling procedure, but also by the idiosyncratic choices of participants who have higher and lower interest and ability to respond and participate in the study (U). Similarly, the

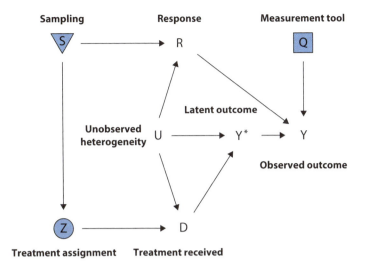

Figure 8.1: Directed acyclic graph illustrating three elements of a data strategy: sampling, assignment, and measurement.

endogenous variable treatment D represents whether participants *actually* receive the treatment, regardless of their assignment Z. D is affected by the treatment assignment procedure (Z), of course. But except in cases when Z fully determines D (no noncompliance), we are concerned that it will be affected by unobserved idiosyncratic features of individuals U. The third researcher node is Q, the measurement procedure. Q affects Y, the observed outcome, measured by the researcher. Y is also affected by a latent variable Y^*, which cannot be directly observed. The measurement procedure provides an imperfect measurement of that latent variable, which is (potentially) affected by treatment D and unobserved heterogeneity U. In the robustness section at the end of the chapter, we explore further variations of this DAG that incorporate threats to inference from noncompliance, attrition, excludability violations, and interference.

8.1 Elements of Data Strategies

In Chapter 7, an inquiry I was characterized by a set of outcomes, a set of treatment conditions, and a set of units, as well as a function that summarizes those outcomes, assessed at those conditions, over those units. The three elements of the data strategy D parallel the first three elements of inquiries: we sample units, assign treatment conditions, and measure outcomes. We next describe menus of approaches that you might use for each of these three parts of your data strategy.

8.1.1 Sampling

Sampling is the process by which units are selected from the population to be studied. The starting point for every sampling strategy should be to consider the units defined in the inquiry. In some cases, all the units to whom the inquiry apply are included in the study, but in others, we consider only a subset.

Why would we ever be content to study a sample and not the full population? For infinite populations, we have no choice. For finite populations the first and best explanation is cost: it's expensive and time-consuming to conduct a full census of the population. Even well-funded research projects face this problem, since money and effort spent answering one question could also be spent answering a second question. A second reason to sample is the diminishing marginal returns of additional data collection. Increasing the number of sampled units from 1,000 to 2,000 will greatly increase the precision of our estimates. Moving from 100,000 to 101,000 will improve things too, but the scale of the improvement is much smaller. Finally, it may simply not be possible to sample some units. Units in the distant past or distant future, for example, are not available to be sampled, even if they are in the set of units that define the inquiry.

Some sampling procedures involve randomization while others do not. Whether a sampling procedure is randomized or not has large implications for the answer strategy. Randomized designs support "design-based inference," which refers to the idea that we rely on known features of the sampling process when producing population-level estimates—much more about this in the next chapter on answer strategies. When randomization breaks down (e.g., if the design encounters attrition) or if nonrandomized designs are used, then we have to fall back on model-based inference to generalize from the sample to the population. Model-based inference relies on researcher beliefs about the nature of the uncontrolled sampling process in order to make inferences about the population. When possible, design-based inference has the advantage of letting us ground inferences in known rather than assumed features of the world. That said, when randomly sampled individuals fail to respond or when we seek to make inferences about *new* populations, we oftentimes fall back to model-based inference.

8.1.1.1 Randomized sampling designs

Owing to the natural appeal of design-based inference, we start off with randomized designs before proceeding to nonrandomized designs. Randomized sampling designs typically begin with a list of all units in a population, then choose a subset to sample using a random process. These random processes can be simple (every unit has an equal probability of inclusion) or complex (first we select regions at random, then villages at random within selected regions, then households within selected villages, then individuals within selected households).

Table 8.1 collects all of these kinds of random sampling together and offers examples of functions in the `randomizr` package you can use to conduct them. The most basic form is simple random sampling. Under simple random sampling, all units in the population have the same probability p of being included in the sample.

8.1 Elements of Data Strategies

Table 8.1: Kinds of random sampling.

Design	Description and `randomizr` R code
Simple random sampling	"Coin flip" or Bernoulli random sampling. All units have the same inclusion probability p `simple_rs(N = 100, p = 0.25)`
Complete random sampling	Exactly n of N units are sampled, and all units have the same inclusion probability n/N `simple_rs(N = 100, p = 0.25)`
Stratified random sampling	Complete random sampling within predefined strata. Units within the same strata have the same inclusion probability n_s / N_s `strata_rs(strata = regions)`
Cluster random sampling	Whole groups of units are brought into the sample together. `cluster_ra(clusters = households)`
Stratified cluster sampling	Cluster random sampling within strata `strata_and_cluster_rs(strata = regions, clusters = villages)`

Multi-stage random sampling	First clusters, then units within
	`cluster_ra(clusters = villages)`
	`strata_ra(strata = villages)`

It is sometimes called coin flip random sampling because it is as though for each unit, we flip a weighted coin that has probability *p* of landing heads up. While quite straightforward, a drawback of simple random sampling is that we can't be sure of the number of sampled units in advance. Although, in expectation, we'll sample $N*p$ units, in practice, sometimes slightly more units will be sampled and sometimes fewer.

Complete random sampling addresses this problem. Under complete random sampling, exactly *n* of *N* units are sampled. Each unit still has an inclusion probability of $p = n/N$, but in contrast to simple random sampling, we are guaranteed that the final sample will be of size n.[1] Complete random sampling represents an improvement over simple random sampling because it rules out samples in which more or fewer than $N*p$ units are sampled. One circumstance in which we might nevertheless go with simple random sampling is when the size of the population is not known in advance, and sampling choices may have to be made "on the fly."

Complete random sampling solves the problem of fixing the total number of sampled units, but it doesn't address the problem that the total number of units with particular characteristics will not be fixed. Imagine a population with N_y young people and N_o old people. If we sample exactly *n* from the population $N_y + N_o$, the number of sampled young people (n_y) and sampled old people (n_o) will bounce around from sample to sample. We can solve this problem by conducting complete random sampling *within* each group of units. This procedure goes by the name

---
[1]To convince yourself of the difference between simple and complete random sampling, run `table(simple_rs(N = 100, prob = 0.5))` a few times and compare the results with `table(complete_rs(N = 100, n = 50))`.

stratified random sampling, since the sampling is conducted separately within the strata of units.[2] In our example, our strata were formed by a dichotomous grouping of people into "young" and "old" categories, but in general, the sampling strata can be defined by any information we have about units before they are sampled. Stratification offers at least three major benefits. First, we defend against sampling surprisingly too few units in some stratum by "bad luck." Second, stratification tends to produce lower variance estimates of many estimands. Finally, stratification allows researchers to "oversample" subgroups of particular interest (see Section 18.4).

Stratified sampling should not be confused with cluster sampling. Stratified sampling means that a fixed number of units from a particular group are drawn into the sample. Cluster sampling means that units from a particular group are brought into the sample *together*. For example, if we cluster sample households, we interview all individuals living in a sampled household. Clustering introduces dependence in the sampling procedure—if one member of the household is sampled, the other members are also always sampled. Relative to a complete random sample of the same size, cluster samples tend to produce higher variance estimates. Just as with individual sampling designs, cluster sampling comes in simple, complete, and stratified varieties with parallel logics and motivations.

Lastly, we turn to multi-stage random sampling, in which we conduct random sampling at multiple levels of a hierarchically structured population. For example, we might first sample regions, then villages within regions, then households within villages, then individuals within households. Each of those sampling steps might be stratified or clustered depending on the researcher's goals. The purpose of a multi-stage approach is typically to balance the logistical difficulties of visiting many geographic areas with the relative ease of collecting additional data once there.

Figure 8.2 gives a graphical interpretation of each of these kinds of random sampling. Here, we imagine a population of 64 units with two levels of hierarchy. For concreteness, we can imagine that the units are individuals nested within 16 households of four people each and the 16 households are nested within four villages of four households each. Starting at the top left, we have simple random sampling at the individual level. The inclusion probability was set to 0.5, so on average, we ought to sample 32 people, but in this particular draw, we actually sampled only 29. Complete random sampling (top center), fixes this problem, so exactly 32 people are sampled—but these 32 are unevenly spread across the four villages. This is addressed with stratified sampling. In the top right, we sample exactly eight people at random from each village of 16 total people.

---

[2]To convince yourself of the difference between complete and stratified sampling, run `age <- rep(c("Y", "O"), 50); table(age, complete_rs(N = 100, n = 50))` a few times and compare the results with `table(age, strata_rs(strata = age))`.

8.1 Elements of Data Strategies   71

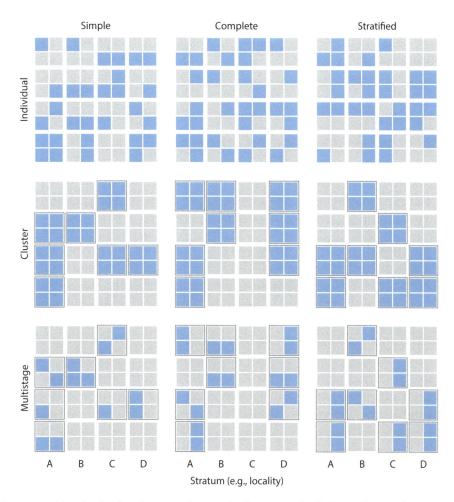

Figure 8.2: Nine kinds of random sampling. In the first row individuals are the sampling units, in the second row clusters are sampled, in the third clusters are sampled and then individuals within these clusters are sampled. In the first column units are sampled independently, in the second units are sampled to hit a target, in the third units are sampled to hit targets within strata.

Moving down to the middle row of the figure, we have three approaches to cluster random sampling. Under simple random sampling at the cluster level, each cluster has the same probability p of inclusion in the sample, so on average we will sample eight clusters. This time, we only sampled seven. This problem can again be fixed with complete random sampling (center facet), but again we have an uneven distribution across villages. Stratified cluster sampling ensures that exactly two households from each village are sampled.

The bottom row of the figure illustrates some approaches to multistage sampling. In the bottom left panel, we conduct a simple random sample of individuals in each sampled cluster. In the bottom center, we draw a complete random sample of individuals in each sampled household. And in the bottom right, we stratify on an individual-level characteristic—we always draw one individual from each row of the household (substantively, we could imagine that "row" could refer to the age of the household members). This doubly stratified multistage random sampling procedure ensures that we sample two households from each village, and within those households, one older member and one younger member.

8.1.1.2 *Nonrandomized sampling designs*

Because nonrandomized sampling procedures are defined by what they don't do—they don't use randomization—the term encompasses a hugely varied set of procedures. We'll consider just a few common ones, since the idiosyncrasies of each nonrandomized approach are hard to systematize.

Convenience sampling refers to the practice of gathering units from the population in an inexpensive way. Convenience sampling might be a good choice when generalizing to an explicit population is not a main goal of the design—for example, when a sample average treatment effect is a theoretically important inquiry. For many decades, social science undergraduates were the most abundant data source available to academics and many important theoretical claims have been established on the basis of experiments conducted with such samples. In recent years, however, online convenience samples like Mechanical Turk, Prolific, or Lucid have mostly supplanted undergraduates as the convenience sample of choice in some disciplines. Convenience sampling may lead to badly biased estimates of population quantities. For example, cable news shows often conduct viewer polls that should not be taken at all seriously. While such polls might promote viewer loyalty (and so might be worth doing from the cable executives' perspective), they do not provide credible evidence about what the population at large thinks or believes.

Many types of qualitative and quantitative research involve convenience sampling. Archival research often involves the "convenience" sample of documents on a certain topic that exist in an archive. The question of how these documents differ from those that would be in a different archive, or how the documents available in archives differ from those that do not ever make it into the archive, importantly shapes what we can learn from them. With the decline of telephone survey response rates, researchers can no longer rely on random digit dialing to obtain a representative sample of people in many countries, and instead must rely on convenience samples from the internet or panels who agree to have their phone numbers in a list. Reweighting techniques in the answer strategy can, in some cases, help recover estimates for the population as a whole if a credible model of the unknown sampling process can be agreed upon.

Next, we consider purposive sampling. Purposive is a catch-all term for rule-based sampling strategies that do not involve random draws, but also are not purely based on convenience and cost. A common example is quota sampling. Sampling purely based on convenience often means we will end up with many units of one type but very few of another type. Quota sampling addresses the problem by continuing to

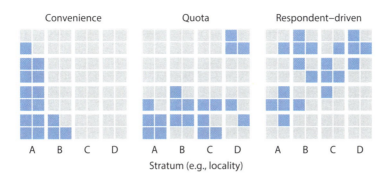

Figure 8.3: Three forms of nonrandom sampling.

search for subjects until target counts (quotas) of each kind of subject are found. Loosely speaking, quota sampling is to convenience sampling what stratified random sampling is to complete random sampling: it fixes the problem that not enough (or too many) subjects of particular types are sampled by employing specific quotas. Importantly, however, we have no guarantee that the sampled units *within* a type are representative of that type overall. Quota samples remain within-stratum convenience samples.

A second common form of purposive sampling is respondent-driven sampling (RDS), which is used to sample from hard-to-reach populations such as HIV-positive needle users. RDS methods often begin with a convenience sample and then systematically obtain contacts for other units who share the same characteristic in order the build a large sample. The hope is that as you move out from the initial sample the new subjects become increasingly representative of the population of interest (Heckathorn, 1997).

Each of these three nonrandom sampling procedures—convenience, quota, and respondent-driven—is illustrated in Figure 8.3. Imagining that village A is easier to reach, we could obtain a convenience sample by contacting everyone we can reach in village A before moving on to village B. This process doesn't yield good coverage across villages. For that, we can turn to quota sampling scheme in which we talk to the five people who are easiest to reach in each of the four villages. Finally, if we conduct a respondent-driven sample, we select a seed that person recruits their four closest friends (who may or may not reside in the same village), who in turn recruit from their friends, and so on.

8.1.1.3 Sampling designs for qualitative research

Another term for sampling is case selection. In case study research, whether qualitative or quantitative, the way we select the (typically small) set of cases is of great importance, and considerable attention has been paid to developing case selection methods.

Advice for selecting cases ranges widely, with many seeming disagreements across scholars (see, for instance, the symposium in Collier et al., 2008). We describe the major strategies used below and highlight some of the goals and assumptions motivating them. The most general advice, however, is that there are likely situations and rationales that could justify any of these strategies. But whether one or the other strategy is right for the problem you face most likely depends on the three other components of your design: what your model set is, what your inquiry is, and what your answer strategy is. Conversely, it is very difficult to assess whether one approach is more appropriate than another without knowing about these other parts of a design because it is hard to tell whether a case will be useful without knowing what you plan to do with it. In short, the case selection decision is one that is usefully made, and justified, by diagnosis.

Geddes (2003) warned that "the cases you choose affect the answers you get." This warning emphasizes the importance of case selection. If we select cases in order to arrive at a particular answer, then the research design doesn't provide good evidence in favor of the answer.

Non-purposive selection. Fearon and Laitin (2008) argue that one good approach is to select randomly. The argument for this approach depends on the purpose and details of the design. If the goal is to use case studies to check the quality of data used in large n analysis, or to explore the sets of pathways that might link a cause to an outcome, then random selection has the virtue of generating a representative set of cases and guards against cherry-picking.

Positive selection. Goertz (2008) argues that one should select multiple cases for which a positive outcome (e.g., a revolution) is unambiguously observed and one should also seek diversity in possible causes. The goal is to have as many opportunities as possible to observe possibly distinct paths leading to an outcome. We have a different perspective on the positive selection procedure, for two reasons. First, the approach presupposes an ability to figure out the causal factors within a case, i.e., it presupposes that one can assess the counterfactual values of outcomes within a case. Second, even if one can do single-case causal inference, Goertz argues that cases in which $X = 0$ and $Y = 0$ are not very useful for figuring out if $X = 1$ causes $Y = 1$. On the contrary, we might believe that the effect of X on Y runs through a positive effect of X on M and a positive effect of M on Y. But if looking at an $X = 0$, $Y = 0$ case we find that, awkwardly, $M = 1$, the evidence casts doubt on the causal importance of X in the $X = Y = 1$ cases. Ultimately, whether the positive selection approach is appropriate in any given instance is a question for diagnosis insofar as it depends on the model, the inquiry, and the answer strategy.

Other purposive strategies. Lieberman (2005) proposes using the predicted values from an initial cross-case regression model in order to select cases for in-depth analysis. Exactly how to select, however, depends on the inquiry and answer strategy. When the inquiry is focused on uncovering the same causal relationship sought in the regression analysis, Lieberman (2005) suggests selecting cases that are relatively well predicted and that maximize variation on the causal variable. He points to Martin (1992) and Swank (2002) as examples of designs employing this strategy. However, Lieberman (2005) advocates a different case selection strategy when the goal is to expand upon the theory initially tested in the regression analysis. In that instance, he recommends choosing cases lying far from the regression line, which are not well predicted and may therefore lead to insights about what alternative considerations were left out of the initial regression.

Seawright and Gerring (2008) use the regression line analogy to describe seven different sampling strategies tailored to suit different inquiries.[3] These include "typical cases" that are representative of the cross-case relationship and can be chosen in order to explore and validate mediating mechanisms. If the researcher's model implies union membership increases welfare spending in democracies through its effects on negotiations with the government, for example, then the researcher might look for evidence of such processes in the cases well predicted by the theory. Diverse cases maximize variation on both X and Y, while extreme cases are located at a maximal distance from other cases on just one dimension—in our example, the researcher chooses the two cases with the highest degree of union strength. While diverse and extreme cases might lie on the regression line, deviant cases are defined by their distance from it. Such cases call for new explanations to account for outcomes. Influential cases are those whose exclusion would most noticeably change the imaginary regression line (i.e., those with the highest leverage in a regression).

Mills methods. Two more approaches correspond to "methods of difference" and "methods of similarity" (Mill, 1869). The method of difference approach selects a set of cases that are similar in a set of pretreatment variables, but nevertheless differ in Y. This gives an opportunity to search for a cause other than those held constant that could explain the variation. The method of similarity approach selects a set of cases that have similar outcomes and discounts causes that vary across these cases and focuses on potential causes that do not. If one characteristic covaries with the outcome, it becomes a candidate for the cause. For example, Skocpol (1979) compares historical periods in France, Russia, the United Kingdom, and Germany that look very similar in many regards. The first two, however, had social revolutions, while the second two did not. The presence of agrarian institutions that provided a degree of political autonomy to the peasants in France and Russia and their absence in the UK and Germany then becomes a possible clue to understanding the underlying causal structure of social revolutions. By contrast, the method of agreement involves examining cases that share the same outcome but diverge on other characteristics. Any characteristics that are *common* to the cases then become candidates for causal attribution. These "methods" are inferential rules given characteristics of cases.

---

[3] See Gerring and Cojocaru (2016) and Plümper, Troeger and Neumayer (2019) for still larger lists.

These methods make sense for identifying possible causes within cases. But they are a dangerous guide to case selection if you want to use covariation to assess the effect of a putative cause, and you select on the basis of both causes and outcomes. Simply put, if we *select* two cases because they differ on the outcome but agree on all but one (observable) characteristic and then apply the method of difference to conclude that the different factor made the difference, then we have effectively *selected* the answer. More generally, if the information used to make an inference is already available prior to data gathering, then there is nothing to be gained from the data gathering.[4] Following Principle 3.1: *Design holistically* will point to the errors of the strategy.

Herron and Quinn (2016) used Monte Carlo simulations to study how well these strategies perform for the specific question of providing leverage on average causal effects. The inquiry is the average treatment effect in the population, and the answer strategy involves, perhaps optimistically, perfectly observing the selected cases' causal types. With these simplifying assumptions, they uncover a clear hierarchy and set of prescriptions: extreme and deviant case selection fare much worse than the other methods in terms of the three diagnosands considered (root-mean-squared error, variance, and bias of the mean of the posterior distribution). By contrast, influential case selection outperforms the other strategies, followed closely by diverse and simple random sampling. As the authors acknowledge, however, this hierarchy might look very different if the inquiry aimed at a different, exploratory quantity (such as discovering the number of causal types that exist).

Other advice focuses less on the values of *X* and *Y* and more on the scope for learning within the case. Humphreys and Jacobs (2015) provide simulations of a process tracing procedure that highlight the importance of "probative value" for case selection. The point is that there is rarely a case selection strategy that fits all problems equally well. The best strategy is the one that optimizes a particular diagnosand given stipulations about the inquiry, the model, and the answer strategy. If you can justify those stipulations and the importance of the diagnosand, then defending the choice of sampling strategy is straightforward.

Finally, Levy (2008) clarifies the logic behind "most likely" and "least likely" case selection strategies—sometimes called "crucial case" designs. The idea here is that we may have beliefs over the heterogeneity of causal effects over cases but uncertainty about the level. If we learn that a causal effect is indeed in operation in a least likely case, we update on our beliefs about it operating in other cases. This is "Sinatra inference" (Levy, 2008): "if I can make it [in New York], I'll make it anywhere." Conversely the most likely case is based on the idea that if I *can't* make it in New York then I can't make it anywhere! Both logics presuppose an answer strategy that can reliably impute counterfactual outcomes.

---

[4]This problem does not arise if cases are selected to be similar on background features other than *X* when *Y is unknown*—in this case there is learning about effects from later observation of *Y*.

8.1.1.4 *Choosing among sampling designs*

The choice of sampling strategy depends on features of the model and the inquiry, and different sampling strategies can be compared in terms of bias, power, and RMSE in design diagnosis. The model defines the population of units we want to make inferences about, and the sampling frame of the sampling strategy should match that as much as possible. The model also points us to important subgroups that we may wish to stratify on, depending on the variability within those subgroups. Whether we select convenience, random, or purposive sampling depends on our budget and logistical constraints as well as the efficiency (power or RMSE) of the design. If there is little bias from convenience sampling, we will often want to select it for cost reasons. If we cannot obtain a convenience sample that has the right composition, we may choose a purposive method that ensures we do. The choice between simple and stratified sampling comes down to the inquiry and to a diagnosis of the RMSE. When the inquiry involves a comparison of subgroups, we will often select stratified sampling. In either, a diagnosis of alternative designs in terms of power or RMSE will guide selection.

8.1.2 Treatment assignment

In many studies, researchers intervene in the world to *set* the level of the causal variable of interest. The procedures used to assign units to treatment are tightly analogous to the procedures explored in the previous section on sampling. Like sampling, assignment procedures fall into two classes, randomized and nonrandomized.

8.1.2.1 *Two-arm trials*

The analogy between sampling and assignment runs deep. All of the sampling designs discussed in the previous section have directly equivalent assignment designs. Simple random sampling is analogous to Bernoulli random assignment, stratified random sampling is analogous to blocked random assignment, and so on. Many of the same design trade-offs hold as well: just like cluster sampling generates higher variance estimates than individual sampling, clustered assignment generates higher variance estimates than individual assignment. While we usually think of randomized assignment designs only, nonrandomized designs in which the researcher applies treatments also occur. For example, researchers sometimes treat a convenience sample, then search out a different convenience sample to serve as a control group. Within-subject designs in which subjects are measured, then treated, then measured again are a second example of a nonrandomized application of treatment.

The analogy between sampling and assignment runs so deep because, in a sense, assignment *is* sampling. Instead of sampling units in or out of the study, we sample from alternative possible worlds. The treatment group represents a sample from the

Table 8.2: Kinds of random assignment.

Design	Description and `randomizr` R code
Simple random assignment	"Coin flip" or Bernoulli random assignment. All units have the same probability of assignment `simple_ra(N = 100, prob = 0.25)`
Complete random assignment	Exactly m of N units are assigned to treatment, and all units have the same probability of assignment m/N `complete_ra(N = 100, m = 40)`
Block random assignment	Complete random assignment within predefined blocks. Units within the same block have the same probability of assignment m_b/N_b `block_ra(blocks = regions)`
Cluster random assignment	Whole groups of units are assigned to the same treatment condition. `cluster_ra(clusters = households)`

Block-and-cluster assignment	Cluster random assignment within blocks of clusters
	`block_and_cluster_ra(blocks = regions,`
	`                     clusters = villages)`

Saturation random assignment	First clusters are assigned to a saturation level, then units within clusters are assigned to treatment conditions according to the saturation level
	`saturation = cluster_ra(clusters = villages,`
	`           conditions = c(0, 0.25, 0.5, 0.75))`
	`block_ra(blocks = villages, prob_unit = saturation)`

world in which all units are treated and the control group represents a sample from the alternative world in which all units are untreated.[5] We can re-encounter the fundamental problem of causal inference through this lens—if a unit is sampled from one possible world, it can't be sampled from any other possible world. Table 8.2 collects together common forms of random assignment.

Figure 8.4 visualizes nine kinds of random assignment, arranged according to whether the assignment procedure is simple, complete, or blocked and according to whether the assignment procedure is carried out at the individual, cluster, or saturation level. In the top left facet, we have simple (or Bernoulli) random assignment, in which all units have a 50% probability of treatment, but the total number of treated units can bounce around from assignment to assignment. In the top center, this problem is fixed: under complete random assignment, exactly m of N units are assigned to treatment and the $N - m$ are assigned to control. While complete random assignment fixes the number of units treated at exactly m, the number of

---
[5] Strictly speaking, this claim only holds under a noninterference assumption; if the usual noninterference assumption is incorrect, we have to redefine potential outcomes in order to recover "stability." Assignment strategies sample from possible worlds of stable potential outcomes that we imagine in M.

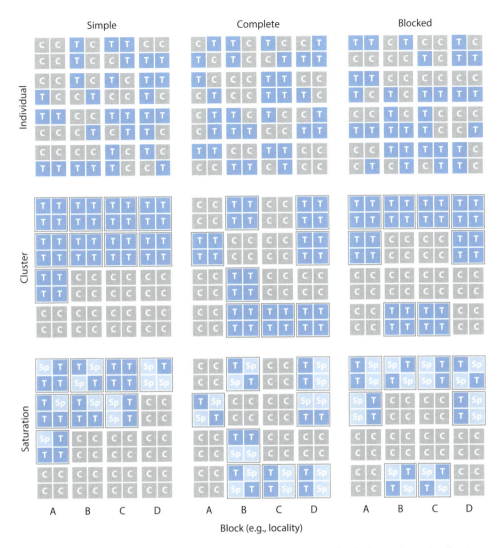

Figure 8.4: Nine kinds of random assignment. In the first row individuals are the units of assignment, in the second row clusters are randomly assigned, in the third clusters are randomly assigned a saturation level and then individuals within these clusters are randomly assigned. In the first column units are assigned independently, in the second units are assigned to hit a target, in the third units are assigned to hit targets within strata.

units that are treated within any particular group of units (defined by a pretreatment covariate) could vary. Under block random assignment, we conduct complete random assignment within each block separately, so we directly control the number treated within each block. Moving from simple to complete random assignment tends to decrease sampling variability a bit, by ruling out highly unbalanced allocations. Moving from complete to blocked can help more, so long as the blocking variable is correlated with the outcome. Blocking rules out assignments in which too many or too few units in a particular subgroup are treated.

Table 8.3: Examples of multi-arm random assignment.

Design	Description and `randomizr` R code
Multi-arm random assignment (complete)	Fixed numbers of units are assigned to three or more conditions `complete_ra(N = 100, m_each = c(40, 30, 30))`

Factorial random assignment (complete)	Units are assigned to receive one treatment, the second treatment, neither, or both
	`Z1 = complete_ra(N = 100, m = 50)`
	`Z2 = block_ra(blocks = Z1, block_m = 25)`
	Equivalently, we could write:
	`Z = complete_ra(N = 100, m_each = c(25, 25, 25, 25))`
	`Z1 = Z %in% c("T1", "T2")`
	`Z2 = Z %in% c("T1", "T3")`

The second row of Figure 8.4 shows clustered designs in which all units within a cluster receive the same treatment assignment. Clustered designs are common for household-level, school-level, or village-level designs, where it would be impractical or unfeasible to conduct individual level assignment. When units within the same cluster are more alike than units in different clusters (as in most cases), clustering increases sampling variability relative to individual level assignment. Just as in individual level designs, moving from simple to complete or from complete to blocked tends to result in lower sampling variability.

The final row of Figure 8.4 shows a series of designs that are analogous to the multi-stage sampling designs shown in Figure 8.2—but their purpose is subtly different in spirit. Multi-stage sampling designs are employed to reduce costs—first clusters are sampled but not all units within a cluster are sampled. A saturation randomization design (sometimes called a "partial population design," see Section 18.9) uses a similar procedure to both contain and learn about spillover effects. Some clusters are chosen for treatment, but some units *within* those clusters are not treated. Units that are untreated in treated clusters can be compared with units that are untreated in untreated clusters in order to suss out intra-cluster spillover effects (Sinclair, McConnell, and Green, 2012). Figure 8.4 shows how the saturation design comes in simple, complete, and blocked varieties.

8.1.2.2 Multi-arm and factorial trials

Thus far we have considered assignment strategies that allocate subjects to just two conditions: either treatment or control. All generalize quite nicely to multi-arm trials (see Table 8.3). Trials that have three, four, or many more arms can of course be

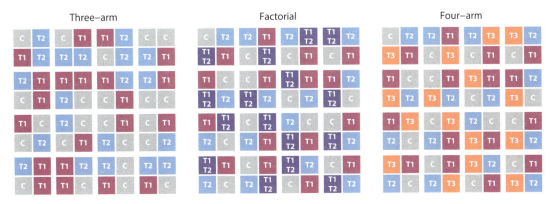

Figure 8.5: Multi-arm random assignment.

simple, complete, blocked, clustered, or feature variable saturation, but we show the complete random assignment versions of multi-arm and factorial assignment here.

Figure 8.5 shows blocked versions of a three-arm trial, a factorial trial, and a four-arm trial.

In the three-arm trial on the left, subjects can be assigned to a control condition or one of two treatments. This design enables three comparisons: a comparison of each treatment to the control condition, but also a comparison of the two treatment conditions to each other. In the four-arm trial on the right, subjects can be assigned to a control condition or one of three treatments. This design supports six comparisons: each of the treatments to control, and all three of the pairwise comparisons across treatments.

The two-by-two factorial design in the center panel shares similarities with both the three-arm and the four-arm trials. Like the three-arm, it considers two treatments T1 and T2, but it also includes a fourth condition in which both treatments are applied. Factorial designs can be analyzed like a four-arm trial, but the structure of the design also enables further analyses. In particular, the factorial structure allows researchers to investigate whether the effects of one treatment depend on the level of the other treatment.

8.1.2.3 Over-time designs

Treatment conditions can also be randomized over multiple time periods, with each unit receiving different treatment conditions in different periods. By focusing on variation in outcomes *within units* rather than across them, these designs can be more efficient than designs that compare across units. Often there is more variation across units than within the same units over time. However, there can be a trade-off in the form of increased bias. Within-unit comparisons must rely on strong stability assumptions such as "no carryover effects" of the treatment condition assigned in

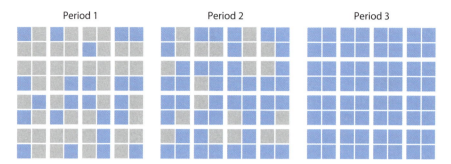

Figure 8.6: Step-wedge random assignment.

the preceding period. If the condition a unit is assigned to in one period affects outcomes in later periods, we cannot isolate the effect of treatment just by considering the treatment it was assigned in this period, we need to know the entire treatment *history*.

A stepped-wedge random assignment procedure involves assigning a subset of units to treatment in the first period, a subset of those who were not treated in the first in the second period, and so on. In the final period, all units are treated. In this design, once you are treated in a period, you are treated in all subsequent periods. For example, once you receive information in a treatment about how to vote, you already have that information in later periods. In Figure 8.6, we illustrate a three-period step-wedge design, in which one third of units are assigned in the first period, a second third are treated in the second period, and the remainder in the third and final period. In such a design, we can make two comparisons: the treatment versus control contrast in each period, and the within-units over-time contrast before and after treatment. By combining these two comparisons, we have a more efficient estimate of the average treatment effect than if we had randomly assigned one half of units to treatment and the other half to control in a single period. However, we must invoke a no carryover assumption that in the second and third periods, potential outcomes are only a function of the current treatment status, not of whether (or not) the unit was treated earlier.

Crossover designs are another common over-time random assignment procedure, in which units are first assigned one condition and then, in a second period, the opposite condition. Such a design is appropriate when units, once treated, do not retain their treatment over time. Crossover designs must also rely on an assumption of no carryover. If this assumption is valid, the design is highly efficient: instead of having half treated and half control in a single period, all units receive treatment in one period and control in the other so we can make comparisons within each period across units with different conditions *and* for all units over time before and after treatment. Whether the crucial no carryover assumption holds is fundamentally not testable: it is an excludability assumption about the unobservable potential outcomes. The assumption may be easier to accept if there is a "washout period" between measurement waves, like buffer rows between crops in agricultural experiments.

8.1.2.4 *Data-adaptive assignment strategies*

We usually think of data strategies as static: a survey asks a fixed set of questions, a randomization protocol has a fixed probability of assignment, sampling designs are designed to yield a fixed number of subjects. But they can also be dynamic. For example, the GRE standardized test many graduate students take is data-adaptive: if you answer the easy questions right, they skip you to harder ones. This process uses fewer questions to figure out test-takers' scores, saving everyone the laborious effort of taking and grading long examinations (see Section 8.1.3.3 for more on data-adaptive measurement).

Data-adaptive designs are also used when the space of possible treatments to choose from is large. We could conduct a static multi-arm trial to evaluate all of them, but experiments with too many conditions tend to have low precision because the sample is spread too thinly across conditions. The usual response to this cost problem is to turn to theory to consider which treatments are most likely to work and test those options only.

"Response-adaptive" designs are an alternative that may be appropriate in these settings. The subject pool is split into sequential "batches." The first batch does the experiment, then the second, and so on. The probabilities of assignment to each condition (or arm) start out equal, but we tweak them between batches. We assign a higher fraction of the second batch to conditions that performed well in the first batch. This process continues until the sample pool is exhausted. Many algorithms for deciding how to update between batches are available, but the most common (Thompson sampling) estimates the probability that each arm is the best arm, then randomly allocates subjects to arms using these probabilities. See Offer-Westort, Coppock and Green (2021) for a recent introduction to this algorithm and elaborations.

8.1.2.5 *Nonrandomized assignment*

Strong causal inferences can sometimes be drawn from treatment allocation strategies that do not involve random assignment. We outline four such strategies below, with their costs and benefits.

A commonly considered strategy is alternating assignment, in which every other participant who arrives is assigned to treatment. The procedure would be identical to block random assignment—blocked on time of treatment—if participants arrived in a randomized order. It is appealing for this similarity, but it is often impossible to demonstrate that order was randomized. In fact, participants who work at different times of day may arrive at different times, and many other correlations between individual characteristics and order may arise. But the real problem comes when there are correlations between those characteristics and the order within each couple of participants. For example, if treatment status is correlated with who goes through the door first, there could be a very strong correlation between individual characteristics and treatment condition. A simple fix for this would be to block units into pairs or quartets as they arrive, then randomize within each block, rather than alternating.

When participants can be assigned a score that represents need, desire, or eligibility for a treatment, with higher score representing higher likelihood of treatment, a common design is to set a cutoff score above which all units are treated and below which none are. With such a cutoff, units very near the cutoff may be very similar to each other, so a regression discontinuity design can be used to estimate the treatment effect by predicting the outcome under control (just below the cutoff) and the outcome under treatment (just above the cutoff). In such a design, the assignment of treatment is deterministic and has no random component. We discuss this design in Section 16.5.

A range of strategies aim to improve upon random assignment by identifying assignments that are optimal in some sense. Bayesian optimal assignment strategies identify individually optimal assignments from a set of multiple treatments, based on past data from experiments and individual characteristics that predict treatment effectiveness. Indeed, from a Bayesian perspective randomization is an unusual choice of procedure for assigning treatment because it suggests that you expect the same learning will emerge from all assignments that you might select via randomization (see Kasy, 2016, and Bai, 2021, for an alternative motivation for randomization in this setting). Diagnosing the properties of these so-called optimal designs is crucial, because, though a treatment assignment may be optimal in terms of the likelihood that each individual receives the treatment most effective for them, the design may be inefficient due to highly variable assignment propensities. Such choices may be appropriate, but in a diagnosis researchers can assess sensitivity to priors and directly trade off design criteria like efficiency with the average expected effectiveness of the treatment assigned to units.

8.1.3 Measurement

Measurement is the part of the data strategy in which variables are collected about the population of units to enable sampling; variables are collected about the sample and outcomes are collected, following any treatment assignment. All variables used in the answer strategy are collected in measurement, aside from any treatment assignment variables and assignment and sample inclusion probabilities.

Descriptive inference is threatened whenever measurements differ from the quantities they are meant to measure. For example, when we want to measure "latent variables" such as fear, support for a political candidate, or economic well-being, we use a measurement technology to imperfectly observe them. We might represent that measurement technology as the function Q that yields the observed outcome Y^{obs}: $Q(Y^*) = Y^{obs}$. Our measurement strategy is a set of such functions for each variable we measure.

Some measurement strategies exhibit little to no measurement error. It's easy enough to measure some plain matters of fact, like whether a country is a member of the European Union (though clerical errors could still crop up). In the social sciences, most measurement strategies are threatened by the possibility of measurement errors due to any number of biases (e.g., recall bias, observer bias, Hawthorne effects, demand effects, sensitivity bias, response substitution, among many others).

We often describe measurement error in two ways, measurement *validity* and measurement *reliability*. Validity is the difference between the observed and latent outcome, $Y^{obs} - Y^*$. Reliability is the consistency of the measurements we would obtain if we were to repeat the measurement many times, which we can operationalize as low variance of the measurements: $\mathbb{V}(Y_1^{obs}, Y_2^{obs}, \ldots, Y_k^{obs})$. We would of course like to always select valid, reliable measurement strategies. When no perfect measure is available, choices among alternative measurement strategies typically reduce to trade-offs between their validity and reliability.

To make these choices, we depend on methodological research whose main inquiries are the reliability and validity of particular measurement procedures. Sometimes measurement studies are presented as "validation" studies that compare a proposed measure to a "ground truth." But even "ground truths" must be measured, usually with an expensive or otherwise unfeasible approach (otherwise there would be no need for the alternative measurement). Further, neither measurement is known to be exactly Y^*, so ultimately validation studies are comparisons of multiple techniques each with its own advantages and disadvantages. This fact does not make these studies useless, but rather underlines that they rely on our faith in these "ground truths."

Researchers select several characteristics of a measurement strategy: who collects the measures, the mode of measurement, how often and when measures are taken, how many different observed measures of the latent outcome Y^* are collected, and how they are summarized into a single measure. These design characteristics may affect validity, reliability, cost, or all three.

Data may be collected by researchers themselves, by participants, or by third parties. In some forms of qualitative research such as participant-observation and interview-based research, the researcher may be the primary data collector. In survey research, interviewers are typically hired agents of the researchers, each of whom may ask questions differently. Participants are sometimes asked to collect data on themselves, through self-administered surveys, journaling, or taking measurements of themselves using thermometers or scales. A primary concern with self-reports is validity: do respondents report their measurements truthfully? A parallel concern is raised when participants do not collect their own data, but are made aware of the fact that they are being measured by others. Finally, data may be collected by agents of governments or other organizations, yielding so-called "administrative" data.

Most of the variety in measurement strategies is how data collectors obtain their data. Data collectors can use observation and ask respondents for self-reports. Increasingly, photos, videos, sound recordings, and even water and soil measurements are used for outcome measurement. The translation of raw data, like videos, into coded data, like counts of the number of police stops, that can be used for analysis is part of Q in the measurement strategy.

8.1.3.1 Multiple measures

We measure the latent outcome Y^* imperfectly with any single measure. In many cases, we have access to multiple imperfect measures of the same Y^*. When possible, collecting all of these different measures and averaging them to construct a single index measure will yield efficiency improvements (see Section 15.4). The average measure can borrow the different strengths of the different measures. When the tools produce answers that are highly correlated, taking multiple measures is unlikely to be worth the cost, because the same information is simply duplicated, but when the correlation is low, it will be worth taking multiple measurements and averaging to improve efficiency. Pilot studies may be usefully tasked with measuring the correlation between items. Index measures are distinct from Y^* outcomes that have multiple dimensions and that typically must be measured with multiple items, one per dimension. An index represents a single measure of Y^* just constructed in a more complex way.

8.1.3.2 Over-time measurement

Data need not be collected at a single time period. The model encodes beliefs about the autocorrelation (correlation over time) of outcomes, and this can help guide whether to collect multiple measurements or just one. If data are expected to be highly variable (low autocorrelation), then taking multiple measurements and averaging them may provide efficiency gains.

When outcomes exhibit high autocorrelation, there will be large precision gains from collecting a baseline measure before a treatment in an experiment. When outcomes exhibit lower autocorrelation, baseline measurements may not be worth the cost.

8.1.3.3 Data-adaptive measurement

Just as we can use data-adaptive methods to hone in on the most effective treatments (Section 8.1.2.4), we can use adaptive measurement techniques to hone in on the most useful measures. Adaptive inventory techniques enable deploying long batteries of survey items, for example, but enumerating the shortest set of items to any given respondent that results in a definitive measurement of Y^*. In the same way as many modern standardized tests condition the choice of survey items on students' past answers in order to hone in quickly on the correct test score, adaptive inventories ask questions that will be maximally informative. The logic is the same as that of using multiple different measures for the same construct: the lower the correlation, or, in other words, the more new information, between two items, the more informative they are. Adaptive inventories select a set of items to enumerate that provide the most uncorrelated information. See Montgomery and Rossiter (2020) for an up-to-date treatment of the adaptive measurement possibilities for constructs measured by long survey batteries.

8.2 Challenges to Data Strategies

Principle 3.2: *Design agnostically* focuses on models, encouraging us to consider plausible variations of the set of variables, their probability distributions, and the relationships between them. The principle has implications for the data and answer strategies also, in particular we should choose D and A such that we have good designs under a wide array of plausible models.

In this section, we discuss four core threats to data strategies and ways to respond to them: noncompliance (failure to treat), attrition (failure to be included in the sample or provide measures), excludability violations (causal effects of random sampling, random assignment, or measurement on the latent outcome), and interference (the dependence of potential outcomes on whether other units are treated). These threats are often discussed in the context of experimental designs, but the core issues they raise are relevant for observational designs also. If serious, these threats may necessitate changes to the inquiry, the answer strategy, or the data strategy itself.

Figure 8.7 adapts Figure 8.1 to introduce each of these threats. The remainder of this section discusses these four threats in turn.

8.2.1 Noncompliance

Noncompliance occurs when the assignment variable Z imperfectly manipulates the treatment variable D. When noncompliance is not a problem, $D = Z$, but in designs that encounter noncompliance $D \neq Z$. One-sided noncompliance occurs when some treated units fail to be treated (and receive the control condition instead). Two-sided noncompliance occurs when some units assigned to treatment do not take treatment and some units assigned to control do take treatment. Noncompliance hampers experimental studies, but also affects observational designs for causal inference in which nature or a nonrandom administrative process affects treatment such as a threshold cutoff, but only imperfectly.

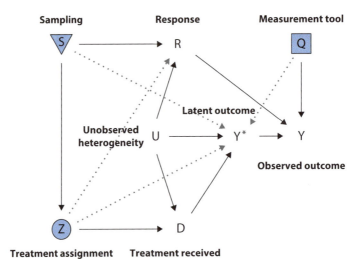

Figure 8.7: Directed acyclic graph of random sampling, random assignment, and measurement with exclusion restriction violations as dotted lines.

In the presence of noncompliance, a change in inquiry is sometimes worth considering. The average difference between those assigned to treatment and those assigned to control no longer targets the average treatment effect, but instead only the effect of *assignment* to treatment. We instead call this inquiry the intent-to-treat effect, and we can estimate it well by comparing the groups as assigned. An alternative inquiry is the complier average treatment effect, which is "local" to the subset of units that comply with treatment (take it when offered).

You can also sometimes use design strategies to limit the risk of noncompliance. The problem is perhaps best solved, when possible, by using strong encouragements. Another strategy is to pre-identify units that you expect are likely to comply and assign treatments from among those units. Or you can include placebos in your data strategy in order to identify compliers. These solutions may also have to be accompanied by a change in inquiry. See Section 18.7 for more on this last strategy.

See Section 18.6 for a discussion of noncompliance in randomized experiments and Section 16.4 for a related discussion of "noncompliance" in observational studies.

8.2.2 Attrition

Attrition occurs when we do not obtain outcome measures for all sampled units. Two types of missing data may result: when a single measure is missing (known as item nonresponse) and when all measures are missing for a participant (known as survey nonresponse). Though these terms were coined by survey researchers, analogous problems can affect non-survey measurement strategies, like missing administrative data, for example.

Whether attrition is a problem depends on whether response (R) is causally affected by variables other than random sampling. If it is not, we say the missingness is completely at random, just as if we had simply added one more random sampling step to the design. Outside of explicit sampling designs, missingness completely at random is rare, though possible, perhaps due to idiosyncratic administrative procedures or computer error. If attrition is completely at random, precision suffers due to a loss of sample size, but bias is unaffected.

If missingness *is* affected by other variables—some units are more likely to respond because of unobserved background characteristics such as being at home when the survey taker calls—then inferences may be biased. Attrition is doubly difficult in experiments, because if treatment affects not just how a unit responds, but *whether* it responds, then treatment-control comparisons on the basis of observed data may be biased.

One approach is to address this weakness in the data strategy via changes to the answer strategy. A bounding approach like the one described in Section 9.2.4 is a design-based answer strategy for drawing inferences despite missingness. Model-based approaches involve reweighting the data by stratum, supposing random missingness within a stratum but not across strata. An example of a data strategy response is to intensively revisit a subset of attritors to gather information about them—including information about why they attrited. For more see the discussion in Section 15.1.1 as well as the combination of data strategy and answer strategy response in Coppock, Gerber, Green, and Kern (2017).

8.2.3 Excludability

Excludability means that when we define potential outcomes, we can exclude extraneous, nontreatment variables from the potential outcomes functions. When we define the treated potential outcome for the latent outcome as $Y^*(D=0)$, we invoke (at least) three important excludability assumptions: no effect of sampling S, no effect of treatment assignment Z (except through treatment D!), and no effect of measurement Q on the latent outcome Y^*. If we did not invoke these assumptions, we would have to define the potential outcome function as $Y^*(D, S, Z, Q)$. When we do invoke the assumptions, we can write simply $Y^*(D)$. The three assumptions are represented as gray dotted lines in Figure 8.7.

The figure asserts no effect of sampling S on latent outcome Y^*. This assumption could be violated if the fact of being *included in the sample* changes your attitudes. For example, if the very act of being asked to be in a focus group causes subjects to reflect on their political beliefs and thereby change them, the sampling excludability assumption would be violated.

Next, we assert no causal effect of assignment Z on outcome Y^*—except through the treatment D. This assumption is constantly under threat! In observational studies using the "instrumental variables" design, excludability is the assumption of no alternative channels through which the instrument affects outcomes except the treatment variable. In the entertainingly titled "Rain, Rain, Go Away: 176 potential exclusion-restriction violations for studies using weather as an instrumental variable," Mellon (2021) discusses how random variation in rainfall has been misused to study the effects of other treatments.

We further assume that Q does not affect Y^*. Hawthorne effects, in which the fact of being measured changes outcomes, are an example a violation of this kind excludability assumption. If outcomes depend on whether subjects know they are being measured or do not, then we cannot exclude the effect of measurement from our effect estimates.

The DAG also encodes the assumption that Z has no effect on Q. How and whether we measure outcomes should not depend on whether a unit is assigned to treatment. This excludability assumption is commonly referred to as the requirement that measurement be parallel across treatment conditions. In this sense a failure of the exclusion restriction can sometimes be thought of as a weakness in a data strategy: a failure to treat or measure cleanly.

To the extent possible, data strategies should try to limit such violations of exclusion restrictions. Strategies include using simple rather than complex treatments, using placebos to identify confounding effects, and maintaining parallelism wherever possible. If we measure outcomes using a face-to-face survey in the treatment group and a mail-back survey in control, then we cannot separate (exclude!) the effect of measurement from the effect of treatment.

8.2.4 Interference

We have four endogenous outcomes in the DAG of a research design in Figure 8.7: R, whether a participant responds to data collection; D, whether a respondent receives treatment; Y^*, the latent outcome; and Y, the observed outcome. Setting aside attrition and noncompliance for the moment, R is a function only of sampling; D of treatment assignment; Y^* of D; and Y of measurement strategy Q.

Interference occurs when these endogenous variables depend not only on whether and how individual units are sampled, assigned to treatment, and measured, but whether and how *other* units are sampled, assigned to treatment, and measured. We usually assume, for example, that $Y_i(Z_i) = Y_i(Z_i, \mathbf{Z}_{-i})$ where Z_{-i} is a vector of the treatment assignments of all units but i. In other words, Y_i, the outcome for unit i, is a function of its own treatment assignment status Z_i, not of other units ($\mathbf{Z}_{-i}$).

We often think of interference when considering how treatments spill from treated to untreated units. But interference can also be induced by sampling: potential outcomes might depend on whether other units are included in the sample. Or by measurement: measurement interference occurs when Y_i^* depends on whether and how other units (or outcomes) are measured. For example, asking about one attitude might affect how subjects respond to a second question.

Interference can sometimes be thought of as reflecting weaknesses in data strategies and data strategies can be deployed—often in combination with modified answer strategies—to make it easier to study interference directly. We discuss examples of such strategies in Sections 18.9 and 18.10.

8.3 Summary

Data strategies are made of up three kinds of empirical strategies: sampling strategies, assignment strategies, and measurement strategies. All research designs have a data strategy—even just downloading a dataset curated by others constitutes a data strategy (the original researcher's data strategy). The blizzard of choices enumerated in this chapter underlines the central importance of the data strategy in developing strong research designs. The data strategy is where we exert researcher control over how, over the conditions under which, and over the population from which we collect the empirical information we will use when generating answers to our research questions.

CHAPTER 9

Choosing an Answer Strategy

The answer strategy is a plan for what to do with the information gathered from the world (or from a model of the world) in order to generate an answer to the inquiry. Qualitative and quantitative methods courses provide guidance about the properties of different strategies and the conditions under which they work well or poorly. Under what conditions should we use ordinary least squares, when should we use logit? When is a machine learning algorithm the appropriate choice and when would a comparative case study be more informative? When is *no* answer strategy worth pursuing because of the fundamental limitations of the data strategy?

Following Principle 3.3: *Design for purpose*, the evaluation of an answer strategy depends on our ultimate goals: what is the answer to be used for? A perfect answer is generally elusive in empirical research, so in practice we often need to select among strategies that come with different strengths and weaknesses. For instance, some might suffer less from bias while others might be more precise. In other words, which answer strategy is best for you depends on what diagnosands you care about.

This chapter first describes the elements of the answer strategy, the most important of which are the type of answer and the approach to assessing the level of uncertainty in the answer. We then describe four distinct approaches to answering a question: point estimation, hypothesis tests, Bayesian posteriors, and interval estimation. Last we identify some general principles for selecting an answer strategy highlighting especially how the choice of A depends on the other three elements of the research design. Principle 3.1 is a reminder to diagnose holistically: we can't choose answer strategies in isolation from the other design elements.

9.1 Elements of Answer Strategies

The three core elements of an answer strategy are the identification of a type of answer, the strategy for conceptualizing and reporting uncertainty about the answer, and a procedure for obtaining both.

9.1.1 Answer characterization

At its most basic an answer strategy delivers a guess at the value of an inquiry. The answer itself, like the inquiry, generally requires a specification of units, outcomes, and conditions. Like the inquiry, it requires a domain.

Domain: We often think of the answer as a number: 55% or an effect of 0.25. But the domain of the answer can be much broader: it could be a logical statement, TRUE or FALSE; a vector of predictions; a statement "This theory is helpful"; even a model. The domain is likely matched with the domain of the inquiry, but it might not be. For instance, the estimand might be 5 and the answer an interval [3, 6]. The rubber hits the road when a diagnosand has to establish the usefulness of an answer; the primary question is whether the usefulness of an answer can be assessed or not.

Units: The units that serve as input to the answer strategy are, likely, either the same as those in the inquiry or good stand-ins. How good is determined by choices in the data strategy: were study units drawn in a random sample from the population? Are some subgroups excluded from the sampling procedure, because they are hard to reach? In some cases, the sampling procedure will be complex and some units will stand in for more than one unit in the population. In this case, the answer strategy should take account of this fact. In some cases the data is measured using units that are not defined at the same "level" as the units that define the inquiry. For instance, you might be interested in women's voting, but have data on polling station level outcomes only. This generates what is called a challenge of ecological inference and your answer strategy should address this.

Outcomes: Answer strategies summarize outcomes that represent measured characteristics of each unit. The outcomes must be measured in the data strategy, and should usually match closely the outcomes used in the inquiry. However, we always have imperfect measures of outcomes; how good is determined by the data strategy. Answer strategies then often involve multiple measured outcomes to best represent an unobserved outcome such as an attitude. The measures might be analyzed separately and interpreted together or formally combined using an indexing method.

Conditions: Inquiries define the treatment conditions over which outcomes are compared. Sometimes outcomes from more than one treatment condition are compared, in the case of causal inquiries, whereas only one is used in the case of descriptive inquiries. The data strategy then determines which treatment conditions are assigned to which units, thus linking units' outcomes to the potential outcomes used in the inquiries. This linking occurs in the answer strategy. Just as sampled units will be analyzed to stand in for units in the population, units assigned to a control group often stand in for the control potential outcome for all units (and the same for treated units). Just as with sampling weights, assignment weights may be used to allow some units to stand in for more than one (or fewer than one) unit in the inquiry when units are assigned to treatments with different probabilities. For descriptive inquiries, all units may be used to stand in for the naturally assigned potential outcome in the inquiry.

9.1.2 Uncertainty

Much empirical work involves *inference*: making guesses about quantities that we cannot directly observe. Sometimes the challenge is descriptive inference, sometimes causal inference, sometimes generalization, and oftentimes all three at once.

In general, when we are doing inference our answers are uncertain and we need to find ways to communicate that uncertainty. Two prominent and clearly distinct perspectives on estimating uncertainty are the Bayesian approach and the frequentist approach.

Bayesian uncertainty. The simplest way of thinking about uncertainty about inferences that arise from data is nicely described by Bayes' rule.

The probability of a quantity of interest θ is given by:

$$\Pr(\theta = \theta' | d = d') = \frac{\Pr(d = d' | \theta = \theta') \Pr(\theta = \theta')}{\sum_{\theta''} \Pr(d = d' | \theta = \theta'') \Pr(\theta = \theta'')},$$

where θ' and θ'' represent particular values of θ, d represents data, and d' represents a particular realization of the data.

Using *MIDA* notation, we might think that a quantity of interest a_{m^*} could take on a range of possible values $a \in A$. Given M and D, we can assess the probability of a particular data realization, d, given any particular value for a. For instance, if a_{m^*} is the share of women in a very large population and you sample m individuals of which d are women, then $\Pr(d = d' | a = a') = \binom{m}{d} a^d (1-a)^{m-d}$. We can then use Bayes rule to calculate $\Pr(a_{m^*} = a' | d = d')$.

Applying the rule over different values of θ we build up a full probability distribution over possible answers. The probability distribution *simultaneously* represents our answer and our certainty in the answer. For instance we might report the mean of the distribution ("posterior mean") as our best guess and the variance as our uncertainty ("posterior variance"). Or we might just report the whole posterior distribution as an answer.

While this approach is intuitive, many are uncomfortable with it. One reason is that the method requires a specification of prior uncertainty $\Pr(\theta = \theta')$. A second reason is philosophical. If we think that the estimand has some particular value, then what does it mean to say something like $\Pr(a_{m^*} = a) = 0.5$? Surely either $a_{m^*} = a$ or $a_{m^*} \neq a$. The Bayesian response is that the probability does not refer to a physical probability but to "degrees of belief": essentially a measure of how confident you are in the claim.

Frequentist uncertainty. Say you wanted to make a statement about your uncertainty about an answer, but did not want to specify prior beliefs about what the answer is. Instead, you want any statements about probability to come from physical processes—actual randomization, for instance. Can you do it?

The short answer is no. You can't escape Bayes' rule if you want to make a claim about the probability that some answer is correct given the data. However, you can do something related.

Leaving $\Pr(\theta = \theta')$ aside you can pick out one element of Bayes' rule from above and report the simpler quantity:

$$\Pr(d = d' | \theta = \theta').$$

In other words: how likely is it that we would see data like this if indeed θ were θ'. You can answer this without thinking of probability as representing strengths of beliefs, but working instead from the idea that θ generates an actual probability distribution over possible data, d. And of course you can do this for many different possible values of θ.

When you go this route you can get a number that you can defend (as Fisher put it: "a reasoned basis for inference"). The basic idea gives rise to a set of useful tools:

- The p-value for a null hypothesis θ_0 corresponds exactly to $\Pr(d = d_{m*} | \theta = \theta_0)$.

- The maximum likelihood approach to estimation corresponds to finding the value θ' for which $\Pr(d = d' | \theta = \theta')$ is greatest.

- The 95% confidence interval is interpretable as the set of values for which $\Pr(d = d' | \theta = \theta') \geq 0.05$.

In short $\Pr(d = d' | \theta = \theta')$ is a powerful quantity and the frequentist approach that uses it is currently the dominant approach in social sciences, and the most commonly used approach in this book also. But it is worth being very clear on what this quantity does and does not do. We seek estimates of uncertainty, but this quantity does *not* provide a statement about your confidence in your answer. Rather it provides a statement about the consistency between possible answers and the data you have. It lets you say that you are certain in your answer to the extent that the world is not as we would expect it to be if other answers were correct. For this reason we often think of it as an approach to ruling out possible answers: an answer is ruled out if the patterns we see are out of line with what the answer would predict.

9.1.3 Procedure

How the outcomes of study units are analyzed and, if relevant, compared across conditions is the method of the answer strategy. This element is the choice of estimator (e.g., OLS or difference-in-means), but also the regression specification and if-then procedures for model selection.

The method should be thought of as a procedure or a function: data goes in, answers come out. The output responds to the inputs. If the events generated by the world had been different, the data produced by the data strategy would be different too. If the data produced by the data strategy had been different, the answers rendered by the answer strategy would be different too. We want to understand how the functions perform as M, I, and D vary.

Critically, when declaring answer strategies as functions, we have to think about more than just the single estimation function that ends up in a published paper. To see this, consider an estimator that is selected through an exploratory procedure in which multiple estimators are compared on the basis of fit statistics. The answer strategy is not this final estimator—it is this entire multi-step if-then procedure. The reason to declare the procedure rather than the final estimator is that the diagnosis of the design may differ. The procedure may be more powerful, if, for example, we assessed multiple sets of covariate controls and selected the specification with the lowest standard error of the estimate. But that procedure would also exhibit poor coverage, since the confidence interval produced by the final estimator does not account for these multiple bites at the apple.

Answer strategies can become multi-stage procedures in unexpected ways. For example, sometimes a planned-on maximum likelihood estimator won't converge when executed on the realized data. In these cases, analysts switch estimators (or sometimes inquiries!). The full set of steps—a decision tree, depending on what is estimable—is the answer strategy we want to declare and compare to alternative decision trees.

This principle extends to settings in which analysts run diagnostic tests, like falsification or placebo tests. If we learn from a sensitivity test that a mediation estimate is very sensitive to unobserved confounding, we might choose not to present it at all. By this logic, the answer strategy includes the sensitivity test and the decision made on the basis of the test. When we inspect the resulting distribution of mediation estimates, some are undefined.

Writing down the full set of if-then choices we might make in the answer strategy depending on revealed data is hard to do. We often imagine answer strategies if things go right, but spend less time imagining what might happen if things go wrong. When things do go wrong—missing data, noncompliance, suspension of the data collection—answer strategies will change. One way to guard against over-correcting to the revealed data is to adopt a *standard operating procedures* document that systematizes these procedures in advance (Green and Lin, 2016).

9.2 Types of Answer Strategies

We identify four distinct types of answers that might be provided by an answer strategy. In each case we describe how information regarding uncertainty is communicated.

9.2.1 Point estimation

9.2.1.1 *Answer*

The most familiar class of answer strategies are point-estimators that produce estimates of scalar parameters. The sample mean of an outcome, the difference-in-means estimate, the coefficient on a variable in a logistic regression, and the estimated number of topics in a text corpus are all examples of point estimates.

To illustrate point estimation in general, we'll try to estimate the average age of the citizens of a small village in Italy. Our model is straightforward—the citizens of the small village all have ages—and the inquiry is the average of them. In our data strategy, we randomly sample three citizens whose ages are then measured via survey to be 5, 15, and 25. Our answer strategy is the sample mean estimator, so our estimate of the population average age is a point estimate of 15.

9.2.1.2 *Uncertainty*

A standard way to report uncertainty of a point estimate is to provide a "standard error." In this case we know that our answer is probably not a good answer. It is almost certainly wrong in the sense that the population average age in the small village is probably not 15 (Italy's population is aging!), but we don't know how wrong because, of course, we don't actually know the value of the inquiry under study. We have instead to evaluate the properties of the procedure. Under a random sampling design—even an egregiously stingy random sampling design that only selects three citizens!—we can justify the approach on the basis of the "bias" diagnosand.[1]

But that doesn't tell us much about how confident we should be in this answer. The design in Declaration 9.1 can be used to generate a view of what answers we might get when we choose just three subjects for our sample given a particular model of the age distribution.[2]

---

[1] Bias is the idea that the average of all the answers you would get if you repeated the data strategy (random sampling) and the answer strategy (taking the sample average) over and over would correspond to the correct answer.

[2] We use a linear regression of the age variable on a constant to estimate the sample mean. Using OLS in this way is a neat trick for estimating sample means along with various uncertainty statistics, discussed in more detail in the next section.

Declaration 9.1 Italian village design.

```
declaration_9.1 <-
  declare_model(N = 100, age = sample(0:80, size = N, replace = TRUE)) +
  declare_inquiry(mean_age = mean(age)) +
  declare_sampling(S = complete_rs(N = N, n = 3)) +
  declare_estimator(age ~ 1, .method = lm_robust)
```

We now diagnose the design by simulating this design repeatedly, plotting the sampling distribution along with the true (true under the model) population mean age, and calculating the bias.

Diagnosis 9.1 Italian village design diagnosis.

```
diagnosis_9.1 <- diagnose_design(declaration_9.1)
```

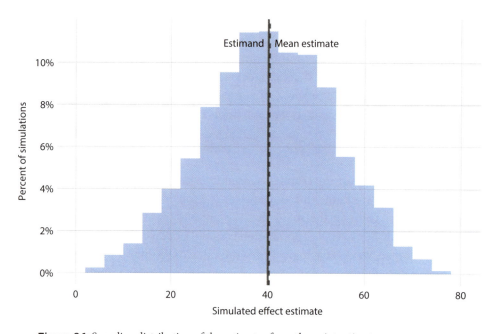

Figure 9.1: Sampling distribution of the estimates from the point estimator answer strategy.

Figure 9.1 shows that we are right on average but usually quite wrong. The average estimate lies right on top of the true value of the estimand (40), but the estimates range enormously widely, from close to zero to close to 80 in some draws. The answer strategy—the sample mean estimator—is just fine; the problem here lies in the data strategy that generates tiny samples. Substantively this does not mean that we now believe we are wrong. But it does tell us that the data is just as consistent with lots of other possibilities as it is with the estimate that we got from a single run of the design.

Imagine we ran the design once and obtained one estimate (20) and its associated standard error (7). The reported standard error seeks to capture the standard deviation of this sampling distribution. In this case the standard deviation of the distribution in Figure 9.1 is about 13. The standard error in this one run, however, is much smaller, which highlights the fact that our estimates of uncertainty are themselves uncertain.

9.2.2 Hypothesis tests

9.2.2.1 Answer

Tests are an elemental kind of answer strategy. Tests yield binary yes/no answers to a binary yes/no inquiry. In some qualitative traditions, hoop tests, straw-in-the-wind tests, smoking gun tests, and doubly decisive tests are common (Van Evera, 1997). These tests are procedures for making analysis decisions in a structured way. Similarly, many forms of quantitative tests have been developed. Sign tests assess whether a test statistic is positive, negative, or zero. Null hypothesis significance tests assess whether a parameter is different from a null value, such as zero. Equivalence tests assess whether a parameter falls within a range, rather than comparing it to a fixed value. Many procedures for conducting tests are also available, with different assumptions about the null hypothesis, the distributions of variables, and the data strategy.

A typical null hypothesis test proceeds by imagining a null model M_0 and imagining the sampling distribution of the empirical answer a_{d_0} under a hypothetical design M_0IDA. That sampling distribution enumerates all the ways the design could have come out if the null model M_0 were the correct one. For a null hypothesis test, we *entertain* the null model and consider its implications. We ask, under M_0 how frequently would we obtain an answer as large as or larger than the empirical answer a_d (or other test statistic)? That frequency is known as a *p*-value.[3] The last step of the test is to turn the *p*-value into a binary decision about statistical significance. The typical threshold in the social sciences is 0.05: hypothesis tests with *p*-values less than 0.05 indicate statistical significance. This threshold is arbitrary, reflecting the inertia of the scientific community much more than some a priori scientific standard. The appropriate threshold value for statistical significance is a matter of furious debate, with some authors calling for the threshold to be lowered to 0.005 to guard against false positives (Benjamin et al., 2018).

We'll illustrate the idea of a hypothesis test in general with the Italian village example. Here, we test against the hypothesis that the average age is 20. If we have strong

---

[3] The *p*-value can be thought of as a diagnosand of the M_0IDA design. If M_0 were true, what fraction of simulations would generate answers as big as some value?

evidence against this hypothesis, we will reject it. If we have weak evidence against the hypothesis, we will fail to reject it. For instance, we might reject 10 and 70 but fail to reject 35 and 45.

Declaration 9.2 Italian village design, continued.

```
declaration_9.2 <-
  declaration_9.1 +
  declare_test(age ~ 1,
               linear_hypothesis = "(Intercept) = 20",
               .method = lh_robust, label = "test")
```

Table 9.1 displays one run of that design. The output can be confusing. By default, most statistical software tests against the null hypothesis that the true parameter value is zero—so the `p.value` in the first row refers to that null hypothesis test. The second row is the test against the hypothesis that the mean is equal to 20. The "estimate" in the second row, 17, is the difference of the observed estimate from 20. The `p.value` in the second row is the one we care about when testing against the null hypothesis that the average age is 20.

```
run_design(declaration_9.2)
```

Table 9.1: Estimates from the test of the mean age equalling 20 from Italian villages example.

estimator	estimate	p.value
estimator	37	0.05
test	17	0.19

Next, we diagnose the modified design, by running the design many times. Figure 9.2 shows how frequently we reject the null that the average age is 20. When the estimate is close to 20, we rarely reject the null, but when the estimate is far from 20, we are more likely to reject it. Again, this diagnosis comes from a design with a weak data strategy of sampling only three citizens at time. We need to see estimates breaking 60 before the testing answer strategy reliably rejects this (false) null hypothesis.

Diagnosis 9.2 Italian village diagnosis, continued.

```
diagnosis_9.2 <- diagnose_design(declaration_9.2)
```

9.2 Types of Answer Strategies   101

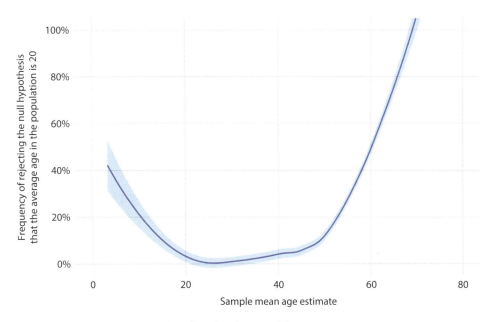

Figure 9.2: Sampling distribution of the test answer strategy.

9.2.2.2 Uncertainty

For tests, uncertainty is expressed by describing the properties of a procedure in terms of error rates. A test is an answer strategy that returns a binary answer to a binary inquiry. The result of a test is an error if the empirical answer a_d does not equal the truth a_{m^*}. Conventionally, a Type 1 error occurs when $a_d = 1$ but $a_{m^*} = 0$ and a Type 2 error occurs when $a_d = 0$ but $a_{m^*} = 1$. A perfect test (i.e., a test about about which we are fully certain) has Type 1 error rate of 0% and a Type 2 error rate of 0% as well. A test about which we are less certain might return $a_d = 1$ 40% of the time when $a_{m^*} = 0$ (a Type I error rate of 40%) and might return $a_d = 1$ 90% of the time when $a_{m^*} = 1$ (a Type II error rate of 10%).

The test reported by the `answer_strategy` function is a null hypothesis significance test against the null hypothesis that the average age in this Italian village is equal to exactly zero. The test returns "yes" if we reject the null and "no" if we fail to reject it. If we use the standard significance threshold of $\alpha = 0.05$ we fail to reject the null model because the `p.value` reported in the table is 0.12. It's a silly test, but silly tests like these are reported by default in many statistical software languages and in many scientific papers to boot. It's a silly test because we always knew the average age was not zero!

Our uncertainty about the decision we made in the hypothesis test to fail to reject is *not* represented by the information in the table. Importantly, the *p*-value does not represent the probability that the null model is correct. The *p*-value is the probability this also goes with the misplaced section estimates of 15 or larger. According to our calculations, draws from the null model will do so 12 percent of the time.

We use this probability along the way to making a decision about whether to reject the null model, but amazingly, a *p*-value does *not* describe our certainty about the significance test!

What does characterize our uncertainty about a significance test? The Type I and type II error rates of the test. The Type I error rate is controlled by the significance threshold. A Type I error occurs if we reject the null model when it is true. If we use $\alpha = 0.05$ and the test correctly accounts for all design elements, then a Type I error should only happen 5% of the time. Type II error rates are harder to learn about. In our case, we failed to reject the null model. To characterize our uncertainty about the test, we also want to calculate the probability that a design like this one would generate Type II errors. To do so, we have to imagine what it means for the null model to be *false*, since they can be false in many ways. One approach is to imagine how the test would perform under a series of non-null models.

Figure 9.4 describes the Type II error rate over a range of non-null models. If the true population mean is around 25 or lower, we fail to reject the null 75% of the time or more. With this comically small sample size, even if the true mean were 75, we would still fail to reject 20% of the time. We are rightly uncertain about this test—it may have a low enough Type I error rate (set as $\alpha = 0.05$), but the Type II errors are way too big.

9.2.3 Bayesian formalizations

9.2.3.1 Answer

Bayesian answer strategies sometimes target the same inquiries as classical approaches, but rather than seeking a point estimate, they try to generate rational beliefs over possible values of the estimand. Rather than trying to provide a single best guess for the average age in a village, a Bayesian answer strategy would try to figure out how likely different answers are given the data. To do so they need to know how likely different age distributions are *before* seeing the data—the priors—and the likelihood of different types of data for each possible age distribution. A Bayesian who knows anything about Italy would likely not be very impressed by the "15" answer given by the point estimator in Section 9.2.1 because, prior to seeing any samples, they would likely expect that the answer had to be bigger than this. Bayesians would chalk the answer "15" down to an unusual draw.

The Bayesian answer strategy specifies a prior distribution over the average age (here a normal distribution centered on 50 to reflect a prior that Italian villages skew older) as well as a lognormal distribution for ages. Here we retain the (median) posterior estimates for average age alongside a standard error based on the posterior variance. In the `.summary` argument we ask the tidier to exponentiate the coefficient estimate and standard error before returning them.

Declaration 9.3 Italian village design à la Bayes.

```
library(rdss) # for helper functions
library(rstanarm)

declaration_9.3 <-
  declare_model(N = 100, age = sample(0:80, size = N, replace = TRUE)) +
  declare_inquiry(mean_age = mean(age)) +
  declare_sampling(S = complete_rs(N = N, n = 3)) +
  declare_estimator(
    age ~ 1,
    .method = stan_glm,
    family = gaussian(link = "log"),
    prior_intercept = normal(50, 5),
    .summary = ~tidy_stan(., exponentiate = TRUE),
    inquiry = "mean_age"
  )
```

Diagnosis 9.3 We can then simulate this design in the same way and examine the distribution of estimates we might get.

```
diagnosis_9.3 <- diagnose_design(declaration_9.3)
```

What we see in Figure 9.3 is that using the same (poor) data strategy as before, a Bayesian answer strategy gets us a somewhat tighter distribution on our answer, but exhibits greater bias: the average estimate is higher than the estimand. We might accept higher bias for lower variance if overall, the root-mean-squared error is lower for the Bayesian approach. See Section 10.4.1 for a further discussion of RMSE. A major difference between the Bayesian and classical approaches is the handling of prior beliefs, which carry a lot of weight in the Bayesian estimation, but no weight in the classical approach.

Bayesian approaches are also used by qualitative researchers drawing case-level inferences from causal process observations. Recent developments in qualitative methods have sought to take Bayes' rule "from metaphor to analytic tool" (Bennett, 2015). This approach characterizes qualitative inference as one in which prior beliefs about the world can be specified numerically and then updated on the basis of evidence observed. At a minimum, writing down such an answer strategy on a computer requires specifying beliefs, expressed as probabilities, about the likelihood of seeing certain kinds of evidence under different hypotheses. We provide an example of such a strategy in the design library in Section 16.1. Herron and Quinn (2016) provide one approach to formalizing a qualitative answer strategy that focuses on understanding an average treatment effect. Humphreys and Jacobs (2015) provide an approach that can be used to formalize answer strategies targeting both causal effect and causal attribution inquiries, while Fairfield and Charman

(2017) formalize a Bayesian approach that treats causal attribution as a problem of attaching a posterior probability to competing alternative hypotheses. Abell and Engel (2021) suggest the use of "supra-Bayesian" methods to aggregate multiple participant-provided narratives in ethnographic studies targeting causal attribution inquiries.

9.2.3.2 Uncertainty

In the Bayes approach, parameter estimates and uncertainty estimates are generated simultaneously. One could imagine introducing uncertainty arising also from uncertainty about the prior or uncertainty about the model, but in practice this is rarely done and in principle can be done by respecifying the prior and the model.

9.2.4 Interval estimation

9.2.4.1 Answer

Instead of seeking a single number as an answer researchers sometimes provide a range or an interval. In this sense a confidence interval is itself a (set valued) estimate. Most often, confidence intervals are built from variance estimates under an appeal to sampling theory. Alternatively, a confidence interval can be formed by "inverting the test," i.e., finding the range of null hypotheses we fail to reject.

Table 9.2 shows the output of the answer strategy from Declaration 9.1, applied to the realized data set. We see the sample mean estimate of 15, the standard error estimate of 6, and the confidence interval from -10 to 40. Numbers inside the confidence interval are answers that are consistent with the data in the sense that we would not think the data unusual if any of these numbers were the true value. Numbers outside the confidence interval are answers that are not consistent with the data in the sense that we would think the data unusual if any of these numbers were the true value. These are 95% confidence intervals which means that we think, applying this procedure, 95% of the time the intervals that we generate will contain the true values.

```
three_italian_citizens <- fabricate(N = 3, age = c(5, 15, 25))
answer_strategy <- declare_estimator(age ~ 1)
answer_strategy(three_italian_citizens)
```

Table 9.2: One draw of the answer strategy.

estimate	std.error	statistic	p.value	conf.low	conf.high
15	5.77	2.6	0.12	-9.84	39.84

9.2 Types of Answer Strategies

Declaration 9.4 Italian village declaration, varying the true mean age parameter.

```
base_declaration <-
  declare_model(N = 100,
                age = round(rnorm(N, mean = true_mean, sd = 23))) +
  declare_inquiry(mean_age = mean(age)) +
  declare_sampling(S = complete_rs(N = N, n = 3)) +
  declare_estimator(age ~ 1, .method = lm_robust)

declaration_9.4 <- redesign(base_declaration,
                            true_mean = seq(0, 100, length.out = 10))
```

Diagnosis 9.4 Diagnosing the Italian village design over many values of the true mean age parameter

```
diagnosis_9.4 <- diagnose_designs(declaration_9.4)
```

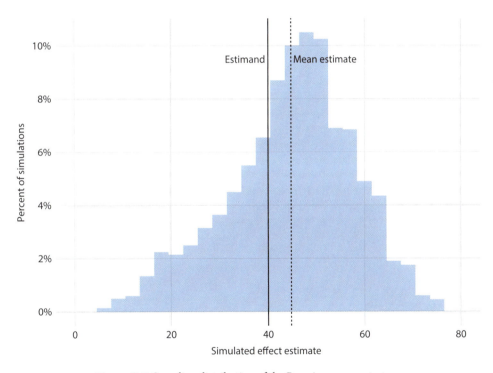

Figure 9.3: Sampling distribution of the Bayesian answer strategy.

A second type of interval estimation is bounding. In many circumstances, the details of the data strategy alone are insufficient to "point-identify" the inquiry, which means we can't generate a point estimate without adding further assumptions. A standard approach is to simply make those further assumptions and move on to reporting point estimates. Under an agnostic approach—we don't know if those assumptions are right because they aren't grounded in the data strategy—we can turn to interval estimation instead.

One way to handle settings in which parameters are not point-identified is to generate "extreme value bounds." These bounds report the best and worst possibilities according to the logical extrema of the outcome variable.

We illustrate interval estimation back in our Italian village, where we have learned the ages of three of the 100 citizens. Suppose we *did not know* whether the data strategy used random sampling; so we can't rely on the guarantee that, under random sampling, the sample mean is unbiased for the population mean. Now we have reason about best and worst case scenarios. Let's agree that the youngest a person can be is zero and the oldest is 110. Starting with an estimate of 15 among three citizens, we can generate lower and upper bound estimates for the average age of the entire 100-person village like this:

```
lower_bound <- (3 * 15 + 97 * 0)/100
upper_bound <- (3 * 15 + 97 * 110)/100
 c(lower_bound, upper_bound)
```

Table 9.3: Extreme value bounds estimate.

Lower bound	Upper bound
0.45	107.15

This procedure generates enormously wide bounds—we already knew before we started that the average age had to be somewhere between 0.45 and 107.15 years. But consider if we had data on 90 of the 100 citizens and among those 90, the average is 44. Now when we generate the bounds, they are still wide but not ridiculously so—the bounds put the average age somewhere between 40 and 50.

```
lower_bound <- (90 * 44 + 10 * 0)/100
upper_bound <- (90 * 44 + 10 * 110)/100
c(lower_bound, upper_bound)
```

Table 9.4: The extreme value bounds are tighter with more data.

Lower bound	Upper bound
39.6	50.6

Extreme value bounds and variations on the idea can be applied when experiments encounter missingness or when we want to estimate effects among subgroups that only reveal themselves in some but not all treatment conditions (see Aronow, Baron and Pinson (2019) or Coppock (2019) for examples). The extreme value bound approach can also be used in qualitative settings in which we can impute some but not all of the missing potential outcomes using qualitative information; the bounds reflect our uncertainty about those missing values (Coppock and Kaur, 2022).

9.2.4.2 Uncertainty

Bounding approaches are built around researcher uncertainty over models; however, it's important to remember that the bounds are themselves estimates that could have come out differently depending on the realization of the data. By this logic, we can attach standard errors and confidence intervals to the bounds (see Coppock et al., 2017, for an example).

9.3 How to Choose an Answer Strategy

Now that we have discussed all four research design elements in detail, we describe how to choose an answer strategy.

The model and the inquiry form the theoretical half of the design, and the data and answer strategies make up the empirical half. Research designs that have *parallel* theoretical and empirical halves tend to be strong (though not all strong designs need be parallel in this way). This principle is motivated by the intersection of two ideas from statistics: the "plug-in principle" and "analyze as you randomize" ("AAYR").

9.3.1 Plug-in principle

The plug-in principle refers to the idea that sometimes the answer strategy function and the inquiry function are very similar in form. The estimand, $I(m) = a_m$, can often be estimated by choosing an A that is very similar to I and then "plugging-in" the realized data d that result from the data strategy for the unobserved data m, i.e., $A(d) = a_d$.

More formally, Aronow and Miller (2019) describe a plug-in estimator as:

> For i.i.d. random variables $X_1, X_2, \ldots, X_n$ with common CDF F, the plug-in estimator of $\theta = T(F)$ is: $\hat{\theta} = T(\hat{F})$,

where $\hat{F}$ is an estimate of F.

9.3.1.1 Illustration of estimates using the plug-in principle

To illustrate the plug-in principle, suppose that our inquiry is the average treatment effect among the N units in the population:

$$I(m) = \frac{1}{N}\sum_{1}^{N}[Y_i(1) - Y_i(0)] = \frac{1}{N}\sum_{1}^{N}Y_i(1) - \frac{1}{N}\sum_{1}^{N}Y_i(0) = \text{ATE}.$$

Here $T()$ is the difference-in-means function.

We can develop a plug-in ATE estimator by replacing the population means—$\frac{1}{N}\sum_{1}^{N}Y_i(1)$ and $\frac{1}{N}\sum_{1}^{N}Y_i(0)$—with sample analogues:

$$A(d) = \frac{1}{m}\sum_{1}^{m}Y_i - \frac{1}{N-m}\sum_{m+1}^{N}Y_i,$$

where units 1 through m reveal their treated potential outcomes and the remainder reveal their untreated potential outcomes.

We could do the same thing for other functions, such as quantiles of the distribution or the variance of the distribution. In general, plug-in estimators are not guaranteed to be unbiased, but they can have nice asymptotic properties, converging to targets as the data increases (for conditions, see Van der Vaart, 2000).

9.3.1.2 Illustration of estimates of uncertainty using the plug-in principle

The plug-in principle can be used also for generating estimates of uncertainty. For instance, if we are interested in understanding the variance of the sampling distribution of estimates that we get from our procedure, we can use the bootstrap. With the bootstrap, we "plug-in" the sample for the population data, then repeatedly *re*sample from our existing data. We can then approximate the true sampling distribution by calculating estimates on each resampled dataset, from which we can estimate the variance. (We use this nonparametric bootstrapping approach when generating estimates of uncertainty of diagnosands; see Section 10.3.3).

As an illustration of the logic of the approach using `DeclareDesign`, we compare the usual standard error estimate that accompanies a difference-in-means estimate with a bootstrapped standard error.

First we set up a design that resamples from Clingingsmith, Khwaja, and Kremer (2009)'s study of the effect of being randomly assigned to go on Hajj on the tolerance of foreigners.

Declaration 9.5 Bootstrapped standard errors.

```
declaration_9.5 <-
  declare_model(data = resample_data(clingingsmith_etal)) +
  declare_estimator(views ~ success, .method = difference_in_means)
```

Diagnosis 9.5 Bootstrap diagnosis

The bootstrapped estimates are gotten by summarizing over multiple runs of the design:

```
diagnosis_9.5 <-
  declaration_9.5 |>
  simulate_design(sims = sims) |>
  summarize(se = sd(estimate))
```

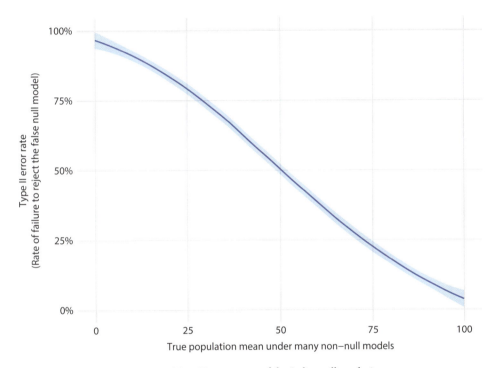

Figure 9.4: Type II error rates of the Italian village design.

Table 9.5: Bootstrapped standard error estimate.

se
0.161

We can compare the standard error estimates using the standard deviation of the bootstrapped estimates to the standard error provided by the difference in means estimator implemented on the original data to see that they are quite close:

```
get_estimates(design = declaration_9.5, data = clingingsmith_etal)
```

Table 9.6: Analytic standard error estimate.

estimate	std.error
0.475	0.163

9.3.2 Analyze as you randomize (AAYR)

Following the plug-in principle only yields good answer strategies under some circumstances. Those circumstances are determined by the data strategy. We need data strategies that sample units, assign treatment conditions, and measure outcomes such that the revealed data can indeed be "plugged into" the inquiry function. Whether a plug-in ATE estimator, the difference in means for example, provides a good answer strategy depends on features of the data strategy. It's a good estimator when units are assigned to treatment with equal probabilities, but it's a bad estimator if the probabilities differ from unit to unit.

When the data strategy introduces distortions like differential probabilities of assignment, the answer strategy function should *not* equal the inquiry function: we can no longer just plug in the observed data. We have to compensate for those distortions, reversing them to reestablish parallelism. In terms of the definition of the plug in principle, we have to do more work to get an estimate of F.

This idea can be summarized as "analyze as you randomize," a dictum attributed to R. A. Fisher. We use known features of the data strategy to adjust the answer strategy. We can undo the distortion introduced by differential probabilities of assignment by weighting units by the inverse of the probability of being in the condition that they are in. If we use an inverse-probability weighted (IPW) estimator, we restore parallelism because even though A no longer equals I, the relationship of D to A once again parallels the relationship of M to I.

9.3.2.1 *Illustration of estimates using the AAYR principle*

Declaration 9.6 illustrates this idea. We declare the theoretical half of the design as MI, then consider the intersection of two data strategies with two answer strategies. D1 has constant probabilities of assignment and D2 has differential probabilities of assignment. A1 is the plug-in estimator, applied to unweighted data, and A2 is the IPW estimator with the inverse probability weights generated by the D2 randomization protocol.

Declaration 9.6 Restoring parallelism design.

```
MI <-
  declare_model(
    N = 100,
    X = rbinom(N, size = 1, 0.5),
    U = rnorm(N),
    potential_outcomes(Y ~ 0.5 * Z+-0.5 * X + 0.5 * X * Z + U)
  ) +
  declare_inquiry(ATE = mean(Y_Z_1 - Y_Z_0))

D1 <-
  declare_assignment(Z = complete_ra(N = N)) +
  declare_measurement(Y = reveal_outcomes(Y ~ Z))
D2 <-
  declare_assignment(Z = block_ra(blocks = X, block_prob = c(0.1, 0.8))) +
  declare_measurement(Y = reveal_outcomes(Y ~ Z))

A1 <- declare_estimator(Y ~ Z, label = "Unweighted")
A2 <-
  declare_step(
    handler = fabricate,
    ipw = 1 / obtain_condition_probabilities(
      assignment = Z,
      blocks = X,
      block_prob = c(0.1, 0.8)
    )
  ) +
  declare_estimator(Y ~ Z, weights = ipw, label = "Weighted")

declaration_9.6 <- list(MI + D1 + A1,
                        MI + D1 + A2,
                        MI + D2 + A1,
                        MI + D2 + A2)
```

Diagnosis 9.6 Restoring parallelism diagnosis

```
diagnosis_9.6 <- diagnose_design(declaration_9.6)
```

We diagnose the bias of all four designs. Figure 9.5 shows that when the answer strategy and the data strategy match (*D1 + A1* and *D2 + A2*), we have no bias. When they do not match (*D1 + A2* and *D2 + A1*), we do. In this case, seeking parallelism in the choice of answer strategy improves the design. Of course, an alternative answer strategy we might call *A3* that implements the weights corresponding to whatever the data strategy says they should be unbiased under both *D1* and *D2*.

This principle applies most clearly to the bias diagnosand, but it applies to others as well. For example, Abadie et al. (2017) recommend that answer strategies include clustered standard errors at the level of sampling or assignment, whichever is higher. The data strategies that include clustering introduce a dependence among units that was not present in the model; clustered standard errors account for this dependence.

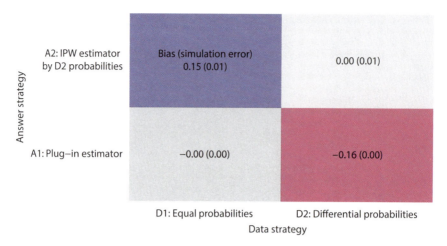

Figure 9.5: When data and answer strategies are mismatched, we obtain bias.

If we did not account for this dependence, our estimated standard error would be a bad estimate of the "standard deviation" diagnosand.

More generally, the principle to "design agnostically" implies that we should choose "agnostic" answer strategies, by which we mean answer strategies that produce good answers under a wide range of models. Selecting answer strategies that are robust to multiple models ensures that we get good answers not only when our model is spot on—which is rare!—but also under many possible circumstances.

Understanding whether the choices over answer strategies—logit or probit or OLS—depend on the model being a particular way is crucial to making a choice. For example, many people have been taught that whenever the outcome variable is binary, OLS is inappropriate and they must use a binary choice model like logit instead. When the inquiry is the probability of success for each unit and we use covariates to model them, how much better logit performs at estimating probabilities depends on the model. When probabilities are all close to 0.5, the two answer strategies both perform well. When the probabilities spread out from 0.5, OLS is less robust and logit beats it (Hellevik, 2009). In the same breath, however, we can consider these same two estimators in the context of a randomized experiment with a binary outcome. Here, OLS can be just as strong as logit, no matter what the distribution of the potential outcomes. In this setting, when designing agnostically, we find that both estimators are robust (see Section 11.2.2).

Designing agnostically has something in common with robustness checks: both share the motivation that we have fundamental uncertainty about the true model. A robustness check is an *alternative* answer strategy that changes some model assumption that the main answer strategy depends on. Presenting three estimates of the same parameter under different answer strategies (logit, probit, and OLS) and making a joint decision based on the set of estimates about whether the main analysis is "robust" is a procedure for assessing "model dependence"—meaning, dependence on *statistical* models. But robustness checks are just answer strategies themselves, and we should declare them and diagnose them to understand whether they are good answer strategies. We want to understand the *properties* of the robustness check, e.g., under what models and how frequently does it correctly describe the main answer strategy as "robust."

9.3.2.2 Illustration of estimates of uncertainty using the AAYR principle

We can illustrate the AAYR principle using the idea of "randomization inference." Randomization inference describes a large class of procedures for generating *p*-values that merit special attention. Randomization inference leverages known features of the randomization procedure to simulate trials under a null model (see Gerber and Green, 2012, chapter 3, for an introduction to randomization inference). In a common case, a randomization inference test proceeds by stipulating a null model under which the counterfactual outcomes of each unit are exactly equal to the observed outcomes, the so-called "sharp null hypothesis of no effect." Under this null hypothesis, the treated and untreated potential outcomes are exactly equal for each unit, reflecting a model in which the treatment has exactly zero effect for each unit.

As described above, a *p*-value is an answer to the question: what is the probability the null model would generate estimates as large or larger in absolute value than the observed estimate? We can answer this question by diagnosing the design under the sharp null model. Importantly, the randomization inference procedure follows the "analyze as you randomize" principle by conducting repeated random assignments according to the original randomization protocol.

We illustrate randomization inference with a voter mobilization experiment reported by Foos et al. (2021). The design was blocked and clustered: voters were clustered by their street, and the assignment was blocked by ward. Wards vary in their size and in the probability of assignment, so we have to recompute inverse probability weights in each draw from the null model.

Here is the observed estimate, indicating that our best guess is that the average effect of the mobilization treatment on voter turnout is 2.8 percentage points.

```
observed_estimate <-
  lm_robust(
    marked_register_2014 ~ treat + ward,
    weights = weights,
    clusters = street,
    data = foos_etal
  )
```

Table 9.7: Results from Foos et al. (2021).

term	estimate
treat	0.028

Here we declare the null model (indicated by `potential_outcomes(Y ~ 0 * Z + marked_register_2014)`) and add it to the data and answer strategies:

Declaration 9.7 Randomization inference under the sharp null.

```r
# number of streets to treat in each ward
block_m = c(71, 47, 60, 48, 35, 39, 63, 32, 52)

declaration_9.7 <-
  declare_model(data = foos_etal
          # this is the sharp null hypothesis
          potential_outcomes(Y ~ 0 * Z + marked_register_2014)) +
  declare_assignment(Z = block_and_cluster_ra(blocks = ward,
                                  clusters = street,
                                  block_m = block_m),
                   probs = obtain_condition_probabilities(
                     assignment = Z,
                     blocks = ward,
                     clusters = street,
                     block_m = block_m
                   ),
                   ipw = 1 / probs) +
  declare_measurement(Y = reveal_outcomes(Y ~ Z)) +
  declare_estimator(Y ~ Z + ward, weights = ipw, clusters = street)
```

Diagnosis 9.7 Randomization inference "diagnosis"

```r
p.value <-
  declare_diagnosands(
    p.value = mean(abs(estimate) >= abs(observed_estimate$coefficients))
  )

diagnosis_9.7 <-
  diagnose_design(
    declaration_9.7,
    diagnosands = p.value
  )

tidy(diagnosis_9.7)
```

Table 9.8: Randomization inference 'diagnosis' to obtain a *p*-value.

design	diagnosand	estimate
declaration_9.7	p.value	0.13

We diagnose the null design with respect to the `p.value` diagnosand: what fraction of simulations under the null model exceed the observed estimate? We find that the `p.value` is 0.13, so the estimate is not deemed statistically significant.

Some naive procedures for generating *p*-values might ignore or otherwise fail to incorporate the important design information (in this example, the blocking and clustering procedures). Randomization inference naturally incorporates this design information by holding the data and answer strategies fixed, while swapping in a null model. Simulating the resulting design yields a sampling distribution under the null, which can then be compared to the observed estimate.

9.4 Summary

The answer strategy describes what we do with the data once we've got it. We use the data to generate estimates that, if we've calibrated our design correctly, will with high frequency come close to the estimand, the value of the inquiry. Answer strategies are defined with respect to units, their conditions, their outcomes, and a summary method for generating estimates. We like to include measures of uncertainty with our estimates; these measures are like estimates of design properties. Answer strategies come in many varieties, but the main four are point estimation, interval estimation, tests, and summaries of Bayesian posterior distributions. Choosing a good answer strategy means staying responsive to the relevant model, inquiry, and data strategy elements.

CHAPTER 10

Diagnosing Designs

Research design diagnosis is the process of evaluating the properties of a research design. We invent the term "diagnosand" to refer to those properties of a research design we would like to diagnose. Many diagnosands are familiar. Power is the probability of obtaining a statistically significant result. Bias is the average deviation of estimates from the estimand. Other diagnosands are more exotic, like the Type-S error rate, which is the probability the estimate has the incorrect sign, conditional on being statistically significant (Gelman and Carlin, 2014). This chapter focuses mainly on the use of Monte Carlo computer simulations to estimate diagnosands, though we touch on analytic design diagnosis as well.

Research designs are strong when the empirical answer a_{d^*} generated by the design is guaranteed to be close to the true answer a_{m^*}. In general, we cannot know either a_{d^*} or a_{m^*} in advance. This problem means we have to assess the performance of our designs, not with respect to the real world, but instead with respect to our unverified and unverifiable beliefs about the world. We can do this using simulation, assessing the properties of research designs by comparing the simulated answer a_d to the answers under the model a_m, over many possible realizations of the design.

Figure 10.1 below is similar to Figure 5.1, which we described when defining the components of a research design. To recapitulate the main points of that discussion: The theoretical half of a research design defines an inquiry I in terms of a model M; the true answer to that question is the inquiry applied to the real world, $I(m^*) = a_{m^*}$; the empirical half of a research design applies the data strategy to the real world to generate a dataset $(D(m^*) = d^*)$, then applies the answer strategy to the realized dataset to generate an answer, $(A(d^*) = a_{d^*})$. The asterisks reflect the fact that *reality* plays an important role in empirical research designs. We commit to the notion that there are *real* answers to the questions we have posed. Our empirical answers are tethered to reality because the data strategy generates information that depends on the real world.

When we simulate and diagnose designs, however, this tether to reality is snipped, and we find ourselves in the bottom half of Figure 10.1. When we simulate, the

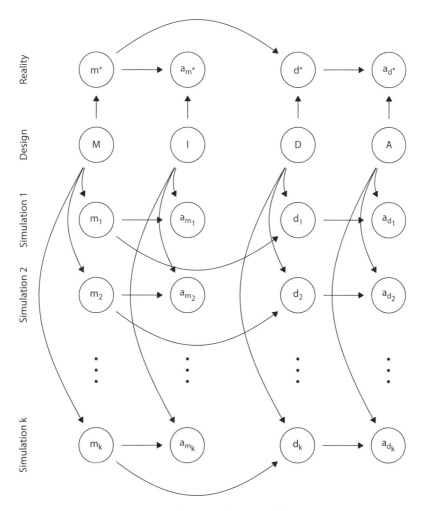

Figure 10.1: Simulations in the *MIDA* framework.

theoretical half of the design entertains many possibilities in the model set *M*, which we label $m_1, m_2, \ldots, m_k$, indexed by *j*. Each of the *k* possibilities generates a different answer to the inquiry: $a_{m_1}, a_{m_2}, \ldots, a_{m_k}$. Importantly, the simulated research design does not have access to the true answer a_{m^*}, but has access only to answers under the *k* considered models.

We pause to address one confusing aspect of our notation. The set of models $m_1, m_2, \ldots, m_k$ could refer to a set of *k* separate theoretical perspectives. Or it could refer to $m_1, m_2, \ldots, m_k$ draws from the same basic model, but the values of the exogenous variables (following the specific meaning described in Section 6.1.1) are different. In other words, our notation doesn't draw a formal distinction between large differences between benchmark models and small ones.

When we simulate, the empirical half of the design is similarly dissociated from reality. We apply the data strategy D to each of the model draws m_j to produce simulated datasets indexed as d_j. These fabricated datasets may be similar to or different from the true dataset d^* that would result if the design were realized (the more similar the better). We apply the answer strategy A to each simulated dataset d_j in order to produce simulated answers a_{d_j}.

A comparison of the top row to the bottom three rows of Figure 10.1 shows how actual research designs differ from simulated research designs. Actual research designs are influenced by reality: we learn about the real world by conducting empirical research. We don't learn about the real world from simulated research designs. Instead, we learn about research designs themselves. We learn how the research design would behave *if* the real world m^* were like the model draw m_1—or like m_{100}. The diagnosis of the design is then a summary of the performance of the model over the multiple models in M. Of course, we only diagnose under the possibilities we consider in M. If the world m^* is not in that set of possibilities, we won't have evaluated the design under the most important setting, i.e., in reality. We want to follow Principle 3.2 to "design agnostically" or, in order words, to consider such a wide range of possibilities that some a_{m_j} will be close enough to a_{m^*}.

With this definition of a diagnosis in hand, we can now sharpen our thinking on when we have a complete design declaration. A design declaration is "diagnosand-complete" when the declaration contains enough information to calculate a specific diagnosand, or a statistic about the design. The "bias" diagnosand requires that all four of M, I, D, and A are specified in sufficient detail because we need to be able to compare the answer under the model (a_m) to the simulated empirical answer (a_d). The "statistical power" diagnosand often does not require the inquiry I to be specified, since we can mechanistically conduct null hypothesis significance tests without reference to inquiries. Neither the "bias" nor "statistical power" diagnosands require any details of confidence interval construction, but without those details, the declaration is not diagnosand-complete for "coverage," which assesses the quality of the standard error estimator by checking how often the confidence intervals cover the true value.

Every design we have ever declared is diagnosand-complete for some diagnosands, but not for others. Diagnosand-completeness for every common diagnosand is not a goal for design declaration. We want to be diagnosand-complete for the set of diagnosands that matter most in a particular research setting.

10.1 Elements of Diagnoses

10.1.1 Diagnosand statistics

Diagnosands are summaries of the distributions of diagnostic statistics. We'll start by defining diagnostic statistics, then move on to describing how to generate the distribution of diagnostic statistics, then how to summarize those distributions in order to estimate diagnosands.

A diagnostic statistic ϕ_j is itself a function of a_{m_j} and a_{d_j}: $\phi_j = g(a_{m_j}, a_{d_j})$. We elide here two important notational annoyances. For the purpose of the following discussion of diagnostic statistics and diagnosands, a_{d_j} can refer to an estimate like a difference-in-means estimate or an associated uncertainty statistic like a standard error or a *p*-value. Importantly, diagnostic statistics can be functions that depend on a_{m_j} only, a_{d_j} only, or both.

Each diagnostic statistic is the result of a different function *g*. For example, the "error" diagnostic statistic is produced by this function: $g(a_{m_j}, a_{d_j}) = a_{d_j} - a_{m_j}$. The "significant" diagnostic statistic is $g(a_{d_j}) = \mathbf{I}[p(a_{d_j}) \leq \alpha]$, where $p()$ is a function of the empirical answer that returns a *p*-value, α is a significance cutoff, and $\mathbf{I}$ is an indicator function that returns 1 when the *p*-value is below the cutoff and 0 when it is above. A diagnostic statistic is something that can be calculated on the basis of a single run of the design.

Typically, diagnostic statistics will be different from simulation to simulation. In other words, ϕ_1 will be different from ϕ_2, ϕ_2 will be different from ϕ_3, and so on. These differences arise partially from the variation in *M*: m_1 is different from m_2, m_2 is different from m_3, and so on. Differences can also arise from the explicitly random procedures in *D*: sampling, assignment, and measurement can all include stochastic elements that will ramify through to the diagnostic statistics. As a result of these sources of variation, a diagnostic statistic is a random variable Φ.

10.1.2 Diagnosands

A diagnosand is a summary of the distribution of Φ, written $f(\Phi)$. For example, the expectation function $\mathbb{E}[\Phi]$ reports the expectation (the mean) of Φ.

Let's now work through two concrete examples of common diagnosands: bias and power (see Section 10.2 for a more exhaustive list).

Consider the diagnosand "bias" in the context of a two-arm randomized trial where the inquiry is the average treatment effect, the data strategy entails complete random assignment, and the answer strategy is the difference-in-means. Bias is the average difference between the estimand and the estimate. Under a single realization m_j of the model *M*, the value of the ATE will be a particular number, which we call a_{m_j}. We simulate a random assignment and measurement of observed outcomes, then apply the difference-in-means estimator. The diagnostic statistic is the error $a_{d_j} - a_{m_j}$; this error is a random variable because each m_j differs slightly. The bias diagnosand is the expectation of this random variable is $\mathbb{E}[a_{d_j} - a_{m_j}]$, where the expectation is taken over the randomization distribution implied by *M* and *D* (or distinct regions of the randomization distribution).

Now consider the diagnosand "power." Like bias, statistical power is an expectation, this time of the "significant" diagnostic statistic $\mathbf{I}(p(a_{d_j}) \leq 0.05)$. Power describes how frequently the answer strategy will return a statistically significant result. Some textbooks define statistical power as one minus the Type II error rate, where a Type II error is the failure to reject the null hypothesis, given that the null hypothesis is false. This definition is accurate, but hard to understand. The phrase "given that the null hypothesis is false" could refer to any number of model possibilities (a_{m_j}'s) in which the null hypothesis does not hold. Our definition of power is instead, "the probability of getting a statistically significant result, conditional on a set of beliefs about the model."

Uncertainty statistics like standard errors can be thought of as empirical estimates of diagnosands describing the quality of your design under some set of models.

Suppose we report that the estimate is equal to 15 and carries with it a standard error of 6. Here we are communicating that we now think our design has the property that, if we were to run it over and over, the standard deviation of our estimates would be 6. That is, if we were to fix the design at a particular m and combine it with I, D, and A, the standard deviation of the estimates across simulations of the design would be 6.

Likewise, estimated p-values can also be thought of as estimates of a peculiar diagnosand: the probability of obtaining a test statistic of a particular value, under a maintained null model. That is, if we were to write down a null model m_0 under which the estimand were in fact zero, then combine it with I, D, and A, we could diagnose that design to learn the fraction of estimates that are as large or larger than 15—a p-value.

Thinking about p-values as diagnosands can be seen most directly in the randomization inference approach to hypothesis testing. Randomization inference often considers "sharp" null hypotheses in which we impute the missing potential outcomes with exactly their observed values, then simulate all the ways the design could come out holding I, D, and A constant. The p-value is the fraction of simulations in which the null model generates estimates that are more extreme than the observed estimate, with variation in estimates arising from different assignments to treatment. See Section 9.3.2.2 for a worked example of this approach.

The payoff from thinking about uncertainty statistics as estimates of diagnosands is in drawing attention to the fact that uncertainty statistics can be poor estimators of diagnosands and to the fact that their performance can be assessed. For example, social scientists criticize one another's choice of standard error—classical or robust, clustered or not, bootstrapped, jackknifed, and on and on. The reason for this debate is that when the procedures we follow to form uncertainty statistics are inappropriate for the design setting, we can be falsely confident in our answers.

10.1 Elements of Diagnoses 121

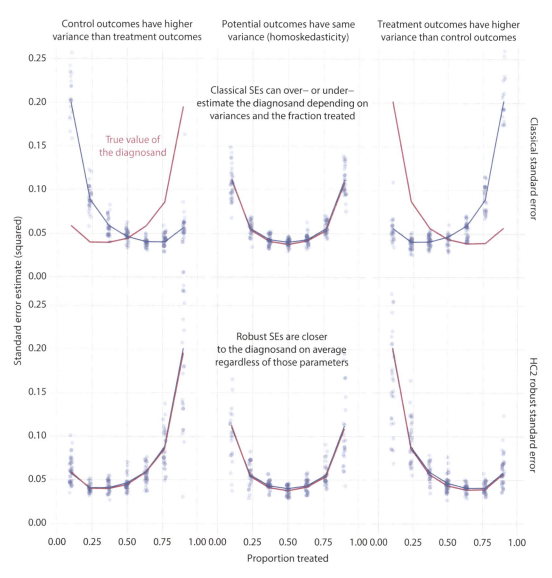

Figure 10.2: Why robust standard errors are preferred to classical standard errors.

Figure 10.2 illustrates what's at stake in the age-old contest between classical standard errors and robust standard errors. Here we are in the context of a two-arm trial under three settings: the control potential outcomes are higher variance, the groups have the same variances, or the treated outcomes have higher variance. The calculation for classical standard errors pools the data from both groups when estimating a variance, thereby assuming "homoskedasticity," a Greek work for having the "same spread." This estimation choice leads to poor performance. Depending on the fraction of the sample that receives treatment, the estimate of the sampling distribution can be upwardly biased (conservative) or downwardly biased (anti-conservative or falsely confident). We're usually worried about standard error estimates being too small because anti-conservatism is probably worse for scientific communication than conservatism.

Robust standard errors are "heteroskedasticity-robust," which means that the estimation does not assume that the two groups have the same error variance. Samii and Aronow (2012) show that a particular variant of robust standard errors (HC2) is exactly equal to the Neyman variance estimator described in Section 10.3.1, which is why HC2 robust standard errors are the default in the lm_robust function. The bottom row of Figure 10.2 shows that the robust standard error estimator hews closely to the true value of the diagnosand in all of the design settings considered. We prefer robust SEs because they do not impose extra model assumptions like homoskedasticity that are not grounded in any particular design feature.

10.2 Types of Diagnosands

As described above, a diagnostic statistic is any summary function of a_m and a_d, and a diagnosand is any summary of the distribution of diagnostic statistics. As a result, there are a great many diagnosands researchers may consider. In Table 10.1, we introduce a nonexhaustive set of diagnostic statistics, and in Table 10.2 a nonexhaustive set of diagnosands.

Table 10.1: Examples of diagnostic statistics.

Diagnostic statistic	Definition
Estimate	a_{d_j}
Estimand under the model	a_{m_j}
p-value	$p(a_{d_j})$
p-value is no greater than α	$\mathbb{I}(p(a_{d_j}) \leq \alpha)$
Confidence interval	$\text{CI}_{1-\alpha}$
Confidence interval covers the estimand under the model	$\text{covers}_{a_m} \equiv \mathbb{I}\{a_m \in \text{CI}_{1-\alpha}\}$
Estimated standard error	$\widehat{\sigma}(A)$
Cost	cost
Proportion of subjects harmed	$\Pr(\text{harm}) \equiv \frac{1}{n}\sum_i \text{harm}_i$

Table 10.2: Examples of diagnosands.

Diagnosand	Description	Formula
Average estimate		$\mathbb{E}(a_d)$
Average estimand		$\mathbb{E}(a_m)$
Power	Probability of rejecting null hypothesis of no effect	$\mathbb{E}(I(p \leq \alpha))$
Null risk	Probability of failing to reject null hypothesis of no effect	$\mathbb{E}(I(p > \alpha))$
Bias	Expected difference between estimate and estimand	$\mathbb{E}(a_d - a_m)$
Variance of the estimates		$\mathbb{V}(a_d)$
True standard error		$\sqrt{\mathbb{V}(a_d)}$
Average estimated standard error		$\widehat{\sigma}(A)$
Root-mean-squared error (RMSE)		$\sqrt{\mathbb{E}(a_d - a_m)}$
Coverage	Probability confidence interval overlaps estimand	$\Pr(\text{covers}_{a_m})$
Bias-eliminated coverage	Probability confidence interval overlaps average estimate (Morris, White, and Crowther, 2021)	$\Pr(\text{covers}_{a_d})$
Type-S error rate	Probability estimate has an incorrect sign, if statistically significant (Gelman and Carlin, 2014)	$\Pr(\text{sgn}(a_d) \neq \text{sgn}(a_m) \mid p \leq \alpha)$
Exaggeration ratio	Expected ratio of absolute value of estimate to estimand, if statistically significant (Gelman and Carlin, 2014)	$\mathbb{E}(\text{abs}(a_d/a_m) \mid p \leq \alpha)$
Type I error	Rejecting the null hypothesis when it is true	$\Pr(p \leq \alpha \mid a_m = a^0)$
Type II error	Failure to reject the null hypothesis when it is false	$\Pr(p \geq \alpha \mid a_m \neq a^0)$

(Continued)

Table 10.2: (*continued*)

Diagnosand	Description	Formula
Sampling bias	Expected difference between population average treatment effect and sample average treatment effect (Imai, King, and Stuart, 2008)	$\mathbb{E}(a_{m_{\text{sample}}} - a_{m_{\text{population}}})$
Expected maximum cost	Maximum cost across possible realizations of the study	max cost
Bayesian learning	Difference between prior and posterior guess of the value of the estimand	$a_{m_{\text{post}}} - a_{m_{\text{pre}}}$
Value for money	Probability that a decision based on estimated effect yields net benefits	
Success	Qualitative assessment of the success of a study	
Minimum detectable effect (MDE)	Smallest effect size for which the power of the design is nominal (e.g., powered at 80%)	$\operatorname{argmin}_{a_{m*}} \Pr(p \leq \alpha) = 0.8$
Robustness	Joint probability of rejecting the null hypothesis across multiple tests	
Maximum proportion of subjects harmed		max Pr(harm)

10.3 Estimation of Diagnosands

10.3.1 Analytic design diagnosis

Diagnosis can be done with analytic, pencil-and-paper methods. In an analytic design diagnosis, we typically derive a formula that returns the value of a diagnosand under a stipulated set of beliefs about the model, inquiry, data strategy, and answer strategy. For example, research design textbooks often contain analytic design diagnoses for statistical power. Gerber and Green (2012) write:

> To illustrate a power analysis, consider a completely randomized experiment where $N > 2$ of N units are selected into a binary treatment. The researcher must now make assumptions about the

distributions of outcomes for treatment and for control units. In this example, the researcher assumes that the control group has a normally distributed outcome with mean μ_c, the treatment group has a normally distributed outcome with mean μ_t, and both group's outcomes have a standard deviation σ. The researcher must also choose α, the desired level of statistical significance (typically 0.05). Under this scenario, there exists a simple asymptotic approximation for the power of the experiment (assuming that the significance test is two-tailed):

$$\beta = \Phi\left(\frac{|\mu_t - \mu_c|\sqrt{N}}{2\sigma} - \Phi^{-1}\left(1 - \frac{\alpha}{2}\right)\right)$$

where β is the statistical power of the experiment, $\Phi(\cdot)$ is the normal cumulative distribution function (CDF), and $\Phi^{-1}(\cdot)$ is the inverse of the normal CDF.

This power formula is usually motivated by a set of assumptions about M, I, D, and A. Under M, it usually assumes that both potential outcomes are normally distributed with group specific means and a common variance. Under I, it usually assumes the average treatment effect. Under D, it usually assumes a particular randomization strategy (simple random assignment). Under A, it usually assumes a particular hypothesis testing approach (equal variance t-test with $N - 2$ degrees of freedom). Whether this set of assumptions is "close enough" will depend on the research setting.

Analytic design diagnosis can be hugely useful, since they cover large families of designs that meet the scope criteria. For example, consider the "standard error" diagnosand $\sqrt{\mathbb{E}[(a_{d_j} - \mathbb{E}[a_{d_j}])^2]}$ for the Sample Average Treatment Effect estimate in a two arm trial with complete random assignment and estimation via difference in means. This has been worked out by statisticians to be $\sqrt{\frac{1}{N-1}\left\{\frac{m\mathbb{V}(Y_i(0))}{N-m} + \frac{(N-m)\mathbb{V}(Y_i(1))}{m} + 2\text{Cov}(Y_i(0), Y_i(1))\right\}}$, where N is the number of units and m is the number in treatment. The Neyman standard error estimator targets this quantity (see Equation 18.2). Many advances in our understanding of the properties of research design come from analytic design diagnosis. For example, Middleton (2008) and Imai, King, and Nall (2009) show that cluster randomized trials with heterogeneous cluster sizes are not unbiased for the ATE, which leads to the design recommendation that clustered trials should block on cluster size. These lessons apply broadly, more broadly perhaps than the lessons learned about a specific design in a specific Monte Carlo simulation.

That said, scholars conducting analytic design diagnosis have only worked out a few diagnosands for a limited set of designs. Since designs are so heterogeneous and can vary on so many dimensions, computer simulation is often the only feasible way to diagnose. We learn a lot from analytic design diagnosis—what the important parameters to consider are, what the important inferential problems are—but they often cannot provide direct answers to practical questions like, how many subjects do I need for my conjoint experiment? For that reason, we turn to design diagnosis via Monte Carlo simulation.

10.3.2 Design diagnosis by simulation

Research design diagnosis by simulation occurs in two steps. First we simulate research designs repeatedly, collecting diagnostic statistics from each run of the simulation. Second, we summarize the distribution of the diagnostic statistics in order to estimate the diagnosands.

Monte Carlo simulations of research designs can be written in any programming language. To illustrate the most common way of simulating a design—a "for" loop—we'll write a concise simulation in base R code. Diagnosis 10.1 conducts the simulation 500 times, each time collecting the *p*-value associated with a regression estimate of the average effect of an outcome on a treatment.

Loops like this one can be implemented in any language and they remain a good tool for design diagnosis. We think, however, writing simulations in this way obscures what parts of the design refer to the model, the inquiry, the data strategy, or the answer strategy. We might imagine Z and Y are generated by a data strategy that randomly assigns Z, then measures Y (though without a language for linking code to design steps, it's a bit unclear). The answer strategy involves running a regression of Y on Z, then conducting a hypothesis test against the null hypothesis that the coefficient on Z is 0. The model and inquiry are left entirely implicit. The inquiry might be the ATE, but it might also be a question of whether the ATE is equal to zero. The model might include only two potential outcomes for each subject, or it might have more, we don't know.

Diagnosis 10.1 By-hand diagnosis example.

```r
sims <- 500
p.values <- rep(NA, sims)

for(i in 1:sims){
  Z <- rbinom(100, 1, 0.5)
  U <- rnorm(100)
  Y <- 0.2 * Z + U
  p.values[i] <- summary(lm(Y ~ Z))$coefficients[2, 4]
}

power <- mean(p.values <= 0.05)
power
```

Table 10.3: By-hand design diagnosis with a for-loop.

power
0.16

10.3 Estimation of Diagnosands

For this reason, we advocate for explicit description of all four research design components. Explicit design declaration can *also* occur in any programming language, but `DeclareDesign` is purpose-built for this task. We begin with the explicit declaration of the same two-arm trial as above. We have 100 subjects with a constant response to treatment of 0.2 units. Our inquiry is the average difference between the treated and untreated potential outcomes—the ATE. We assign treatment using complete random assignment and estimate treatment effects using the difference-in-means.

Declaration 10.1 Example of declaration using `DeclareDesign`.

```
declaration_10.1 <-
  declare_model(
    N = 100,
    U = rnorm(N),
    potential_outcomes(Y ~ 0.2 * Z + U)
  ) +
  declare_inquiry(ATE = mean(Y_Z_1 - Y_Z_0)) +
  declare_assignment(Z = complete_ra(N)) +
  declare_measurement(Y = reveal_outcomes(Y ~ Z)) +
  declare_estimator(Y ~ Z, .method = difference-in-means, inquiry = "ATE")
```

Diagnosis 10.2 Diagnosis in `DeclareDesign`.

We can now diagnose the declared design. For comparison with the loop, we calculate just one diagnosand: statistical power. Both approaches return approximately the same answer. Any difference between the two can be attributed to simulation error, which is why `DeclareDesign` by default returns a bootstrapped standard error for each diagnosand estimate. If we were to increase the number of simulations for both approaches dramatically (100,000 simulations would be plenty), the differences would vanish.

```
diagnosands <- declare_diagnosands(power = mean(p.value <= 0.05))

diagnosis <-
  diagnose_design(declaration_10.1,
                  diagnosands = diagnosands)

diagnosis
```

Table 10.4: Design diagnosis using `DeclareDesign`.

power	se(power)	n_sims
0.1615	0.0083482	2000

Backing up, we now construct that same diagnosis step-by-step. We build up from a single simulation run of the design to the distribution of simulations, to summaries of that distribution.

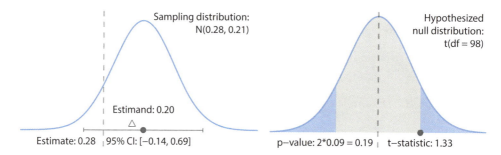

Figure 10.3: Visualization of one draw from a design diagnosis.

```
set.seed(343)

simulation_10.1 <-
  simulate_design(declaration_10.1, sims = 10) |>
  mutate(significant = p.value <= 0.05)
```

We can run this simulation a single time with `run_design`:

```
run_design(declaration_10.1)
```

Table 10.5: One simulation draw.

estimand	estimate	std.error	df	p.value	conf.low	conf.high
0.2	0.278	0.209	98	0.186	−0.136	0.692

Figure 10.3 shows the information we might obtain from a single run of the simulation. The filled point is the estimate a_{d_j}. The open triangle in the left panel is the estimand a_{m_j}. The bell-shaped curve is our normal-approximation-based estimate of the sampling distribution. The standard deviation of this estimated distribution is our estimated standard error, which expresses our uncertainty. The confidence interval around the estimate, shown in the left panel, is another expression of our uncertainty: We're not sure where a_{d_j} is, but if things are going according to plan, confidence intervals constructed this way will bracket a_{m_j} 95% of the time.

From this single draw, we can't yet estimate diagnosands, but we can calculate diagnostic statistics. The estimate was higher than the estimand in this draw, so the error is $0.45 - 0.20 = 0.25$. Likewise, the squared error is $(0.45 - 0.20)^2 = 0.0625$. The *p*-value is 0.01. This corresponds to the sum of the volumes of the two shaded areas in the right panel. It is above the threshold of 0.05, so the "statistical significance" diagnostic statistic is equal to FALSE. The confidence interval stretches from 0.11 to 0.79, and since the value of the estimand (0.20) is between those bounds, the "covers" diagnostic statistic is equal to TRUE.

To calculate the distributions of the diagnostic statistics, we have to simulate designs not just once, but many times over. The bias diagnosand is the average error over many runs of the simulation. The statistical power diagnosand is the fraction of runs in which the estimate is significant. The coverage diagnosand is the frequency with which the confidence interval covers the estimand.

Figure 10.4 visualizes 10 runs of the simulation. We can see that some of the draws produce statistically significant estimates (the shaded areas are small and the confidence intervals don't overlap with zero), but not all. We get a sense of the *true* standard error (the standard deviation of the estimates over multiple runs of the design) by seeing how the point estimates bounce around. We get a feel for the difference between the estimates of the standard error and true standard error. Design diagnosis is the process of learning about the many ways the study might come out, not just the one way that it will.

In Diagnosis 10.3, one line of code does all of these steps at once. We simulate the design (500 times by default) to calculate the diagnostic statistics, then we summarize them in terms of bias, the true standard error, RMSE, power, and coverage.

Diagnosis 10.3 Design diagnosis in one step.

```
diagnosis_10.3 <-
  diagnose_design(
    declaration_10.1,
    diagnosands = declare_diagnosands(
      bias = mean(estimate - estimand),
      true_se = sd(estimate),
      power = mean(p.value <= 0.05),
      coverage = mean(estimand <= conf.high &
                      estimand >= conf.low)
    )
  )
```

Table 10.6: Diagnosand estimates with bootstrapped standard errors in parentheses.

bias	true se	power	coverage
−0.00 (0.00)	0.20 (0.00)	0.17 (0.01)	0.96 (0.00)

130   Chapter 10: Diagnosing Designs

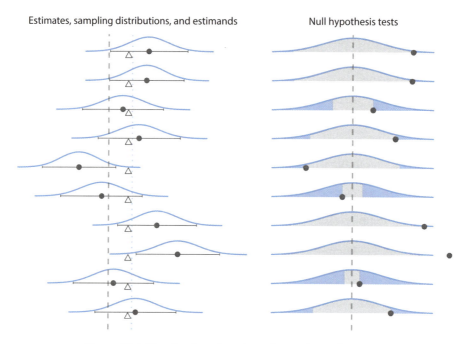

Figure 10.4: Visualization of ten draws from a design diagnosis.

10.3.3 Simulation error

We use Monte Carlo simulation to estimate diagnosands. We only get estimates—not the exact value—of diagnosands under a particular model set because of simulation error. Simulation error declines as we conduct more simulations. When we conduct many thousands of simulations, we're relatively certain of the value of the diagnosand. If we conduct just tens of simulations, we are much more uncertain.

We can characterize our uncertainty regarding the diagnosand estimate by calculating a standard error. If the Monte Carlo standard error is large relative to the estimated diagnosand, then we need to increase the number of simulations. Unlike empirical settings where additional data collection can be very expensive, in order to get more observations of diagnostic statistics, we can just increase the number of simulations. Computation time isn't free—but it's cheap.

The standard error of diagnosand estimates can be calculated using standard formulas. If the diagnosand can be written as a population mean, and the simulations are fully independent, then we can estimate the standard error as $\frac{\text{sd}(\phi)}{\sqrt{k}}$, where k is the number of simulations. The power diagnosand summarizes a binary diagnostic statistic (is the estimate significant or not?). Binary variables that take a value of 1 with probability p have variance $p(1-p)$. So with 1,000 independent simulations, the standard error for the mean of a binary diagnostic statistic is $\frac{\sqrt{p(1-p)}}{\sqrt{1000}}$. This level of simulation uncertainty is often acceptable (in the worst case when $p = 0.5$, the

95% confidence interval is approximately 4 * 0.016 = 6.4 percentage points wide), but if it isn't, you can always increase the number of simulations.

Since some diagnosands are more complex than a population mean (i.e., we can't characterize the estimation error with simple formulas), the `diagnose_design()` function uses the nonparametric bootstrap.

10.4 How to Diagnose Designs

10.4.1 Exploring design trade-offs

Choosing among designs means choosing which diagnosands are important—and not all diagnosands are equally important for every study. For example, in a descriptive study whose goal is to estimate the fraction of people in France who are left-handed, statistical power is likely irrelevant. A hypothesis test against the null hypothesis that zero percent of the people in France are left-handed is preposterous (though we could of course have other policy relevant hypotheses). A much more important diagnosand for this study would be RMSE (root-mean-squared error), which is a measure of how well estimated the estimand is that incorporates both bias and variance.

Often, we need to look at several diagnosands in order to understand what might be going wrong. If our design exhibits "undercoverage" (e.g., a procedure for constructing "95%" confidence interval only covers the estimand 50% of the time), that might be because the standard errors are too small or because the point estimator is biased, or some combination of the two. In really perverse instances, we might have a biased point estimator which, thanks to overly wide confidence intervals, just happens to cover the estimand 95% of the time.

Many research design decisions involve trading off bias and variance. In trade-off settings, we may need to accept higher variance in order to decrease bias. Likewise, we may need to accept a bit of bias in order to achieve lower variance. The trade-off is captured by mean-squared error, which is the average squared distance between a_d and a_m. Of course, we would ideally like to have as low a mean-squared error as possible, that is, we would like to achieve low variance and low bias simultaneously.

To illustrate, consider the following three designs as represented by three targets. The inquiry is the bullseye of the target. The data and answer strategies combine to generate a process by which arrows are shot toward the target. On the left, we have a very bad archer: even though the estimates are unbiased in the sense that they hit the bullseye "on average," very few of the arrows are on target. In the middle, we have an excellent shot: they are both on target and low variance. On the right, we have an archer who is very consistent (low variance) but biased. The mean squared error is highest on the left and lowest in the middle.

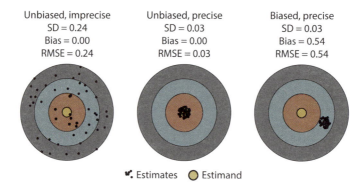

Figure 10.5: Visualization of the bias and variance of three 'estimators' of the bullseye.

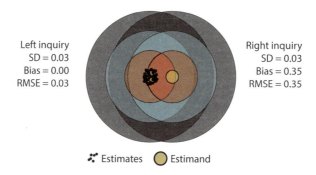

Figure 10.6: The bias, variance, and RMSE of an answer strategy depend on the inquiry.

The archery metaphor is common in research design textbooks because it effectively conveys the difference between variance and bias, but it does elide an important point. It really matters *which target* the archer is shooting at. Figure 10.6 shows a bizarre double-target representing two inquiries. The empirical strategy is unbiased and precise for the left inquiry, but it is clearly biased for the right inquiry. When we are describing the properties of an answer strategy, we have to be clear about which inquiry it is associated with.

MSE is an exactly equal weighting of variance and bias (squared). Yet many other weightings of these two diagnosands are possible, and different researchers will vary in their weightings.

In evaluating a research design through diagnosis, we must construct a weighting of all relevant diagnosands. We can think of this as our research design utility function. Our utility function describes how important it is to study big questions, to shift beliefs in a research field, to overturn established findings, to obtain unbiased answers, and to get the sign of the inquiry right. When we compare across empirical designs, we compare them on this utility function that aggregates all the diagnosands according to their importance.

For example, we too often consider the diagnosand *power* on its own. This diagnosand is the probability of getting a statistically significant result, which of course depends on many things about your design, including, crucially, the unknown magnitude of the parameter to be estimated. But considering power alone is also misleading: no researcher wants to design a study that is 80% powered but returns highly biased estimates. Another way of saying this is that researchers always care about both power and bias. How much they care about each feature determines the weight of power and bias in their utility function.

Diagnosands need not be about hypothesis testing or even statistical analysis of the data at all. We often trade off how much we learn from a research design with its cost in terms of money and our time. We have financial and time budgets that provide hard constraints to our designs. Many researchers wish to select cheaper (or shorter) designs in order to carry out more studies or finish their degree sooner. Time and cost are also diagnostic statistics! We may wish to explore the maximum cost of a study or the average amount of time it would take.

Ethical considerations also often enter the process of assessing research designs, if implicitly. We can explicitly incorporate them into our utility function by caring about harm to subjects and the degree of informed consent. When collecting data, researchers often encounter a trade-off between informing subjects about the purpose of the study (an ethical consideration, or a requirement of the IRB) on the one hand and the bias that comes from Hawthorne or demand effects on the other. We can incorporate these considerations in a research design diagnosis by specifying diagnostic statistics related to the amount of disclosure about the purposes of research or the number of subjects harmed in the research. See Section 21.1.1 for an example.

10.4.2 Diagnosis under model uncertainty

We are always uncertain about the model in M. If we were certain of M (or there was no real dispute about it), there would be no need to conduct new empirical research. Research design diagnosis can incorporate this uncertainty by evaluating the performance of the design under alternative models. For example, if we are unsure of the exact value of the intra-cluster correlation (ICC), we can simulate the design under a range of plausible ICC values. If we are unsure of the true average treatment effect, we can diagnose the power of the study over a range of plausible effect sizes. Uncertainty over model inputs like the means, variances, and covariances in data that will eventually be collected is a major reason to simulate under a range of plausible values.

We illustrate diagnosis under model uncertainty with the declaration below. Here we have a 200-unit two-arm trial in which we explicitly describe our uncertainty over the value of the true average treatment effect. In the `potential_outcomes` call, we have Y ~ runif(1, 0, 0.5) * Z + U, which indicates that the treatment effect in each run of the simulation is one draw from uniform distribution between 0.0 and 0.5.

Declaration 10.2 Declaration including model uncertainty.

```
declaration_10.2 <-
  declare_model(
    N = 200, U = rnorm(N),
    # this runif(n = 1, min = 0, max = 0.5)
    # generates 1 random ATE between 0 and 0.5
    potential_outcomes(Y ~ runif(n = 1, min = 0, max = 0.5) * Z + U)) +
  declare_inquiry(ATE = mean(Y_Z_1 - Y_Z_0)) +
  declare_assignment(Z = complete_ra(N, prob = 0.5)) +
  declare_measurement(Y = reveal_outcomes(Y ~ Z)) +
  declare_estimator(Y ~ Z, inquiry = "ATE")
```

Diagnosis 10.4 Diagnosis under model uncertainty.

Figure 10.7 shows how the statistical power of this design varies over the set of model possibilities. We plot the possible effect sizes we entertain in the model on the horizontal axis and the statistical power on the vertical axis. We also plot a loess curve that flexibly smooths over the full distribution of effect sizes. We see that at low levels of the effect size, statistical power is quite poor. With only 200 subjects, we couldn't achieve 80% statistical power unless the true effect size were approximately 0.45 standard deviations. The effect size at which a design achieves 80% power is often referred to as the minimum detectable effect size (MDE). This exercise shows how the MDE diagnosand is a summary of a design that admits uncertainty over

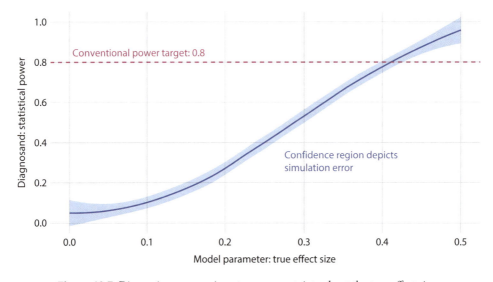

Figure 10.7: Diagnosing an experiment over uncertainty about the true effect size.

the effect size. We return to this example in Section 11.1.1, when we redesign this study to learn how the MDE changes at different sample sizes.

What is "the" power of this design? Under one view, the true power of the design is whichever value for power is associated with the effect size. But under an agnostic view, the ex ante "power" of the design is a weighted average of all these power values, weighted by the researcher's prior beliefs over the distribution of possible effect sizes.

10.4.3 Adjudicating between competing models

The principle to design agnostically extends to *competing* models. Imagine that you believe *M*1 is true but that your scholarly rival believes *M*2 is true. Suppose that under *M*1, the treatment affects *Y*1 but not *Y*2. Your rival posits the reverse: Under *M*2, the treatment affects *Y*2 but not *Y*1. In the spirit of scientific progress, the both of you engage in an "adversarial collaboration." You design a study together. The design you choose should, first, demonstrate *M*1 is true if it is true and, second, demonstrate *M*2 is true if *it* is true. In order to come to an agreement about the properties of the design, you will need to simulate the design under both models.

Declaration 10.3 Declaration of competing models.

```
M1 <-
  declare_model(
    N = 200,
    U = rnorm(N),
    potential_outcomes(Y1 ~ 0.2 * Z + U),
    potential_outcomes(Y2 ~ 0.0 * Z + U)
  )
M2 <-
  declare_model(
    N = 200,
    U = rnorm(N),
    potential_outcomes(Y1 ~ 0.0 * Z + U),
    potential_outcomes(Y2 ~ 0.2 * Z + U)
  )
IDA <-
  declare_inquiry(ATE1 = mean(Y1_Z_1 - Y1_Z_0),
                  ATE2 = mean(Y2_Z_1 - Y2_Z_0)) +
  declare_assignment(Z = complete_ra(N)) +
  declare_measurement(Y1 = reveal_outcomes(Y1 ~ Z),
                      Y2 = reveal_outcomes(Y2 ~ Z)) +
  declare_estimator(Y1 ~ Z, inquiry = "ATE1", label = "DIM1") +
  declare_estimator(Y2 ~ Z, inquiry = "ATE2", label = "DIM2")

declaration_10.3a <- M1 + IDA
declaration_10.3b <- M2 + IDA
```

Diagnosis 10.5 Diagnosis of competing models.

To diagnose these alternative models, we count how frequently each perspective receives support. If we define support by statistical significance (other metrics are of course possible), then your model is supported if the effect of treatment on $Y1$ is significant but the effect on $Y2$ is not significant. If the reverse pattern is obtained, your rival can claim victory. Two kinds of split decisions are possible: neither estimate is significant, or both are. By simulation, we can estimate the rates of these four possibilities, under both your beliefs and those of your theoretical adversary.

```
diagnosis_10.5 <-
  diagnose_design(
    list(declaration_10.3a, declaration_10.3b)
  )
```

Table 10.7: Design diagnosis under two alternative theories.

design	Only theory 1 supported	Only theory 2 supported	Both supported	Neither supported
design_1	0.2610	0.026	0.0260	0.687
design_2	0.0255	0.260	0.0255	0.689

The diagnosis shows that the study is responsive to the truth. When theory 1 is correct, the design is more likely to yield empirical evidence in favor of it; the reverse holds when theory 2 is correct. That said, the major concern facing this adversarial collaboration is that the study is too small to resolve the dispute. About two thirds of the time—regardless of who is right!—neither theory receives support. This problem can be ameliorated either by elaborating more tests of each theoretical perspective or by increasing the size of the study.

10.5 Summary

Diagnosis is the process of estimating the properties of research designs under uncertain beliefs about the world. We simulate under many alternative designs because we want to choose designs that are strong under a large range of model possibilities. Each run of a design generates a diagnostic statistic. We learn about the distribution of the diagnostic statistic by running the design repeatedly. Diagnosands are summaries of the distribution of diagnostic statistics. Which diagnosands are most important will vary from study to study, and depend on the relative weight you place on one diagnosand versus another. Analytic design diagnosis is possible and can be quite powerful—we nevertheless recommend full simulation of research designs in order to learn about a range of diagnosands.

CHAPTER 11

Redesigning

Redesign is the process of choosing the single empirical design to be implemented from a large family of possible designs. To make this choice, we systematically vary aspects of the data and answer strategies to understand their impact on the most important diagnosands. Redesign entails diagnosing many possible empirical designs over the range of plausible models, and comparing them.

A sample size calculation is the prototypical result of a redesign. Holding the model, inquiry, and answer strategy constant, we vary the "sample size" feature of the data strategy in order to understand how a diagnosand like the width of the confidence interval changes as we change N. We then choose the N that we will in fact use in our study.

Not surprisingly, most designs get stronger as we allocate more resources to them. The expected width of a confidence interval could always be tighter, if only we had more subjects. Standard errors could always be smaller, if only we took more pretreatment measurements. At some point, though, the gains are not worth the increased costs, so we settle for an affordable design that meets our scientific goals well enough. (Of course, if the largest affordable design has poor properties, no version of the study is worth implementing). The knowledge-expense trade-off is a problem that every empirical study faces. The purpose of redesign is to explore this and other trade-offs in a systematic way.

11.1 Redesigning over Data Strategies

A redesign over a data strategy choice can be illustrated with a "power curve." We want to learn the power of a test at many sample sizes, either so we can learn the price of precision, or so we can learn what sample size is required for a minimum level of statistical power.

We start with a minimal design declaration: we draw samples of size N and measure a single binary outcome Y, then conduct a test against the null hypothesis that the true proportion of successes is equal to 0.5.

Chapter 11: Redesigning

Declaration 11.1 A baseline declaration intended to be redesigned over *N*.

```
N <- 100

declaration_11.1 <-
  declare_model(N = N) +
  declare_measurement(Y = rbinom(n = N, size = 1, prob = 0.55)) +
  declare_test(handler =
                 label_estimator(function(data) {
                   test <- prop.test(x = table(data$Y), p = 0.5)
                   tidy(test)
                 }))
```

To construct a power curve, we redesign our baseline declaration over values of *N* that vary from 100 to 1,000.

Diagnosis 11.1 Diagnosing over a redesign

```
diagnosis_11.1 <-
  declaration_11.1 |>
  redesign(N = seq(100, 1000, 100)) |>
  diagnose_designs()
```

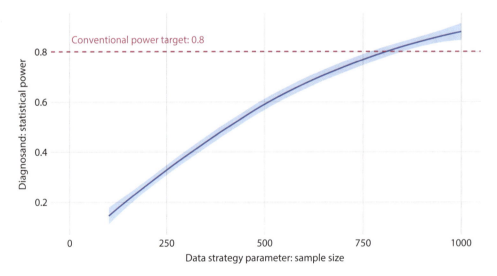

Figure 11.1: Redesigning with respect to sample size.

Redesigns are often easiest to understand graphically, as in Figure 11.1. At each sample size, we learn the associated level of statistical power. We might then choose the least expensive design (sample size 800) that meets a minimum power standard (0.8).

11.1.1 Redesigning under model uncertainty

When we diagnose studies, we do so over the many theoretical possibilities we entertain in the model. Through diagnosis, we learn how the values of the diagnosands change depending on model parameters. When we redesign, we explore a *range* of empirical strategies over the set of model possibilities. Redesign might indicate that one design is optimal under one set of assumptions, but that a different design would be preferred if a different set holds.

We illustrate this idea with an analysis of the minimum detectable effect (MDE) and how it changes at different sample sizes. The MDE diagnosand is complex. Whereas most diagnosands can be calculated with respect to a single possible model in M, the MDE is defined with respect to a collection of possible models. It is obtained by calculating the statistical power of the design over a range of possible effect sizes (holding the empirical design constant), then reporting the effect size that is associated with (typically) 80% statistical power.

MDEs can be a useful heuristic for thinking about the multiplicity of possibilities in the model. If the minimum detectable effect of a study is enormous—a one standard deviation effect, say—then we don't have to think much harder about our beliefs about the true effect size. If we think it implausible that effects could be as large as 1 SD, even if we are otherwise very uncertain, we can immediately conclude that the design is too small.

Declaration 11.2 contains uncertainty over the true effect size. This uncertainty is encoded in the `runif(n = 1, min = 0, max = 0.5)` command, which corresponds to our uncertainty over the ATE. It could be as small as 0.0 SDs or as large as 0.5 SDs, and we are equally uncertain about all the values in between. We redesign over three values of N: 100, 500, and 1,000, then simulate each design. Each run of the simulation features a different true ATE somewhere between 0.0 and 0.5.

Declaration 11.2 Uncertainty over effect size design.

```
N <- 100
declaration_11.2 <-
  declare_model(
    N = N, U = rnorm(N),
    # this runif(n = 1, min = 0, max = 0.5)
    # generates 1 random ATE between 0 and 0.5
    potential_outcomes(Y ~ runif(n = 1, min = 0, max = 0.5) * Z + U)) +
  declare_inquiry(ATE = mean(Y_Z_1 - Y_Z_0)) +
  declare_assignment(Z = complete_ra(N, prob = 0.5)) +
  declare_measurement(Y = reveal_outcomes(Y ~ Z)) +
  declare_estimator(Y ~ Z, inquiry = "ATE")
```

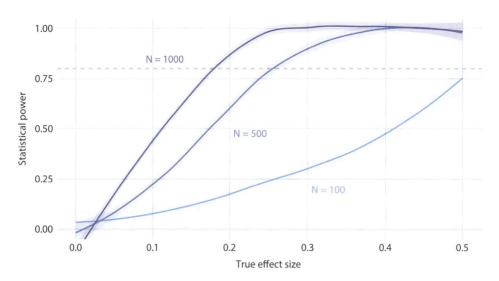

Figure 11.2: Redesigning an experiment over model uncertainty about the true effect size.

Diagnosis 11.2 Redesigning under uncertainty

```
diagnosis_11.2 <-
  declaration_11.2 |>
  redesign(N = c(100, 500, 1000)) |>
  diagnose_designs()
```

Figure 11.2 summarizes the simulations by smoothing over effect sizes: the loess curves describe the fraction of simulations that are significant at each effect size.[1] The MDEs for each sample size can be read off the plot by examining the intersection of each curve with the dotted line at 80% statistical power. At `N = 1000`, the MDE is approximately 0.175 SDs. At `N = 500`, the MDE is larger, at approximately 0.225 SDs. If the design only includes 100 units, the MDE is some value higher than 0.5 SDs. We could of course expand the range of effect sizes considered in the diagnosis, but if we believe effect sizes above 0.5 SDs are unlikely, we don't even need to—we'll need a design larger that 100 units in any case.

This diagnosis and redesign shows how our decisions about the data strategy depend on beliefs in the model. If we think the true effect size is likely to be 0.225 SDs, then a design with 500 subjects is a reasonable choice, but if it is smaller than that, we'll want a larger study. Small differences in effect size have large consequences for design. Researchers who arrive at a plot like that in Figure 11.2 through redesign should be inspired to sharpen up their prior beliefs about the true effect size, either through literature review, meta-analysis of past studies, or piloting (see Section 21.4).

---

[1] `DeclareDesign` tip: this procedure is more computationally efficient than an alternative, which would be to conduct simulations of each design at specific effect sizes across the plausible range.

11.1.2 Redesigning over two data strategy parameters

Sometimes, we have a fixed budget (in terms of financial resources, creative effort, or time), so the redesign question isn't about how much to spend, but how to spend across competing demands. For example, we might want to find the sample size `N` and the fraction of units to be treated (`prob`) that minimize a design's error subject to a fixed budget. Data collection costs $2 per unit and treatment costs $20 per treated unit. We need to choose how many subjects to sample and how many to treat. We might rather add an extra 11 units to the control units (additional cost $2 * 11 = $22) than add one extra unit to the treatment group (additional cost $2 + $20 = $22).

We solve the optimization problem:

$$\underset{N,N_t}{\operatorname{argmin}} \qquad E_M(L(a^d - a^m | D_{N,m}))$$

$$\text{s.t.} \qquad 5N + 20m \leq 5000,$$

where L is a loss function, increasing in the difference between a^d and a^m.

We can explore this optimization with a bare-bones declaration of a two-arm trial that depends on two separate data strategy parameters, `N` and `prob`:

Declaration 11.3 Bare-bones two-arm trial.

```
N <- 100

declaration_11.3 <-
  declare_model(N = N, U = rnorm(N),
                potential_outcomes(Y ~ 0.2 * Z + U)) +
  declare_inquiry(ATE = mean(Y_Z_1 - Y_Z_0)) +
  declare_assignment(Z = complete_ra(N = N, prob = prob)) +
  declare_measurement(Y = reveal_outcomes(Y ~ Z)) +
  declare_estimator(Y ~ Z, inquiry = "ATE")
```

We redesign, varying those two parameters over reasonable ranges: 100 to 1,000 subjects, with probabilities of assignment from 0.1 to 0.5. The redesign function smartly generates designs with all combinations of the two parameters. We want to consider the consequences of these data strategy choices for two diagnosands: cost and a very common loss function, mean-squared error.

Diagnosis 11.3 Redesigning over two parameters

```
diagnosands <-
  declare_diagnosands(cost = unique(N * 2 + prob * N * 20),
                      rmse = sqrt(mean((estimate - estimand) ^ 2)))

diagnosis_11.3 <-
  declaration_11.3 |>
```

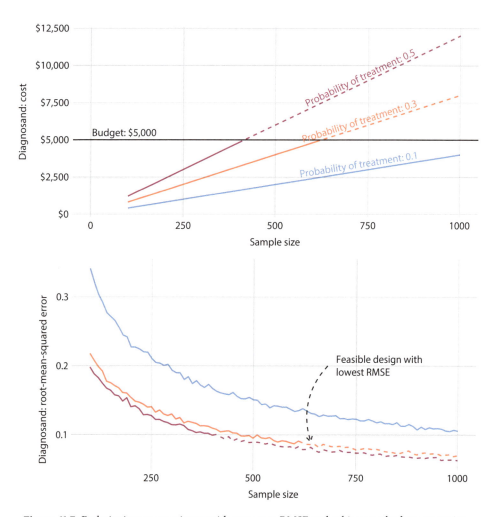

Figure 11.3: Redesigning an experiment with respect to RMSE and subject to a budget constraint.

```
redesign(N = seq(100, 1000, 25),
         prob = seq(0.1, 0.5, 0.2)) |>
  diagnose_designs(diagnosands = diagnosands)
```

The diagnosis is represented in Figure 11.3. The top panel shows the cost of empirical designs, at three probabilities of assignment over many sample sizes. The bottom panel shows the RMSE of each design. According to this diagnosis, the best combination that can be achieved for less than $5,000 is `N = 600` with `prob = 0.3`. This conclusion is in mild tension with the common design advice that under many circumstances, balanced designs are preferable (see Section 10.3.1 in the design library for an in-depth discussion of this point). Here, untreated subjects are so much less expensive than treated subjects that we want to tilt the design toward having a larger control group. How far to tilt depends on model beliefs as well as the cost structure of the study.

11.2 Redesigning over Answer Strategies

Redesign can also take place over possible answer strategies. An inquiry like the average treatment effect could be estimated using many different estimators: difference-in-means, logistic regression, covariate-adjusted ordinary least squares, the stratified estimator, doubly robust regression, targeted maximum likelihood regression, regression trees—the list of possibilities is long. Redesign is an opportunity to explore how alternative analysis approaches work.

11.2.1 Redesigning over model flexibility

A key trade-off in the choice of answer strategy is the bias-variance trade-off. Some answer strategies exhibit higher bias but lower variance while others have lower bias but higher variance. Choosing which side of the bias-variance trade-off to take is complicated and the process for choosing among alternatives must be motivated by the scientific goals at hand.

A common heuristic for trading off bias and variance is the mean-squared error (MSE) diagnosand. Mean-squared error is equal to the square of bias plus variance, which is to say, MSE weighs (squared) bias and variance equally. Sometimes, researchers choose among alternative answer strategies by minimizing MSE. If in your scientific context, bias is more important than variance, you might choose an answer strategy that accepts slightly more variance in exchange for a decrease in bias.

To illustrate the bias-variance trade-off, Declaration 11.4 describes a setting in which the goal is to estimate the conditional expectation of some outcome variable Y with respect to a covariate X. The true conditional expectation function (produced by the custom `dip` function) is not smooth, but we estimate it with smooth polynomial functions of increasing order.

Declaration 11.4 Conditional expectation function design.

```
library(purrr)

dip <- function(x) (x <= 1) * x + (x > 1) * (x - 2) ^ 2 + 0.2
x_range <- seq(from = 0, to = 3, length.out = 50)
polynomial_degrees <- 1:6

declaration_11.4 <-
  declare_model(
    N = 100,
    X = runif(N, 0, 3)) +
```

```
declare_inquiry(
  X = x_range, inquiry = str_c("X_", X), estimand = dip(X),
  data = NULL, handler = tibble
) +
declare_measurement(Y = dip(X) + rnorm(N, 0, .5)) +
declare_estimator(handler = function(data) {
  map(polynomial_degrees, ~lm(Y ~ poly(X, .), data = data)) |>
    set_names(nm = str_c("A", polynomial_degrees)) |>
    map_dfc(~predict(., newdata = tibble(X = x_range))) |>
    bind_cols(tibble(X = x_range)) |>
    mutate(inquiry = str_c("X_", X)) |>
    pivot_longer(cols = starts_with("A"),
                 names_to = "estimator",
                 values_to = "estimate")
})
```

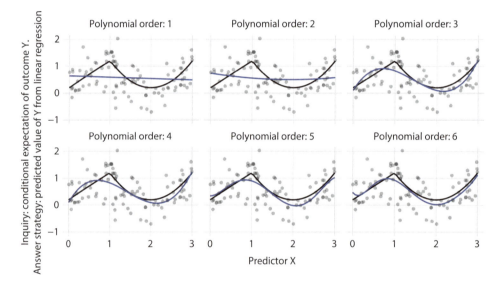

Figure 11.4: Estimating a CEF (black line) with polynomials of increasing order (blue line).

Figure 11.4 shows one draw of this design—the predictions of the CEF made by six regressions of increasing flexibility. A polynomial of order 1 is just a straight line, a polynomial of order 2 is a quadratic, that of order 3 is a cubic, etc. Aronow and Miller (2019) show (Theorem 4.3.3) that even nonlinear CEFs can be approximated up to an arbitrary level of precision by increasing the order of the polynomial regression used to estimate it, given enough data. The figure provides some intuition for why. As the order of the polynomial increases, the line becomes more flexible and can accommodate unexpected twists and turns in the CEF.

Increasing the order of the polynomial decreases bias, but this decrease comes at the cost of variance. Figure 11.5 shows how, when the order increases, bias goes down while variance goes up. Mean-squared error is one way to trade these two diagnosands off one another. Here, MSE gains from increasing flexibility disappear after a polynomial order of 3. If we were to care much more about bias than variance, perhaps we would choose a polynomial of even higher order.

Diagnosis 11.4 Conditional expectation function diagnosis

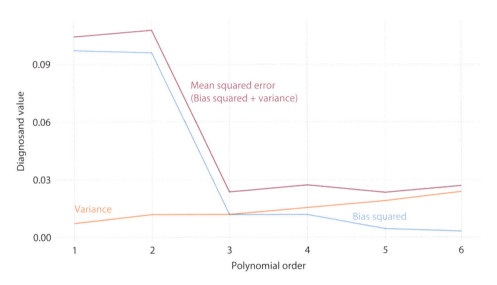

Figure 11.5: The bias-variance trade-off when choosing the flexibility of polynomial approximations to the CEF.

11.2.2 Redesigning over estimators: Logit, probit, or OLS?

A perennial debate among social scientists is whether to use a binary choice model like logit or probit when the outcome is binary, or if the workhorse OLS estimator is preferable. Unsurprisingly, who is right in this debate depends on other features of the research design. For example, in an observational descriptive study in which the inquiry is a prediction for the probability of success among a particular group of units, explicitly accounting for the binary nature the outcome variable is important; OLS can generate predictions that lie outside the theoretically permissible 0 to 1 range when the treatment is not binary. However, in a two-arm trial in which the inquiry is the average treatment effect, it is not possible for a comparison of treatment and control group means (as estimated by OLS) to generate a nonsense treatment effect estimate in the sense of being outside the theoretically permissible -100 to $+100$ percentage point range.

Declaration 11.5 Choosing logit, probit, or OLS.

```
library(margins)

tidy_margins <- function(x) {
  tidy(margins(x, data = x$data), conf.int = TRUE)
}

declaration_11.5 <-
  declare_model(
    N = 100,
    U = rnorm(N),
    potential_outcomes(Y ~ rbinom(N, 1, prob = 0.2 * Z + 0.6))) +
  declare_inquiry(ATE = mean(Y_Z_1 - Y_Z_0)) +
  declare_assignment(Z = complete_ra(N, prob = 0.5)) +
  declare_measurement(Y = reveal_outcomes(Y ~ Z)) +
  declare_estimator(Y ~ Z,
                    inquiry = "ATE",
                    term = "Z",
                    label = "OLS") +
  declare_estimator(
    Y ~ Z,
    .method = glm,
    family = binomial("logit"),
    .summary = tidy_margins,
    inquiry = "ATE",
    term = "Z",
    label = "logit"
  ) +
  declare_estimator(
    Y ~ Z,
    .method = glm,
    family = binomial("probit"),
    .summary = tidy_margins,
    inquiry = "ATE",
    term = "Z",
    label = "probit"
  )
```

Diagnosis 11.5 Redesigning alternative estimators over sample sizes

```
diagnosis_11.5 <-
  declaration_11.5 |>
  diagnose_designs()
```

Figure 11.6 displays the distribution of average treatment effect estimates from this design, over three answer strategies (OLS, logit, and probit). All three sampling distributions, including the distribution for OLS, are centered on the estimand, despite the binary nature of the outcome variable.

11.3 Summary

We use the redesign process to learn about design trade-offs. Most often, the trade-off is some measure of design quality like power against cost. We want to trade quality off against cost until we find a good enough study for the budget. Sometimes

11.3 Summary

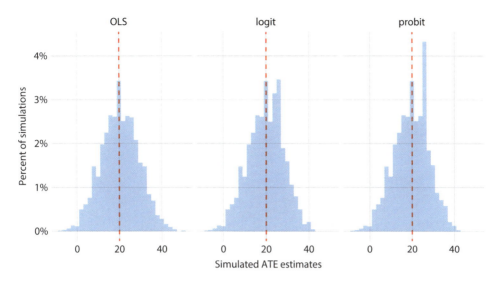

Figure 11.6: Sampling distribution of three estimators.

the trade-off is across design parameters—holding budget fixed, should we sample more clusters or should we sample more people within clusters? Sometimes the trade-off is across diagnosands—more flexible answer strategies may exhibit lower bias, but higher variance. Minimizing RMSE weighs bias and variance equally, but other weightings are possible. Tradeoffs across diagnosands are implicit in many design decisions, but design diagnosis and redesign can help make those trade-offs explicit.

CHAPTER 12

Design Example

We illustrate the declare-diagnose-redesign framework with a study of political motivations among office-seekers in Pakistan. Gulzar and Khan (2021) conducted an experiment that estimated the effects of two alternative incentives for becoming a politician: helping the community or generating personal benefits. The researchers randomly assigned eligible citizens to receive different encouragements to stand for office and measured the rates of running for office, the types of people who chose to run, and the congruence of elected politicians' policy positions with those of the general population.

By contrast with the stylized designs we've described to this point in the book, this design is moderately complex. We have multiple inquiries and a layered data strategy that has important implications for the answer strategy. The reason we selected it is that we want to show how one would actually apply the declare-diagnose-redesign framework in a complex, real-world setting.

12.1 Declaration in Words

The model describes the units under study: citizens who are eligible to run for office in villages in the study region. The model also includes citizens' individual characteristics and their potential outcomes depending on which encouragement they receive. The model set includes four theories of political motivation: politicians respond only to encouragements that focus on themselves, only to encouragements that focus on others, to neither, or to both. Among theories that include room for both motivations, some claim that personal motivations are more powerful than community-minded motivations, while others claim the reverse. The potential outcomes are defined in terms of subjects' underlying ("latent") probability of running for office, which is tightly related to the binary choice to run or not to run.

The two inquiries for this study are the average treatment effects of each encouragement, defined as the average difference in potential outcomes between receiving and not receiving each encouragement to run. The authors consider a third inquiry—the difference between these two average treatment effects—but we'll leave that complication to the side for the moment. It's worth highlighting what the inquiry is not. The inquiry is not "why" actual politicians run for office or what the features of the job are that attract candidates. The answers to the average treatment effect inquiries may shed light on those questions, but that inquiry is not directly targeted.

The data strategy for this study includes sampling, treatment assignment, and measurement. The sampling step takes place in two stages. First, the researchers sample 192 villages and then they sample 48 citizens who are eligible to stand for election from each village. In the assignment step, the authors allocate participants to a personal benefits encouragement, a prosocial encouragement, or no encouragement (control). All eligible citizen in a village are assigned to the same treatment condition, which is to say that this experiment uses cluster random assignment. Lastly, in the measurement step, the authors record the decision to run for office by checking whether a participant's name appears on the official candidate lists released by the Election Commission of Pakistan. In contrast to the latent probability outcome in the model, the outcome variable as measured by the data strategy is binary.

The answer strategy is an ordinary least squares regression of outcome variable on the treatment variable, with standard errors clustered at the village level. The clustering of the errors reflects the clustered assignment of treatments. This mirroring is an example of how choices in the answer strategy should reflect choices in the data strategy.

12.2 Declaration in Code

With `declare_model`, we describe a hierarchical structure with 660 villages, each of which is home to many citizens who are eligible to run for elected office. Each citizen harbors three potential outcomes. `Y_Z_neutral` is the citizen's latent probability of standing for election if treated with a neutral appeal, `Y_Z_personal` is the probability if treated with an appeal that emphasizes the personal return to office, and `Y_Z_social` is the probability if treated with an appeal that underlines the benefits to the community. Our simplified model assumes a constant treatment effect of about 3 percentage points for the personal appeal and 4 percentage points for the social appeal.[1]

---

[1] Readers may wonder where 3 and 4 percentage points are declared in the code. We use the `pnorm` function to define a latent variable representing the potential to run for office. The measured binary outcome `Y_observed` springs from this latent outcome `Y_latent`. The effect sizes of 0.10 and 0.15 in the latent outcome translate in this setting to 3 and 4 percentage point effects on a binary scale. See Section 13.1.2 for further discussion.

```
model_12.1 <-
  declare_model(
    villages = add_level(N = 660, U_village = rnorm(N, sd = 0.1)),
    citizens = add_level(
      N = 100,
      U_citizen = rnorm(N),
      potential_outcomes(
        Y ~ pnorm(
          U_citizen + U_village +
            0.10 * (Z == "personal") +
            0.15 * (Z == "social")),
        conditions = list(Z = c("neutral", "personal", "social"))
      )
    )
  )
```

We have two inquiries, representing the average treatment effects in the population for the personal and social appeals compared to the neutral appeal, defined as the average differences in potential outcomes:

```
inquiry_12.1 <-
  declare_inquiry(
    ATE_personal = mean(Y_Z_personal - Y_Z_neutral),
    ATE_social = mean(Y_Z_social - Y_Z_neutral)
  )
```

The data strategy consists of four steps: sampling of villages, sampling of citizens, treatment assignment, and outcome measurement. In sampling, we sample 192 villages and 48 of the eligible citizens from each village. In assignment, we cluster assign 25% of the villages to the neutral condition, 37.5% to the personal appeal, and 37.5% to the social appeal. The measurement step maps the "revealed," but still latent, probability of running to the observed binary choice to run or not.

```
n_villages <- 192
citizens_per_village <- 48

data_strategy_12.1 <-
  declare_sampling(
    S_village = cluster_rs(clusters = villages, n = n_villages),
    filter = S_village == 1) +
  declare_sampling(
    S_citizen = strata_rs(strata = villages, n = citizens_per_village),
    filter = S_citizen == 1) +
  declare_assignment(
    Z = cluster_ra(
      clusters = villages,
      conditions = c("neutral", "personal", "social"),
      prob_each = c(0.250, 0.375, 0.375))) +
  declare_measurement(
    Y_latent = reveal_outcomes(Y ~ Z),
    Y_observed = rbinom(N, 1, prob = Y_latent)
  )
```

The answer strategy consists of an ordinary least squares regression (as implemented by `lm_robust`) of the outcome on the treatments. The standard errors are clustered at the village level in order to account for the clustering in the assignment procedure. The regression will return three coefficients: an intercept and two treatment effect estimates. We ensure that the estimators are mapped to the relevant inquiries by explicitly linking them.

```
answer_strategy_12.1 <-
  declare_estimator(Y_observed ~ Z, term = c("Zpersonal", "Zsocial"),
                    clusters = villages,
                    .method = lm_robust,
                    se_type = "stata",
                    inquiry = c("ATE_personal", "ATE_social"))
```

When we concatenate all four elements with the + operator, we get a design:

Declaration 12.1 Gulzar and Khan (2021) design.

```
declaration_12.1 <-
  model_12.1 +
  inquiry_12.1 +
  data_strategy_12.1 +
  answer_strategy_12.1
```

12.3 Diagnosis

To diagnose the design, we first define a set of diagnosands: bias, statistical power, the root-mean-squared error, and total cost. The total cost calculation is in an arbitrary unit and reflects an assumption that sampling an additional village incurs a cost that is ten times larger than the cost of sampling an additional subject within a village.

```
diagnosands <-
  declare_diagnosands(
    bias = mean(estimate - estimand),
    rmse = sqrt(mean((estimate - estimand) ^ 2)),
    power = mean(p.value <= 0.05),
    cost = mean(10 * n_villages + 1 * n_villages * citizens_per_village)
  )
```

We then diagnose the design by simulating the design over and over, then calculating the diagnosands based on simulations data.

Diagnosis 12.1 Diagnosis of Gulzar and Khan (2022)

```
diagnosis_12.1 <-
  diagnose_design(declaration_12.1, diagnosands = diagnosands)
```

152   Chapter 12: Design Example

Table 12.1: Diagnosis of the simplified Gulzar and Khan design.

inquiry	term	bias	rmse	power
ATE_personal	Zpersonal	0	0.014	0.482
ATE_social	Zsocial	0	0.014	0.839

The diagnosis reveals that the design is unbiased for both inquiries. The power of the design for the social treatment is above the standard 80% threshold but it is not for the personal treatment (given the reference model we specified). The table gives us a sense of what effect sizes the design is powered for, since the only difference in the design between these two inquiries is the assumed effect size in the model.

12.4   Redesign

Two of the most important design decisions in this study are the number of sampled villages and the number of sampled citizens per village. Due to the assumed large fixed costs of traveling to each village, an additional sampled village is more expensive than an additional sampled citizen. In order to best allocate constrained study resources, we need to understand the gains from changes to the data strategy along each margin. Here, we redesign the study across possible combinations of numbers of villages and citizens per village.

Diagnosis 12.2 Diagnosis of redesigned Gulzar and Khan (2022)

```
diagnosis_12.2 <-
  declaration_12.1 |>
  redesign(n_villages = c(192, 500),
           citizens_per_village = c(25, 50, 75, 100)) |>
  diagnose_designs(diagnosands = diagnosands)
```

In Figure 12.1, we illustrate the results of our redesign exercise across all four diagnosands. The number of citizens per village is plotted on the horizontal axis and the value of the diagnosand is shown on the vertical axis. The plot is faceted by diagnosand and each line represents a different possible number of villages. We focus here on the social treatment only.

What we see is that bias is invariant to these choices. The study is unbiased regardless of the number of villages and the number of citizens interviewed per village. However, our other three diagnosands do change. Power is increasing in the number of citizens per village, and is always higher with more villages. We might reject designs with 192 villages with only 25 citizens per village, because they fall below the 80%

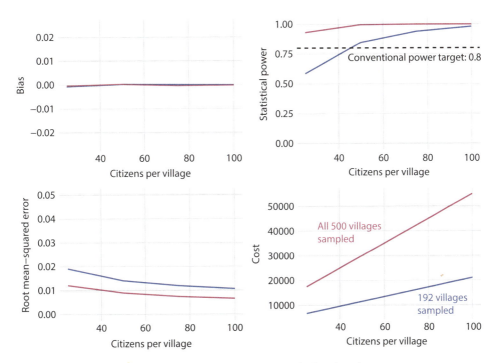

Figure 12.1: Redesign of Gulzar and Khan (2020).

power threshold (in fact, the number chosen by the researchers, 48, is just over the threshold, suggesting that under this model their choice would be the most cost-effective design that meets a conventional power target). Root-mean-squared error, a measure capturing both bias and efficiency of the design, is improving (decreasing) in the number of citizens per village and the number of villages. Cost is, of course, increasing in both sample size parameters. We can use the cost parameters to make decisions about what sample sizes to choose accounting for both scientific diagnosands of the design (i.e., power) and cost at the same time.

CHAPTER **13**

Designing in Code

The software package `DeclareDesign` provides tools for declaration, diagnosis, and redesign in code using the R statistical package. We introduce each step of the process sequentially in this chapter. The first goal is to get you started using the software for many common types of designs and to illustrate how the software works for a few less common ones. The second aim is to deepen understanding of the four elements of research design and our algorithm for selecting one. By working through each part in code, you get a second shot at grappling with how to build and assess research designs.

13.1 Model

In this section, we describe how to declare models in practice in the `DeclareDesign` code language. We start with declarations of units and the hierarchical structures that contain them, then move on to declarations of the characteristics of units. An important feature of models is the set of potential outcomes associated with each unit, so we spend some time describing a few approaches for thinking about them. This section is meant as a reference guide, so it covers common settings and a few uncommon ones as well.

13.1.1 Units

The model is first defined by the units under study. If there are 1,000 people who live in a city that you wish to learn about, but you don't know anything else about them, you can declare:

```
M <- declare_model(N = 1000)
```

Units often sit within multiple, sometimes overlapping geographic and social hierarchies. Households live on blocks that make up neighborhoods. Workers have jobs at firms and also often are represented by unions that sometimes represent workers in multiple firms (a non-nested hierarchy). These hierarchies are important to declare in the model as they often form the basis for why units are similar or different. Within `declare_model`, we define hierarchy using `add_level`, which adds a new level of hierarchy. This model declaration creates 100 households of varying sizes, then creates the appropriate number of individuals within households.

```
M <-
  declare_model(
    households = add_level(
      N = 100,
      N_members = sample(c(1, 2, 3, 4), N,
                         prob = c(0.2, 0.3, 0.25, 0.25), replace = TRUE)
    ),
    individuals = add_level(
      N = N_members,
      age = sample(18:90, N, replace = TRUE)
    )
  )
```

Panel data have a different structure. For example, in a country-year panel dataset, we observe every country in every year. To create data with this structure, we first declare a country-level dataset, then a years-level dataset, then we join them. The join is accomplished in the `cross_levels` call, which defines the variables we join by with `by = join_using(countries, years)`. In `cross_levels`, we also create the observation-level outcome variable, which is a function in this case of a country shock, a year shock, an observation shock, and a time trend.

```
M <-
  declare_model(
    countries = add_level(
      N = 196,
      country_shock = rnorm(N)
    ),
    years = add_level(
      N = 100,
      time_trend = 1:N,
      year_shock = runif(N, 1, 10),
      nest = FALSE
    ),
    observation = cross_levels(
      by = join_using(countries, years),
      observation_shock = rnorm(N),
      Y = 0.01 * time_trend + country_shock + year_shock + observation_shock
    )
  )
```

13.1.2 Unit characteristics

We can describe the characteristics of units by either supplying existing data or generating simulated data.

Here is an example of the simulation approach. We imagine 100 units with a characteristic X that is uniformly distributed between 0 and 100.

156   Chapter 13: Designing in Code

```
M <-
  declare_model(
    N = 100,
    X = runif(N, min = 0, max = 100)
  )
```

You can use any of the enormous number of data simulation functions available in R for this purpose. Here we gather six functions we tend to use in our own declarations, but they are by no means exhaustive. Each function has arguments that govern exactly how the data are created; we chose arbitrary values here to show how they work. Figure 13.1 shows what these six look like for a 1,000 unit model.

```
M <-
  declare_model(
    N = 1000,
    X1 = rnorm(N, mean = 5, sd = 2),
    X2 = runif(N, min = 0, max = 5),
    X3 = rbinom(N, size = 1, prob = 0.5),
    X4 = rbinom(N, size = 5, prob = 0.5),
    X5 = rlnorm(N, meanlog = 0, sdlog = 1),
    X6 = sample(c(1, 2, 3, 4, 5), N, replace = TRUE)
  )
```

Binary variables are very important in the social sciences, but they can be particularly tricky to make, so we'll spend a little more time on them. In a common way of thinking, binary variables are translations from latent, continuous variables into observed binary outcomes.

We can draw binary outcomes in one of three ways. First, we can simulate binary outcomes using the `rbinom` function, as we have already seen. The function `rbinom(N, size = 1, prob = 0.5)` flips 1 coin for each of N subjects with a constant latent probability of success across units.

```
M1 <-
  declare_model(
    N = 1000,
    Y = rbinom(N, 1, prob = 0.5)
  )
```

If you believe the latent probability varies across units, you might want to set up a latent variable first before the call to `rbinom`. A major reason to do it this way is to build in correlation between the binary outcome Y and some other variable, like X in this model declaration.

```
M2 <-
  declare_model(
    N = 1000,
```

13.1 Model

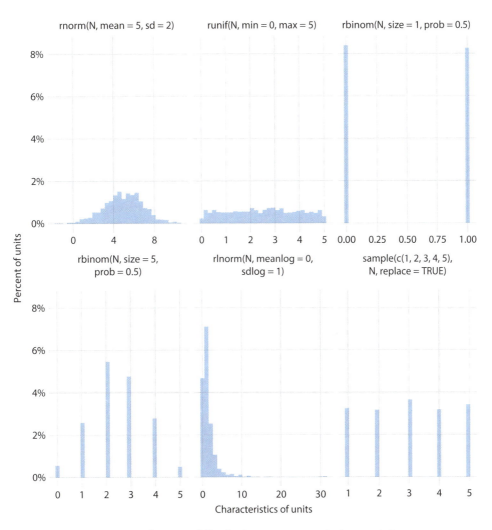

Figure 13.1: Six types of distributions to capture unit characteristics.

```
    latent = runif(N, min = 0, max = 1),
    Y = rbinom(N, 1, prob = latent),
    X = latent + rnorm(N)
)
```

A third way to create binary variable skips the call to rbinom altogether and creates a binary variable by assessing whether the latent variable exceeds some threshold, here 0.75. A major reason to do this is when we want to control the sources of randomness. The latent variable is random because of the call to the runif function. If we pass the resulting latent probabilities to rbinom as in M2, then we add a *second* layer of randomness, the coin flips. If one layer is enough, then M3 might be a more appropriate model declaration.

Chapter 13: Designing in Code

```r
M3 <-
  declare_model(
    N = 1000,
    latent = runif(N, min = 0, max = 1),
    Y = if_else(latent > 0.75, 1, 0)
  )
```

13.1.2.1 Building in correlations between simulated variables

Most social science variables are interrelated. The correlations between variables may affect the quality of a research design in many ways. If we control for a variable in a regression to improve power, how much power we gain depends on the correlation between that variable and the outcome.

Here we walk through two main ways to create correlated variables. The first way is simply to make one variable a function of another:

```r
M1 <-
  declare_model(
    N = 1000,
    X1 = rnorm(N),
    X2 = X1 + rnorm(N)
  )
```

The second way uses an explicit draw from a *multivariate* distribution. The mvrnorm function in the MASS package generates draws from the multivariate normal distribution. We have to give it a two dimensional mean (mu) and a variance-covariance matrix (Sigma). The draw_multivariate function is a wrapper that makes these functions (which return more than one column of data!) play nicely with declare_model.

```r
M2 <-
  declare_model(
    draw_multivariate(c(X1, X2) ~ MASS::mvrnorm(
      N = 1000,
      mu = c(0, 0),
      Sigma = matrix(c(1, 0.3, 0.3, 1), nrow = 2)
    )))
```

13.1.2.2 Building in correlations within clusters

A second important form of correlation is correlation within clusters, described by the intra-cluster correlation coefficient (ICC). When ICC is low, units are not much more similar to other units in their cluster than they are to units in other clusters. When it is high, clusters are more homogeneous within themselves and more heterogeneous across themselves. For more on clustered designs for surveys and for experiments, see Section 15.2 and Section 18.3.

We can introduce ICC using the `draw_normal_icc` function:

```
M <-
  declare_model(households = add_level(N = 1000),
                individuals = add_level(
                  N = 4,
                  X = draw_normal_icc(
                    mean = 0,
                    clusters = households,
                    ICC = 0.65
                  )
                ))
```

13.1.2.3 Drawing on baseline data

In some cases, you will be in possession of baseline data about the units you plan to study. In the model, you can replace simulations with these data, as long as your goal is to make inferences just about those units you have data for. If you have a census of the dwelling characteristics of all houses in Philadelphia and you plan to conduct a survey of homeowner attitudes toward a new tax based on a sample stratified by dwelling type, you don't need to simulate data for the dwelling characteristics. They are known. You will still need to simulate the data on attitudes, which you have not yet collected.

```
M <-
  declare_model(
    data = baseline_data,
    attitudes = sample(1:5, N, replace = TRUE)
  )
```

13.1.2.4 Drawing on data about similar units

More commonly, you may have data on similar units from past studies or from a pilot study of your own. In these cases, you will not want to take their data as fixed, but resample from the data to simulate the population you are now drawing from. For example, if your baseline data is a random sample of households in Philadelphia, you may want to resample from that data to construct a simulated population of Philadelphia from which you can sample.

```
M <-
  declare_model(
    data = baseline_data,
    N = 619505,
    handler = resample_data
  )
```

Drawing on past data holds several advantages. The natural correlations with clusters and across background characteristics are already built into your data. Using past data makes declaring your model easier, and in some cases can provide more realistic simulation of the data you end up collecting.

13.1.2.5 Unknown heterogeneity

Most declarations include unobserved variables, or unknown heterogeneity. These represent the lurking variables that confound our inferences and the variation in outcomes not correlated with observed values. In virtually every declaration in the book, we include a U term to represent these unobserved values.

At the point of declaration we face problems immediately: how much heterogeneity do we introduce, where, and of what kind?

M1 shows how to make rather benign unknown heterogeneity. U is normally distributed and only affects Y. The observed binary variable X is independent of U and affects Y in its own way.

```
M1 <-
  declare_model(
    N = 100,
    U = rnorm(N),
    X = rbinom(N, size = 1, prob = 0.5),
    Y = 0.1 * X + U
  )
```

M2 is more worrisome. U now affects X as well, by affecting the probability of X equaling 1. See Section 16.2 for designs that face this sort of problem.

```
M2 <-
  declare_model(
    N = 100,
    U = rnorm(N),
    X = rbinom(N, size = 1, prob = pnorm(U)),
    Y = 0.1 * X + U
  )
```

A further question for U is how much it should vary. This question is tougher to answer. U is an important source of variation in outcomes, so it needs to be calibrated in a way that the simulated data look like the data you expect to generate or encounter in the world. So our best advice here is to follow Principle 3.2: *Design agnostically* to figure out the conditions under which your design works well.

13.1.3 Potential outcomes

We declare "potential" outcomes when describing counterfactual quantities.

Table 13.1: One draw of two potential outcomes.

ID	Y_Z_0	Y_Z_1
001	0	0
002	0	1
003	0	0
004	0	1
005	0	0

The most straightforward way to declare potential outcomes is to make one variable per potential outcome. Here the two potential outcomes come from coin flip distributions with different success probabilities.

```
M <-
  declare_model(
    N = 100,
    Y_Z_0 = rbinom(N, size = 1, prob = 0.5),
    Y_Z_1 = rbinom(N, size = 1, prob = 0.6)
  )
```

The `potential_outcomes` function can do the same thing, but using R's "formula" syntax, allowing us to write down potential outcomes in a "regression-like" way.

```
M <-
  declare_model(
    N = 100,
    potential_outcomes(Y ~ rbinom(N, size = 1, prob = 0.1 * Z + 0.5))
  )

M()
```

By default, `potential_outcomes` imagines you are making two potential outcomes with respect to a treatment variable Z that can take on two values, 0 and 1.

But we can use `potential_outcomes` to describe multiple treatment conditions:

```
M <-
  declare_model(
    N = 100,
    potential_outcomes(
      Y ~ rbinom(N, 1, prob = 0.1 * (Z == 1) + 0.2 * (Z == 2)),
      conditions = list(Z = c(0, 1, 2))
    )
  )
M()
```

Table 13.2: One draw of three potential outcomes.

ID	Y_Z_0	Y_Z_1	Y_Z_2
001	0	0	1
002	0	0	0
003	0	0	0
004	0	0	0
005	0	1	0

Or to describe multiple treatment factors (see Section 18.5 on factorial experiments):

```r
M <-
  declare_model(
    N = 100,
    potential_outcomes(
      Y ~ rbinom(N, 1, prob = 0.1 * Z1 + 0.2 * Z2 + 0.1 * Z1 * Z2),
      conditions = list(Z1 = c(0, 1), Z2 = c(0, 1))
    )
  )
M()
```

Table 13.3: One draw of four potential outcomes.

ID	Y_Z1_0_Z2_0	Y_Z1_1_Z2_0	Y_Z1_0_Z2_1	Y_Z1_1_Z2_1
001	0	0	1	1
002	0	0	0	1
003	0	0	0	1
004	0	0	0	0
005	0	0	0	0

13.1.3.1 Effect sizes

We often want to consider a range of plausible effect sizes, for example when estimating the minimum detectable effect of a design. A strategy we commonly use is to sample the treatment effect in the model declaration itself, and then draw the potential outcomes using that single number. When we diagnose many times, then we will get many different treatment effects (here, `tau`), which we can then summarize in a diagnosis. Section 13.6.1 describes how to create a plot of the power across values of `tau`.

```
M <-
  declare_model(
    N = 100,
    tau = runif(1, min = 0, max = 1),
    U = rnorm(N),
    potential_outcomes(Y ~ tau * Z + U)
  )
```

Where do our expectations about effect sizes, and the minimal plausible effect size, come from? We may conduct meta-analyses of past studies when there are sufficiently many with at least one relevant estimate of the same effect, or a systematic review or literature review when they are less comparable, but we want to find a range (see Section 19.3 for a discussion of meta-analyses). We may be tempted to conduct a pilot study to estimate the effect size. We need to be careful when doing so about what to infer and how much to update from small pilot studies, as we discuss in Section 21.4, but we can often shrink our uncertainty over models. In the absence of pilot studies or past studies to draw on, we need to make educated guesses and understand under what true effect sizes our design will perform well and when it will not follow Principle 3.1: *Design holistically*.

13.1.3.2 Effect heterogeneity

Sometimes, the inquiry centers on treatment effect heterogeneity by subgroups. This heterogeneity has to be present in the model in order for the simulation to pick it up. Here we declare effect heterogeneity according to a binary covariate X. This example really shows off the utility of the formula syntax in the `potential_outcomes` function. We can write in our expectations about heterogeneity as if they were regression coefficients. Here, the "interaction term" is equal to `0.1`.

```
M <-
  declare_model(
    N = 100,
    U = rnorm(N),
    X = rbinom(N, 1, prob = 0.5),
    potential_outcomes(Y ~ 0.3 * Z + 0.2 * X + 0.1 * Z * X + U)
  )
```

13.1.3.3 Correlation between potential outcomes

Treated and untreated potential outcomes are typically highly correlated. When treatment effects are exactly homogeneous, the correlation is equal to 1. Rarely are potential outcomes *negatively* correlated, but it can occur. The sign and magnitude of the correlation especially affects the standard errors of estimates for causal effects (for more discussion of the correlation of potential outcomes in experiments and also standard error estimators, see Section 10.3.1).

We described some complexities of generating binary variables above. They transfer over to the generation of correlated potential outcomes in special ways. In the declarations below, `M1` generates uncorrelated potential outcomes, because the draws from `rbinom` are independent of one another. In `M2`, we still use `rbinom`, but with a transformation of the normally distributed variable into a probability via `pnorm`. This allows the potential outcomes to be correlated because they are both influenced by the same latent variable. Finally, in `M3`, we generate highly correlated potential outcomes because we peel off the layer of randomness introduced by `rbinom`.

```
M1 <-
  declare_model(
    N = 100,
    potential_outcomes(Y ~ rbinom(N, 1, prob = 0.2))
  )

M2 <-
  declare_model(
    N = 100,
    latent = rnorm(N),
    potential_outcomes(Y ~ rbinom(N, 1, prob = pnorm(latent + 0.2 * Z)))
  )

M3 <-
  declare_model(
    N = 100,
    latent = rnorm(N),
    potential_outcomes(Y ~ if_else(latent + 0.2 * Z > 0.5, 1, 0))
  )
```

13.2   Inquiry

An inquiry is a summary function of events generated by a model. When we declare inquiries in code, we declare this summary function. Here, we declare a causal inquiry, the `mean` of the differences in two potential outcomes described in the model:

```
M <- declare_model(N = 100, U = rnorm(N), potential_outcomes(Y ~ Z + U))
I <- declare_inquiry(ATE = mean(Y_Z_1 - Y_Z_0))
```

Descriptive inquiries can be declared in a similar way: they are just functions of outcomes rather than comparisons of potential outcomes.

```
M <- declare_model(N = 100, Y = rnorm(N))
I <- declare_inquiry(mean_Y = mean(Y))
```

13.2.1 Inquiries among subsets of units

We often want to learn about an inquiry defined among a subgroup of units. For example, if we are interested in the conditional average treatment effect (CATE) among units with X = 1, we can use the subset argument.

```
M <-
  declare_model(
    N = 100,
    U = rnorm(N),
    X = rbinom(N, 1, prob = 0.5),
    potential_outcomes(Y ~ 0.3 * Z + 0.2 * X + 0.1 * Z * X + U)
  )
I <-
  declare_inquiry(CATE = mean(Y_Z_1 - Y_Z_0),
                  subset = X == 1)
```

Equivalently, we could use R's [] syntax for subsetting:

```
I <- declare_inquiry(CATE = mean(Y_Z_1[X == 1] - Y_Z_0[X == 1]))
```

13.2.2 Inquiries with continuous potential outcomes

"Non-decomposable" inquiries are not as simple as an average over the units in the model. A common example arises with continuous potential outcomes. The regression discontinuity design described in Section 16.5 has an inquiry that is defined by two continuous functions of the running variable. The control function is a polynomial function representing the potential outcome under control and the treatment function is a different polynomial representing treated potential outcomes. The inquiry is the difference in the two functions evaluated at the cutoff point on the running variable. We declare it as follows:

```
cutoff <- 0.5
control <- function(X) {
  as.vector(poly(X, 4, raw = TRUE) %*% c(0.7, -0.8, 0.5, 1.0))}
treatment <- function(X) {
  as.vector(poly(X, 4, raw = TRUE) %*% c(0.0, -1.5, 0.5, 0.8)) + 0.15}

I <- declare_inquiry(LATE = treatment(cutoff) - control(cutoff))
```

13.2.3 Multiple inquiries

In some designs, we are interested in the value of an inquiry for many units or for many types of units.

We can enumerate them one by one, to describe the average treatment effect, two conditional average treatment effects, and the difference between them.

```
I <- declare_inquiry(
    ATE = mean(Y_Z_1[X == 1] - Y_Z_0[X == 1]),
    CATE_X0 = mean(Y_Z_1[X == 0] - Y_Z_0[X == 0]),
    CATE_X1 = mean(Y_Z_1[X == 1] - Y_Z_0[X == 1]),
    Difference_in_CATEs = CATE_X1 - CATE_X0
)
```

In the multilevel regression and poststratification (MRP) design in Section 15.3, we want to know what the average opinion is in each state.

We declare an inquiry at the county level below. We rely on `group_by` and `summarize` from `dplyr` to write a function `MRP_inquiry` that uses a pipeline to group the data into counties and take the average of individual values. Now, our design targets an inquiry for each state.

```
M <-
  declare_model(
    counties = add_level(N = 5, county_mean = rnorm(N)),
    individuals = add_level(N = 50, Y = rnorm(N, mean = county_mean))
  )

MRP_inquiry <-
  function(data) {
    data |>
      group_by(counties) |>
      summarize(mean_Y = mean(Y)) |>
      ungroup()
  }

I <- declare_inquiry(handler = MRP_inquiry)
```

We discuss further in Section 13.4 how to link inquiries to answer strategies, including the case of multiple inquiries.

13.3 Data Strategy

The three data strategy functions, `declare_sampling`, `declare_assignment`, and `declare_measurement`, share most features in common. All three add variables to the running data frame. `declare_sampling` is special in that it has a filter argument that determines which (if any) of the units should be dropped from the data and which should be retained as the sample. `declare_assignment` and `declare_measurement` work in the exact same way as one another. The reason we separate them is to insist on the features of the data strategy, not for a deep programming reason.

13.3.1 Sampling

Declaring a sampling procedure involves constructing a variable indicating whether a unit is sampled or not and then filtering to sampled units. By default, you should create a variable S and `declare_sampling` will filter to sampled units by selecting those for which S == 1. You can rename your sampling variable or you can create more sampling variables to develop multistage sampling procedures, though you will need to alter the `filter` argument to reflect your changed procedure.

```
D <- declare_sampling(S = complete_rs(N = 100, n = 10))
```

For a multistage sample of districts, then villages, then households, we start out with all the data and sample at each stage then combine the three sampling indicators to form the final indicator S.

```
D <-
  declare_sampling(
    # sample 20 districts
    S_districts = cluster_rs(clusters = districts, n = 20),
    # within each district, sample 50 villages
    S_villages  = strata_and_cluster_rs(
      strata = districts,
      clusters = villages,
      strata_n = 10
    ),
    # within each village select 25 households
    S_households  = strata_and_cluster_rs(
      strata = villages,
      clusters = households,
      strata_n = 25
    ),
    S = S_districts == 1 & S_villages == 1 & S_households == 1,
    filter = S == 1
  )
```

You could also perform each of these steps in separate calls, and the data will be filtered appropriately step-to-step.

```
D <-
  declare_sampling(S = cluster_rs(clusters = districts, n = 20)) +
  declare_sampling(S = strata_and_cluster_rs(
    strata = districts,
    clusters = villages,
    strata_n = 10
  )) +
  declare_sampling(S = strata_and_cluster_rs(
    strata = villages,
    clusters = households,
    strata_n = 25
  ))
```

For many sampling designs, the probabilities of inclusion are not constant across units. We often need to adjust the answer strategy by reweighting the data according to the inverse of the inclusion probabilities. For common sampling designs in `randomizr`, we provide a built-in function for calculating these. If you use your own sampling function, you will need to calculate them yourself. Here we show how to include probabilities from a stratified sampling design.

```r
M <-
  declare_model(N = 100,
                X = rbinom(N, 1, prob = 0.5))

D <-
  declare_sampling(
    S = strata_rs(strata = X, strata_prob = c(0.2, 0.5)),
    S_inclusion_probability = 
      strata_rs_probabilities(strata = X,
                              strata_prob = c(0.2, 0.5))
  )
```

13.3.2 Treatment assignment

The declaration of treatment assignment procedures works similarly to sampling, but we don't drop any units. Treatment assignment probabilities often come into play just like sampling inclusion probabilities. You can use `randomizr` to calculate them for many common designs in a similar fashion, except that for treatment assignment in order to know with what probability you were assigned to the condition you are in we have to know what condition you are in. To obtain condition assignment probabilities we can declare:

```r
D <-
  declare_assignment(
    Z = complete_ra(N, m = 50),
    Z_condition_probability = 
      obtain_condition_probabilities(assignment = Z, m = 50)
  )
```

13.3.3 Measurement

Measurement procedures can be declared with `declare_measurement`. A common use is to generate an observed measurement from a latent value:

```r
M <- declare_model(N = 100, latent = runif(N))
D <- declare_measurement(observed = rbinom(N, 1, prob = latent))
```

13.3.3.1 Revealing potential outcomes

A very common use of `declare_measurement` in this book is for the "revelation" of potential outcomes according to treatment assignments. We build potential outcomes in `declare_model`, randomly assign in `declare_assignment`, then reveal outcomes in `declare_measurement`. We use the `reveal_outcomes` function to pick out the right potential outcome to reveal for each unit.

```
M <-
  declare_model(
    N = 100,
    potential_outcomes(Y ~ rbinom(N, size = 1, prob = 0.1 * Z + 0.5))
  )

D <-
  declare_assignment(Z = complete_ra(N, m = 50)) +
  declare_measurement(Y = reveal_outcomes(Y ~ Z))
```

13.3.3.2 Index creation

Many designs use multiple measures of the same outcome, which are then combined into an index. For example, here's a design with three measures of Y that we will combine using factor analysis. Here we use the `fa` function from the `psych` package, which can be installed with `install.packages('psych')`.

```
library(psych)

D <-
  declare_measurement(
    index = fa(
      r = cbind(Y_1, Y_2, Y_3),
      nfactors = 1,
      rotate = "varimax"
    )$scores
  )
```

13.4 Answer Strategy

An answer strategy is a function that provides answers to an inquiry. Declaring one in code involves selecting that function and linking the answer or answers it returns to one or more inquiries.

The functions we declare in `DeclareDesign` for answer strategies differ from those for the other elements of research design to reflect the two-step nature of many answer strategies. Often, first a statistical model (e.g., a linear regression) is fit to data, and then summaries of that model fit (e.g., the coefficient on a variable X, its standard error, *t*-statistic, *p*-value, and confidence interval) are combined to form an answer and its associated measures of uncertainty.

13.4.1 Statistical method functions

In `DeclareDesign`, we call these two steps `.method` and `.summary` (these arguments are preceded by `.`'s to avoid argument conflicts). The `.method` argument in `declare_estimator` can take almost any modelling function in R (e.g., `lm` for linear regression) and `.summary` consists of a summary function that calculates statistics from the fit such as `tidy` or `glance`. You can write your own `.method` or `.summary` functions. When your answer strategy does not fit this two-step structure, you can (as with all `declare_` functions) write your own handler.

We break down each part of a standard answer strategy declaration using the example of a linear regression of the effect of a variable Z on an outcome Y in Declaration 13.1. The first argument in our `declare_estimator` step defines the method we will use, here `lm_robust`, which is our function in the `estimatr` package for running linear regressions with robust standard errors. The second is the main argument for `lm_robust`, the formula for the regression specification, in this case Y on Z with no controls.

Declaration 13.1 Linear regression design.

```
declaration_13.1 <-
  declare_model(N = 100,
                U = rnorm(N),
                potential_outcomes(Y ~ 0.2 * Z + U)) +
  declare_inquiry(ATE = mean(Y_Z_1 - Y_Z_0)) +
  declare_assignment(Z = complete_ra(N)) +
  declare_measurement(Y = reveal_outcomes(Y ~ Z)) +
  declare_estimator(
    Y ~ Z,
    .method = lm_robust,
    .summary = tidy,
    term = "Z",
    inquiry = "ATE",
    label = "OLS"
  )
```

```
draw_estimates(declaration_13.1)
```

Table 13.4: The estimate from one draw of the linear regression design.

term	estimator	estimate	std.error	statistic	p.value	conf.low	conf.high	df	outcome	inquiry
Z	OLS	0.03	0.2	0.16	0.87	−0.36	0.43	98	Y	ATE

13.4.2 Tidying statistical modelling function output

Let's unpack the `.summary` argument. In this case we send the `tidy` function from the `broom` package (the default). Understanding what `tidy` does opens a window into the way we match estimates and estimands. The tidy function takes many model fit objects and returns a data frame in which rows represent estimates and columns represent statistics about that estimate. The columns typically include the estimate itself (`estimate`), an estimated standard error (`std.error`), a test statistic of some kind reported by the model function such as a t-statistic or Z-statistic (`statistic`), a p-value based on the test statistic (`p.value`), a confidence interval (`conf.low`, `conf.high`), and the degrees of freedom of the test statistic if relevant (`df`).

A key column in the output of tidy is `term`, which represents which coefficient (term) is being described in that row. We will often need to use the term column in conjunction with the name of the estimator to link estimates to inquiries when there is more than one. If in the regression we pull out two coefficients (e.g., for treatment indicator 1 and for treatment indicator 2), we need to be able to link those to separate inquiries representing the true effect of treatment 1 and the true effect of treatment 2. Term is our tool for doing so. The default is for term to pick the first coefficient that is not the intercept, so for the regression Y ~ Z there will be an intercept and then the coefficient on Z, which is what will be picked.

The `inquiry` argument defines which inquiry or inquiries the estimates will be linked to. In this case, we link to a single inquiry, the ATE. You can also declare an estimator that shoots at multiple inquiries: `declare_estimator(Y ~ Z, .method = lm_robust, term = "Z", inquiry = c("ATE", "ATT"))`, useful for learning how well an estimator does for different targets. When we run the answer strategy on data, we get two additional pieces of information tacked on to the model summary data frame: the name of the estimator, which comes from the `label` argument, and the inquiry. The unit of analysis of a diagnosis is the inquiry-estimator pair, so if you link an estimator to multiple inquiries, then there will be a row for each inquiry.

We can use other summary functions to obtain other summaries of the fitted model. For example `glance` will provide model fit statistics such as the R-squared:

```
A <- declare_estimator(Y ~ Z,
                       .method = lm_robust,
                       .summary = glance)

declaration_13.1 |>
  draw_data() |>
  A()
```

When neither `tidy` nor `glance` works well for your answer strategy, you can write your own summary function. Below, we build up a tidy function for the `lm` model from scratch. (One is already built into the `broom` package, but we do so here to

Table 13.5: The model fit statistics from one draw of the linear regression design.

r.squared	adj.r.squared	statistic	p.value	df.residual	nobs	se_type
0	−0.01	0.16	0.69	98	100	HC2

illustrate how you can write your own for a function that does not already have one.) Before you start to write your own summary function, check whether one exists on the Broom website.

There are three steps for a tidy function:

1. Pull out statistics from the model fit object. You can extract out any statistics and transform them in any relevant way.

2. Return a data frame (or `tibble`).

3. Name your estimates in a common format that works across all tidy functions. The estimate column should be called "estimate," the standard error column "std.error," etc., as described earlier. However, if you want to add other statistics from the model fit that you will diagnose, you can, and you can name them whatever you want.

```
tidy_lm <- function(fit) {
  # calculate estimates by grabbing the coefficients from the model fit
  estimate <- coef(lm)

  # get the names of the coefficients (e.g., "(Intercept)", "Z")
  #    we will call these "term" to represent regression terms
  term <- names(estimates)

  # calculate the standard error by grabbing the variance-covariance
  #    matrix, then pulling the diagonal elements of it and taking the
  #    square root to transform from variances to standard errors
  std.error <- sqrt(diag(vcov(lm)))

  # return a tibble with term, estimate, and std.error
  tibble(term = term, estimate = unlist(estimate), std.error = std.error)
}

declare_estimator(
  Y ~ Z,
  .method = lm,
  .summary = tidy_lm
)
```

In other cases, you may want to build on functions that interoperate with the `broom` functions to do specialized summary tasks like calculating marginal effects or predicted effects. The `margins` function from the `margins` package calculates marginal effects and the `predictions` function from the `predictions` package constructs predictions. These two functions are especially useful and work well with the `tidy` workflow. To calculate marginal effects, run margins and then tidy as your model summary:

```
tidy_margins <- function(x) {
  tidy(margins(x, data = x$data), conf.int = TRUE)
}
declare_estimator(
  Y ~ Z + X,
  .method = glm,
  family = binomial("logit"),
  .summary = tidy_margins,
  term = "Z"
)
```

13.4.3 Custom answer strategies

If your answer strategy does not use a `.method` function, you'll need to provide a function that takes `data` as an input and returns a data frame with the estimate. Set the handler to be `label_estimator(your_function_name)` to take advantage of `DeclareDesign`'s mechanism for matching inquiries to estimators. When you use `label_estimator`, you can provide an inquiry, and `DeclareDesign` will keep track of which estimates match each inquiry. (It simply adds a column to your tidy estimates data frame for the name of the estimator and the inquiry.) For example, to calculate the mean of an outcome, you could write your own estimator in this way:

```
my_estimator <-
  function(data) {
    data.frame(estimate = mean(data$Y))
  }
declare_estimator(handler = label_estimator(my_estimator),
                  label = "mean",
                  inquiry = "Y_bar")
```

Often you may want to construct a test as part of your answer strategy that does not target an inquiry. Our `declare_test` function works just like `declare_estimator`, except you need not include an inquiry. The `label_test` infrastructure works just like `label_estimator` for custom test functions.

13.5 Declaration

To construct a research *design* object that we can operate on—diagnose, redesign, draw data from, etc.—we add research design elements together with the + operator. In Declaration 13.2, we first create each design step separately, then concatenate the steps. This style of declaration is useful when you want to mix and match design elements. Usually, though, we just add steps together without creating each step first.

Declaration 13.2 Declaration of two-arm randomized experiment.

```
model <-
  declare_model(N = 1000,
                U = rnorm(N),
                X = U + rnorm(N, sd = 0.5),
                potential_outcomes(Y ~ 0.2 * Z + U))
inquiry <-
  declare_inquiry(ATE = mean(Y_Z_1 - Y_Z_0))
sampling <-
  declare_sampling(S = simple_rs(N, prob = 0.2),
                   filter = S == 1)
assignment <-
  declare_assignment(Z = complete_ra(N))
measurement <-
  declare_measurement(Y = reveal_outcomes(Y ~ Z))
answer_strategy <-
  declare_estimator(Y ~ Z, inquiry = "ATE", label = "DIM") +
  declare_estimator(Y ~ Z + X, inquiry = "ATE", label = "OLS")

# as separate elements
declaration_13.2 <-
  model +
  inquiry +
  sampling +
  assignment +
  measurement +
  answer_strategy

# equivalently, and more compactly:
declaration_13.2 <-
  declare_model(N = 1000,
                U = rnorm(N),
                X = U + rnorm(N, sd = 0.5),
                potential_outcomes(Y ~ 0.2 * Z + U)) +
  declare_inquiry(ATE = mean(Y_Z_1 - Y_Z_0)) +
  declare_sampling(S = simple_rs(N, prob = 0.2),
                   filter = S == 1) +
  declare_assignment(Z = complete_ra(N)) +
  declare_measurement(Y = reveal_outcomes(Y ~ Z)) +
  declare_estimator(Y ~ Z, inquiry = "ATE", label = "DIM") +
  declare_estimator(Y ~ Z + X, inquiry = "ATE", label = "OLS")
```

Order matters in declaring designs. We can think of the order of the declaration as the temporal order in which the elements are realized. Below, since the inquiry comes before sampling and assignment, the inquiry is a *population* inquiry, the population average treatment effect.

```
model +
  declare_inquiry(PATE = mean(Y_Z_1 - Y_Z_0)) +
  sampling +
  assignment +
  measurement +
  answer_strategy
```

We could instead define our inquiry as a *sample* average treatment effect by putting the inquiry after sampling:

```
model +
  sampling +
  declare_inquiry(SATE = mean(Y_Z_1 - Y_Z_0)) +
  assignment +
  measurement +
  answer_strategy
```

13.6 Diagnosis

Once a design is declared in code, diagnosing it is usually the easy part. `diagnose_design` handles all the details and bookkeeping for you. In this section, we outline how to conduct a diagnosis using our default tools for standard diagnoses and also how you might operate directly on the simulations for more complicated analyses.

Diagnosis 13.1 Diagnosis of two-arm randomized experiment

Here we use `diagnose_design` to diagnose the design. By default, we conduct 500 simulations and characterize simulation error with 100 bootstraps of the diagnosands. `reshape_diagnosis` prepares the output for nice printing.

```
diagnosis_13.1 <-
  diagnose_design(declaration_13.2,
                  sims = 500,
                  bootstrap_sims = 100)
reshape_diagnosis(diagnosis_13.1)
```

We can "tidy" the results of the diagnosis for easier printing and plotting of the results. Here, each row is an estimate of a diagnosand and then uncertainty statistics such as the standard error and 95% confidence interval around the diagnosand estimate.

Table 13.6: Design diagnosis of two-arm randomized experiment.

Estimator	Mean Estimand	Mean Estimate	Bias	SD Estimate	RMSE	Power	Coverage
DIM	0.20	0.20	−0.00	0.14	0.14	0.29	0.96
	(0.00)	(0.00)	(0.00)	(0.00)	(0.00)	(0.01)	(0.00)
OLS	0.20	0.20	−0.00	0.06	0.06	0.87	0.95
	(0.00)	(0.00)	(0.00)	(0.00)	(0.00)	(0.01)	(0.00)

```r
tidy(diagnosis_13.1)
```

13.6.1 Working directly with the simulations data frame

In some cases, it is useful to operate directly on the simulations produced by `diagnose_design`. For example, we might want to calculate diagnosands manually or plot simulations.

```r
simulations_df <- get_simulations(diagnosis_13.1)
```

Once we have the simulations, we can summarize them using `dplyr` tools:

```r
simulations_df |>
  group_by(design, inquiry, estimator, term, outcome) |>
  summarize(
    bias = mean(estimate - estimand),
    rmse = sqrt(mean((estimate - estimand)^2)),
    power = mean(p.value <= 0.05),
    coverage = mean(estimand <= conf.high & estimand >= conf.low)
  )
```

Plotting simulations using `ggplot2` is often a great way to gain a deeper sense of the properties of the design.

The answer strategy for Declaration 13.1 includes two estimators, so our aim here is to create histograms of the sampling distribution for each of them. This goal is best accomplished using `geom_histogram`, then faceting by estimator using `facet_wrap`. We often want to overlay the true value of the estimand on these plots, which we do here with `geom_vline`. Notice that in order to do so, we have to create a `summary_df` that includes the value of the estimand. The resulting plot in Figure 13.2 shows that both the adjusted and unadjusted estimators are unbiased, but that the sampling distribution of the adjusted estimator is tighter.

```r
# first create summary for vertical lines
summary_df <-
  simulations_df |>
  group_by(estimator) |>
  summarize(estimand = mean(estimand))

# then plot simulations
ggplot(simulations_df) +
  geom_histogram(aes(estimate),
                 bins = 40, fill = "#72B4F3") +
```

Table 13.7: Tidied diagnosis of two-arm randomized experiment.

design	inquiry	estimator	outcome	term	diagnosand	estimate	std.error	conf.low	conf.high
declaration_13.2	ATE	DIM	Y	Z	mean_estimand	0.20	0.00	0.20	0.20
declaration_13.2	ATE	DIM	Y	Z	mean_estimate	0.20	0.00	0.19	0.20
declaration_13.2	ATE	DIM	Y	Z	bias	0.00	0.00	−0.01	0.00
declaration_13.2	ATE	DIM	Y	Z	sd_estimate	0.14	0.00	0.13	0.14
declaration_13.2	ATE	DIM	Y	Z	rmse	0.14	0.00	0.13	0.14
declaration_13.2	ATE	DIM	Y	Z	power	0.29	0.01	0.27	0.31
declaration_13.2	ATE	DIM	Y	Z	coverage	0.96	0.00	0.95	0.97
declaration_13.2	ATE	OLS	Y	Z	mean_estimand	0.20	0.00	0.20	0.20
declaration_13.2	ATE	OLS	Y	Z	mean_estimate	0.20	0.00	0.20	0.20
declaration_13.2	ATE	OLS	Y	Z	bias	0.00	0.00	0.00	0.00
declaration_13.2	ATE	OLS	Y	Z	sd_estimate	0.06	0.00	0.06	0.06
declaration_13.2	ATE	OLS	Y	Z	rmse	0.06	0.00	0.06	0.06
declaration_13.2	ATE	OLS	Y	Z	power	0.87	0.01	0.86	0.89
declaration_13.2	ATE	OLS	Y	Z	coverage	0.95	0.00	0.94	0.96

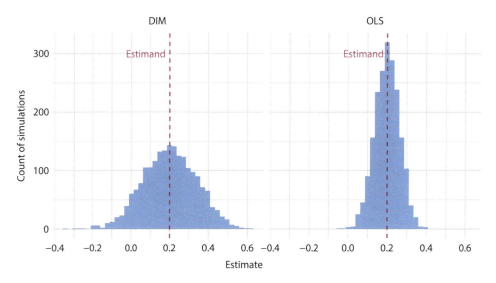

Figure 13.2: Example visualization of a diagnosis.

```
geom_vline(data = summary_df,
           aes(xintercept = estimand),
           lty = "dashed", color = "#C6227F") +
annotate("text", y = 300, x = 0, label = "Estimand",
         color = "#C6227F", hjust = 1) +
facet_wrap(~ estimator) +
labs(x = "Estimate", y = "Count of simulations") +
theme_minimal()
```

Diagnosing over model uncertainty is a crucial part of diagnosis. We want to understand when our design performs well and when it does not. A classical example of this in wide practice is the power curve. In a power curve (see Figure 13.3), we display the power of a design (the probability of achieving statistical significance) along different possible effect sizes. In this setting, plotting the simulations directly with an indicator for whether that simulation's estimate is statistically significant is the easiest way to learn about the properties of the design.

```
design <-
  declare_model(
    N = 200,
    U = rnorm(N),
    potential_outcomes(Y ~ runif(1, 0.0, 0.5) * Z + U)
  ) +
  declare_inquiry(ATE = mean(Y_Z_1 - Y_Z_0)) +
  declare_assignment(Z = complete_ra(N)) +
  declare_measurement(Y = reveal_outcomes(Y ~ Z)) +
  declare_estimator(Y ~ Z, inquiry = "ATE")

simulations_df <-
  diagnose_design(design) |>
```

```
  get_simulations() |>
  mutate(significant = if_else(p.value <= 0.05, 1, 0))

ggplot(simulations_df) +
  stat_smooth(aes(estimand, significant),
              method = 'loess', color = "#3564ED",
              fill = "#72B4F3", formula = 'y ~ x') +
  geom_hline(yintercept = 0.8, color = "#C6227F", linetype = "dashed") +
  annotate("text", x = 0, y = 0.85,
           label = "Conventional power threshold = 0.8",
           hjust = 0, color = "#C6227F") +
  scale_y_continuous(breaks = seq(0, 1, 0.2)) +
  coord_cartesian(ylim = c(0, 1)) +
  theme(legend.position = "none") +
  labs(x = "Model parameter: true effect size",
       y = "Diagnosand: statistical power") +
  theme_minimal()
```

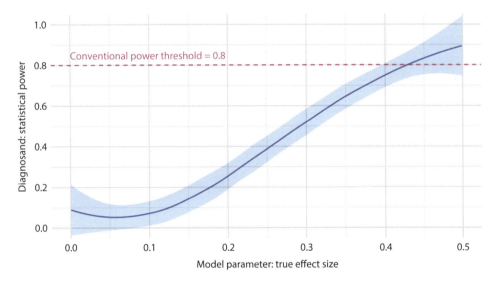

Figure 13.3: Example visualization of a diagnosis.

13.7 Redesign

The basic principle of redesign is that we need to create a list of designs which then get passed to `simulate_designs` or `diagnose_designs`. (The plural versions of these functions are identical to their singular counterparts; we provide both just to allow the code to speak for itself a little more easily).

You can make lists of designs to redesign across directly with `list`:

```
designs <- list(design1, design2)
```

More often, you'll vary designs over a parameter with `redesign`. Any quantity that you define in the global environment and use in a declaration step can become a parameter like this and then altered via redesign. Here, we're imagining we've already declared a `design` that has an `N` parameter that we allow to have three values.

```
designs <- redesign(design, N = c(100, 200, 300))
```

Whichever way you create `designs`, you can then diagnose all of the designs in the list with:

```
designs <- diagnose_designs(designs)
```

PART

Research Design Library

CHAPTER **14**

Research Design Library

This section of the book enumerates a series of common social science research designs. Each entry will include a description of the design in terms of its model, inquiry, data strategy, and answer strategy, first in words then in code. We'll often diagnose designs over the range of values of some design parameters in order to point out especially interesting or important features of the design.

Our goal in this section is not to provide a comprehensive accounting of all empirical research designs. It's also not to describe any of the particular designs in exhaustive detail, because we are quite sure that in order for these designs to be useful for any practical purpose, they will need to be modified. The entries in the design library are not recipes that will automatically produce high-quality research. Instead, we hope that the entries provide inspiration for how to tailor a particular class of design to your own research setting.

The design library is also a corpus of design elements and code that can be mixed and matched to fit your particular research setting. We do not have a stepped-wedge experimental design with blocking, but you can create one by combining elements from the stepped-wedge design and the block-randomized experimental design.

We've organized the library by inquiry and by data strategy. Inquiries can be descriptive or causal; data strategies can be observational or experimental. Crossing these two pairs gives rise to four categories of research design: observational descriptive, experimental descriptive, observational causal, and experimental causal. Table 14.1 offers examples of each class of design. We dedicate chapters to each of these four as well as a chapter for "complex" designs—designs that involve multiple stages, multiple inquiries, or inferences from multiple distinct projects.

Table 14.1: Research design types with examples.

	Data strategy: Observational	Data strategy: Experimental
Inquiry: Descriptive	Sample survey or case study	List experiment or participant observation
Inquiry: Causal	Regression discontinuity design or process tracing	Randomized controlled trial

CHAPTER 15

Observational : Descriptive

An observational design for descriptive inference usually has an inquiry like a population mean, covariance, or distribution as the main research goal. In an observational research design, the data strategy includes sampling and measurement components, but no treatments are allocated by the researcher. Put differently, in an observational design for descriptive inference, researchers seek to measure and summarize the world. This class of research designs encompasses a huge portion of research activity—many surveys fall into this class, as do large-scale data collections of economic and sociopolitical indicators, classic case studies focused on "thick description," and many text analysis projects.

15.1 Simple Random Sampling

> We declare a design in which a researcher takes a simple random sample of a population and uses a survey instrument to measure a latent quantity. The inquiry is the population average of the measured quantity. We show how to declare this design and an approach to incorporate concerns about nonrandom nonresponse in the design.

Descriptive inquiries like the population mean of one variable or the population correlation between two variables are defined with respect to a specific group of units: the population about which we want to draw inferences.

One approach to studying a population is to conduct a census in which we record data on all N units (written with an uppercase N to represent the population). A census has the clear advantage of being comprehensive, but it usually comes at an overwhelming and prohibitive cost.

To avoid those costs, we collect data from only n units (written with a lowercase n), where the sample size n is smaller than the population size N. When the n units we sample are chosen at random, we can obtain unbiased estimates of many descriptive inquiries.[1]

Imagine we seek to estimate the average political ideology of adult residents of the small town of Portola, California (population 2,100). Under our model M, the latent ideology Y^* is drawn from a standard normal distribution.

The data strategy D has two components: a survey question Q and a sampling procedure S. The survey question asks subjects to place themselves on a left-right scale that varies from 1 (most liberal) to 7 (most conservative). We approximate this measurement procedure with a function that "cuts" the latent ideology into seven separate groups. This survey question will introduce measurement error insofar as it does not distinguish among people with different latent ideologies who, because of our measurement tool, place themselves at the same place on the seven-point scale.[2] Our main hope for this measurement procedure is that all of the people who give themselves higher scores are indeed more conservative than those who give themselves lower scores. The sampling procedure is "complete" random sampling. We draw a sample of exactly $n = 100$, where every member of the population has an equal probability of inclusion in the sample, $\frac{n}{N}$.

The model and data strategy are represented by the DAG in Figure 15.1. The DAG shows that the observed outcome Y is a function of the latent score Y^* and the survey question Q. The observed outcome Y is only measured for sampled units, i.e., units that have $S = 1$. This simple diagram represents important design assumptions. First, no arrow leads from Y^* to S. If such an arrow were present, then units with higher or lower latent ideologies would be more likely to be sampled. Second, an arrow does lead from Y^* to Y, indicating that we assume the measured variable does indeed respond to the latent variable. Finally, the diagram includes an explicit role for the survey question, which helps us to consider how alternative wordings of Q might change the observed variable Y.

We imagine here that our inquiry I is the population mean of the *measured* variable Y: $\frac{1}{N}\sum_1^N Y_i = \bar{Y}$, rather than the more ambitious target, the mean of the latent variable Y^*. In this sense, our inquiry is "data-strategy dependent," since we are interested in the expected value of what we *would* measure for any member of the population were we to sample them and apply question Q.

Our answer strategy is the sample mean estimator: $\widehat{\bar{Y}} = \frac{1}{n}\sum_1^n Y_i$, implemented here as an ordinary least squares regression to facilitate the easy calculation of auxiliary statistics like the standard error of the estimate and the 95% confidence interval.

---

[1] But not all. Hedayat, Cheng and Pajda-De La O (2019) prove that unbiased estimators of the population minimum, maximum, and even median do not exist for any sampling procedure except a census. The intuition behind this result is easiest to see for a maximum: unless the random sample happens to contain the unit with the highest value of the outcome, the estimate will necessarily fall below the maximum.

[2] Why do we choose this strategy? Respondents may have trouble placing them on a finer scale, and we cannot ask them on an infinitely fine scale.

15.1 Simple Random Sampling

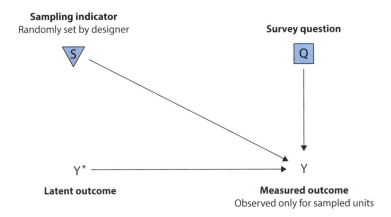

Figure 15.1: Directed acyclic graph for the simple random sampling design.

We incorporate these design features into Declaration 15.1. The `portola` object is a fixed population of 2,100 units with a latent ideology `Y_star`. The declaration of the measurement strategy comes before the declaration of the inquiry, showing how the inquiry is data strategy-dependent.

Declaration 15.1 Simple random sampling design.

```
set.seed(343) # fix random seed to yield a fixed population of units
portola <-
  fabricate(
    N = 2100,
    Y_star = rnorm(N)
  )

declaration_15.1 <-
  declare_model(data = portola) +
  declare_measurement(Y = as.numeric(cut(Y_star, 7))) +
  declare_inquiry(Y_bar = mean(Y)) +
  declare_sampling(S = complete_rs(N, n = 100)) +
  declare_estimator(Y ~ 1, inquiry = "Y_bar")
```

Two main diagnosands for the simple random sampling design are bias and root-mean-squared error. We want to know if we get the right answer on average and we want to know, on average, how far off from the truth we are.

Diagnosis 15.1 Simple random sampling diagnosis

```
diagnosands <-
  declare_diagnosands(
    bias = mean(estimate - estimand),
    rmse = sqrt(mean((estimate - estimand) ^ 2))
  )
diagnosis_15.1 <- diagnose_design(declaration_15.1,
                                  diagnosands = diagnosands)
```

Table 15.1: Complete random sampling design diagnosis.

Bias	RMSE
0.00	0.11
(0.00)	(0.00)

The diagnosis in Table 15.1 indicates that under complete random sampling, the sample mean estimator of the population mean is unbiased and that the root-mean-squared error is manageable at 0.11.

15.1.1 What can go wrong

A serious threat to descriptive inference in a randomized sampling design like this is nonresponse. Missingness due to nonresponse can lead to bias if missingness is correlated with outcomes. Sometimes this bias is referred to as "selection bias" in the sense that some units select out of responding when sampled.

Depending on what information is available about the missing units, various answer strategy fix-ups are available to analysts. For example, if we have demographic or other covariate information about the missing units, we can search for similar-seeming units in the observed data, then impute their missing outcomes. This approach depends on the strong assumption that units with the same covariate profile have the same average outcome, regardless of whether they go missing. The imputation process is often done on the basis of a regression model; multiple imputation methods attempt to incorporate the additional uncertainty that accompanies the modeling technique. Answer strategies that employ inverse probability weights adjust for nonresponse by upweighting types of units we have too few of (relative to a population target) and downweighting units we have too many of.

Avoiding—or dynamically responding to—missingness in the data strategy can be preferable to the addition of modeling assumptions in the answer strategy. Avoiding missingness often means extra effort and expense, such as adding monetary incentives for participation, making multiple rounds of attempted contact, and attempting contact through a variety of modes (phone, mail, email, direct message, text, or in-person visit). The best way to allocate extra effort will vary from context to context, as will the payoff from doing so. Our recommendation is to reason about the plausible response rates that would result from different levels of effort, then to consider how to optimize the bias-effort trade-off. Sometimes, achieving zero bias would be far too costly, so we would be willing to tolerate some bias because effort is too expensive.

Declaration 15.2 builds in a dependence between the latent outcome Y^* and the probability of responding to the survey. That probability also responds to researcher effort. The diagnosis shows how effort translates into higher response rates and lower bias:

Declaration 15.2 Survey nonresponse design.

```
effort <- 0 # baseline of no extra effort

declaration_15.2 <-
  declare_model(data = portola) +
  declare_measurement(Y = as.numeric(cut(Y_star, 7))) +
  declare_inquiry(Y_bar = mean(Y)) +
  declare_sampling(S = complete_rs(N, n = 100)) +
  declare_measurement(
    R = rbinom(n = N, size = 1, prob = pnorm(Y_star + effort)),
    Y = if_else(R == 1, Y, NA_real_)
  ) +
  declare_estimator(Y ~ 1, inquiry = "Y_bar") +
  declare_estimator(R ~ 1, label = "Response Rate")
```

Diagnosis 15.2 Survey nonresponse diagnosis

```
diagnosis_15.2 <-
  declaration_15.2 |>
  redesign(effort = seq(0, 5, by = 0.5)) |>
  diagnose_designs()
```

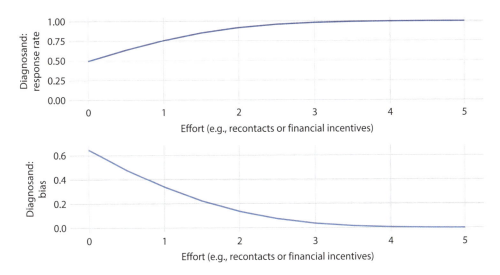

Figure 15.2: Redesigning the random sampling design over researcher effort.

15.1.2 Design Examples

- Bradley et al. (2021) compare "big data" convenience sample surveys (n = 75,000 and 250,000) of COVID-19 vaccine uptake to a 1,000 person simple random sampling design with an inverse probability weighting answer strategy, finding strong support for random sampling over "big data."

- Simple random sampling is also used when researchers need to take manual measurements of a large number of observations. Merkley and Stecula (2021) hand-code a simple random sample of 3,000 newspaper articles about climate change out of the many hundreds of thousands of articles about climate change identified by an automatic search process, allowing them to characterize their population of observations without hand-coding each one.

15.2   Cluster Random Sampling

> We declare a design in which a researcher takes a clustered random sample of a population and uses the design to ask whether they should invest in sampling more clusters or in more individuals per cluster. The design includes a budget constraint that affects how many individuals can be sampled within clusters as a function of the number of clusters sampled.

Researchers often cannot randomly sample at the individual level because it may, among other reasons, be too costly or logistically impractical. Instead, they may choose to sample clusters at random first, then randomly sample units within clusters. Clusters might be schools, localities, or households.

How does clustering change the research design relative to the individual-level design? First, we need to elaborate the model M to make the clustering hierarchy explicit. In the declaration below, we imagine our research site is two states in Nigeria. Localities are nested within states and individuals are nested within localities. Second, we want to respect this hierarchy when thinking about the distribution of outcomes. Individuals living in the same locality are likely to share political viewpoints, either through the explicit transmission of political views or because of common exposure to political influence. The "intra-cluster correlation," or ICC, is an extremely important statistic for the design of cluster-sampled studies. It describes what fraction of the total variation in the outcome can be attributed to the across-cluster differences in average outcomes.

In the declaration below, the latent outcome `Y_star` describes a subject's latent political preferences. This latent outcome is a function of locality differences and individual differences. The variances of these two shocks (difference parameters) are determined by the `ICC` parameter. If ICC were equal to 1, the variance across localities would be equal to 1, and all individuals within a locality would have exactly the same political preferences. If ICC were equal to 0, then the variation in preferences would be entirely at the individual level.

```
ICC <- 0.4

two_nigerian_states <-
  fabricate(
    state = add_level(N = 2,
                      state_name = c("taraba", "kwara"),
                      state_mean = c(-0.2, 0.2)),
    locality = add_level(
      N = 500,
      locality_shock = rnorm(N, state_mean, sqrt(ICC))
    ),
    individual = add_level(
      N = 100,
      individual_shock = rnorm(N, sd = sqrt(1 - ICC)),
      Y_star = locality_shock + individual_shock
    )
  )
```

Many different cluster sampling designs are possible, but a standard choice is a two-stage design in which first, some but not all clusters are sampled, and second, some but not all units within a cluster are sampled. The sampling at either stage may be stratified by covariates at the appropriate level. The first stage can be stratified by cluster-level covariates and the second stage can be stratified by individual-level covariates in order to improve precision. In this declaration, we form cluster-level strata by state.

The two-stage random-sampling design raises an important trade-off: Should we invest in sampling more clusters or in more individuals per cluster? Typically, adding the marginal cluster is more expensive than adding the marginal individual. We formalize the trade-off with a "budget function" that returns the largest individual level inclusion probability that is budget-compatible with a given cluster sampling probability:

```
budget_function <-
  function(cluster_prob){
    budget = 20000
    cluster_cost = 20
    individual_cost = 2
    n_clusters = 1000
    n_individuals_per_cluster = 100

    total_cluster_cost <-
      cluster_prob * n_clusters * cluster_cost

    remaining_funds <- budget - total_cluster_cost

    sampleable_individuals <-
      cluster_prob * n_clusters * n_individuals_per_cluster

    individual_prob =
      (remaining_funds/individual_cost)/sampleable_individuals
    pmin(individual_prob, 1)
  }
```

We use the output of this function to determine the probability of an individual being sampled, conditional on their cluster being sampled.

Lastly, the answer strategy must also respect the data strategy by clustering standard errors at the highest level at which units are sampled, which in this case is the locality.

Declaration 15.3 Cluster random sampling design.

```
declaration_15.3 <-
  declare_model(data = two_nigerian_states) +
  declare_measurement(Y = as.numeric(cut(Y_star, 7))) +
  declare_inquiry(Y_bar = mean(Y)) +
  declare_sampling(
    S_cluster = strata_and_cluster_rs(
      strata = state,
      clusters = locality,
      prob = cluster_prob
    ),
    filter = S_cluster == 1
  ) +
  declare_sampling(
    S_individual =
      strata_rs(strata = locality,
                prob = budget_function(cluster_prob)),
    filter = S_individual == 1
  ) +
  declare_estimator(Y ~ 1,
                    clusters = locality,
                    se_type = "stata",
                    inquiry = "Y_bar")
```

We redesign Declaration 15.3 over various levels of the cluster-level probability of sampling, which in turn sets the probability of sampling at the individual level. Figure 15.3 shows that for a good while, adding additional clusters yields precision gains. At some point, however, the cost to sample size within cluster is too large, and we start seeing precision loss around a probability of 0.75 of a cluster being sampled. The precise combination of design parameters that minimize the standard deviation of the sampling distribution will depend on nearly every aspect of the design declaration, but the most important are the total budget, the relative costs of clusters and individuals, and the ICC. When the ICC is 0, we should invest in few clusters and many individuals. When the ICC is 1, we should invest in many clusters and few individuals.

Diagnosis 15.3 Cluster random sampling diagnosis

```
designs <- redesign(declaration_15.3,
                    cluster_prob = seq(0.1, 0.9, 0.1))
diagnosis_15.3 <- diagnose_design(designs)
```

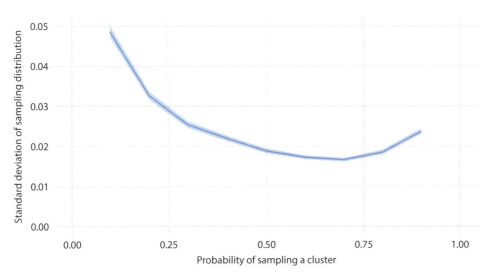

Figure 15.3: Trading off the number of clusters and the number of individuals per cluster.

15.2.1 Design examples

- Stokes (2005) uses a stratified cluster sampling design to estimate the prevalence of vote buying in Argentina. The strata were provinces and the clusters were census tracts. A simple random sample of individuals residing in selected census tracts were ultimately interviewed.

- Paler, Marshall, and Atallah (2018) use a multistage clustered sampling design to study Lebanese citizens' willingness to sign a petition condemning sectarian politics. The clusters were localities (villages in rural areas, neighborhoods in urban areas), which were stratified by population size. Within selected localities, simple random samples of households were drawn; within households, a single adult was selected at random. The study also included a randomized treatment that manipulated whether petition signatures were public or private.

15.3 Multilevel Regression and Poststratification

> We declare a design in which researchers reweight the responses of different units in a sample in order to better estimate a population-level quantity. Reweighting depends on how much units are thought to "represent" other nonsampled units and requires making decisions about how much units of different types should be pooled together. Design performance of a partially pooled model is compared against designs that involve no pooling and full pooling.

Multilevel regression and poststratification (MRP) is a technique used primarily for "small area estimation." In the prototypical setting, we conduct a nationally representative survey of public opinion, but our goal is to generate estimates of the average level of public opinion for many subnational units. In the United States context, these "small area" units are often the 50 states. The main problem is that in a national poll of 2,000 Americans, we might only have four respondents from small states like Alaska, Wyoming, or Vermont, but more than 100 from large states like California, New York, or Texas. Accordingly, it is harder to estimate opinion in small states than in large states. The key insight of an MRP design is that we can "borrow strength" across states and kinds of people in order to improve state level estimates.

In an MRP design, the answer strategy includes two steps: a multilevel regression step and a poststratification step. The regression model generates estimates of the average opinion for classes of people within each state. The precise flavor of regression model can vary from application to application. In the simple example below, we use a generalized linear mixed effects model with an individual-level covariate and random effects by state, but regression models of substantial complexity are sometimes used to model important nuances in how opinions covary with individual and state-level characteristics (see, e.g., Bisbee, 2019).

The regression model generates estimates of the average opinion for classes of people within each state. The poststratification step reweights these estimates to *known* proportions of each class of person within each state. The knowledge of these proportions has to come from outside the survey. The US census is the usual source of these population proportions in the American context, though any reliable source of this information is suitable.

In Declaration 15.4, we begin with a dataset of the 50 states that describes what fraction of people in each state has graduated from high school. This code block also establishes the true state means that will be summarized by our inquiry. In the model, we draw a nationally representative sample of size 2,000, respecting the fraction of people within each state with a high school degree. The poststratification weights are built from that fraction as well. The binary public opinion variable `policy_support` is a function of the high school covariate, an individual-level shock, and a state-level shock. The inquiry is the mean policy support at the state level. The tricky part of this design is the two-step answer strategy. The first step is handled by the multilevel regression function `glmer`. The second step is handled by the `post_stratification_helper` function (available in the `rdss` companion package), which obtains predictions from the model, then reweights them according to the poststratification weights.

Declaration 15.4 Multilevel regression and poststratification design.

```
library(rdss) # for helper functions
library(lme4)
```

```r
states <-
  as_tibble(state.x77) |>
  transmute(
    state = rownames(state.x77),
    prop_of_US = Population / sum(Population),
    # results in exactly 2,000 due to rounding
    state_n = round(prop_of_US * 1998.6),
    prob_HS = `HS Grad` / 100,
    state_shock = rnorm(n = n(), sd = 0.5),
    state_mean = prob_HS * pnorm(0.2 + state_shock) +
      (1 - prob_HS) * pnorm(state_shock)
  )
declaration_15.4 <-
  declare_model(
    data = states[rep(1:50, states$state_n), ],
    HS = rbinom(n = N, size = 1, prob = prob_HS),
    PS_weight =
      case_when(HS == 0 ~ (1 - prob_HS),
                HS == 1 ~ prob_HS),
    individual_shock = rnorm(n = N, sd = 0.5),
    policy_support =
      rbinom(N, 1, prob = pnorm(0.2 * HS + individual_shock + state_shock))
  ) +
  declare_inquiry(
    handler = function(data) {
      states |> transmute(
        state,
        inquiry = "mean_policy_support",
        estimand = state_mean
      )
    }
  ) +
  declare_estimator(handler = label_estimator(function(data) {
    model_fit <- glmer(
      formula = policy_support ~ HS + (1 | state),
      data = data,
      family = binomial(link = "logit")
    )
    post_stratification_helper(model_fit, data = data,
                               group = state, weights = PS_weight)
  }),
  label = "Partial pooling",
  inquiry = "mean_policy_support")
```

Figure 15.4 shows one draw from this design, plotting the MRP estimates against the true level of opinion.

15.3.1 Redesign over answer strategies

The strengths of the MRP design are best appreciated by contrasting MRP's partial pooling approach to two alternatives: no pooling and full pooling. Under no pooling, we estimate each state mean separately with a national adjustment for the individual-level high school covariate. Under full pooling, we only adjust for high school and ignore state information altogether. Here we add both estimators to the design and diagnose.

Chapter 15: Observational : Descriptive

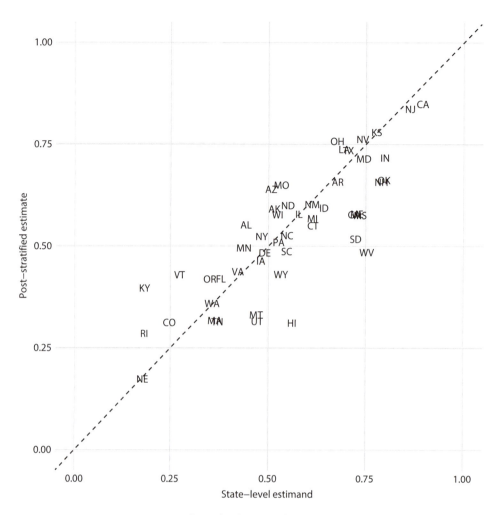

Figure 15.4: Estimates of state-level option plotted against their true levels.

Declaration 15.5 Redesign over answer strategies.

```
declaration_15.5 <-
  declaration_15.4 +
  declare_estimator(
    handler = label_estimator(function(data) {
      model_fit <- lm_robust(
        formula = policy_support ~ HS + state,
        data = data
      )
      post_stratification_helper(model_fit, data = data,
                                 group = state, weights = PS_weight)
    }),
    label = "No pooling",
    inquiry = "mean_policy_support") +
  declare_estimator(
    handler = label_estimator(function(data) {
      model_fit <- lm_robust(
```

15.3 Multilevel Regression and Poststratification

```
        formula = policy_support ~ HS,
        data = data
    )
    post_stratification_helper(model_fit, data = data,
                               group = state, weights = PS_weight)
}),
label = "Full pooling",
inquiry = "mean_policy_support")
```

Diagnosis 15.4 Diagnosing over answer strategies

```
diagnosis_15.4 <- diagnose_design(declaration_15.5)
```

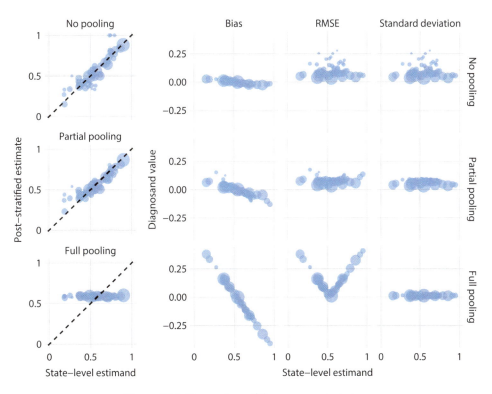

Figure 15.5: Comparison of three answer strategies.

Figure 15.5 compares the three estimators. The first column of facets shows one draw of the estimates against the estimands. The main thing to notice here is that the full pooling estimate is more or less a flat line—regardless of the estimand, the estimates are just above 50%. Relative to partial pooling, the no pooling estimates are further spread around the 45 degree line, with small states bouncing around the most.

On the right side of the figure, we see the bias, RMSE, and standard deviation diagnosands for each inquiry under all three answer strategies. Under no pooling, bias is very low, but the RMSE and standard deviation for small states is very high. Under full pooling, the standard deviation is very low, but bias is very positive for states with low support and very negative for states with high support. The resulting RMSE has a funny "V" shape—we only do well for states that happen to have opinion that is very close to the national average.

Partial pooling represents a Goldilocks compromise between full and no pooling. Yes, we have some positive bias for low-opinion states and negative bias for high-opinion states, but variance has been brought under control. As a result, the RMSE for both small and large states is small.

15.3.2 Design examples

- Lax and Phillips (2009) apply multilevel regression and poststratification to 41 national polls conducted between 1999 and 2008 to generate state-level estimates of gay rights attitudes in the US.
- Tausanovitch and Warshaw (2013) apply multilevel regression and poststratification to large polls of Americans' policy preferences to generate estimates of policy opinions at the Congressional district, state legislative district, and municipality levels.

15.4 Index Creation

> We declare a design is which we take multiple measures and combine them to learn about a latent, unobservable quantity. The design diagnosis shows that it is possible to generate interpretable conditional estimates of this quantity and assess bias even though the metric of the unobservable quantity is unknown. The diagnosis highlights how subtle differences in scale construction generate different biases.

Models often specify a latent variable (`Y_star`) that we can't observe directly. The measurement procedures we use involve imperfect proxies (`Y_1`, `Y_2`, `Y_3`): observed values for these proxies may be related to the latent variables but are often on different scales. A common strategy for addressing measurement error is to combine multiple measures of the same latent variable into an index. The basic intuition for this procedure is that when we combine multiple measures, the errors attending to each measure will tend to cancel one another out. When this happens, the index itself has lower measurement error than any of the constituent parts.

The first difficult feature of such problems is that we do not have access to the *scale* on which `Y_star` is measured and so it may seem like a hopeless exercise to try to assess whether we have good or bad estimates of `Y_star` when we combine the measured data.

One way around this is to normalize the scale of both the latent variable and the measured variable so that they have a mean of 0 and a standard deviation of 1. But in that case, we are guaranteed that our estimate of the mean of the normalized variable will be unbiased because we will certainly estimate a mean of 0! That may be—but as we show in the declaration below, if your model is correct this approach may still be useful for calculating other quantities (such as conditional means) that you don't get right just by construction.

A second challenge is deciding which measurements to combine into the index. We clearly only want to create indices using measurements of the same latent variable, but it can hard to be sure ex ante whether a given measurement is a good proxy for a given latent variable. Just relying on whether the measurements are positively correlated or not is not sufficient, because measurements can be correlated even if they are not measurements of the same underlying variable. Ultimately we have to rely on theory to make these decisions, as uncomfortable as that may make us.

In Declaration 15.6, our inquiry is the average level of the latent variable among units whose binary covariate X is equal to 1.

In the declaration below, Y_star has a normal distribution but it is not centered on 0. The measured variables Y_1, Y_2, Y_3 are also normally distributed but each has its own scale; they are all related to Y_star, though some more strongly than others. Many procedures for combining these measured variables into an index exist. Here we'll consider a few of the common approaches:

- Y_avg is constructed by first scaling each of these measured variables, then averaging them. This is akin to the approach used in Kling, Liebman, and Katz (2007).

- Y_avg_adjusted is the same as Y_avg, but we scale the measured values by features of the units with X = 0.

- Y_avg_rescaled is the same as Y_avg, but instead of taking an equally weighted average of the scaled components, we rescale their sum by its mean and standard deviation.

- Y_first_factor extracts the first factor from a principal components analysis, which, intuitively, seeks to find a weighting that minimizes the distance to the measured variables.

Declaration 15.6 Latent variable design.

```
declaration_15.6 <-
  declare_model(
    N = 500,
    X = rep(0:1, N / 2),
```

```
    Y_star = 1 + X + 2 * rnorm(N)
  ) +
  declare_inquiry(Y_bar_X1 = mean(scale(Y_star)[X == 1])) +
  declare_measurement(
    Y_1 = 3 + 0.1 * Y_star + rnorm(N, sd = 5),
    Y_2 = 2 + 1.0 * Y_star + rnorm(N, sd = 2),
    Y_3 = 1 + 0.5 * Y_star + rnorm(N, sd = 1),
    Y_avg = ((scale(Y_1) + scale(Y_2) + scale(Y_3)))/3,
    Y_avg_adjusted = (
      # rescaling according to the X = 0 group
      (Y_1 - mean(Y_1[X == 0])) / sd(Y_1[X == 0]) +
      (Y_2 - mean(Y_2[X == 0])) / sd(Y_2[X == 0]) +
      (Y_3 - mean(Y_3[X == 0])) / sd(Y_3[X == 0])
    ) / 3,
    Y_avg_rescaled = scale((scale(Y_1) + scale(Y_2) + scale(Y_3))),
    Y_first_factor = princomp( ~ Y_1 + Y_2 + Y_2, cor = TRUE)$scores[, 1]
  ) +
  declare_estimator(
    cbind(Y_avg, Y_avg_adjusted, Y_avg_rescaled, Y_first_factor) ~ 1,
    .method = lm_robust,
    inquiry = "Y_bar_X1",
    subset = X == 1,
    term = TRUE,
    label = "Average"
  )
```

In Figure 15.6 we show that the correlation between all the indices and the underlying quantity is quite good, even though the strength of the correlations for some of the components is weak. Trickier, however, is being sure we have an interpretable *scale*.

Diagnosis 15.5 Latent variables diagnosis over alternative answer strategies

```
diagnosis_15.5 <- diagnose_design(declaration_15.6,
                                  make_groups = vars(outcome))
```

Figure 15.7 shows the distribution of estimates from different approaches to generating indices. A few features stand out from the distribution of estimates.

The simple averaging of the normalized scales also generates estimates that are too small. Rescaling the scaled components instead of taking the average helps only a small amount. The principal component version appears to do especially poorly, but there is a simple reason for this: the method does not presuppose knowledge of the *direction* of the scale of the latent variable and can come up with an index that reverses the actual scale of interest. Avoiding this requires an interpretative step after the principal components analysis is implemented (more subtly, the averaging approach also has an interpretative step *before* averaging, when components are introduced with a metric that presupposes a positive correlation with the underlying quantity). Even accounting for the different sign patterns however, the estimates are too small.

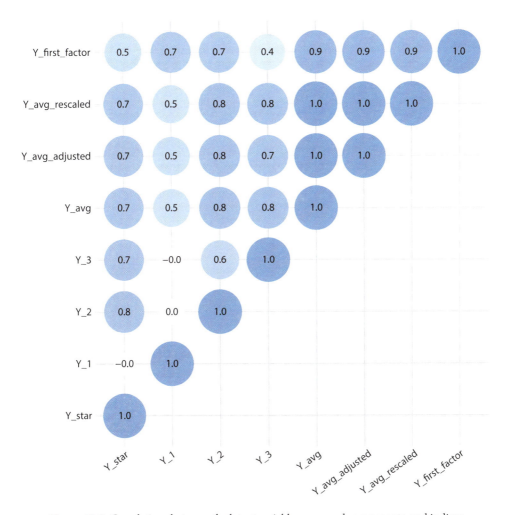

Figure 15.6: Correlations between the latent variable, measured components, and indices.

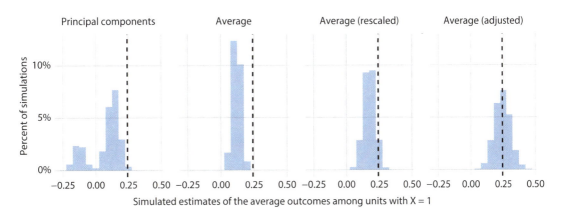

Figure 15.7: Distribution of estimates from different approaches to generating indices.

Scaling by units with $X = 1$ does best in this case. The key insight here is that the total variation in the latent variable combines the variation within groups and between them: we want to measure outcomes on a scale benchmarked to the within-group variation and so have to take out the between-group variation when rescaling.

Overall, we see from the diagnosis that we *can* do quite well here in recovering the conditional mean of the standardized latent variable. But we see risks here. We declared a design under optimistic conditions in which we knew the relevant components and these were all related to the latent variable in a simple way. Even in this case we had difficulty getting the answer right.

15.4.1 Design examples

- Jefferson (2022) introduces the "Respectability Politics Scale," which is a six-item additive index. Responses on 1–7 Likert scales are rescaled to the 0–1 range, then averaged.

- Broockman and Kalla (2016) conduct a randomized experiment in which the main outcome is an index of attitudes toward transgender people, which is constructed by taking the first factor from a factor analysis of multiple survey questions.

CHAPTER 16

Observational : Causal

In an observational design, researchers do not themselves assign units to conditions; the natural processes of the world are responsible for the observed treatment conditions. Causal inference from observational research designs is the art of imagining what outcomes treated units would have expressed if they had not been treated—and the outcomes of the untreated units if they had been treated.

Observational causal inference is hard because it depends on the world generating just the right circumstances. This is true for all five of the observational designs we describe in this chapter. Process tracing requires observation of just the right clues to the causal mystery. Selection-on-observables requires measurement of a set of variables that collectively close all the backdoor paths from treatment to outcome. A difference-in-difference design requires a very specific kind of over-time stability—that untreated potential outcomes move exactly in parallel. Instrumental variables designs require nature to randomly assign something we can measure. Regression discontinuity designs require a cutoff that determines who is treated and who is not that we can observe and understand.

Many other innovative designs have been developed to try to estimate causal quantities from observational research designs. These generally seek clever innovations in A in order to have as few assumptions on M as possible. We refer readers to Angrist and Pischke (2008) and Dunning (2012) for excellent overviews of the design theory behind many of these methods.

16.1 Process Tracing

> We declare a qualitative design in which researchers seek to learn about the effect of a cause on a single unit. The diagnosis helps evaluate the gains from different within-case data gathering strategies.

In qualitative research we are often interested in learning about the causal effect for a single unit. For example, for a country unit that underwent sanctions (an "event") and subsequently complied, we want to know the causal effect of the sanctions on government compliance. To do so, we need to know what would have happened if the event did not happen, the *counter*factual outcome that did not occur as opposed to the factual outcome that did. Due to the fundamental problem of causal inference, we cannot observe what would have happened if that counterfactual condition had arisen. We have to guess—or infer—what would have happened. Social scientists have developed a large array of tools for guessing missing counterfactual outcomes—what would have happened in the counterfactual condition, if the event had not happened.[1]

A common inquiry in this setting is whether an outcome was *due* to a cause. For instance in a case with $X = 1, Y = 1$, this "causal attribution" inquiry or "Cause of Effect" inquiry can be written $\text{CoE} := 1 - Y(0)|X = 1 \& Y = 1$. For a unit with $X = 1$ and $Y = 1$, $\text{CoE} = 1$ if $Y(0) = 0$.

"Process tracing" is a prominent strategy for assessing causes of effects (Bennett and Checkel, 2015; Fairfield and Charman, 2017). Here, following, for example, Humphreys and Jacobs (forthcoming), we think of process tracing as a procedure in which researchers provide a theory in the form of a causal model that is rich enough to characterize the probability of observing ancillary data ("Causal process observations" (Brady, 2004)) given underlying causal relations. When equipped with prior beliefs, such a model in turn lets one use Bayes' rule to form posterior beliefs over causal relations after observing these data.

For intuition, say we are interested in whether a policy caused a change in economic outcomes. We theorize that for the policy to matter, it at least had to be implemented. So if we find out that the policy was not implemented we infer that it did not matter. We make theory-dependent inferences that are reasonable *insofar as* the theory itself is reasonable. In this example, if there were plausible channels through which a policy might have mattered even if not implemented, then our conclusion would not be warranted.

To illustrate design choices for a process tracing study we consider a setting in which we have already observed X, Y data and are interested in figuring out whether Y takes on the value it does *because* X took on the value it did.

More specifically we imagine a model with two ancillary variables, M and W. We posit that X causes Y via M—with negative effects of X on M and of M on Y ruled out. And we posit that W is a cause of both M and Y. Specifically, our model asserts that if $W = 1$ then X causes M and M causes Y for sure. Under this model M and W each serves as a "clue" for the causal effect of X on Y.

Using the language popularized by Van Evera (1997), M provides a "hoop" test: if you look for data on M and find that $M = 0$ when $X = 1$ and $Y = 1$ then you infer

---

[1] We are also interested in the opposite case sometimes: we have a unit that did not experience an event, and we want to know the causal effect of *not* having it. In this case, we need to guess what would have happened if the event did happen. The same tools apply in reverse.

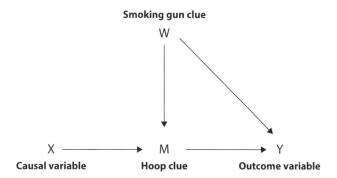

Figure 16.1: Directed acyclic graph of a process tracing model.

that X did not cause Y. If on the other hand you examine W and find that $W = 1$ then you have a "smoking gun" test: you infer that X did indeed cause Y. However, if you find both $M = 0$ and $W = 1$, then you know your model is wrong.

The model can be described using the `CausalQueries` package thus:

```
library(rdss) # for helper functions
library(CausalQueries)

causal_model <- make_model("X -> M -> Y <- W -> M") |>
  set_restrictions("(M[X=1] < M[X=0]) | (M[X=1, W=1] == M[X=0, W=1])") |>
  set_restrictions("(Y[M=1] < Y[M=0]) | (Y[M=1, W=1] == Y[M=0, W=1])")

strategies = c("X-Y", "X-Y-M", "X-Y-W",  "X-Y-W-M")
```

The DAG of the causal model is shown in Figure 16.1.

This model definition describes the DAG but also specifies a set of restrictions on causal relations. By default, flat priors are then placed over all other possible causal relations, though of course other prior beliefs could also be specified.

We now have all we need to assess what inferences we might make given different sorts of observations on W and M.

Table 16.1 shows three types of quantities: beliefs upon observing $X = 1$, $Y = 1$, conditional inferences upon observing additional data on M or W, and the conditional probability of seeing different outcomes for M or W.

We see here that M provides a hoop test since we are certain that X does not cause Y when $M = 0$, but we are uncertain when $M = 1$. (Moreover, we already expect to see $M = 1$ given what we have seen for X and Y.) W provides a smoking gun test since we are certain that X causes Y when $M = 1$ but uncertain otherwise. Since we have access to both conditional inferences and the probability of seeing different types of data, we have enough data in Table 16.1 to calculate how different strategies will perform.

Chapter 16: Observational : Causal

Table 16.1: Beliefs about the probability X caused Y upon observing $X = 1, Y = 1$, updated inferences upon observing additional data on M or W, and the conditional probability of seeing different outcomes for M or W given observation of $X = 1, Y = 1$.

Query	Value
Prob(CoE=1 | X = 1, Y=1)	0.71
Prob(CoE=1 | X = 1, Y = 1, M=0)	0.00
Prob(CoE=1 | X = 1, Y = 1, M=1)	0.77
Prob(CoE=1 | X = 1, Y = 1, W=0)	0.20
Prob(CoE=1 | X = 1, Y = 1, W=1)	1.00
Prob(M=1 | X = 1, Y = 1)	0.93
Prob(W=1 | X = 1, Y = 1)	0.64

We think it useful to fold these quantities into a design declaration so that research consumers can access the data strategies and answer strategies in the same way as they would for any other problem.

Declaration 16.1 provides a flexible process tracing design. You can use this design with a different causal model and substitute in different causal queries and process tracing strategies. Given a background causal model, the design first draws a "causal type"—that is, a case together with all its causal relations. The value of the estimand (CoE) can then be calculated and the observable data corresponding to the type revealed. The estimation uses a custom function, which simply returns the inferences on the query—like those in Table 16.1—given different possible observed values for all nodes. No data strategy is provided explicitly as the data strategy is tied up here in the estimation, that is, the estimation step describes what data will be used.

Declaration 16.1 Process tracing design declaration.

```
declaration_16.1 <-
  declare_model(draw_causal_type(causal_model)) +
  declare_inquiry(
    CoE = query_distribution(
      causal_model,
      query = "Y[X=1] - Y[X=0]",
      parameters = causal_type)) +
  declare_measurement(
    handler = function(data)
      causal_model |>
      make_data(parameters = data$causal_type))  +
  declare_estimator(
```

```
    handler = label_estimator(process_tracing_estimator),
    causal_model = causal_model,
    query = "Y[X=1] - Y[X=0]",
    strategies = strategies)
```

Diagnosis 16.1 Process tracing diagnosis

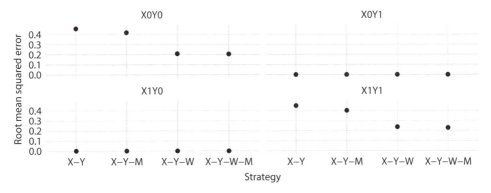

Figure 16.2: Inferences from four different process tracing data strategies on whether X caused Y given four different observed X, Y data patterns.

Given such a model, a case in which $X = Y = 1$ (for instance), and limited resources, we now want to know whether we would be better gathering data on M or W or both.

The answers are given in Figure 16.2. Here we show the expected error from inferences given each process tracing strategy. We break up the diagnoses according to the X, Y data already observed—thus illustrating how an unconditional model can be used to assess designs even after some data is observed. Across the four possible data patterns we see equivalent implications for settings in which we are interested, in one case with $X = Y = 1$, and in one case with $X = Y = 0$. For the cases with $X \neq Y$ we already know—because of the monotonicity restrictions in the model—that X did not cause Y and so we learn nothing from all strategies.

We see only modest declines in expected errors from observation of the mediator M (consistent with the manual calculation above), but large declines from observing W. If we have already observed W, the gains from observing M are still more slight. Broadly this confirms a more general observation that mediators can often provide limited traction for learning about causes of effects relative to moderators (Dawid, Humphreys, and Musio, 2022).

16.1.1 Design examples

- Revkin and Ahram (2020) consider the "rebel social contract," in which rebel groups offer citizens political protections and social benefits in return for citizens' allegiance. The authors use the presence of formal complaints by citizens about the Islamic State in Iraq and Syria as a hoop test for the causal model of exchange of protections for allegiance.

- Snyder and Borghard (2011) attempted to apply a smoking gun test to audience cost theory, but could find no clear-cut cases of settings in which "the public was opposed to military action before a threat was issued and then explicitly punished the leader for not following through with a threat with which it disagreed."

16.2 Selection-on-Observables

> We declare a design in which a researcher tries to address concerns about confounding by conditioning on other observable variables. In the design, the researcher has to specify how the other variable create a risk of confounding and how exactly they will take account of these variables to minimize bias.

When we want to learn about causal effects, but treatments are allocated by the world and not by the researcher, we are sometimes stuck. It is possible that a comparison of treated units to control units will generate biased inferences because of selection—the problem that certain types of units "select" into treatment and others into control. If the average potential outcomes of the groups that come to be treated or untreated are not equal, then a comparison of the realized outcomes of the two groups is not guaranteed to yield unbiased causal inferences.

Sometimes, however, we know enough about selection in order to condition on the variables that cause it. A selection-on-observables design stipulates a family of models M of the world that describe which variables are responsible for selection, then employs a data strategy that measures those variables, rendering them "observable." In the answer strategy, we draw on substantive knowledge of the causal process to generate an "adjustment set," or a set of variables that can account for selection into treatment. In the language of causal path diagrams, an adjustment set is a set of variables that, when conditioned upon, closes all backdoor paths from the treatment to the outcome. We can condition on the adjustment set using a variety of alternative answer strategies, for example, through regression adjustment, stratification, or matching.

The quality of causal inferences we draw comes down to whether our claims about selection into treatment are correct. If we've missed a cause (missed a backdoor path), then our inferences will be prone to bias. It is the nature of the selection-on-observables design that we can't know if our claims about the processes that cause selection are correct or not; the design amounts to a leap of faith in the theoretical model.

The problems don't end there. We risk bias if we fail to adjust for X under some models—but we will also risk bias if we *do* adjust for X under other models. In

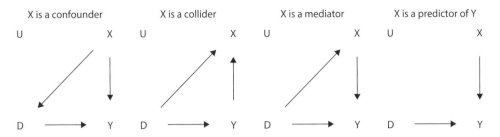

Figure 16.3: Four roles for an observable variable X.

Figure 16.3 we illustrate four of the possible roles for an observable variable X: as a confounder of the relationship between D and Y; as a collider, which is affected by both D and Y; as a mediator of the relationship between D and Y; and as a predictor of Y with no connection to D. We set aside in these DAGs the possible roles of an unobservable variable U that would introduce additional problems of confounding.

If X is a confounder, failing to adjust for it in studying the relationship between the treatment D and outcome Y will lead to a risk of confounding bias. We often think of the fourth DAG as the alternative to this, where X is a predictor of Y but has no link to D. In this circumstance, we still want to adjust for X to seek efficiency improvements by soaking up additional variation in Y, but failing to do so will not introduce bias. If the true model is definitely represented by either the first or fourth DAG, we should clearly choose to adjust for X. In the first case, we should adjust to close the backdoor path, and in the fourth case, we will do no worse in terms of bias and may in fact increase precision.

However, the middle two DAGs present problems if we *do* adjust for X. In the first, X is a collider: it is affected by both D and Y. Adjusting for X if this is the true model introduces collider bias, because we open a backdoor path between D and Y through X. We also introduce bias if we control for X if the mediator model (DAG 3) is the true model, wherein D affects X and Y and X affects Y (i.e., X is a mediator for the relationship between D and Y). But the reason here is different: controlling for a mediator adjusts away part of the true treatment effect.

In a selection-on-observables design, we must get many features of the model correct, not only about the factors that affect D. We must be sure of all the arrows into X, D, and Y and the order of the causal arrows. In some cases, in natural experiments where selection processes are not randomized by researchers but are nevertheless known, these assumptions can be sustained. In others, we will be making heroic assumptions.

Declaration 16.2 explores these considerations, with a model defining the relationship between a causal factor of interest D, outcome Y, and an observable confounder X; the average treatment effect as the inquiry; a simple measurement strategy; and two estimators with and without adjustment for X. We use exact matching as our adjustment strategy.

Declaration 16.2 Matching design declaration.

```r
library(MatchIt)

exact_matching <-
  function(data) {
    matched <- matchit(D ~ X, method = "exact", data = data)
    match.data(matched)
  }

declaration_16.2 <-
  declare_model(
    N = 100,
    U = rnorm(N),
    X = rbinom(N, 1, prob = 0.5),
    D = rbinom(N, 1, prob = 0.25 + 0.5 * X),
    Y_D_0 = 0.2 * X + U,
    Y_D_1 = Y_D_0 + 0.5
  ) +
  declare_inquiry(ATE = mean(Y_D_1 - Y_D_0)) +
  declare_step(handler = exact_matching) +
  declare_measurement(Y = reveal_outcomes(Y ~ D)) +
  declare_estimator(Y ~ D,
                    weights = weights,
                    .method = difference_in_means,
                    label = "Matched difference-in-means") +
  declare_estimator(Y ~ D,
                    .method = difference_in_means,
                    label = "Raw difference-in-means")
```

We declare beliefs about the selection process and how D, Y, and X are related. The model needs to include potential outcomes for the main outcome of interest (Y) and a specification of the assignment of the key causal variable (in this case, D). Here, we have defined the assignment process as a function of an observable variable X. In fact, X is the only variable that affects selection into treatment: X is a binary variable (i.e., two groups), and the probability of treatment is 0.4 when $X = 0$ and 0.6 when $X = 1$. In addition, we define the potential outcomes for Y, which invoke confounding by X because it affects both D and Y. We only invoke one possible relationship between X, Y, and D, and so do not consider the possibilities of colliders or mediators.

In our model, U is not a confounder, because it affects Y but not D; this is a strong excludability assumption on which our causal inferences depend. The assumption is strong because ruling out all unobservable confounders is typically impossible. Most causal factors in nature are affected by many variables, only some of which we can imagine and measure. The first estimator, with adjustment, uses the weights from the exact matching estimator. The matching procedure adjusts for differences in the probability of selection into treatment according to X. The second, unadjusted, estimator does not control for X. It suffers from unobserved confounding, because X predicts both treatment and the outcome.

Diagnosis 16.2 Matching design diagnosis

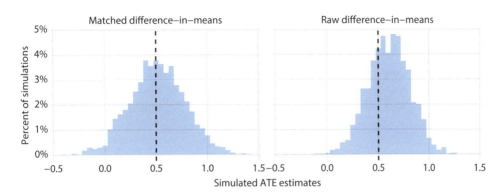

Figure 16.4: Sampling distribution of two estimators.

In Figure 16.4, we see that the raw, unmatched estimate is upwardly biased (by about 20% of the average estimate) and that the matched estimate is unbiased. If we fail to adjust for the observable features of the selection process, we have biased answers. But if we do control in this case, we obtain unbiased answers. However, as highlighted earlier, these results depend on the plausibility of our model, which in this case involves observed confounding of the relationship between D and Y by X. If there was *unobservable* confounding from U, or if X were a collider or mediator, there would be bias even if we control for X.

16.2.1   Design examples

- Bateson (2012) uses a selection-on-observables design to estimate the causal effect of crime victimization on political participation from regional barometer survey data. The main specification is justified by the argument that all backdoor paths are closed using Ordinary Least Squares regression and a robustness check uses a nearest-neighbor matching approach under equivalent assumptions.

- Prillaman (2022) uses a matching design to compare Indian villages that featured women's self-help groups to those that did not on rates of women's political participation.

16.3   Difference-in-Differences

> We declare a differences-in-differences design in which the effect of a treatment is assessed by comparing changes over time for a unit that gets treated to changes over time in the same period for a unit the does not get treated. The declaration and diagnosis help clarify when effect heterogeneity threatens causal inferences drawn from this design.

The difference-in-differences design compares the pre-to-posttreatment difference in treated units to that in untreated units. By focusing on the difference over time, unit-specific characteristics of treated units are subtracted out. We use the over-time change in the untreated units to account for the changes over time in the treated units that are not due to the treatment. Suppose outcomes were rising over time for all units but we only looked at the pre-to-post difference in the treatment group. We might falsely infer the treatment increased outcomes. The logic of the difference-in-differences design is that we can subtract off first unit-specific characteristics and then trends affecting all units in order to adjust our causal effect estimates.

The difference-in-differences design relies on a strong assumption in M: the parallel trends assumption. This assumption asserts that the *changes* (not the levels) in untreated potential outcomes are the same for treated and untreated units. Because this assumption depends on the values of the unrealized (and thus unobservable) control potential outcomes in the treated units after treatment, it cannot be tested. A widely used diagnostic is to look at the trends in outcomes between the treated and control unit *before* treatment; this is only an indirect test because the parallel trends assumption concerns the unobserved control trend of the actually treated unit.

The design has been commonly used for analyses of two periods (before and after) and two groups (treated and untreated), such as a policy change in one state compared to another before and after the policy change. Today, difference-in-differences is often used in many-period, many-group settings with observational panel data. Here, the logic of the two-period, two-group design is extended through analogy. Parallel trends between treated and control groups are assumed *on average* across treated groups and periods. Unfortunately, the analogy holds only under limited circumstances, a fact only recently appreciated.

Declaration 16.3 describes a 20-period, 20-unit design in which eventually treated units become treated at different times, a common setting in empirical social science often referred to as the staggered adoption design. The treatment effect of interest might be a state-level policy adopted in 20 states at some point within a 20-year period, so we draw on comparisons before and after policy adoption within states and comparisons across states that have and have not yet adopted treatment. We use the `did_multiplegt_tidy` function (available in the `rdss` companion package) to prepare the output from the `DIDmultiplegt` package that implements the estimation procedure suggested by de Chaisemartin and d'Haultfoeuille (2020).

Declaration 16.3 Difference-in-differences design.

```
library(rdss) # for helper functions
library(DIDmultiplegt)

N_units <- 20
N_time_periods <- 20
```

```r
declaration_16.3 <-
  declare_model(
  units = add_level(
    N = N_units,
    U_unit = rnorm(N),
    D_unit = if_else(U_unit > median(U_unit), 1, 0),
    D_time = sample(1:N_time_periods, N, replace = TRUE)
  ),
  periods = add_level(
    N = N_time_periods,
    U_time = rnorm(N),
    nest = FALSE
  ),
  unit_period = cross_levels(
    by = join_using(units, periods),
    U = rnorm(N),
    potential_outcomes(Y ~ U + U_unit + U_time +
                         D * (0.2 - 1 * (D_time - as.numeric(periods))),
                       conditions = list(D = c(0, 1))),
    D = if_else(D_unit == 1 & as.numeric(periods) >= D_time, 1, 0),
    D_lag = lag_by_group(D, groups = units, n = 1, order_by = periods)
  )
) +
  declare_inquiry(
    ATT = mean(Y_D_1 - Y_D_0),
    subset = D == 1
  ) +
  declare_inquiry(
    ATT_switchers = mean(Y_D_1 - Y_D_0),
    subset = D == 1 & D_lag == 0 & !is.na(D_lag)
  ) +
  declare_measurement(Y = reveal_outcomes(Y ~ D)) +
  declare_estimator(
    Y ~ D, fixed_effects = ~ units + periods,
    .method = lm_robust,
    inquiry = c("ATT", "ATT_switchers"),
    label = "twoway-fe"
  ) +
  declare_estimator(
    Y = "Y",
    G = "units",
    T = "periods",
    D = "D",
    handler = label_estimator(did_multiplegt_tidy),
    inquiry = c("ATT", "ATT_switchers"),
    label = "chaisemartin"
  )
```

We define hierarchical data with time periods nested within groups, such that each of the 20 units have 20 time periods from 1 to 20. We assign units to be treated at some point in the period (`D_unit`), and confound treatment assignment with unobservable unit-specific features `U_unit`. (If there were no confounding, we would not need the parallel trends assumption.) In addition, the timing of treatment is randomly assigned (`D_time`). The assignment `D` then is jointly determined by whether the unit is treated and whether the current period is after the assigned `D_time`. We allow for unit-specific variation (`U_unit`) and time-specific variation (`U_time`), which affect the outcome as well as unit-period characteristics

(U). Potential outcomes are a function of these unit-, time-, and unit-time-specific characteristics, and a treatment effect that varies according to when units are treated (more on the importance of this treatment effect heterogeneity below).

The difference-in-differences design typically targets the average treatment effect on the treated (ATT) inquiry. We leverage over time comparisons within units to isolate the causal effect of treatment, and difference out time-varying characteristics by subtracting off the change in untreated units. Unfortunately, except under extremely limited circumstances—exactly homogeneous treatment effects—we will not be sure to be able to recover unbiased estimates of the ATT. We can, however, under some circumstances and with some estimators, recover the ATT for a specific subgroup: units in those periods that just switched from untreated to treated. We declare the ATT for these "switchers" as the inquiry.

So many answer strategies have been proposed in recent years to address bias in the difference-in-differences design that we cannot summarize them in this short entry. Instead, we illustrate how to assess the properties of two particular estimators under a range of conditions. First, we define the standard two-way fixed effects estimator with fixed effects by time and unit. The two-way fixed effects fits the empirical goal of difference-in-differences: the time fixed effects net out time-varying unit-invariant variables such as seasonality and time trends. The unit fixed effects net out unit-varying variables that are time-invariant, like race or gender at birth of individuals and long-term histories of violence in territories. However, the two-way fixed effects estimator relies on comparisons between units that are treated and units that are *not yet* treated. When treatment effects differ across units depending on when they are treated (as they do in the design here), then those comparisons can be biased: part of the treatment effect will be subtracted out of the estimate. Our second estimator, proposed by de Chaisemartin and d'Haultfoeuille (2020), addresses this problem when estimating the ATT among switchers.

Diagnosis 16.3 Difference-in-differences diagnosis

```
diagnosis_16.3 <- diagnose_design(declaration_16.3)
```

Figure 16.5 shows that the two-way fixed effects estimator is biased for both the ATT and the ATT on the switchers. By contrast, the de Chaisemartin and d'Haultfoeuille (2020) estimator is unbiased for the ATT on the switchers. Neither estimator recovers unbiased estimates of the ATT. The next section explains why.

Diagnosis 16.4 Redesigning over alternative models of treatment effect heterogeneity

The issues with the two-way fixed effects estimator emerge when treatment effects differ for units that are treated later versus earlier. Following Principle 3.2: *Design*

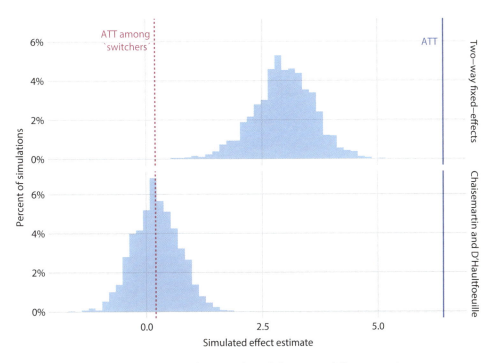

Figure 16.5: Sampling distributions of two difference-in-differences estimators.

agnostically, we declare a model with homogeneous treatment effects, as well as two kinds of time-varying heterogeneous treatment effects: one in which effects are lower for units treated later and one in which effects are higher for units treated later.

The timing of treatment, nature of heterogeneous effects, and answer strategies interact to determine the properties of the design. Figure 16.6 shows the diagnosis under all three sets of potential outcomes, and examines both the ATT and the ATT for switchers inquiries. We consider both the two-way fixed effects estimator and the de Chaisemartin and d'Haultfoeuille (2020) estimator.

When treatment effects happen to be homogeneous (middle panel), both estimators recover unbiased estimates of both the ATT and the ATT for switchers, which of course are equal to one another because of treatment effect homogeneity. However, when treatment effects vary with the timing of treatment (left or right panels), the two-way fixed effects estimator is biased for both inquiries. The de Chaisemartin and d'Haultfoeuille (2020) estimator is also biased for the ATT, but remains unbiased for the ATT among switchers regardless of the pattern of treatment effect heterogeneity.

16.3.1 Design examples

- Paglayan (2019) uses a difference-in-differences design to estimate the causal effect of collective bargaining rights for teachers on education spending in American states.

216   Chapter 16: Observational : Causal

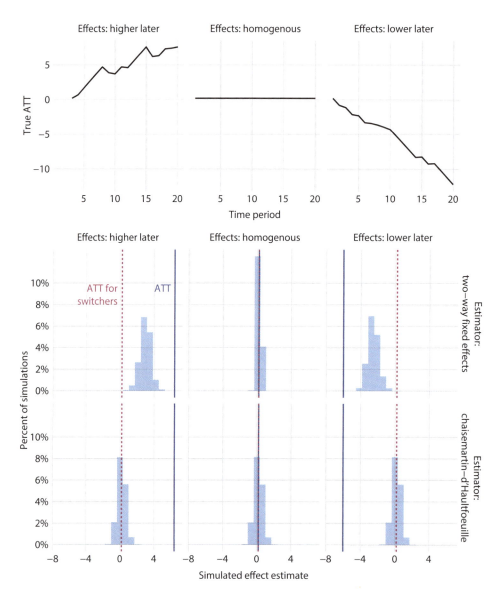

Figure 16.6: Diagnoses of two generalized difference-in-differences estimators under three types of potential outcomes.

- Carreri and Dube (2017) uses a difference-in-differences design to estimate the effect of changes in the international price of oil on the election of right-wing politicians in oil-dependent countries.

16.4 Instrumental Variables

> We declare a design in which a researcher addresses confounding concerns by using an instrumental variable. Under the right conditions, the approach can generate unbiased estimates for treatment effects for units whose treatment status is sensitive to the instrument.

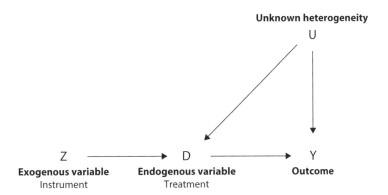

Figure 16.7: Directed acyclic graph of an instrumental variables design.

When we cannot credibly assert that we have controlled for all confounding variables as in a selection-on-observables design (see Section 16.2), and when we do not think the parallel trends assumption is likely to hold in a difference-in-differences design (see Section 16.3), we might have to give up on our goal of drawing causal inferences.

But occasionally, the world yields an opportunity to sidestep unobserved confounding by generating as-if random variation in a variable that itself affects the treatment variable but does not directly affect the outcome. We call the variable that is as-if randomly assigned by the world an "instrument."

Instruments are special. They are variables that are "as-if" randomly assigned by nature, the government, or other individuals or groups. Usually, genuine random assignments have to be crafted by researchers as part of a deliberate data strategy. Experimenters go to great lengths to randomly expose some units but not others to treatments. When the world provides credibly random variation in an instrumental variable, it's a rare and valuable opportunity. By virtue of as-if random assignment, we can learn about the average causal effects of the instrument itself without any further consternation. Conditional on geography and season, weather conditions are plausibly as-if randomly assigned, so we can learn about the average effects of rainfall on many outcomes, like crop yields, voter turnout, and attendance at sporting events. Conditional on gender and birth year, draft numbers in the US were actually randomly assigned by the government, so we can learn about the average effects of being drafted on educational attainment, future earnings, or public policy preferences.

We illustrate the logic of instrumental variables with the DAG shown in Figure 16.7. An instrument Z affects an endogenous treatment D which subsequently affects an outcome Y. Many other common causes, summarized in terms of unknown heterogeneity U, affect both D and Y. It is because of this unmeasured confounding that we cannot learn about the effect of D on Y directly using standard tools.

We can naturally imagine an inquiry that represents the effect of the instrument (Z) on an outcome of interest, such as the effect of features of the draft number

Table 16.2: Compliance types.

Type	$D_i(Z_i=0)$	$D_i(Z_i=1)$
Never-taker	0	0
Complier	0	1
Defier	1	0
Always-taker	1	1

on future earnings. In the terminology of instrumental variables, this inquiry is called the "reduced form" or the "intention-to-treat" (ITT) effect. If it's really true that the instrument is randomly assigned by the world, estimation of the reduced form effect is straightforward: we estimate the causal effect of Z on Y using, for example, a difference-in-means estimator. Sometimes, we are also interested in the "first-stage" effect of the instrument on the treatment variable. Similarly, we can target this inquiry by studying the causal effect of Z on D, for example, by using the difference-in-means estimator again.

The trouble comes when we want to leverage the random assignment of the instrument (Z) to learn about the average causal effect of the treatment variable (D) on the outcome (Y), where D is not randomly assigned but rather affected by Z and also other variables. To do so, we need to understand better how the instrument affects whether units are *treated* and then how both affect the outcome of interest. We need to understand "compliance" with the instrument.

We can define the compliance types of units in terms of the combinations of values the potential outcomes of D take on as a function of the values of the instrument Z. The combinations are made up of the value of the treatment if unit i is assigned to control ($D_i(Z_i=0)$) and the value if it is assigned to treatment ($D_i(Z_i=1)$). With a binary instrument and binary treatment, there are four possible potential outcome values and thus four types, enumerated in Table 16.2. These compliance types are sometimes known as "principal strata" (Frangakis and Rubin, 2002).

Never-takers are those who never take the treatment, no matter what the value of the instrument. Compliers take the value of the treatment they are assigned by the instrument. Defiers do exactly the opposite. When the instrument assigns them to take the treatment, defiers refuse it, but if it assigns them not to, they do take treatment. As their name suggests, always-takers take the treatment regardless of the value of the instrument.

With these types in mind, we can now define a new inquiry that we will be able to target with instrumental variables under a special set of assumptions: a "local" average treatment effect (LATE) among compliers. The "local" qualifier indicates that the effect applies only to the specific group of units whose treatment status changes as a result of the instrument. The LATE is $\mathbb{E}[Y_i(D_i = 1) - Y_i(D_i = 0) | D_i(Z_i = 1) > D_i(Z_i = 0)]$. This quantity is the average treatment effect among the compliers. The LATE is different from the ATE because it does not average over the effects for never-takers, always-takers, and defiers, but the ATE does.

We can adopt an instrumental variables answer strategy—using two-stage least squares, for example—to estimate the LATE. Angrist, Imbens, and Rubin (1996) show that this LATE estimand can be identified under the following five assumptions:

1. Exogeneity of the instrument: $Y_i(D_i = 1), Y_i(D_i = 0), D_i(Z_i = 1), D_i(Z_i = 0) \perp\!\!\!\perp Z_i | X_i$. Substantively, this assumption requires that (possibly conditional on observed covariates in X) the instrument is as-if randomly assigned, so it is jointly independent of the treated and untreated potential outcomes as well as the potential values the treatment variable D would take on, depending on the values of the instrument Z. Exogeneity is usually justified on the basis of qualitative knowledge about why as-if random assignment is a reasonable assumption to make. The assumption can be bolstered—but not directly tested—with design checks like whether pretreatment values of the covariates are balanced across the levels of the instrument.

2. Excludability of the instrument: $Y_i(D_i(Z_i), Z_i) = Y_i(D_i(Z_i))$. We can "exclude" the instrument from the potential outcomes function $Y_i()$, so the only relevant argument is the value of the treatment variable. Substantively, this means that Z has exactly no effect on Y except by changing the value of D, or in other words, we are willing to assume "total mediation." Under the exclusion restriction, the effect of the instrumental variable is wholly mediated by the treatment variable. The validity of the exclusion restriction cannot be demonstrated empirically and typically must be asserted on qualitative grounds. Since the reduced form of the instrument can be estimated for many different outcome variables, one piece of evidence that can bolster the exclusion restriction is that the instrument does not affect other plausible causal precedents of the outcome variable. If it does affect other variables that might, in turn, affect the outcome, the exclusion restriction might be an implausible assumption.

3. Noninterference: $Y(D_i(Z_i), D_{-i}, Z_{-i}) = Y(D_i(Z_i))$. Like any non-interference assumption, here we assert that for any particular unit, other units' values of the instrument or the treatment do not affect the outcome.

4. Monotonicity: $D_i(Z_i = 1) \geq D_i(Z_i = 0), \forall_i$. This assumption states that the effect of the instrument on the treatment either is zero or is positive for all units. Monotonicity rules out defiers. Monotonicity is usually quite plausible (it's tough to imagine a person who *would* serve in the military if not drafted but *would not* serve if drafted!), but it's not possible to affirm empirically. An empirical test that demonstrates a positive effect of the instrument on

the treatment for one group but a negative effect for a different group could, however, falsify the monotonicity assumption.

5. Nonzero effect of the instrument on the treatment. If the instrument does not affect the treatment, then it is useless for learning about the effects of the treatment on the outcome, simply because it generates no compliers. If there are no compliers, the LATE itself is undefined.

If all five of these assumptions are met, it can be shown that the inquiry LATE = $\frac{\text{ATE}_{Z \to Y}}{\text{ATE}_{Z \to D}} = \frac{\text{Reduced Form}}{\text{First Stage}}$. It is the quotient of the ATE of the instrument on the outcome divided by the ATE of the instrument on the treatment. This expression underlines the importance of the fifth assumption: if the instrument doesn't affect the treatment, the first stage is equal to zero and the ratio is undefined.

Many of the five assumptions are represented in the DAG in Figure 16.7. The exogeneity of the instrument is represented by the exclusion of a causal effect of U on Z. The omission of an arrow from Z to Y directly invokes the exclusion restriction. Noninterference is typically not directly represented in DAGs. The nonzero effect of the instrument on the treatment is represented by the causal arrow from Z to D.

Moving to the answer strategy, a plug-in estimator of the LATE is the difference-in-means of the outcome according to the instrument divided by the difference-in-means of the treatment according to the instrument. Equivalently, we can use two-stage least squares, which will yield the identical answer as the ratio of the difference-in-means estimates when no covariates are included in the regression.

With the four elements of the design in hand, we declare the model in code, invoking each of the five assumptions in doing so:

Declaration 16.4 Instrumental variables design.

```
declaration_16.4 <-
  declare_model(
    N = 100,
    U = rnorm(N),
    potential_outcomes(D ~ if_else(Z + U > 0, 1, 0),
                       conditions = list(Z = c(0, 1))),
    potential_outcomes(Y ~ 0.1 * D + 0.25 + U,
                       conditions = list(D = c(0, 1))),
    complier = D_Z_1 == 1 & D_Z_0 == 0
  ) +
  declare_inquiry(LATE = mean(Y_D_1 - Y_D_0), subset = complier == TRUE) +
  declare_assignment(Z = complete_ra(N, prob = 0.5)) +
  declare_measurement(D = reveal_outcomes(D ~ Z),
                      Y = reveal_outcomes(Y ~ D)) +
  declare_estimator(Y ~ D | Z, .method = iv_robust, inquiry = "LATE")
```

The exclusion restriction is invoked in omitting a causal direct effect of Z in the Y potential outcomes. We invoke the monotonicity and nonzero effect of Z on D in the D potential outcomes, which have an effect of Z of 1. We invoke the noninterference assumption by excluding effects of the instrument values from other units in the definition of the D and Y potential outcomes. And we invoke the ignorability of Z by randomly assigning it in the assignment step. Of course you can and should vary this design to assess performance when these assumptions are violated.

How can you use this declaration? Many instrumental variables designs involve historical data, such that most remaining design choices are in the answer strategy. Declaring and diagnosing the design can yield insights about how to construct standard errors and confidence intervals and about the implications of analysis procedures in which data-dependent tests are run before fitting instrumental variables models—and only fit if the tests pass. But other instrumental variables papers involve prospective data collection, in which an instrument is identified and outcome data (and possibly instrument and treatment data) are collected anew. In such settings, the design diagnosis and redesign tools are just as useful as in any prospective research design: to help select sampling and measurement procedures, from the sample size to the number of outcomes to be collected. The key in this case is to build in the features of the instrument, the potential outcomes of treatment receipt, and the potential outcomes of the ultimate outcome of interest, and to explore violations of the five assumptions in the model.

16.4.1 Design examples

- Nellis and Siddiqui (2018) instrument for the share of secular legislators with the as-if randomly assigned victory of secularist candidates in close elections. The authors use this instrument to study the causal effect of secular legislators on religious violence in Pakistan.

- Stokes (2016) studies the causal effects of wind turbines on voting for incumbents, instrumenting for the presence or absence of wind turbines with plausibly exogenous differences in wind speeds across localities.

16.5 Regression Discontinuity Designs

> We declare a design in which the assignment of a treatment is determined by whether a characteristic of a unit exceeds a certain threshold value. We demonstrate through diagnosis the bias-variance trade-off at the heart of the choice of answer strategies that target the local average treatment effect inquiry, defined right at the cutoff.

Regression discontinuity designs exploit substantive knowledge that treatment is assigned in a particular way: everyone above a threshold is assigned to treatment and everyone below it is not. Even though researchers do not control the assignment, substantive knowledge about the threshold serves as a basis for a strong causal identification claim.

Thistlewhite and Campbell introduced the regression discontinuity design in the 1960s to study the impact of scholarships on academic success (Thistlethwaite and Campbell, 1960). Their insight was that students with a test score just above a scholarship cutoff were plausibly comparable to students whose scores were just below the cutoff, so any differences in future academic success could be attributed to the scholarship itself.

Just like instrumental variables, regression discontinuity designs identify a local average treatment effect: in this case, the average effect of treatment local to the cutoff. The main trouble with the design is the vanishing amount of data available as we approach the cutoff, so any answer strategy needs to use data that is some distance away from the cutoff. The further away from the cutoff we move, the larger the threat of bias, because units become less and less similar.

Regression discontinuity designs have four components: a running variable X, a cutoff, a treatment variable D, and an outcome Y. The cutoff determines which units are treated, depending on the value of the running variable. If the goal is to study the causal effects of winning an election on the likelihood of future elections, the running variable might be the Democratic party's margin of victory at time $t-1$, the treatment D might be whether the Democratic party won the election in time $t-1$, outcome Y might be the Democratic vote margin at time t.

A major assumption required for the regression discontinuity design is that the conditional expectation functions—functions that define the expected value of the outcome at every level of the running variable—for both treatment and control potential outcomes are continuous at the cutoff.[2]

The regression discontinuity design is closely related to the selection-on-observables design in that we exploit precise knowledge of the assignment mechanism. In Figure 16.8, we illustrate the DAG for the RD design, which includes a treatment with a known assignment mechanism (that units with $X >$ cutoff are treated and the others are not). The running variable X is a common cause both of treatment and the outcome, and so must be adjusted for (indicated by the dashed box) in order to identify the effect of treatment on the outcome and avoid confounding bias.

Figure 16.9 illustrates the major features of the model for the regression discontinuity using simulated data. The untreated units (blue points) are plotted to the left of the cutoff (vertical line), and the treated units (red points) are plotted to the right. The true conditional expectation functions for both the treated and untreated potential outcomes are displayed as colored lines, dashed where they are unobservable, and solid where they are observable.

---

[2] An alternative motivation for some designs that do not rely on continuity at the cutoff is called "local randomization."

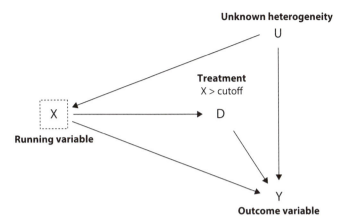

Figure 16.8: Directed acyclic graph for the regression discontinuity design.

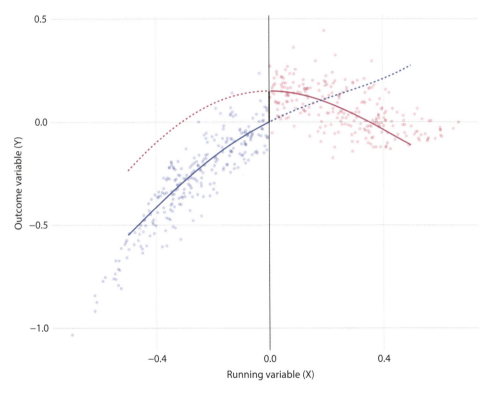

Figure 16.9: Data from a regression discontinuity design. On the x-axis is the running variable, which defines the cutoff between control (here, below 0 on the running variable) and treatment (above 0). The outcome Y is on the y-axis. We illustrate smooth potential outcomes by showing the observed data curve (solid) and the counterfactual potential outcome (dashed).

The inquiry in a regression discontinuity design is the effect of the treatment exactly at the cutoff. Formally, it is the difference in the conditional expectation functions of the control and treatment potential outcomes when the running variable is exactly zero. The thicker black vertical line segment in the plot shows this difference.

The data strategy is to collect the outcome data for all units within an interval (bandwidth) around the cutoff. The choice of bandwidth involves a trade-off between bias and variance. The wider we make the bandwidth, the more data we have, and thus the more precision we may be able to achieve. However, the claim of causal identification comes from the comparability of units *just* above and *just* below the threshold. Units far from the cutoff are less likely to be comparable: at a minimum they differ in their values of the running variable and if that is correlated with other unobserved heterogeneity then they may differ in that too. Thus, the more units we compare further from the threshold, the more likely we are to induce bias in our estimates of the treatment effect. The ultimate bandwidth chosen for analysis is a function of the data collected in the data strategy and the bandwidth chosen in the answer strategy, which is often the output of an automated process.

Declaration 16.5 Regression discontinuity design.

```
library(rdss) # for helper functions
library(rdrobust)

cutoff <- 0.5
control <- function(X) {
  as.vector(poly(X, 4, raw = TRUE) %*% c(.7, -.8, .5, 1))}
treatment <- function(X) {
  as.vector(poly(X, 4, raw = TRUE) %*% c(0, -1.5, .5, .8)) + .15}

declaration_16.5 <-
  declare_model(
    N = 500,
    U = rnorm(N, 0, 0.1),
    X = runif(N, 0, 1) + U - cutoff,
    D = 1 * (X > 0),
    Y_D_0 = control(X) + U,
    Y_D_1 = treatment(X) + U
  ) +
  declare_inquiry(LATE = treatment(0.5) - control(0.5)) +
  declare_measurement(Y = reveal_outcomes(Y ~ D)) +
  declare_estimator(
    Y, X, c = 0,
    term = "Bias-Corrected",
    .method = rdrobust_helper,
    inquiry = "LATE",
    label = "optimal"
  )
```

Regression discontinuity answer strategies approximate the treated and untreated conditional expectation functions to the left and right of the cutoff. The choice of

16.5 Regression Discontinuity Designs

answer strategy involves two key choices: the bandwidth of data around the threshold that is used for estimation, and the model used to fit that data. We declare the local polynomial regression discontinuity estimator with the robust bias-corrected inference procedures described in Calonico, Cattaneo and Titiunik (2014), which fits a nonparametric model to the data and chooses an optimal bandwidth that minimizes bias. This robust estimator is now widely used in practice, because it navigates the bias-variance trade-off in selecting bandwidths and statistical model specifications in a data-driven manner. The procedure also obviates the need for researchers to select these parameters themselves.

Figure 16.10 illustrates the trade-off in bandwidth selection for a one-degree polynomial (linear interaction). We see the bias-variance trade-off directly. The bias increases the wider the bandwidth and the more we are relying on data further from the threshold, whereas the variance (here, the standard deviation of the estimates) gets smaller the more we add data by widening the bandwidth.

Declaration 16.6 Regression discontinuity designs with varying bandwidths.

```
declaration_16.6 <-
  declaration_16.5 +
  declare_estimator(
    Y ~ X * D,
    subset = X > -1*bandwidth & X < bandwidth,
    .method = lm_robust,
    inquiry = "LATE",
    label = "linear"
  )
```

Diagnosis 16.5 Regression discontinuity diagnosis across varying bandwidths

```
diagnosis_16.5 <-
  declaration_16.6 |>
  redesign(bandwidth = seq(from = 0.05, to = 0.5, by = 0.05)) |>
  diagnose_designs
```

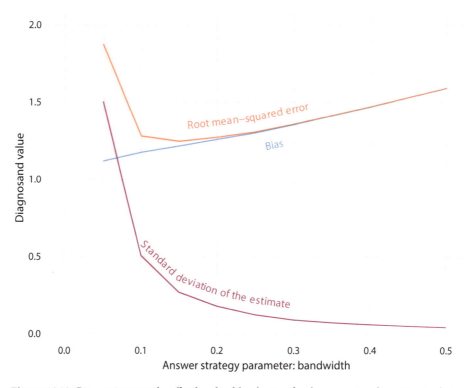

Figure 16.10: Bias-variance trade-off in bandwidth selection for the regression discontinuity design.

16.5.1 Design examples

- Kirkland (2021) uses a regression discontinuity design to estimate the effect of just electing a mayor with a business background on infrastructure and redistribution spending.

- Carnegie and Samii (2019) uses a regression discontinuity design to compare countries that are just-eligible for lender status to those that are just-ineligible on human rights and democracy policies.

CHAPTER 17

Experimental : Descriptive

We use experiments to target descriptive inquiries when units do not naturally reveal a characteristic that we want to measure. Instead, we must assign units into more than one condition that we can use to figure out what characteristic the units hold. Each experiment we discuss is simply another kind of measurement tool (albeit often a very useful one!). Importantly, the fact that we are using an experiment does not switch our inquiry from descriptive to causal. In each entry in this chapter, we define the inquiry as a summary of unit characteristics in the population, and not as a function of potential outcomes.

We study four kinds of experiments for descriptive inference. Audit experiments estimate the fraction of units that discriminate. List experiments estimate the prevalence rate of holding a sensitive characteristic such as drug use or support for an insurgent group. Conjoint experiments measure (aggregations of) preferences over choices such as candidates for election. Experimental behavioral games measure trust.

We need audit experiments because we typically cannot identify whether someone discriminates naturally by measuring a single interaction with another person. We need to see how that person interacts with multiple others, some that they might discriminate against and some not, and then compare their behaviors. We also cannot ask people if they discriminate in a survey and expect useful answers: people typically do not think of themselves as discriminatory. Trust games are motivated by the same idea: people may think of themselves as more trusting than they are. The list experiment is motivated by a related concern: people may not answer sensitive questions when they think others can learn their answer and might punish them socially or physically for giving a sensitive answer. If we measured these sensitive characteristics by asking, people might misreport their answers, so we use the experiment to ask in a way that provides plausible deniability (but still allows us to estimate the prevalence rate). Conjoint experiments address the problem that it is difficult to learn about multidimensional preferences over choices by asking about a single choice. In each case, the experiment allows us to randomize people into multiple conditions that let us figure out a descriptive characteristic we could not otherwise measure.

17.1 Audit Experiments

> We declare an audit experiment design in which the name of a citizen requesting service from government is randomized to be Latino-sounding or White-sounding and the government official either responds or does not. We then declare an augmented design in which a treatment to reduce discrimination is cross-randomized. The declaration highlights the behavioral assumptions that must be made to interpret the estimated treatment effect of the name as discrimination, and the diagnosis of the anti-discrimination treatment highlights how large a sample would be required for high power.

Audit experiments are used to measure discrimination against one group in favor of another group. The design is used commonly to measure whether job applications that are otherwise similar but come from candidates from different genders, races, or social backgrounds receive the same rate of job interview invitations. The same approach has been applied to a very wide range of settings, including education, housing, and requests to politicians.

The audit experiment design we'll explore in this chapter has data and answer strategies that are identical to the two-arm trial for causal inference described in Section 18.1. The difference between an audit study and the typical randomized experiment lies in the model and inquiry. In a two-arm trial, a common (causal) inquiry is the average difference between the treated and untreated potential outcomes, the ATE. In an audit experiment, by contrast, the inquiry is descriptive: what is the fraction of the sample that discriminates?

We can hear our colleagues objecting now—the inquiry in an audit study can of course be conceived of as causal! It's the average effect of signaling membership in one social group on a resume versus signaling membership in another. We agree, of course, that this interpretation is possible and technically correct. But when we think of the inquiry as descriptive, we usefully put our focus on the behaviors of people who do and do not discriminate.

Consider White, Nathan, and Faller (2015), which seeks to measure discrimination against Latinos by election officials through assessing whether election officials respond to emailed requests for information from putatively Latino or White voters. We imagine three types of election officials: those who would always respond to the request (regardless of the emailer's ethnicity), those who would never respond to the request (again regardless of the emailer's ethnicity), and officials who discriminate against Latinos. Here, discriminators are defined by their behavior: they would respond to the White voter but not to the Latino voter. These three types are given in Table 17.1.

Our descriptive inquiry is the fraction of the sample that discriminates: $\mathbb{E}[\text{Type}_i =$ Anti Latino discriminator]. Under the behavioral assumptions about these three

Table 17.1: Audit experiment response types.

Type	$Y_i(Z_i = \text{White})$	$Y_i(Z_i = \text{Latino})$
Always-responder	1	1
Anti-Latino discriminator	1	0
Never-responder	0	0

types enumerated in Table 17.1 (whether these types would respond depending on the ethnicity of the sender), $\mathbb{E}[\text{Type}_i = \text{Anti Latino discriminator}] = \mathbb{E}[Y_i(Z_i = \text{White}) - Y_i(Z_i = \text{Latino})]$. Because this is the expected difference between two outcomes, we can use a randomized experiment that randomizes ethnicity to measure this descriptive quantity. In the data strategy, we randomly sample from the $Y_i(Z_i = \text{White})$'s and from the $Y_i(Z_i = \text{Latino})$'s, then in the answer strategy, we take a difference-in-means, generating an estimate of the fraction of the sample that discriminates.

Some finer points about these behavioral assumptions. First, we assume that always-responders and never-responders do not engage in discrimination. It could be that some never-responders don't respond to Latino voters out of racial animus, but do not respond to White voters out of laziness. In this model, such officials would be not be classified as anti-Latino discriminators by assumption. Second, we assume that there are no anti-White discriminators. If there were, then the difference-in-means would not be unbiased for the fraction of anti-Latino discriminators. Instead, it would be unbiased for "net" discrimination, i.e., how much more election officials discriminate against Latinos versus how much they discriminate against Whites. Anti-Latino discrimination and net discrimination are theoretically separate inquiries. To assess whether the no anti-White discriminators assumption is appropriate in a given setting, substantive knowledge is needed. It is not an assumption that can be directly tested empirically (unless of course *most* discrimination goes in this direction).

Declaration 17.1 connects the behavioral assumptions we make about subjects to the randomized experiment we use to infer the value of a descriptive quantity. Only never-responders fail to respond to the White request while only always-responders respond to the Latino request. The inquiry is the proportion of the sample that is an anti-Latino discriminator. The data strategy involves randomly assigning the putative ethnicity of the voter making the request and recording whether it was responded to. The answer strategy compares average response rates by randomly assigned group.

Declaration 17.1 Audit experiment design.

```
declaration_17.1 <-
  declare_model(
```

```r
    N = 500,
    type = sample(
      size = N,
      replace = TRUE,
      x = c("Always-responder",
            "Anti-Latino discriminator",
            "Never-responder"),
      prob = c(0.30, 0.05, 0.65)
    ),
    # Behavioral assumptions represented here:
    Y_Z_white = if_else(type == "Never-Responder", 0, 1),
    Y_Z_latino = if_else(type == "Always-Responder", 1, 0)
  ) +
  declare_inquiry(
    anti_latino_discrimination = mean(type == "Anti-Latino discriminator")
  ) +
  declare_assignment(Z = complete_ra(
    N, conditions = c("latino", "white"))) +
  declare_measurement(Y = reveal_outcomes(Y ~ Z)) +
  declare_estimator(Y ~ Z, inquiry = "anti_latino_discrimination")
```

17.1.1 Intervening to decrease discrimination

Butler and Crabtree (2017) prompt researchers to "move beyond measurement" in audit studies. Under the model assumptions in the design, audit experiments measure the level of discrimination, but of course they do not do anything to reduce it. To move beyond measurement, we intervene in the world to reduce discrimination in a treatment group but not in a control group, then measure the level of discrimination in both arms using the audit experiment technology.

This two-stage design is illustrated in Declaration 17.2. The first half of the design is about causal inference: we want to learn about the effect of the intervention on discrimination. The second half of the design is about descriptive inference—*within each treatment arm*. We incorporate both stages of the design in the answer strategy, in which the coefficient on the interaction of the intervention indicator with the audit indicator is our estimator of the effect on discrimination.

Declaration 17.2 Audit experiment intervention study design.

```r
declaration_17.2 <-
  # This part of the design is about causal inference
  declare_model(
    N = 5000,
    type_D_0 = sample(
      size = N,
      replace = TRUE,
      x = c("Always-Responder",
            "Anti-Latino Discriminator",
            "Never-Responder"),
      prob = c(0.30, 0.05, 0.65)
    ),
    type_tau_i = rbinom(N, 1, 0.5),
    type_D_1 = if_else(
      type_D_0 == "Anti-Latino Discriminator" &
```

17.1 Audit Experiments

```
    type_tau_i == 1,
    "Always-Responder",
    type_D_0
  )
) +
declare_inquiry(
  ATE = mean((type_D_1 == "Anti-Latino Discriminator") -
             (type_D_0 == "Anti-Latino Discriminator"))
) +
declare_assignment(D = complete_ra(N)) +
declare_measurement(type = reveal_outcomes(type ~ D)) +
# This part is about descriptive inference in each condition!
declare_model(
  Y_Z_white = if_else(type == "Never-Responder", 0, 1),
  Y_Z_latino = if_else(type == "Always-Responder", 1, 0)
) +
declare_assignment(
  Z = complete_ra(N, conditions = c("latino", "white"))) +
declare_measurement(Y = reveal_outcomes(Y ~ Z)) +
declare_estimator(Y ~ Z * D, term = "Zwhite:D", inquiry = "ATE")
```

Even at 5,000 subjects, the power to detect the effect of the intervention is quite poor, at approximately 15%. This low power stems from the small treatment effect (reducing discrimination by 50% from 5.0% to 2.5%) and from the noisy measurement strategy.

Diagnosis 17.1 Audit experiment intervention study diagnosis

```
diagnosis_17.1 <- diagnose_design(declaration_17.2)
```

Table 17.2: Audit experiment power analysis.

power	se(power)	n_sims
0.15	0.01	2000

17.1.2 Avoiding posttreatment bias

Coppock (2019) discusses how to avoid posttreatment bias when studying how the audit treatment affects the "quality" of responses, such as the tone of an email or the enthusiasm of the hiring callback. Here our inquiry is effect of the sender type on tone rather than a descriptive inquiry about the fraction of receivers who discriminate. Interestingly, this causal effect is not defined among the discriminators, because they never send emails to Latinos, so those emails never have a tone. The tone inquiry is defined only among always-responders, but estimating this effect without bias is tricky.

17.1.3 Design examples

- Birkelund et al. (2022) conduct harmonized audit experiments in six countries to measure employment discrimination on the basis of gender.

- Fang, Guess, and Humphreys (2019) "move beyond measurement" by randomizing a New York City government intervention designed to stop housing discrimination, which was then measured by an audit study design.

17.2 List Experiments

> We declare a list experiment design, highlighting that the inquiry is a descriptive one despite the use of an experiment. We then declare a design comparing the list experiment to direct questioning in estimating the prevalence of a sensitive item, and clarify when one survey technology is preferred to the other as a function of sensitivity bias levels and sample size.

Sometimes, subjects might not tell the truth about certain attitudes or behaviors when asked directly. Responses may be affected by sensitivity bias, or the tendency of survey subjects to misreport their answers for fear of negative repercussions if some individual or group learns their true response (Blair, Coppock, and Moor, 2020). In such cases, standard survey estimates based on direct questions will be biased. One class of solutions to this problem is to obscure individual responses, providing protection from social or legal pressures. When we obscure responses systematically through an experiment, we can often still identify average quantities of interest. One such design is the list experiment (introduced in Miller, 1984), which asks respondents for the count of the number of "yes" responses to a series of questions including the sensitive item, rather than for a yes or no answer on the sensitive item itself. List experiments give subjects cover by aggregating their answer to the sensitive item with responses to other questions.

For example, Creighton and Jamal (2015) study preferences for religious discrimination in immigration policy among Americans. They worried that direct measures of Americans' willingness to grant citizenship to Muslims would be distorted by sensitivity bias, so they turned to a list experiment. Subjects in the control and

Table 17.3: Creighton and Jamal (2015) list experiment conditions.

Control	Treatment
The federal government increasing assistance to the poor.	The federal government increasing assistance to the poor.
Professional athletes making millions of dollars per year.	Professional athletes making millions of dollars per year.
Large corporations polluting the environment.	Large corporations polluting the environment.
	Granting citizenship to a legal immigrant who is Muslim.

treatment groups were asked: "Below you will read [three/four] things that sometimes people oppose or are against. After you read all [three/four], just tell us HOW MANY of them you OPPOSE. We don't want to know which ones, just HOW MANY."

The treatment group averaged 2.123 items while the control group averaged 1.904 items, for a difference-in-means estimate of 0.219. Under the usual assumptions of randomized experiments, the difference-in-means is an unbiased estimator for the average treatment effect of *being asked* to respond to the treated list versus the control list. But our (descriptive) inquiry is the proportion of people who would grant citizenship to a legal immigrant who is Muslim.

For the difference-in-means to be an unbiased estimator for that inquiry, we invoke two additional assumptions (Imai, 2011):

- **No design effects**: The count of "yes" responses to the control items is the same whether a respondent is assigned to the treatment or control group.

- **No liars**: Subjects with the sensitive trait truthfully increment their count when assigned to the treatment group.

Under these two extra assumptions, the list experimental estimate of the prevalence of opposition to granting Muslim immigrants citizenship is 21.9%.

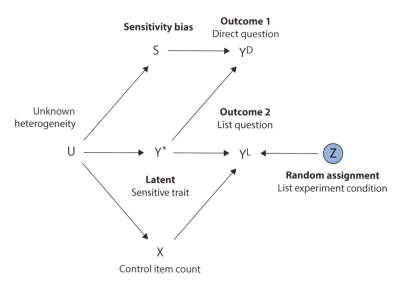

Figure 17.1: Directed acyclic graph for the list experiment.

Figure 17.1 represents the list experimental design. The no liars assumption is represented by the lack of an edge from sensitivity bias S to the list experiment outcome Y^L. The no design effects assumption is not represented on the DAG.

Declaration 17.3 describes a list experimental design. The model includes subjects' true attitude (`Y_star`) and whether or not their direct question answers are contaminated by sensitivity bias (`S`). These two variables combine to determine how subjects will respond when asked directly about support for the policy. The potential outcomes model combines three types of information to determine how subjects will respond to the list experiment: their responses to the three control items (`control_count`), their true attitude (`Y_star`), and whether they are assigned to see the treatment or the control list (`Z`). Our definition of the potential outcomes embeds the no liars and no design effects assumptions.

The inquiry is the prevalence rate of the sensitive item. In the data strategy, we randomly assign 50% of our 500 subjects to treatment and the remainder to control. In the survey, we ask subjects the list experiment question (`Y_list`). Our answer strategy estimates the prevalence rate by calculating the difference-in-means in the list outcome between treatment and control.

Declaration 17.3 List experiment design.

```
declaration_17.3 <-
  declare_model(
    N = 500,
    control_count = rbinom(N, size = 3, prob = 0.5),
    Y_star = rbinom(N, size = 1, prob = 0.3),
    potential_outcomes(Y_list ~ Y_star * Z + control_count)
  ) +
  declare_inquiry(prevalence_rate = mean(Y_star)) +
  declare_assignment(Z = complete_ra(N)) +
  declare_measurement(Y_list = reveal_outcomes(Y_list ~ Z)) +
  declare_estimator(Y_list ~ Z, .method = difference_in_means,
                    inquiry = "prevalence_rate")
```

Diagnosis 17.2 List experiment diagnosis

```
diagnosands <- declare_diagnosands(
  bias = mean(estimate - estimand),
  mean_CI_width = mean(conf.high - conf.low)
)
diagnosis_17.2 <- diagnose_design(declaration_17.3,
                                  diagnosands = diagnosands)
```

Table 17.4: Diagnosis of a list experiment.

Bias	Mean CI width
−0.002	0.325

We see in the diagnosis that the list experiment generates unbiased estimates of the prevalence rate, but it is extremely imprecise: the average width of the confidence

17.2 List Experiments

interval is enormous at 33 percentage points. If the estimate from a list experiment using this design is 25%, this would imply a confidence interval ranging from about 9% to 41% holding the sensitive item, ranging from rare to common and thus providing only a limited amount of information about the prevalence rate.

The diagnosis above shows that the list experiment (under its assumptions) is unbiased but has high variance. In the presence of sensitivity bias, direct questions are biased, but has much lower variance. The choice between these two technologies therefore amounts to a bias-variance trade-off (see Blair, Coppock and Moor, 2020, for more on this point). Declaration 17.3 wraps up both approaches in one design so we can compare them.

Declaration 17.4 Comparing list experiments with direct questions.

```r
declaration_17.4 <-
  declare_model(
    N = N,
    U = rnorm(N),
    control_count = rbinom(N, size = 3, prob = 0.5),
    Y_star = rbinom(N, size = 1, prob = 0.3),
    W = case_when(
      Y_star == 0 ~ 0L,
      Y_star == 1 ~ rbinom(N, size = 1, prob = proportion_hiding)
    ),
    potential_outcomes(Y_list ~ Y_star * Z + control_count)
  ) +
  declare_inquiry(prevalence_rate = mean(Y_star)) +
  declare_assignment(Z = complete_ra(N)) +
  declare_measurement(Y_list = reveal_outcomes(Y_list ~ Z),
                      Y_direct = Y_star - W) +
  declare_estimator(Y_list ~ Z,
                    inquiry = "prevalence_rate", label = "list") +
  declare_estimator(Y_direct ~ 1,
                    inquiry = "prevalence_rate", label = "direct")
```

Diagnosis 17.3 Comparison of list experiment and direct questions diagnosis

Diagnosing this design, we see that at low levels of sensitivity bias and low sample sizes, the direct question is preferred on RMSE grounds. This is because though the direct question is biased for the prevalence rate in the presence of any sensitivity bias (positive `proportion_hiding`), it is much more precise than the list experiment. When we have a large sample size, then we begin to prefer the list experiment for its low bias. At high levels of sensitivity bias, we prefer the list experiment on RMSE grounds despite its inefficiency, because bias will be so large.

```r
diagnosis_17.3 <-
  declaration_17.4 |>
  redesign(proportion_hiding = seq(from = 0, to = 0.3, by = 0.1),
           N = seq(from = 500, to = 2500, by = 500)) |>
  diagnose_design()
```

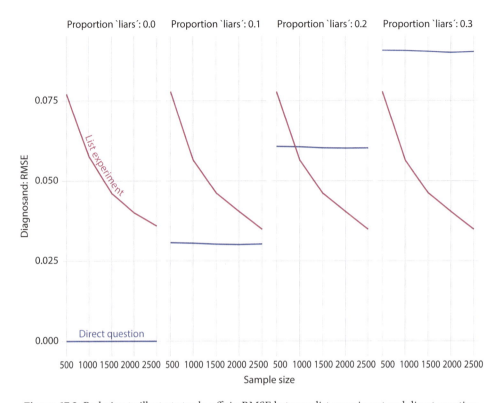

Figure 17.2: Redesign to illustrate trade-offs in RMSE between list experiment and direct question.

17.2.1 Design Examples

- Coppock (2017) compares direct question and list experimental estimates of support for Donald Trump during the 2016 election, finding no evidence for "shy" Trump supporters who misreport their support for Trump for fear of being perceived as racist or sexist by enumerators.

- Cruz (2019) uses a list experiment to estimate the rate of vote buying in the Philippines, though comparison to direct question estimates yields no evidence of sensitivity bias.

17.3 Conjoint Experiments

> We declare a forced-choice conjoint experiment design in which respondents choose one of two profiles in three sets of tasks, each with three attributes. The design highlights the complexity of defining the inquiries for conjoints, and their lower power at common sample sizes.

Conjoint survey experiments have become hugely popular in political science and beyond for describing multidimensional preferences over profiles (Hainmueller, Hopkins, and Yamamoto 2014). The designs have been used to study preferences over political candidates, types of immigrants to admit, neighborhoods to live in, policies to select, and many more questions. Conjoint experiments come in two basic varieties: the single profile design and the forced-choice design. Throughout this chapter, we'll discuss these studies in the context of hypothetical candidate experiments, in which candidates are described in terms of a number of attributes each of which can take on multiple values, known as levels. In the single profile design, subjects are asked to rate one profile at a time using, for example, a 1–7 support scale. In a forced-choice conjoint experiment, subjects are shown two profiles at a time, then asked to make a binary choice between them. Forced choice conjoint experiments are especially useful for studying electoral behavior because they closely mirror the real-world behavior of choosing between two candidates at the ballot box. A similar logic applies to purchasing behavior when consumers have to choose one product over another. Occasionally, forced-choice conjoint experiments are applied even when no real-world analogue for the binary choice exists. For example, we rarely face a binary choice between two immigrants or between two refugees.

We take the unorthodox position that conjoint experiments target descriptive, rather than casual, inquiries. The reason can be most easily seen in the single profile design case. For concreteness, imagine subjects are presented with one profile at a time that describes the age (young, middle-aged, old), gender (woman, man), and employment sector (public, private) of a candidate for office and are asked to rate their support for the candidate on a 1–7 Likert scale. This set of attributes and levels generates $2 * 3 * 2 = 12$ possible profiles. We *could* ask subjects to rate all 12, but we typically ask them instead to rate only a random subset. If our goal were to estimate the average ratings of each of the 12 profiles, clearly we would be targeting descriptive quantities.

The most common inquiry in conjoint experimentation is the Average Marginal Component Effect or AMCE, which summarizes the average difference in preferences between two levels of one attribute, averaging over all of the levels of the other attributes. The AMCE for gender, for example, considers the average difference in preference for women candidates versus men candidates among young candidates who work in the private sector, among middle-aged candidates who work in the public sector, and so on for all six combinations. The overall AMCE is a weighted average of all six of these average preference differences, where the weights are given by the relative frequency of each type of candidate. Despite its name, we think of the AMCE as a descriptive quantity. We of course agree there is a sense in which the AMCE is a causal quantity, since it is the average effect on preferences of describing a hypothetical candidate as a man or a woman. But we can see this quantity as descriptive if we just imagine asking subjects about both candidates and describing the difference in their preferences. We then could aggregate these descriptive differences across profiles. The only reason we don't ask about all possible profiles is that there are far too many to get through in a typical survey, so we ask subjects about a random subset.

Just like single-profile conjoints, forced-choice conjoints also target descriptive inquiries, but the inquiry is one step removed from raw preferences over profiles. Instead, we aim to describe the fraction of pairwise contests that a profile would win, averaging over all subjects in the experiment. That is, we aim to describe a profile's average win rate. We can further describe the differences in the average win rate across profiles, for example, among young candidates who work in the private sector, what is the average difference in win rates for women versus men? Just as in the single profile case, the AMCE is a weighted average of these differences, weighted by the relative frequency of each type of candidate.

Here, again, we *could* think of the AMCE as a causal effect, i.e., the average effect of describing a profile as a woman versus a man. But we can also imagine asking subjects to consider all $12 * 12 = 144$ possible pairwise contests, then using those binary choices to fully describe subject preferences over contests. A forced-choice conjoint asks subjects to rate just a random subset of those contests, since asking about all of them would be impractical.

One final wrinkle about the AMCE inquiries, in both the single-profile and forced-choice cases: they are "data-strategy-dependent" inquiries in the sense that AMCEs average over the distribution of the other profile attributes, and that distribution is controlled by the researcher.[1] The AMCE of gender for profiles that do not include partisanship is different from the AMCE of gender for profiles that include partisanship due to masking (discussed below). Further, and more subtly, the AMCE of gender for profiles that are 75% public sector and 25% private sector is different from the AMCE of gender for profiles that are 50% public sector and 50% private sector, because those relative frequencies are part of the very definition of the inquiry. For contrast, consider a vignette-style hypothetical candidate experiment in which all or most of the other candidate features are fixed, save gender. In that design, we estimate an ATE of gender under only one set of conditions, but in the conjoint design, the AMCE averages over ATEs under many sets of conditions. There is a great benefit in doing so: our inferences are not specific to that one set of conditions. But it also means that what conditions inferences depends crucially on researcher choices about which characteristics are chosen and the randomization scheme.

The data strategy for conjoints, then, requires making these four choices, in addition to the usual measurement, sampling, and assignment concerns:

1. Which attributes to include in the profiles,
2. Which levels to include in each attribute (and in what proportion),

---

[1] The AMCE need not be data-dependent. We could write down one distribution of profiles in the model to establish the AMCE inquiry, then randomly sample the profiles shown to respondents for a different distribution. This would be a headache, because the estimator would need to be reweighted to successfully target the AMCE inquiry. Better to bring the data strategy in line with the model in the first place.

3. How many profiles subjects are asked to rate at a time, and

4. How many sets of profiles subjects are asked to rate in total.

The right set of attributes is governed by the "masking/satisficing" trade-off (Bansak et al., 2021). If we don't include an important attribute (like partisanship in a candidate choice experiment), we're worried that subjects will partially infer partisanship from other attributes (like race or gender). If so, partisanship is "masked," and the estimates for the effects of race or gender will be biased by these "omitted variables." But if we include too many attributes in order to avoid masking, we may induce "satisficing" among subjects, whereby they only take in a little bit of information, enough to make a "good enough" choice among the candidates.

The right set of levels to include is a tricky choice. We want to include all of the most important levels, but every additional level harms statistical precision. If an attribute has three levels, it's like we're conducting a three-arm trial, so we'll want to have enough subjects for each arm. The more levels, the lower the precision.

How many profiles to rate at the same time is also tricky. Our point of view is that this choice should be guided by the real-world analogue of the survey task. If we're learning about binary choices between options in the real world, then the forced-choice, paired design makes good sense. If we're learning about preferences over many possibilities, the single profile design may be more appropriate. That said, the paired design can yield precision gains over the single profile design in the sense that subjects rate two profiles at the same time, so we effectively generate twice as many observations for perhaps less than twice as much cognitive effort.

Finally, the right number of choice tasks usually depends on the survey budget. We can always add more conjoint tasks and the only cost is the opportunity cost of asking a different question of the survey that may serve another scientific purpose. If we're worried that respondents will get bored with the task, we can always throw out profile pairs that come later in the survey. Bansak et al. (2021) suggest that you can ask many tasks without much loss of data quality.

The declaration of conjoint experiments is complex, so we provide a series of helper functions specifically for forced-choice conjoint design in the `rdss` companion software package.

We begin by establishing the number of subjects and the number of tasks they will accomplish. We then establish the attributes and their levels (this design assumes complete random assignment of all attributes with equal probabilities). Finally, we describe a utility function that governs subject preferences. This function can be simple, as we have it here, or it can be complex, building in differences in preferences by subject type or other details.

In Declaration 17.5, we imagine a forced-choice candidate choice conjoint in which the attributes are gender, party, and region. We sample 500 subjects and ask them to complete three tasks each.

Declaration 17.5 Conjoint experiment design.

```
library(rdss) # for helper functions
library(cjoint)

# Design features
N_subjects <- 500
N_tasks <- 3

# Attributes and levels
levels_list =
  list(
    gender = c("Man", "Woman"),
    party = c("Left", "Right"),
    region = c("North", "South", "East", "West")
  )

# Conjectured utility function
conjoint_utility <-
  function(data){
    data |>
      mutate(
        U = 0.25*(gender == "Woman")*(region %in% c("North", "East")) +
          0.5*(party == "Right")*(region %in% c("North", "South")) +
          uij)
  }

declaration_17.5 <-
  declare_model(
    subject = add_level(N = N_subjects),
    task = add_level(N = N_tasks, task = 1:N_tasks),
    profile = add_level(
      N = 2,
      profile = 1:2,
      uij = rnorm(N, sd = 1)
    )
  ) +
  declare_inquiry(handler = conjoint_inquiries,
                  levels_list = levels_list,
                  utility_fn = conjoint_utility) +
  declare_assignment(handler = conjoint_assignment,
                     levels_list = levels_list) +
  declare_measurement(handler = conjoint_measurement,
                      utility_fn = conjoint_utility) +
  declare_estimator(choice ~ gender + party + region,
                    respondent.id = "subject",
                    .method = amce)
```

Diagnosis 17.4 Diagnosis of the conjoint experiment design

```
diagnosis_17.4 <- diagnose_design(declaration_17.4)
```

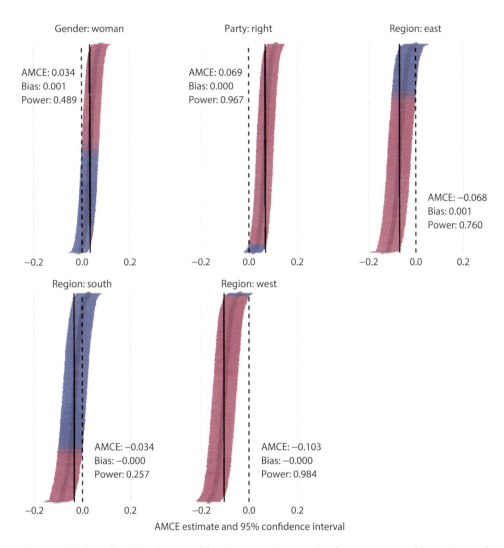

Figure 17.3: Sampling Distribution of five AMCE estimators. Bands are constructed by sorting and stacking the confidence intervals generated from many simulations. Statistical significance of estimates indicated by color.

Figure 17.3 shows the sampling distribution of the five AMCE estimators. All five are unbiased, but with only 500 subjects evaluating three pairs of candidates, the power for the smaller AMCEs is less than ideal.

17.3.1 Design examples

- Kao and Revkin (2022) uses a conjoint experiment in an Iraqi city that was controlled by the Islamic State to understand residents' preferences over punishments for civilian collaborators, depending on the type of collaboration they engaged in.

- Aguilar, Cunow, and Desposato (2015) conduct a candidate choice experiment to measure the difference in how voters evaluate candidates depending on whether they are identified as a man or a woman in Brazil.

17.4 Behavioral Games

> We declare a trust game and explore the implications of using deception in the game setup. The diagnosis highlights how the choices in the first round of a game, which are not randomized, affect our ability to study the behaviors of the player in the second round without bias.

Behavioral games are often used to study difficult-to-measure characteristics of subjects like risk attitudes, altruism, prejudice, and trust. The approach involves using labs or other mechanisms to control contexts. A high level of control brings two distinct benefits. First, it can eliminate noise: we obtain estimates under a particular well-defined set of conditions rather than estimates generated from averaging over a range of possibly unknown conditions. Second, more subtly, it can prevent various forms of confounding. For instance, outside the lab we might observe how people act when they work on tasks with an out-group member. But we only observe the responses among those that *do* work with out-group members, not among those that do not. By studying behaviors in a controlled setting we can see how people *would* react when put into particular situations.

The approach holds enormous value. But, as highlighted by Green and Tusicisny (2012), it also introduces many subtle design choices. Many of these can be revealed through declaration and diagnosis.

We illustrate using the "trust" game, in which we specify three common inquiries and use a standard design in Declaration 17.6. The design is successful at generating unbiased estimates of the first inquiry but runs into problems with the other two.

The trust game has been implemented hundreds of times to understand levels and correlates of social trust. Following the meta-analysis given in Johnson and Mislin (2011) we consider a game in which one player (Player 1, the "trustor") can invest some share of $1. Whatever is invested is then doubled. A second player (Player 2, "the trustee") can then decide what share of the doubled amount to keep for themselves and what share to return to the trustor.

As described by Johnson and Mislin (2011), "trust" is commonly measured by the share given and "trustworthiness" is measured by the share returned. With the *MIDA* framework in mind, we will be more specific and define the inquiry independently of the measurement. We define "trust" as the share that *would* be invested by a trustor when confronted with a random trustee, whereas "trustworthiness" is the average share that *would* be returned over a range of possible investments.

17.4 Behavioral Games

To motivate M we assume the following decision-making model. We assume that each person i seeks to maximize a weighted average of logged payoffs:

$$u_i = (1-a_i)\log(\pi_i) + a_i \log(\pi_{-i}),$$

where π_i, π_{-i} denotes the monetary payoffs to $i, -i$ and a_i ("altruism") captures the weight players place on the (logged) payoffs of other players.

Let x denote the amount sent by the trustor from the endowment 1.

The trustee then maximizes:

$$u_2 = (1-a_2)\log((1-\lambda)2x) + a_2 \log((1-x) + \lambda 2x),$$

where λ denotes the share of $2x$ that the trustee returns. Maximizing with respect to λ yields:

$$\lambda = a_2 + (1-a_2)\frac{x-1}{2x}$$

in the interior. Taking account of boundary constraints,[2] we have best response function:

$$\lambda(x) := \max\left(0, a_2 + (1-a_2)\frac{x-1}{2x}\right)$$

Interestingly, the share sent back is increasing in the amount sent because player 2 has greater incentive to compensate player 1 for their investment. If the full amount is sent then the share sent back is simply a_2.

Given this, the trustor chooses x to maximize:

$$u_1 = (1-a_1)\log\left(1 - x + \lambda(x)2x\right) + a_1 \log\left((1-\lambda(x))2x\right).$$

In the interior this reduces to:

$$u_1 = (1-a_1)\log\left((1+x)a_2\right) + a_1 \log\left((1-a_2)(1+x)\right),$$

with greatest returns at $x = 1$.

For ranges in which no investment will be returned, utility reduces to:

$$u_1 = (1-a_1)\log(1-x) + a_1 \log(2x),$$

which is maximized at: $x = a_1$.

The global maximum depends on which of these yields higher utility.

Figure 17.4 shows the returns to the trustor from different investments given their own and the trustee's other-regarding preferences. We see that when other-regarding preferences are weak for both players, the largest payoffs arise when

---
[2] $a_2 + (1-a_2)\frac{x-1}{2x} \geq 0$ requires $x \geq \frac{1-a_2}{1+a_2}$

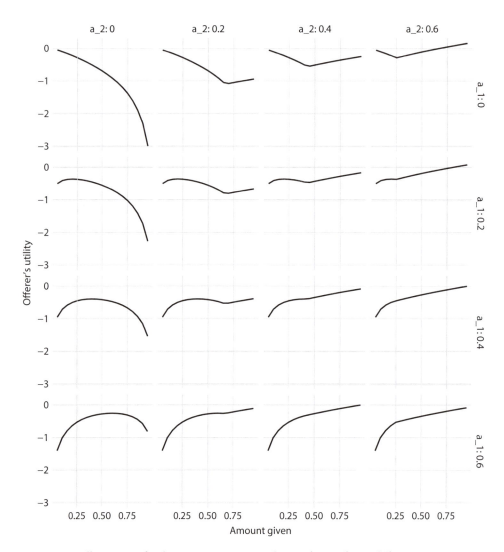

Figure 17.4: Illustration of utility in a trust game to player 1 from offering different amounts given preferences of both players and anticipated reactions of player 2.

nothing is given and nothing is returned. When other regarding preferences are strong for player 1, they optimally offer substantial amounts even when nothing is expected in return. When other-regarding preferences are sufficiently strong for player 2, player 1 invests fully in anticipation of a return.

The predictions of this model are then used to define the inquiry and predict outcomes in the model declaration. The model part of the design includes information on underlying preferences. For this we make use of a set of functions that characterize stipulated beliefs about behavior.

```
invested <- function(a_1, a_2) {
  u_a = (1 - a_1) * log(1 - a_1) + a_1 * log(2 * a_1)   # give a1
```

17.4 Behavioral Games

```
    u_b = (1 - a_1) * log(2 * a_2) + a_1 * log(2 * (1 - a_2)) # give 1
    ifelse(u_a > u_b, a_1, 1)
}
average_invested <- function(a_1)
  mean(sapply(seq(0, 1, .01), invested, a_1 = a_1))

returned <- function(x1, a_2 = 1/3)
  ((2 * a_2 * x1 - (1 - a_2) * (1 - x1)) / (2 * x1)) *
  (x1 > (1 - a_2) / (1 + a_2))

average_returned <- function(a_2)
  mean(sapply(seq(0.01, 1, .01), returned, a_2 = a_2))
```

The inquiries for this design are the expected share offered to different types of trustees, the expected returns, averaged over possible offers, and the expected action by a trustee when the full amount is invested. The data strategy involves assigning players to pairs and orderings. The first player in each pair is assigned to the trustor role and the second to the trustee role. For the answer strategy, we simply measure average behavior across subjects. As a wrinkle, we include the possibility that the experimenter confronts the returners with random offers rather than the ones actually made by their partners. This aspect of the design is controlled by an argument called `deceive` and turns out to be important for inference.

Declaration 17.6 Trust game design.

```
rho     <- 0.8
n_pairs <- 200
deceive <- FALSE

declaration_17.6 <-

  declare_model(N = 2 * n_pairs,
                a = runif(N)) +

  declare_inquiries(
    trusting = mean(sapply(a, average_invested)),
    trustworthy = mean(sapply(a, average_returned))) +

  declare_assignment(pair = complete_ra(N = N, num_arms = n_pairs),
                     role = 1 + block_ra(blocks = pair)) +
  declare_step(
    id_cols = pair,
    names_from = role,
    values_from = c(ID, a),
    handler = pivot_wider) +

  declare_measurement(invested = invested(a_1, a_2)) +

  declare_estimator(
    invested ~ 1,
    .method = lm_robust,
    inquiry = "trusting",
    label = "trusting") +
```

Table 17.5: Trust game sample data.

pair	ID_2	ID_1	a_2	a_1	invested	returned
T1	357	026	0.69	0.51	1.00	0.69
T2	298	103	0.60	0.22	1.00	0.60
T3	362	390	0.65	0.09	1.00	0.65
T4	249	224	0.50	0.96	0.96	0.49
T5	152	304	0.32	0.33	1.00	0.32
T6	250	244	0.94	0.21	1.00	0.94

```
declare_measurement(invested = deceive*runif(N) + (1-deceive)*invested,
                    returned = returned(invested, a_2)) +
  declare_estimator(
    returned ~ 1,
    .method = lm_robust,
    inquiry = "trustworthy",
    label = "trustworthy")
```

A few features are worth highlighting. First, the inquiries are defined using a set of hypothetical responses under the model using a specified response function. However the inquiry is robust to the model in the sense that it remains well defined even if you stipulate very different behaviors. Second, the declaration involves a step where we shift from a "long" data frame with a row per subject to a "wide" data frame with a row per game. Third, the design orders steps so that an estimation stage is implemented before a measurement stage; this is a little unusual but it is done in this way to allow the researchers to analyze Player 1 investment decisions before (possibly) replacing them with fabricated decisions.

A sample of data that might be produced by this design is shown in Table 17.5.

We have a row for each game, we have the (unobserved) a_i, a_j parameters as well as actions by both players in the data.

Diagnosis 17.5 illustrates the properties of the trust game design.

Diagnosis 17.5 Trust game diagnosis

```
diagnosis_17.5 <-
  declaration_17.6 |>
  redesign(deceive = c(TRUE, FALSE)) |>
  diagnose_design()
```

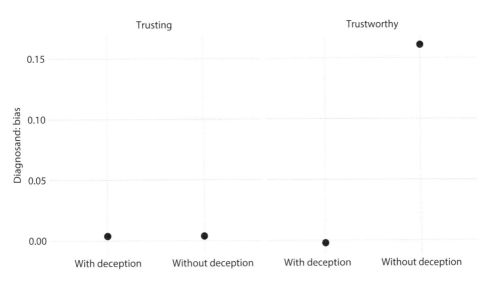

Figure 17.5: Diagnosis of bias in the analysis of trust games with and without deception.

We see that we do well for the first inquiry whether or not deception is used. The first inquiry—*trusting*—is after all a simple measurement of choices albeit in a controlled setting. But we do poorly for the second and third inquiries.

Whether we have bias in the measure of *trustworthy* depends on the use of deception, however, and so presents researchers with a serious design challenge.

There are two distinct reasons for the bias when Player 2 is confronted with the investments made by Player 1. First, the stage 2 distribution of investments differs from the distribution specified in the definition of the inquiry. Although we have assigned roles randomly, the choices confronting Player 2 are not random: they reflect the particular assignments generated by Player 1's choices. These player-generated assignments are generally higher than those specified in the definition of the inquiry, resulting in higher returns than would arise from random offers. A second source of bias is self-selection in stage 2. Even if the distribution of offers confronting the trustees in the second stage were correct, we could still suffer from a problem that the trustees that are sent larger investments are sent those investments partly *because* trustors expect them to return a large share.

These problems are, we think, very common in games that involve the analysis of decisions that depend on prior decisions. Switching out the offers solves both of these problems but at the cost of deception.

Many experimental labs have developed quite strong norms against the use of deception. Some alternatives might exist that could be functionally equivalent. One approach would be to limit the information that players have about each other. We assumed in this design that players had enough information on each other to figure out a_{-i}. Say instead that information on players were coarsened—for instance, so that players know only each other's gender and ethnicity. In this case we might have a small set of "types" for Player 1 and Player 2. Conditional on the type pair, the variation in offers is as-if random with respect to a Player 2's characteristics and one could assess the average response of each Player 2 type to each offer received from a Player 1 type. This approach would address the selection problem. The problem of nonrandom offers could be sidestepped by redefining the inquiry to be responses *conditional* on particular offers (such as the return of a 100% investment).

Another approach is to in fact do a mixture of reporting and randomization and *advise* Player 2 players that with some probability (say 50%) they will be confronted with a random investment and with some probability they will see the actual investment made by Player 1.

17.4.1 Design examples

- Avdeenko and Gilligan (2015) use a trust game to measure outcomes in a randomized controlled trial of the effects of local public infrastructure projects in Sudan.

- Iyengar and Westwood (2015) use both dictator and trust games to measure partisan antipathy in the United States.

CHAPTER 18

Experimental : Causal

An inquiry is causal if it involves a comparison of counterfactual states of the world and a data strategy is experimental if it involves explicit assignment of units to treatment conditions. Experimental designs for causal inference combine these two elements. The designs in this section aim to estimate causal effects and the procedure for doing so involves actively allocating treatments.

Many experimental designs for causal inference in the social sciences take advantage of researcher control over the assignment of treatments to assign them *at random*. In the archetypal two-arm randomized trial, a group of N subjects are recruited, m of them are chosen at random to receive treatment and the remaining $N - m$ of them do not receive treatment and serve as controls. The inquiry is the average treatment effect, the answer strategy is the difference-in-means estimator. The strength of the design can be appreciated by analogy to random sampling. The m outcomes in the treatment group represent a random sample from the treated potential outcomes among all N subjects, so the sample mean in the treatment group is a good estimator of the true average treated potential outcome; an analogous claim holds for the control group.

The randomization of treatments to estimate average causal effects is a relatively recent human invention. While glimmers of the idea appeared earlier, it wasn't until at least the 1920s that explicit randomization appeared in agricultural science, medicine, education, and political science (Jamison, 2019). Only a few generations of scientists have had access to this tool. Sometimes critics of experiments will charge, "you can't randomize [important causal variables]." There are of course practical constraints on what treatments researchers can control, be they ethical, financial, or otherwise. We think the main constraint is researcher creativity. The scientific history of randomized experiments is short—just because it hasn't been randomized *yet* doesn't mean it can't be. (By the same token, just because it *can* be randomized doesn't mean that it should be.)

Randomized experiments are rightly praised for their desirable inferential properties, but of course they can go wrong in many ways that designers of experiments should anticipate, and whose effects they should minimize. These problems include problems in the data strategy (randomization implementation failures, excludability violations, noncompliance, attrition, and interference between units), problems in the answer strategy (conditioning on posttreatment variables, failure to account for clustering, p-hacking), and even problems in the inquiry (estimator-inquiry mismatches). Of course, all these problems apply a fortiori to nonexperimental studies, but they are important to emphasize for experimental studies since they are often characterized as being "unbiased" without qualification.

The designs in this chapter proceed from the simplest experimental design—the two-arm trial—up through very complex designs such as the randomized saturation design.

18.1 Two-Arm Randomized Experiments

> We declare a canonical two-arm trial, motivate key diagnosands for assessing the quality of the design, use diagnosis and redesign to explore the properties of two-arm trials, and discuss key risks to inference.

All two-arm randomized trials have in common that subjects are randomly assigned to one of two conditions. Canonically, the two conditions include one treatment condition and one control condition. Some two-arm trials eschew the pure control condition in favor of a placebo control condition, or even a second treatment condition. The uniting feature of all these designs is that the model includes two and only two potential outcomes for each unit and that the data strategy randomly assigns which of these potential outcomes will be revealed by each unit.

A key choice in the design of two-arm trials is the random assignment procedure. Will we use simple random assignment (coin flip, or Bernoulli) or will we use complete random assignment? Will the randomization be blocked or clustered? Will we "restrict" the randomization so that only randomizations that generate acceptable levels of balance on pretreatment characteristics are permitted? We will explore the implications of some of these choices in the coming sections, but for the moment, the main point is that saying "treatments were assigned at random" is insufficient. We need to describe the randomization procedure in detail in order to know how to analyze the resulting experiment. See Section 8.1.2 for a description of many different random assignment procedures.

In this chapter, we'll consider a canonical two-arm trial design, with complete random assignment in a fixed population, which uses difference-in-means to estimate the average treatment effect. We'll now unpack this shorthand into the components of M, I, D, and A.

The model specifies a fixed sample of N subjects. Here we aren't imagining that we are first sampling from a larger population. We have in mind a fixed set of units from which we will conduct our experiment: we are conducting "finite sample inference." Under the model, each unit is endowed with two latent potential outcomes: a treated potential outcome and an untreated potential outcome. The difference between them is the individual treatment effect. In the canonical design, we assume that potential outcomes are "stable," in the sense that all N units' potential outcomes are defined with respect to the same treatment and that units' potential outcomes do not depend on the treatment status of other units. This assumption is often referred to as the "stable unit treatment value assumption," or SUTVA (Rubin, 1980).

Because the model specifies a fixed sample, the inquiries are also defined at the sample level. The most common inquiry for a two-arm trial is the sample average treatment effect, or SATE. It is equal to the average difference between the treated and untreated potential outcomes for the units in the sample: $\mathbb{E}_{i \in N}[Y_i(1) - Y_i(0)]$. Two-arm trials can also support other inquiries like the SATE among a subgroup (called a conditional average treatment effect, or CATE), but we'll leave those inquiries to the side for the moment.

The data strategy uses complete random assignment, in which exactly m of N units are assigned to treatment ($Z_i = 1$) and the remainder are assigned to control ($Z_i = 0$). We measure observed outcomes in such a way that we measure the treated potential outcome in the treatment group and untreated potential outcomes in the control group: $Y_i = Y_i(1) \times Z_i + Y_i(0) \times (1 - Z_i)$. This expression is sometimes called the "switching equation" because of the way it "switches" which potential outcome is revealed by the treatment assignment. It also embeds the crucial assumption that units reveal the potential outcome they are assigned to reveal. If the experiment encounters noncompliance, this assumption is violated. It's also violated if "excludability" is violated, i.e., if something other than treatment moves with assignment to treatment. For example, if the treatment group is measured differently from the control group, excludability would be violated.

The answer strategy is the difference-in-means estimator with so-called Neyman standard errors. In mathematical notation, if units are ordered with treated units first and control units after, we can write both as:

$$\widehat{DIM} = \frac{\sum_1^m Y_i}{m} - \frac{\sum_{m+1}^N Y_i}{N-m} \quad (18.1)$$

$$\widehat{se(DIM)} = \sqrt{\frac{\widehat{Var}(Y_i(1))}{m} + \frac{\widehat{Var}(Y_i(0))}{N-m}}. \quad (18.2)$$

The estimated standard error can be used as an input for two other statistical procedures: null hypothesis significance testing via a t-test and the construction of a 95% confidence interval.

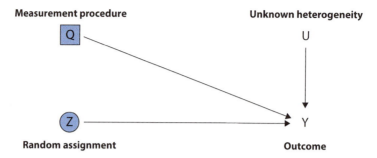

Figure 18.1: Directed acyclic graph of a two-arm randomized experiment.

The DAG corresponding to a two-arm randomized trial is very simple. An outcome Y is affected by unknown factors U and a treatment Z. The measurement procedure Q affects Y in the sense that it measures a latent outcome and records the measurement in a dataset. No arrows lead into Z because it is randomly assigned. No arrow leads from Z to Q, because we assume no excludability violations wherein the treatment changes how units are measured. This simple DAG confirms that the average causal effect of Z on Y is nonparametrically identified because no backdoor paths lead from Z to Y.

Declaration 18.1 Canonical two-arm trial design.

```
declaration_18.1 <-
  declare_model(N = 100,
                U = rnorm(N),
                potential_outcomes(Y ~ 0.2 * Z + U)) +
  declare_inquiry(ATE = mean(Y_Z_1 - Y_Z_0)) +
  declare_assignment(Z = complete_ra(N, prob = 0.5)) +
  declare_measurement(Y = reveal_outcomes(Y ~ Z)) +
  declare_estimator(Y ~ Z, .method = difference_in_means, inquiry = "ATE")
```

Diagnosing this two-arm trial design, we see that, as expected, we encountered no bias, but encountered high variance. In the model, we set the ATE at 0.2 standard units, but the true standard deviation of the estimator (the true standard error) is nearly the same value, at 0.19 standard units. We have low statistical power, at 16%. Two approaches to increasing the precision of the estimate include increasing the sample size and including prognostic pretreatment covariates in the answer strategy. We explore both of these approaches in the next section.

Diagnosis 18.1 Two arm-trial diagnosis.

```
diagnosis_18.1 <- diagnose_design(declaration_18.1)
```

Table 18.1: Bias, power, and true standard error (standard deviation of the estimate) for a two-arm randomized trial.

Bias	Power	SD Estimate
−0.01	0.17	0.20
(0.00)	(0.01)	(0.00)

18.1.1 Using covariates to increase precision

When treatments are randomized, whether we adjust for pretreatment covariates makes little difference for bias. By contrast, when treatments are not randomized, we often do need to adjust for covariates in order to account for the confounding introduced by "omitted variables" (see Section 16.2).

The purpose of adjusting for covariates in an experimental study is to increase precision. The more predictive the covariates are of the outcome, the more they improve the precision of the estimates.

One way to think about how much the inclusion of covariates will help precision is to summarize their predictive power in a statistic like the R^2. The R^2 value from a regression of the outcome on the covariates alone (i.e., without the treatment indicator) gives an understanding of how jointly predictive the covariates are. If R^2 is close to 0, including the covariates will make almost no difference for precision. If R^2 is close to 1, we can achieve dramatic increases in precision and statistical power.

Declaration 18.2 draws a summary covariate X and unobserved heterogeneity U from a multivariate normal distribution with a specified covariance between the two variables. By redesigning over the values of that correlation, we can learn how covariate adjustment affects precision depending on the level of R^2. The answer strategy uses the estimator proposed in Lin (2013) for reasons explained in the next section.

Declaration 18.2 Two-arm trial with covariate adjustment.

```
N <- 100
r_sq <- 0

declaration_18.2 <-
  declare_model(N = N,
                draw_multivariate(c(U, X) ~ MASS::mvrnorm(
                  n = N,
                  mu = c(0, 0),
                  Sigma = matrix(c(1, sqrt(r_sq), sqrt(r_sq), 1), 2, 2)
                )),
                potential_outcomes(Y ~ 0.1 * Z + U)) +
  declare_inquiry(ATE = mean(Y_Z_1 - Y_Z_0)) +
  declare_assignment(Z = complete_ra(N)) +
```

```
declare_measurement(Y = reveal_outcomes(Y ~ Z)) +
declare_estimator(
  Y ~ Z, covariates = ~X, .method = lm_lin, inquiry = "ATE"
)
```

Diagnosis 18.2 Two-arm trial diagnosis.

```
diagnosis_18.2 <-
  declaration_18.2 |>
  redesign(r_sq = seq(0.0, 0.9, by = 0.2)) |>
  diagnose_designs()
```

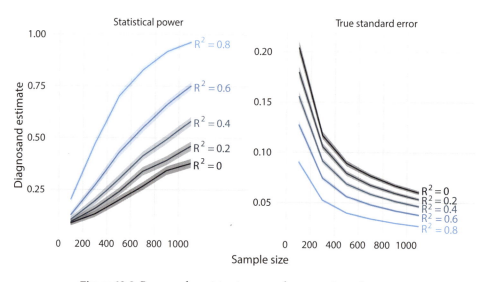

Figure 18.2: Power and precision increases from covariate adjustment.

Figure 18.2 plots sample size on the horizontal axis and diagnosand estimates on the vertical axis. In the left-hand panel, we see that, as usual, statistical power increases with sample size. Different values of R^2 are distinguished by colored lines. Higher values of R^2 lead to higher statistical power. The gains can be dramatic. The no-adjustment benchmark is represented by the $R^2 = 0$ line. We achieve approximately the same statistical power as a 1,000 unit experiment with no adjustment when the pretreatment covariates yield an R^2 of 0.8 and we have just 200 units. The right panel tells a similar story, though it emphasizes that the marginal benefits of covariate adjustment get smaller as the sample size gets bigger. In any real experimental scenario, designers should take care to generate informed guesses about the probable R^2 of the covariates and then explore the trade-offs between pretreatment data collection and additional sample size.

18.1.2 Can controlling for covariates hurt precision?

Freedman (2008) critiques the practice of using covariates in an OLS regression to adjust experimental data. While the difference-in-means estimator is unbiased for the average treatment effect, the covariate-adjusted OLS estimator exhibits a small sample bias (sometimes called "Freedman bias") that diminishes quickly as sample sizes increase. More worrying is the critique that covariate adjustment can even hurt precision.

Lin (2013) unpacks the circumstances under which this precision loss occurs and offers an alternative estimator that is guaranteed to be at least as precise as the unadjusted estimator. The trouble occurs when the correlation of covariates with the outcome is quite different in the treatment condition from that in the control condition and when designs are strongly imbalanced in the sense of having large proportions of treated or untreated units. We refer the reader to this excellent paper for details and the connection between covariate adjustment in randomized experiments and covariate adjustment in random sampling designs. In sum, the Lin estimator deals with the problem by performing covariate adjustment in each arm of the experiment separately, which is equivalent to the inclusion of a full set of treatment-by-covariate interactions. In a clever bit of regression magic, Lin shows how first preprocessing the data by de-meaning the covariates renders the coefficient on the treatment regressor an estimate of the overall ATE. The `lm_lin` estimator in the `estimatr` package implements this preprocessing in one step.

Declaration 18.3 will help us to explore the precision of three estimators under a variety of circumstances. We want to understand the performance of the difference-in-means, OLS, and Lin estimators depending on how different the correlation between X and the outcome is by treatment arm, and depending on the fraction of units assigned to treatment.

Declaration 18.3 Lin estimator design.

```
prob = 0.5
control_slope = -1

declaration_18.3 <-
  declare_model(N = 100,
                X = runif(N, 0, 1),
                U = rnorm(N, sd = 0.1),
                Y_Z_1 = 1*X + U,
                Y_Z_0 = control_slope*X + U
  ) +
  declare_inquiry(ATE = mean(Y_Z_1 - Y_Z_0)) +
  declare_assignment(Z = complete_ra(N = N, prob = prob)) +
  declare_measurement(Y = reveal_outcomes(Y ~ Z)) +
  declare_estimator(Y ~ Z,
                    inquiry = "ATE", label = "DIM") +
  declare_estimator(Y ~ Z + X, .method = lm_robust,
                    inquiry = "ATE", label = "OLS") +
  declare_estimator(Y ~ Z, covariates = ~X, .method = lm_lin,
                    inquiry = "ATE", label = "Lin")
```

Diagnosis 18.3 Lin estimator diagnosis.

```
diagnosis_18.3 <-
  diagnosis_18.3 |>
  redesign(
    control_slope = seq(-1, 1, 0.5),
    prob = seq(0.1, 0.9, 0.1)) |>
  diagnose_designs()
```

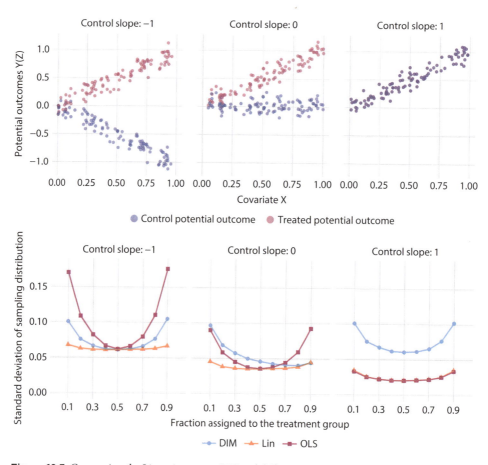

Figure 18.3: Comparing the Lin estimator to OLS and difference-in-means, varying fraction assigned to treatment and correlation of potential outcomes with the covariate.

Figure 18.3 considers a range of designs under three possible models. The three models are described by the top row of facets. In all cases, the slope of the treated potential outcomes with respect to X is set to 1. All the way to the left, the slope with respect to the control potential outcomes is set to -1, and all the way to the right is set to $+1$. The bottom row of facets shows the performance of three estimators along a range of treatment assignment probabilities.

When the control slope is −1, we can see Freedman's precision critique. The standard error of the OLS is *larger* than difference-in-means for many designs, though they coincide when the fraction treated is 50%. This problem persists in some form until the slope of the control potential outcome with respect to X gets close enough to the slope of the treated potential outcomes with respect to X.

All along this range, however, the Lin estimator dominates OLS and difference-in-means. Regardless of the fraction assigned to treatment and the model of potential outcomes, the Lin estimator achieves equal or better precision than either difference-in-means or OLS. These results highlight the gains that can be made by including covariate controls in your ex ante design, as long as you use the right answer strategy. They do not provide support for the more worrying practice of selecting controls ex post based on how they affect your results.

18.1.3 Examples

- Peyton, Sierra-Arévalo, and Rand (2019) conduct a two-arm randomized experiment in which treatment households were assigned to receive a nonenforcement visit from police and control households were not. Outcomes were measured via a follow-up survey.

- Balcells, Palanza, and Voytas (2022) use a two-arm randomized experiment to study the effects of a visit to a transitional justice museum in Chile on support for democratic institutions.

18.2 Block-Randomized Experiments

> We declare a block-randomized trial in which subjects are assigned to treatment and control conditions within groups. We use design diagnosis to assess the variance reductions that can be achieved from block randomization.

In a block-randomized experimental design, homogeneous sets of units are grouped together into blocks on the basis of covariates. The ideal blocking would group together units with identical potential outcomes, but since we don't have access to any outcome information at the moment of treatment assignment, let alone the full set of potential outcomes, we have to make do with grouping together units on the basis of covariates we hope are strongly correlated with potential outcomes. The stronger the correlation between a blocking variable and the potential outcomes, the more effective the blocking in terms of increasing precision.

Blocks can be formed in many ways. They can be constructed based on the levels of a single discrete covariate. We might be able to do better by blocking on the intersection of the levels of two discrete covariates. We could coarsen a continuous variable in order to create strata. We could even create matched quartets of units, partitioning the sample into sets of four units that are as similar as possible on many covariates. In any of these cases, we then randomize units *within* blocks to treatment. All of these procedures fall under the rubric of block random assignment. Methodologists have crafted many algorithms for creating blocks, each with their own trade-offs in terms of computational speed and efficiency guarantees.

In Declaration 18.4, we block our assignment on a binary covariate X. We assign different fractions of each block to treatment to illustrate the notion that probabilities of assignment need not be constant across blocks, and if they aren't, we need to weight units by the inverse of the probability of assignment to the condition that they are in. In the answer strategy, we adjust for blocks using the Lin (2013) regression adjustment estimator including IPW weights.

Declaration 18.4 Block randomized two-arm trial design.

```
declaration_18.4 <-
  declare_model(
    N = 500,
    X = rep(c(0, 1), each = N / 2),
    U = rnorm(N, sd = 0.25),
    potential_outcomes(Y ~ 0.2 * Z + X + U)
  ) +
  declare_assignment(
    Z = block_ra(blocks = X, block_prob = c(0.2, 0.5)),
    probs =
      obtain_condition_probabilities(assignment = Z,
                                     blocks = X,
                                     block_prob = c(0.2, 0.5)),
    ipw = 1 / probs
  ) +
  declare_measurement(Y = reveal_outcomes(Y ~ Z)) +
  declare_estimator(
    Y ~ Z,
    covariates = ~ X,
    .method = lm_lin,
    weights = ipw,
    label = "Lin"
  )
```

18.2.1 Why does blocking help?

Why does blocking increase the precision with which we estimate the ATE? One piece of intuition is that blocking rules out "bad" random assignments that exhibit imbalance on the blocking variable. If $N=12$ and $m=6$, complete random assignment allows `choose(12, 6)` = 924 possible permutations. If we form two blocks of six units and conduct block random assignment, then there are `choose(6, 3) * choose(6, 3)` = 400 remaining possible assignments. The assignments that are ruled are those in which too many or too few units in a block are assigned to treatment, because blocking requires that exactly m_B units be treated in each block B. When potential outcomes are correlated with the blocking variable,

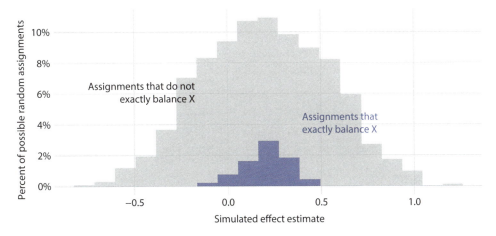

Figure 18.4: Sampling distribution under complete random assignment, by covariate balance.

those "extreme" assignments produce estimates that are in the tails of the sampling distribution associated with complete random assignment.[1]

Diagnosis 18.4 Diagnosis comparing block random assignment and complete random assignment.

This intuition behind blocking is illustrated in Figure 18.4, which shows the sampling distribution of the difference-in-means estimator under *complete* random assignment. The histogram is shaded according to whether the particular random assignment is permissible under a procedure that blocks on the binary covariate X. The sampling distribution of the estimator among the set of assignments that are permissible under blocking is more tightly distributed around the true average treatment effect than the estimates associated with assignments that are not perfectly balanced. Here we can see the value of a blocking procedure—*it rules out by design* those assignments that are not perfectly balanced.

18.2.2 Design examples

- Kalla, Rosenbluth, and Teele (2018) conduct an audit experiment among legislators in which the gender of a student asking for advice about starting a career in politics is randomized. Units are block-randomized into treatments on the basis of the legislators' own gender and their state.

- Lyall, Zhou, and Imai (2020) use a block-randomized design to evaluate the effect of vocational training and cash transfers on support for combatants among youth in Afghanistan. Matched quartet blocks were created on

---
[1] One mistake sometimes made by new experimenters is to conduct *simple* random assignment within each block. None of the gains from blocking described here apply if simple random assignment is conducted in each block, because that procedure produces the identical randomization distribution as a simple random assignment procedure without any blocking (provided that the probability of assignment is the same in each block).

the basis of district, gender, employment status, displacement status, and exposure to violence.

18.3 Cluster-Randomized Experiments

> We declare a cluster-randomized trial in which subjects are assigned to treatment and control conditions in groups. We use design diagnosis to quantify how the magnitude of the efficiency losses from clustering depends on the intra-cluster correlation.

When whole groups of units are assigned to treatment conditions together, we say that the assignment procedure is clustered. A common example is an education experiment in which the treatment is randomized at the classroom level. All students in a classroom are assigned to either treatment or control together; assignments do not vary within the classroom. Clusters can be localities, like villages, precincts, or neighborhoods. Clusters can be households if treatments are assigned at the household level.

Typically, cluster randomized trials exhibit higher variance than the equivalent individually randomized trial. How much higher variance depends on a statistic that can be hard to think about, the intra-cluster correlation (ICC) of the outcome. The total variance can be decomposed into the variance of the cluster means $\sigma^2_{between}$ plus the individual variance of the cluster-demeaned outcome σ^2_{within}. The ICC is a number between 0 and 1 that describes the fraction of the total variance that is due to the between variance: $ICC = \frac{\sigma^2_{between}}{\sigma^2_{between} + \sigma^2_{within}}$. If ICC equals 1, then all units within a cluster express the same outcome, and all of the variation in outcomes is due to cluster-level differences. If ICC equals zero, then the cluster means are all identical, but the individuals vary within each cluster. When ICC is 1, the effective sample size is equal to the number of clusters. When ICC is 0, the effective sample size is equal to the number of individuals. Since ICC is usually somewhere between these two values, we can see that clustering decreases the effective sample size from the number of individuals. The size of this decrease depends on how similar outcomes are within a cluster compared to how similar outcomes are across clusters.

For these reasons clustered random assignment is not usually a desirable feature of a design. Sometimes, however, it is useful or even *necessary* for logistical or ethical reasons for subjects to be assigned together in groups.

To demonstrate the consequences of clustering, Declaration 18.5 shows a design in which both the untreated outcome Y_Z_0 and the treatment effect tau_i exhibit intra-cluster correlation. The inquiry is the average treatment effect over individuals, which can be defined without reference to the clustered structure of the data. The data strategy employs clustered random assignment. We highlight two features of the clustered assignment. First, the clustered nature of the data does not itself *require* clustered assignment. In principle, one could assign treatments at the individual level or subgroup level even if outcomes are correlated within groups. Second, surprisingly, random assignment of clusters to conditions does not guarantee unbiasedness of outcomes when clusters are of unequal size (Middleton, 2008; Imai, King, and Nall, 2009). The bias stems from the possibility that potential outcomes could be correlated with cluster size. With uneven cluster sizes, the total number of units (the denominator in the mean estimation) in each group bounces around from assignment to assignment. Since the expectation of a ratio is not, in general, equal to the ratio of expectations, any dependence between cluster size and potential outcomes will cause bias. We can address this problem by blocking clusters into groups according to cluster size. If all clusters in a block are of the same size, then the overall size of the treatment group will remain stable from assignment to assignment. For this reason the design below uses clustered assignment blocked on cluster size.

Declaration 18.5 Blocked and clustered randomized trial.

```
ICC <- 0.9

declaration_18.5 <-
  declare_model(
    cluster =
      add_level(
        N = 10,
        cluster_size = rep(seq(10, 50, 10), 2),
        cluster_shock =
          scale(cluster_size + rnorm(N, sd = 5)) * sqrt(ICC),
        cluster_tau = rnorm(N, sd = sqrt(ICC))
      ),
    individual =
      add_level(
        N = cluster_size,
        individual_shock = rnorm(N, sd = sqrt(1 - ICC)),
        individual_tau = rnorm(N, sd = sqrt(1 - ICC)),
        Y_Z_0 = cluster_shock + individual_shock,
        Y_Z_1 = Y_Z_0 + cluster_tau + individual_tau
      )
  ) +
  declare_inquiry(ATE = mean(Y_Z_1 - Y_Z_0)) +
  declare_assignment(Z = block_and_cluster_ra(clusters = cluster,
                                              blocks = cluster_size)) +
  declare_measurement(Y = reveal_outcomes(Y ~ Z)) +
  declare_estimator(Y ~ Z,
                    clusters = cluster,
                    inquiry = "ATE")
```

Diagnosis 18.5 Redesigning over values of ICC.

```
diagnosis_18.5 <-
  declaration_18.5 |>
  redesign(ICC = seq(0.1, 0.9, by = 0.4)) |>
  diagnose_designs()
```

262   Chapter 18: Experimental : Causal

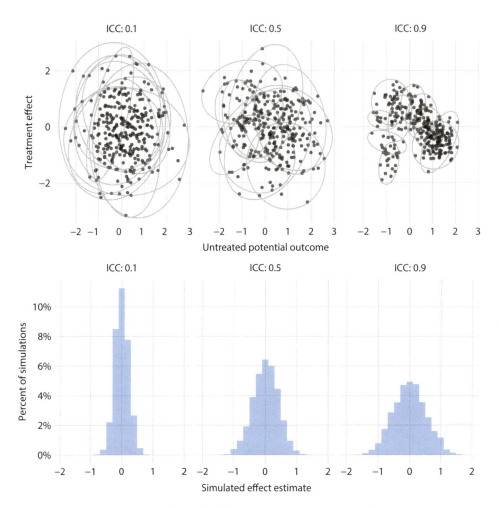

Figure 18.5: Sampling distribution under differenct ICCs.

Figure 18.5 shows the sampling distribution of the difference-in-means estimator under cluster random assignment at three levels of intra-cluster correlation ranging from 0.1 to 0.9.

The top row of panels plot the treatment effect on the vertical axis and the untreated potential outcome on the horizontal axis. Clusters of units are circled. At low levels of ICC, the circles all overlap, because the differences across clusters are smaller than the differences within a cluster. At high levels of ICC, the differences across clusters are more pronounced than differences within a cluster. The bottom row of panels shows that the sampling distribution of the difference-in-means estimator spreads out as the ICC increases. At low levels of ICC, the standard error is small; at high levels the standard error is high.

This diagnosis clarifies the *costs* of cluster assignment. These costs are greatest when there are few clusters and when units within clusters have similar potential outcomes. Diagnosis can be further used to compare these costs to advantages and assess the merits of variations in the design that seek to alter the number or size of clusters.

18.3.1 Design examples

- Mousa (2020) studies the effects of inter-group contact on tolerance by cluster assigning players in a Christian football league in Iraq to play with four new Muslim teammates or four new Christian teammates, where the clusters are the teams.

- Paluck and Green (2009) cluster-assigned communities in Rwanda to radio programs encouraging dissent and disobedience to authorities and measured individual-level outcomes via survey.

18.4 Subgroup Designs

> We declare and diagnose a design that is targeted at understanding the difference in treatment effects between subgroups. The design combines a sampling strategy that ensures reasonable numbers within each group of interest and a blocking assignment strategy to minimize variance.

Subgroup designs are experimental designs that have been tailored to a specific inquiry, the difference-in-CATEs. A CATE is a "conditional average treatment effect," or the average treatment effect conditional on membership in some group. A difference-in-CATEs is simply the difference between two CATEs.

For example, studies of political communication often have the *difference* in response to a party cue by subject partisanship as the main inquiry, since Republican subjects tend to respond positively to a Republican party cue, whereas Democratic subjects tend to respond negatively.

Subgroup designs share much in common with factorial designs, discussed in detail in Section 18.5. The main source of commonality is the answer strategy for the difference-in-CATEs inquiry. In subgroup designs and factorial designs, the usual approach is to inspect the interaction term from an OLS regression. The two designs differ because in the subgroup design, the difference-in-CATEs is a descriptive difference. We don't randomly assign partisanship, so we can't attribute the difference in response to treatment to partisanship, which could just be a marker for the true causes of the difference in response. But this makes it no less important a quantity of interest. In the factorial design, we randomize the levels of all treatments, so the differences-in-CATEs carry with them a causal interpretation.

Since we don't randomly assign membership in subgroups, how can we optimize the design to target the difference-in-CATEs? Our main data strategy choice comes in sampling. We need to obtain sufficient numbers of both groups in order to generate sharp enough estimates of each CATE, the better to estimate their difference. For example, at the time of this writing, many sources of convenience samples (Mechanical Turk, Lucid, Prolific, and many others) appear to under-represent

Republicans, so researchers sometimes need to make special efforts to increase their numbers in the eventual sample.[2]

Declaration 18.6 describes a fixed population of 10,000 units, among whom people with X = 1 are relatively rare (only 20%). In the `potential_outcomes` call, we build in both baseline differences in the outcome, and also responses to treatment that are oppositely signed across the two subgroups. Those with X = 0 have a CATE of 0.1 and those with X = 1 have a CATE of 0.1 - 0.2 = -0.1. The true difference-in-CATEs is therefore 20 percentage points.

If we were to draw a sample of 1,000 at random, we would expect to yield only 200 people with X = 1. Here we improve upon that through stratified sampling. We deliberately sample 500 units with X = 1 and 500 with X = 0, then block-random-assign the treatment within groups defined by X.

Declaration 18.6 Subgroup design declaration.

```
set.seed(343)
fixed_pop <-
  fabricate(N = 10000,
            X = rbinom(N, 1, 0.2),
            potential_outcomes(
              Y ~ rbinom(N, 1,
                         prob = 0.7 + 0.1 * Z - 0.4 * X - 0.2 * Z * X))
  )

total_n <- 1000
n_x1 <- 500
# Note: n_x2 = total_n - n_x1

declaration_18.6 <-
  declare_model(data = fixed_pop) +
  declare_inquiry(
    CATE_X1 = mean(Y_Z_1[X == 1] - Y_Z_0[X == 1]),
    CATE_X0 = mean(Y_Z_1[X == 0] - Y_Z_0[X == 0]),
    diff_in_CATEs = CATE_X1 - CATE_X0
  ) +
  declare_sampling(
    S = strata_rs(strata = X, strata_n = c(total_n - n_x1, n_x1))
  ) +
  declare_assignment(Z = block_ra(blocks = X)) +
  declare_measurement(Y = reveal_outcomes(Y ~ Z)) +
  declare_estimator(Y ~ Z + X + Z * X,
                    term = "Z:X",
                    inquiry = "diff_in_CATEs")
```

Diagnosis 18.6 Subgroup design diagnosis.

To show the benefits of stratified sampling for experiments, we redesign over many values of under- and over-sampling units with X = 1, holding the total sample size fixed at 1000. The top panel of Figure 18.6 shows the distribution of difference-in-CATE estimates at each size of the X = 1 group. When very small or very large

---
[2] Klar and Leeper (2019) make a similar point when specifically advocating for oversampling minority groups in experimental studies of intersectionality.

fractions of the total sample have $X = 1$, the variance of the estimator is much larger than when the two groups have the same size.

The bottom panel of the figure shows how three diagnosands change over the oversampling design parameter. Bias is never a problem—even small subgroups will generate unbiased difference-in-CATE estimates. As suggested by the top panel, the standard error is minimized in the middle and is largest at the extremes. Likewise, statistical power is maximized in the middle, but drops off surprisingly quickly as we move away from evenly balanced recruitment.

```
diagnosis_18.6 <-
  declaration_18.6 |>
  redesign(n_x1 = seq(20, 980, by = 96)) |>
  diagnose_designs()
```

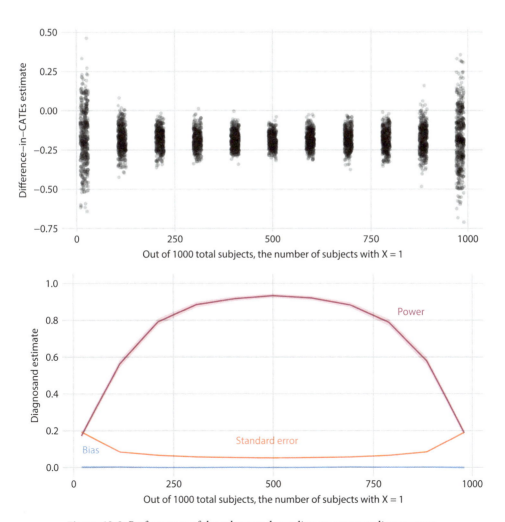

Figure 18.6: Performance of the subgroup depending on oversampling strategy.

18.4.1   Design examples

- Collins (2021) conducts a survey experiment that measures the effects of school board meeting style (standard, participatory, or deliberative) on willingness to attend meetings. The author hypothesized that the effects of participatory and deliberative meeting styles would be larger for non-white subjects, which motivated an oversample of this type of respondent. The final sample included 1,061 non-White subjects and 1,122 White subjects, so the design was well poised to estimate the conditional average effects of the treatments for both groups, which ended up being quite similar.

- Swire et al. (2017) conduct an experimental study of misinformation and corrections that compares Republican and Democratic subjects beliefs in false statements. These authors oversampled Republicans from the Mechanical Turk platform, since usual samples from the platform underrepresent Republicans. Republicans believed false claims more when they were attributed to President Trump and Democrats believed them less; this difference-in-CATEs is especially precisely estimated because of the oversample. Both partisan groups responded to *corrections* of false claims by believing them less, by similar amounts.

18.5   Factorial Experiments

> We declare and diagnose a simple factorial design in which two different treatments are crossed. The design allows for unbiased estimation of a number of estimands, including conditional effects and interaction effects. We highlight the difficulty of achieving statistical power for interaction terms and the risks of treating a difference between a significant conditional effect and a nonsignificant effect as itself significant.

In factorial experiments, researchers randomly assign the level of not just one treatment, but multiple treatments. The prototypical factorial design is a "two-by-two" factorial design in which factor 1 has two levels and so does factor 2. Similarly, a "three-by-three" factorial design has two factors, each of which has three levels. We can entertain any number of factors with any number of levels. For example, a "two-by-three-by-two" factorial design has three factors, two of which have two levels and one of which has three levels. Conjoint experiments are highly factorial, often including six or more factors with two or more levels each (see Section 17.3).

Factorial designs can help researchers answer many inquiries, so it is crucial to design factorials with a particular set in mind. Let's consider the two-by-two case, which is complicated enough. Let's call the first factor $Z1$ and the second factor $Z2$,

18.5 Factorial Experiments

each of which can take on the value of 0 or 1. Considering only average effects, this design can support at least seven separate inquiries:

1. the average treatment effect (ATE) of Z1,
2. the ATE of Z2,
3. the conditional average treatment effect (CATE) of Z1 given Z2 = 0,
4. the CATE of Z1 given Z2 = 1,
5. the CATE of Z2 given Z1 = 0,
6. the CATE of Z2 given Z1 = 1, and
7. The difference-in-CATEs: the difference between inquiry (4) and inquiry (3), which is numerically equivalent to the difference between inquiry (6) and inquiry (5)

The reason we distinguish between the ATE of Z1 versus the CATEs of Z1 depending on the level of Z2 is that the two factors may "interact." When factors interact, the effects of Z1 are heterogeneous in the sense that they differ depending on the level of Z2. We often care about the difference-in-CATEs inquiry when we think the effects of one treatment will depend on the level of another treatment.

However, if we are not so interested in the difference-in-CATEs, then factorial experiments have another good justification—we can learn about the ATEs of each treatment for half price, in the sense that we apply treatments to the same subject pool using the same measurement strategy. Conjoint experiments are a kind of factorial design (discussed in Section 17.3) that often target average treatment effects that average over the levels of the other factors.

Here we declare a factorial design with two treatments and a normally distributed outcome variable. We imagine that the CATE of Z1 given Z2 = 0 is 0.2 standard units, the CATE of Z2 given Z1 = 0 is equal to 0.1, and the interaction of the two treatments is 0.1.

Declaration 18.7 Two-by-two factorial design.

```
CATE_Z1_Z2_0 <- 0.2
CATE_Z2_Z1_0 <- 0.1
interaction <- 0.1
N <- 1000

declaration_18.7 <-
  declare_model(
    N = N,
    U = rnorm(N),
    potential_outcomes(Y ~ CATE_Z1_Z2_0 * Z1 +
```

```
                        CATE_Z2_Z1_0 * Z2 +
                        interaction * Z1 * Z2 + U,
                     conditions = list(Z1 = c(0, 1),
                                       Z2 = c(0, 1)))) +
  declare_inquiry(
    CATE_Z1_Z2_0 = mean(Y_Z1_1_Z2_0 - Y_Z1_0_Z2_0),
    CATE_Z1_Z2_1 = mean(Y_Z1_1_Z2_1 - Y_Z1_0_Z2_1),
    ATE_Z1 = 0.5 * CATE_Z1_Z2_0 + 0.5 * CATE_Z1_Z2_1,

    CATE_Z2_Z1_0 = mean(Y_Z1_0_Z2_1 - Y_Z1_0_Z2_0),
    CATE_Z2_Z1_1 = mean(Y_Z1_1_Z2_1 - Y_Z1_1_Z2_0),
    ATE_Z2 = 0.5 * CATE_Z2_Z1_0 + 0.5 * CATE_Z2_Z1_1,

    diff_in_CATEs_Z1 = CATE_Z1_Z2_1 - CATE_Z1_Z2_0,
    #equivalently
    diff_in_CATEs_Z2 = CATE_Z2_Z1_1 - CATE_Z2_Z1_0
  ) +
  declare_assignment(Z1 = complete_ra(N),
                     Z2 = block_ra(Z1)) +
  declare_measurement(Y = reveal_outcomes(Y ~ Z1 + Z2)) +
  declare_estimator(Y ~ Z1, subset = (Z2 == 0),
                    inquiry = "CATE_Z1_Z2_0", label = "1") +
  declare_estimator(Y ~ Z1, subset = (Z2 == 1),
                    inquiry = "CATE_Z1_Z2_1", label = '2') +
  declare_estimator(Y ~ Z2, subset = (Z1 == 0),
                    inquiry = "CATE_Z2_Z1_0", label = "3") +
  declare_estimator(Y ~ Z2, subset = (Z1 == 1),
                    inquiry = "CATE_Z2_Z1_1", label = "4") +
  declare_estimator(Y ~ Z1 + Z2, term = c("Z1", "Z2"),
                    inquiry = c("ATE_Z1", "ATE_Z2"), label = "5") +
  declare_estimator(Y ~ Z1 + Z2 + Z1*Z2, term = "Z1:Z2",
                    inquiry = c("diff_in_CATEs_Z1", "diff_in_CATEs_Z2"),
                    label = "6")
```

Diagnosis 18.7 Two-by-two factorial diagnosis.

We now redesign this factorial over many sample sizes, considering the statistical power for each of the inquiries. Figure 18.7 shows that depending on the inquiry, the statistical power of this design can vary dramatically. The average treatment effect of *Z1* is relatively large at 0.25 standard units, so power is above the 80% threshold at all the sample sizes we consider. The ATE of *Z2* is smaller, at 0.15 standard units, so power is lower, but not dramatically so. Both ATEs use all *N* data points, so power is manageable for the average effects. The conditional average effects generally fare worse, mainly because each is estimated on only half the sample. The power for the 0.1 standard unit difference-in-CATEs is abysmal at all sample sizes considered here. This diagnosis underlines Principle 3.1: *Design holistically*. The power of a factorial design is not just one number—we have to calculate power for each inquiry separately, as they can differ dramatically.

```
diagnosis_18.7 <-
  declaration_18.7 |>
  redesign(N = seq(500, 3000, 500)) |>
  diagnose_designs()
```

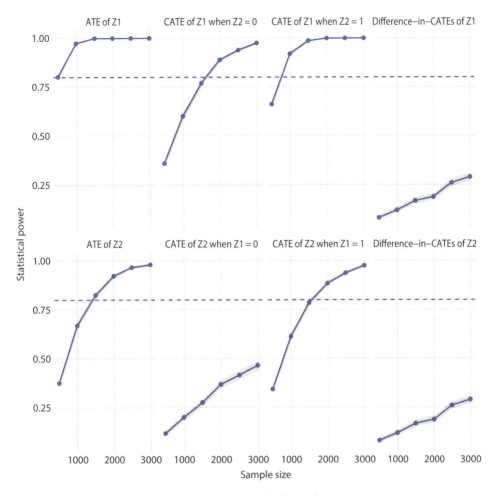

Figure 18.7: Power curves for factorial inquires.

18.5.1 Avoiding misleading inferences

The very poor power for the difference-in-CATEs sometimes leads researchers to rely on a different answer strategy for considering whether the effects of Z1 depend on the level of Z2. Sometimes, researchers will consider the statistical significance of each of Z1's CATEs separately, then conclude the CATEs are "different" if the effect is significant for one CATE but not the other. This is a bad practice and we'll show why.

Here we diagnose over the true values of the Z1 ATE, setting the true interaction term to 0. Our diagnostic question will be, how frequently do we conclude the two CATEs are different, using two different strategies. The first is the usual approach, i.e., we consider the statistical significance of the interaction term. The second considers whether one, but not the other, of the two CATE estimates is significant.

Diagnosis 18.8 Redesign over models.

```
diagnosis_18.8 <-
  declaration_18.7 |>
  redesign(
    CATE_Z1_Z2_0 = seq(0, 0.5, 0.05),
    CATE_Z2_Z1_0 = 0.2,
    interaction = 0
  ) |>
  diagnose_designs()
```

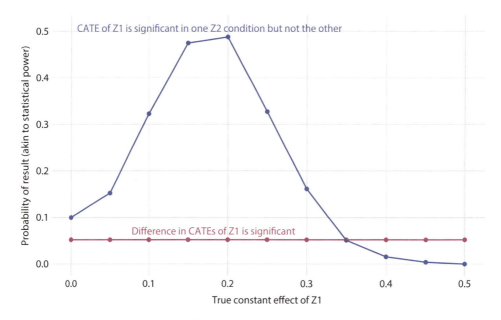

Figure 18.8: Comparing the significance of CATE estimates generates misleading inferences.

Figure 18.8 shows that the error rate when we consider the statistical significance of the interaction term is nominal. Only 5% of the time do we falsely reject the null that the difference-in-CATEs is zero, which is what we expect when we adopt an $\alpha = 0.05$ threshold. But when we claim "treatment effect heterogeneity!" when one CATE is significant but not the other, we make egregious errors. When the true (constant) average effect of *Z1* approaches 0.2, we falsely conclude that the treatment has heterogeneous effects nearly 50% of the time!

18.5.2   Design examples

- Karpowitz, Monson, and Preece (2017) use a two-by-two factorial design in their experimental study of interventions to increase the number of women elected officials. The first factor is a "demand" treatment in which caucus meetings of party members are read a letter encouraging them to vote for women. The second factor is a "supply" treatment in which caucus leaders encourage specific women to stand for election. Caucus meetings could be assigned to the demand treatment, the supply treatment, both, or neither. Both treatments increase the number of women elected. The difference-in-CATEs (the interaction term) is negative, suggesting diminishing marginal returns to the interventions, though it is imprecisely estimated.

- Wilke (2021) conducts a field experiment in South Africa in which treated households are assigned to receive an alarm that directly alerts police to criminal activity, in order to understand how increased access to formal policing channels may discourage mob violence. Outcomes are measured via survey, and embedded in the survey were two additional information treatments about how the police fight crime or fight mob violence. The design is therefore a $2 \times 2 \times 2$ design, and indeed the author finds that the mob violence information treatment is more effective among those assigned an alarm in the field experiment.

18.6 Encouragement Designs

> We declare an encouragement design in which units are assigned to be encouraged to take up a treatment and the average treatment effect is measured among those who comply with the encouragement. The declaration highlights the many changes to the design that are needed to consider noncompliance and what inquiries can be estimated with the design.

In many experimental settings, we cannot require units we *assign* to take treatment to actually *take* treatment. Nor can we require units assigned to the control group not to take treatment. Instead, we have to content ourselves with "encouraging" units assigned to the treatment group to take treatment and "encouraging" units assigned to the control group not to.

Encouragements are often only partially successful. Some units assigned to treatment refuse treatment and some units assigned to control find a way to obtain treatment after all. In these settings, we say that experiments encounter "noncompliance." This section will describe the most common approach to the design and analysis of encouragement trials, and will point out potential pitfalls along the way.

Any time a data strategy entails contacting subjects in order to deliver a treatment like a bundle of information or some good, noncompliance is a potential problem. Emails go undelivered, unopened, and unread. Letters get lost in the mail. Phone calls are screened, text messages get blocked, direct messages on social media are ignored. People don't come to the door when you knock, either because they aren't home or because they don't trust strangers. Noncompliance

Table 18.2: Compliance types.

Compliance Type	$D_i(Z_i=0)$	$D_i(Z_i=1)$
Never-taker	0	0
Complier	0	1
Defier	1	0
Always-taker	1	1

can affect non-informational treatments as well: goods may be difficult to deliver to remote locations, subjects may refuse to participate in assigned experimental activities, or research staff might simply fail to respect the realized treatment schedule.

Experimenters who anticipate noncompliance should make compensating adjustments to their research designs (relative to the canonical two-arm design). These adjustments ripple through M, I, D, and A.

18.6.1 Changes to the model

The biggest difference in M relative to the two arm trial is that we now need to provide beliefs about compliance types, also called "principal strata" (Frangakis and Rubin, 2002). In a two-arm trial, subjects can be one of four compliance types, depending on how their treatment status responds to their treatment assignment. The four types are described in Table 18.2. $D_i(Z_i=0)$ is a potential outcome—it is the treatment status that unit i would express if assigned to control. Likewise, $D_i(Z_i=1)$ is the treatment status that unit i would express if assigned to treatment. These potential outcomes can each take on a value of 0 or 1, so their intersection allows for four types. For always-takers, D_i is equal to 1 regardless of the value of Z—they always take treatment. Never-takers are the opposite—D_i is equal to 0 regardless of the value of Z_i. For always-takers and never-takers, assignment to treatment *does not change* whether they take treatment.

Compliers are units that take treatment if assigned to treatment and do not take treatment if assigned to control. Their name "compliers" connotes that something about their disposition as subjects makes them "compliant" or otherwise docile, but this connotation is misleading. Compliance types are generated by the confluence of subject behavior and data strategy choices. Whether or not a subject answers the door when the canvasser comes calling is a function of many things, including whether the subject is at home and whether they open the door to canvassers. Data strategies that attempt to deliver treatments in the evenings or on weekends might generate more (or different) compliers than those that attempt treatment during working hours.

The last compliance type to describe are defiers. These strange birds refuse treatment when assigned to treatment, but find a way to obtain treatment when assigned to control. Whether or not "defiers" exist turns out to be a consequential assumption that must be made in the model.

A unit's compliance type is usually not possible to observe directly. Subjects assigned to the control group who take take treatment ($D_i(0) = 1$) could be defiers or always-takers. Subjects assigned to the treatment group who do not take treatment ($D_i(1) = 0$) could be defiers or never-takers. Our inability to be sure of compliance types is another facet of the fundamental problem of causal inference. Even though a subject's compliance type (with respect to a given design) is a stable trait, it is defined by how the subject would act in multiple counterfactual worlds. We can't tell what type a unit is because we would need to see whether they take treatment when assigned to treatment and also when assigned to control.

18.6.2 Changes to the inquiry

The inclusion of compliance types in the model accompanies changes to the inquiry. Always-takers and never-takers present a real problem for causal inference. Even with the power to randomly assign, we can't change what treatments these units take. As a result, *we don't get to learn* about the effects of treatment among these groups. Even if our inquiry were the average effect of treatment among the never-takers, the experiment (as designed) would not be able to generate empirical estimates of it.[3] Our inquiry has to fall back to the average effects among those units whose treatment status we can affect: the compliers.

This inquiry is called the complier average causal effect (the CACE). It is defined as $\mathbb{E}[Y_i(1) - Y_i(0) | d_i(1) > d_i(0)]$. Just like the average treatment effect, it refers to an average over individual causal effects, but this average is taken over a specific subset of units, the compliers. Compliers are the only units for whom $d_i(1) > d_i(0)$, because for compliers, $d_i(1) = 1$ and $d_i(0) = 0$. When assignments and treatments are binary, the CACE is mathematically identical to the local average treatment effect (LATE) described in Chapter 16.4. Whether we write CACE or LATE sometimes depends on academic discipline, with LATE being more common among economists and CACE more common among political scientists. An advantage of "CACE" over "LATE" is that it is specific about which units the effect is "local" to—it is local to the compliers.

---

[3] We write "as designed" because compliance types are defined with respect to a particular design. If it were possible to induce the never-takers to take treatment (i.e., under a different data strategy, these units might be compliers), this inquiry would not necessarily be out of reach.

When experiments encounter noncompliance, the CACE may well be the most important inquiry for theory, since it refers to an average effect of the causal variable, at least for a subset of the units in the study. However, two other common inquiries are important to address here as well.

The first is the intention-to-treat (ITT) inquiry, which is defined as $\mathbb{E}[Y_i(D_i(Z=1), Z=1) - Y_i(D_i(Z=0), Z=0)]$. The encouragement itself (Z) has a total effect on Y that is mediated in whole or in part by the treatment status. Sometimes the ITT is the policy-relevant inquiry, since it describes what would happen if a policy maker implemented the policy in the same way as the experiment, *inclusive* of noncompliance. Consider an encouragement design to study the effectiveness of a tax webinar on tax compliance. Even if the webinar is very effective among people willing to watch it (the CACE is large), the main trouble faced by the policy maker will be getting people to sit through the webinar. The ITT describes the average effect of *inviting* people to the webinar, which could be quite small if very few people are willing to join.

The second additional inquiry is the compliance rate, sometimes referred to as the ITT_D. It describes the average effect of assignment on treatment, and is written $\mathbb{E}[(D_i(Z=1) - D_i(Z=0))]$. A small bit of algebra shows that the ITT_D is equal to the fraction of the sample that are compliers minus the fraction that are defiers.

These three inquiries are tightly related. Under five very important assumptions discussed in Section 16.4 on instrumental variables (see also Angrist, Imbens, and Rubin 1996), we can write:

$$\text{CACE} = \frac{\text{ITT}}{\text{ITT}_\text{D}}.$$

In an experimental setting, the "exogeneity of the instrument" assumption is guaranteed by features of the data strategy. Since we use random assignment, we know for sure that the "instrument" (the encouragement) is exogenous. Excludability of the instrument refers to the idea that the effect of the encouragement on the outcome is fully mediated by the treatment. This assumption could be violated if the mere act of encouragement changes outcomes. Stated differently, if never-takers or always-takers reveal *different* potential outcomes in treatment and control ($Y_i(D_i(Z=1), Z=1) \neq Y_i(D_i(Z=0), Z=0)$), it must be because encouragement itself changes outcomes. Noninterference in this setting means that units' treatment status and outcomes do not depend on the assignment or treatment status of other units. In an experimental context, the assumption of monotonicity rules out the existence of defiers. This assumption is often made plausible by features of the data strategy (perhaps it is impossible for those who are not assigned to treatment to obtain treatment) or by theoretical considerations ("defiant" responses to encouragement are behaviorally unlikely). The final assumption—nonzero effect of the instrument on the treatment—can also be bolstered by features of the data strategy. In order to learn about the effects of treatment, data strategies must successfully encourage at least some units to take treatment.

18.6.3 Changes to the data strategy

When experimenters expect that noncompliance will be a problem, they should take steps to mitigate that problem in the data strategy. Sometimes doing so just means trying harder: investigating the patterns of noncompliance, attempting to deliver treatment on multiple occasions, or offering subjects incentives for participation. "Trying harder" is about turning more subjects into compliers by choosing a data strategy that encounters less noncompliance.

A second important change to the data strategy is the explicit measurement of treatment status as distinct from treatment assignment. For some designs, measuring treatment status is easy. We just record which units were treated and which were untreated. But in some settings, measuring compliance is trickier. For example, if treatments are emailed, we might never know if subjects read the email. Perhaps our email service will track read receipts, in which case one facet of this measurement problem is solved. We won't know, however, how many subjects read the subject line—and if the subject line contains any treatment information, then even subjects who don't click on the email may be "partially" treated. One approach is to measure compliance in the most conservative way: if treatment emails bounce altogether, then subjects are not treated.

In multi-arm trials or with continuous rather than binary instruments, noncompliance becomes a more complex problem to define and address through the data strategy and answer strategy. We must define complier types according to all of the possible treatment conditions. For multi-arm trials, the complier types for the first treatment may not be the same for the second treatment; in other words, units will comply at different rates to different treatments. Apparent differences in complier average treatment effects and intent-to-treat effects, as a result, may reflect not differences in treatment effects but different rates of compliance.

18.6.4 Changes to the answer strategy

Estimation of the CACE is not as straightforward subsetting the analysis to compliers (since we cannot observe who they are!). A plug-in estimator of the CACE with good properties takes the ratio of the ITT estimate to the ITT_d estimate. Since the ITT_d must be a number between 0 and 1, this estimator "inflates" the ITT by the compliance rate. Another way of thinking about this is that the ITT is deflated by all the never-takers and always-takers, among whom the ITT is by construction 0, so instead of "inflating", we are "re-inflating" the ITT to the level of the CACE. Two-stage least squares in which we instrument the treatment with the random assignment is a numerically equivalent procedure when treatment and assignments are binary. Two-stage least squares has the further advantage of being able to seamlessly incorporate covariate information to increase precision.

Two alternative answer strategies are biased and should be avoided. An "as-treated" analysis ignores the encouragement Z and instead compares units by their revealed treatment status D. This procedure is prone to bias because those who come to be treated may differ systematically from those who do not. The "per protocol" analysis is similarly biased. It drops any unit that fails to comply with its assignment, but those who take treatment in the treatment group (compliers and always-takers) may differ systematically from those who do not take treatment in the control group (compliers and never-takers). Both the "as-treated" and "per-protocol" answer strategies suffer from a special case of posttreatment bias, wherein conditioning on a post-assignment variable (treatment status) essentially de-randomizes the study.

Declaration 18.9 elaborates the model to include the four compliance types, setting the share of defiers to zero to match the assumption of monotonicity. It imagines that the potential outcomes of the outcomes Y with respect to the treatment D are different for each compliance type, reflecting the idea that compliance type could be correlated with potential outcomes. The declaration also links compliance type to the potential outcomes of the treatment D with respect to the randomized encouragement Z. We then move on to declaring two inquiries (the CACE and the ATE) and three answer strategies (two-stage least squares, as-treated analysis, and per-protocol analysis).

Declaration 18.8 Encouragement design.

```
declaration_18.8 <-
  declare_model(
    N = 100,
    type =
      rep(c("Always-Taker", "Never-Taker", "Complier", "Defier"),
          c(0.2, 0.2, 0.6, 0.0)*N),
    U = rnorm(N),
    # potential outcomes of Y with respect to D
    potential_outcomes(
      Y ~ case_when(
        type == "Always-Taker" ~ -0.25 - 0.50 * D + U,
        type == "Never-Taker" ~ 0.75 - 0.25 * D + U,
        type == "Complier" ~ 0.25 + 0.50 * D + U,
        type == "Defier" ~ -0.25 - 0.50 * D + U
      ),
      conditions = list(D = c(0, 1))
    ),
    # potential outcomes of D with respect to Z
    potential_outcomes(
      D ~ case_when(
        Z == 1 & type %in% c("Always-Taker", "Complier") ~ 1,
        Z == 1 & type %in% c("Never-Taker", "Defier") ~ 0,
```

```
      Z == 0 & type %in% c("Never-Taker", "Complier") ~ 0,
      Z == 0 & type %in% c("Always-Taker", "Defier") ~ 1
    ),
    conditions = list(Z = c(0, 1))
  )
) +
declare_inquiry(
  ATE = mean(Y_D_1 - Y_D_0),
  CACE = mean(Y_D_1[type == "Complier"] - Y_D_0[type == "Complier"])) +
declare_assignment(Z = conduct_ra(N = N)) +
declare_measurement(D = reveal_outcomes(D ~ Z),
                    Y = reveal_outcomes(Y ~ D)) +
declare_estimator(
  Y ~ D | Z,
  .method = iv_robust,
  inquiry = c("ATE", "CACE"),
  label = "Two stage least squares"
) +
declare_estimator(
  Y ~ D,
  .method = lm_robust,
  inquiry = c("ATE", "CACE"),
  label = "As treated"
) +
declare_estimator(
  Y ~ D,
  .method = lm_robust,
  inquiry = c("ATE", "CACE"),
  subset = D == Z,
  label = "Per protocol"
)
```

Figure 18.9 represents the encouragement design as a DAG. No arrows lead into Z, because the treatment was randomly assigned. The compliance type C, the assignment Z, and the unobserved heterogeneity U conspire to set the level of D. The outcome Y is affected by the treatment D of course, but also by compliance type C and the unobserved heterogeneity U. The required exclusion restriction that Z only affects Y through D is represented by the *lack* of an arrow from Z to Y. The deficiencies of the as-treated and per-protocol analysis strategies can be learned from the DAG as well. D is a collider, so conditioning on it would open up backdoor paths between Z, C, and U, leading to bias of unknown direction and magnitude.

Diagnosis 18.9 Diagnosis of encouragement design.

The design diagnosis shows the sampling distribution of the three answer strategies and compares it to two potential inquiries: the complier average causal effect and the average treatment effect. Our preferred method, two-stage least squares, is *biased* for the ATE. Because we can't learn about the effects of treatment among never-takers or always-takers, any estimate of the true ATE will be necessarily be prone to bias, except in the happy circumstance that never-takers and always-takers happen to be just like compliers in terms of their potential outcomes.

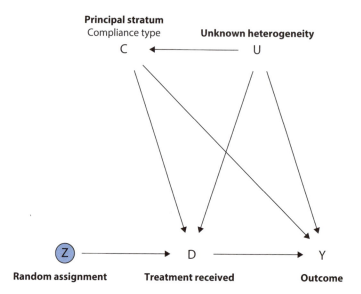

Figure 18.9: Directed acyclic graph of the encouragement design.

Two-stage least squares does a much better job of estimating the complier average causal effect. Even though the sampling distribution is wider than those for the per-protocol and as-treated analysis, it is at least centered on a well-defined inquiry. By contrast, the other two answer strategies are biased for either target.

```
diagnosis_18.9 <- diagnose_design(declaration_18.8)
```

18.6.5   Design examples

- Scacco and Warren (2018) randomize young men in Nigeria to participate in a vocational training program—84% of subjects assigned to the training participated, but the remainder did not. The authors attempted to measure outcomes for all subjects, regardless of treatment or compliance status and estimated intention-to-treat effects in all cases.

- Blair et al. (2022) randomize communities in Colombia to receive a program aimed at improving local governance through enhanced cooperation between state and local agencies. Some communities assigned to participate in the program did not participate, or did not participate fully. The authors present the intention-to-treat estimates of treatment effects as well as complier average causal effect estimates, varying the definition of compliance to include or exclude partial compliance. (Defining compliance as "any compliance including partial compliance" is the conservative choice, as defining partial compliers as noncompliers could violate excludability.)

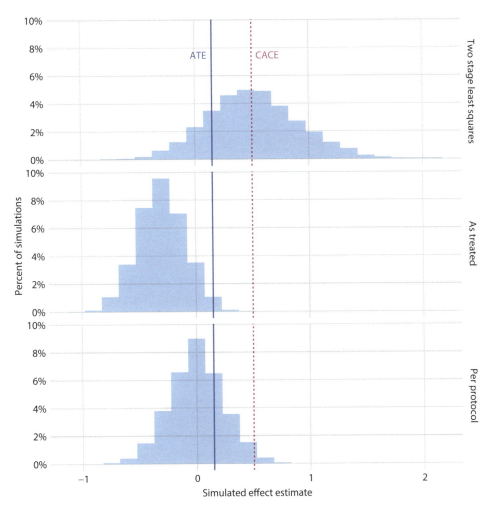

Figure 18.10: Sampling distributions of the two-stage least squares, per protocol, and as-treated answer strategies.

18.7 Placebo-Controlled Experiments

We compare an encouragement design to a placebo-controlled trial in which units are selected into treatment based on whether they receive *either* treatment or a placebo treatment with a similar deployment method. At low levels of compliance, the diagnosis reveals the placebo-controlled design is preferred, but then the encouragement design is preferred as compliance increases.

In common usage, the notion of a placebo is a treatment that carries with it everything about the bona fide treatment—except the active ingredient. We're used to thinking about placebos in terms of the "placebo effect" in medical trials. Some portion of the total effect of the actual treatment is due to the mere act of *getting treated*, so the administration of placebo treatments can difference this portion off.

Placebo-controlled designs abound in the social sciences, too; for similar purposes (see Porter and Velez, 2021). Media treatments often work through a bundle of priming effects and new information; a placebo treatment might include only the prime but not the information. The main use of placebos is to difference off the many small excludability violations involved in bundled treatments to better understand the main causal variable of interest.

In this chapter, we study the use of placebos for a different purpose: to combat the negative design consequences of noncompliance in experiments. As described in the previous chapter, a challenge for experiments that encounter noncompliance is that we do not know for sure who the compliers are. Compliers are units that would take treatment if assigned to treatment, but would not do so if assigned to control. Compliers are different from always-takers and never-takers in that assignment to treatment actually changes which potential outcome they reveal.

In the placebo-controlled design, we attempt to deliver a real treatment to the treatment group and a placebo treatment to the placebo group, then conduct our analysis among those units that accept either treatment. This design solves two problems at once. First, it lets us answer a *descriptive* question: "Who are the compliers?" Second, it lets answer a *causal* question: "What is the average effect of treatment among compliers?"

Employing a placebo control can seem like an odd design choice—you go through the effort of contacting a unit but at the very moment you get in touch, you deliver a placebo message instead of the treatment message. It turns out that despite this apparent waste, the placebo-controlled design can often lead to more precise estimates than the standard encouragement design. Whether it does or not depends in large part on the underlying compliance rate.

Declaration 18.9 actually includes two separate designs. Here we'll directly compare the standard encouragement design to the placebo-controlled design. They have identical models and inquiries, so we'll just declare those once, before declaring the specifics of the empirical strategies for each design. The model has no always takers, which is a reasonable assumption if the treatment can only be provided through the researchers. When we use this model for the placebo design we will also assume that the compliance types are the same for both the treatment and the placebo conditions—that is, there is no differential selection conditional on contact.

Declaration 18.9 Comparing the encouragement and placebo-controlled designs.

```
compliance_rate <- 0.2

MI <-
  declare_model(
    N = 400,
    type = sample(x = c("Never-Taker", "Complier"),
                  size = N,
```

18.7 Placebo-Controlled Experiments

```
                 prob = c(1 - compliance_rate, compliance_rate),
                 replace = TRUE),
    U = rnorm(N),
    # potential outcomes of Y with respect to D
    potential_outcomes(
      Y ~ case_when(
        type == "Never-Taker" ~ 0.75 - 0.25 * D + U,
        type == "Complier" ~ 0.25 + 0.50 * D + U
      ),
      conditions = list(D = c(0, 1))
    ),
    # potential outcomes of D with respect to Z
    potential_outcomes(
      D ~ if_else(Z == 1 & type == "Complier", 1, 0),
      conditions = list(Z = c(0, 1))
    )
  ) +
  declare_inquiry(
    CACE = mean(Y_D_1[type == "Complier"] -
                Y_D_0[type == "Complier"])
  )
```

Here, again, are the data and answer strategies for the encouragement design (simplified from the previous chapter to focus on the one-sided compliance case, in which units can fail to take treatment but cannot take treatment if assigned to control). We conduct a random assignment among all units, then reveal treatment statuses and outcomes according to the potential outcomes declared in the model. The two-stage least squares estimator operates on all N units to generate estimates of the CACE.

```
declaration_18.9_encouragement <-
  MI +
  declare_assignment(Z = complete_ra(N)) +
  declare_measurement(D = reveal_outcomes(D ~ Z),
                      Y = reveal_outcomes(Y ~ D)) +
  declare_estimator(
    Y ~ D | Z,
    .method = iv_robust,
    inquiry = "CACE",
    label = "2SLS among all units"
  )
```

By contrast, here are the data and answer strategies for the placebo-controlled design. In a typical canvassing experiment setting, the expensive part is sending canvassing teams to each household, regardless of whether a treatment or a placebo message is delivered when the door opens. So in order to keep things "fair" across the placebo-controlled and encouragement designs, we're going to hold fixed the number of treatment attempts by sampling 200 of the 400 individuals to participate. Then among that subset, we conduct a random assignment to treatment or placebo. When we attempt to deliver the placebo or the treatment, we will either succeed or fail, which gives us a direct measure of whether a unit is a complier—made possible by the assumption that there are no always takers and that compliance types are the same in the treatment and placebo condition. This measurement is represented in the `declare_measurement` step, where an observable X now corresponds to compliance type. We conduct our estimation directly conditioning on the subset of the sample we have measured to be compliers.

```
declaration_18.9_placebo <-
  MI +
  declare_sampling(S = complete_rs(N, n = 200)) +
  declare_assignment(Z = complete_ra(N)) +
  declare_measurement(X = if_else(type == "Complier", 1, 0),
                      D = reveal_outcomes(D ~ Z),
                      Y = reveal_outcomes(Y ~ D)) +
  declare_estimator(
    Y ~ Z,
    subset = X == 1,
    .method = lm_robust,
    inquiry = "CACE",
    label = "OLS among compliers"
  )
```

Diagnosis 18.10 Diagnosing the encouragement and placebo-controlled designs.

We diagnose both the encouragement design and the placebo-controlled design over a range of possible levels of noncompliance, focusing on the standard deviation of the estimates (the standard error) as our main diagnosand. Figure 18.11 shows the results of the diagnosis. At high levels of compliance, the standard encouragement design actually outperforms the placebo-controlled design. But when compliance is low, the placebo-controlled design is preferred. Which design is preferable in any particular scenario will depend on the compliance rate as well as other design features like the total number of attempts and the fraction treated (see Broockman, Kalla, and Sekhon, 2017).

```
diagnosis_18.10_encouragment <-
  declaration_18.9_encouragment |>
  redesign(compliance_rate = seq(0.1, 0.9, by = 0.1)) |>
  diagnose_designs(sims = sims, bootstrap_sims = bootstrap_sims)

diagnosis_18.10_placebo <-
  declaration_18.9_placebo |>
  redesign(compliance_rate = seq(0.1, 0.9, by = 0.1)) |>
  diagnose_designs(sims = sims, bootstrap_sims = bootstrap_sims)
```

18.7.1 Design examples

- Broockman and Kalla (2016) use a placebo-controlled design in their study of a transphobia-reduction canvassing treatment. Households were assigned either a placebo (a conversation about recycling) or the treatment; analysis was conducted among those who opened the door to the canvasser.

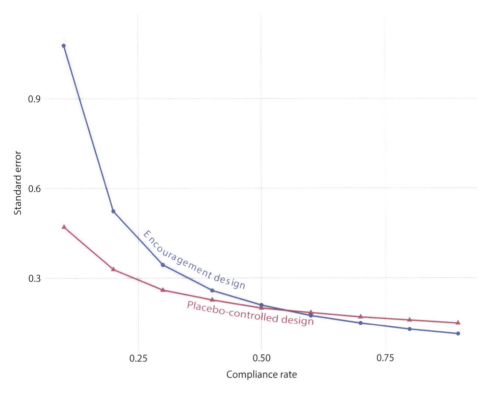

Figure 18.11: Comparison of the placebo-controlled design to a standard encouragment design.

- Wilke, Green, and Cooper (2020) extend the placebo-controlled design in a media experiment in Uganda. Film festival attendees were assigned to watch public service announcements on one or two of three topics; posttreatment attitudes about all three topics were measured for all subjects. Subjects who saw the treatment on a given topic served as placebo controls for subjects who saw treatments on other topics. Under the maintained placebo assumption that treatments on one topic won't affect attitudes on other topics, this design allows for efficient, unbiased inference for the effects of multiple treatments on their targeted outcomes.

18.8 Stepped-Wedge Experiments

> We declare a stepped-wedge design in which units are assigned a *sequence* of treatments across multiple periods. In each period, one third are treated successively. Diagnosis of this design and of similar-cost standard two-arm trials suggests that a double-sized two-arm trial is preferable in terms of power but that the stepped-wedge experiment is useful when the number of study units is limited.

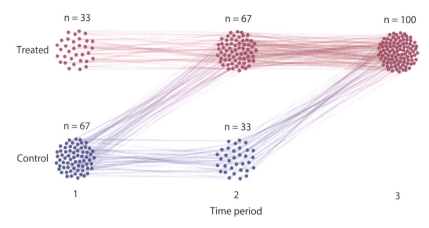

Figure 18.12: Illustration of random assignment in a stepped-wedge design.

We often face an ethical dilemma in allocating treatments to some units but not others, since we would rather not withhold treatment from anyone. However, practical constraints often make it impossible to allocate treatments to everyone at the same time. In these circumstances, a stepped-wedge experiment, also known as a waitlist design, can help. Under a stepped-wedge design, we follow an allocation rule that randomly assigns a portion of units to treatment in each of one or more periods, and then in a final period everyone is allocated treatment. We conduct posttreatment measurement after each period except for the last one. Figure 18.12 illustrates the allocation procedure. A common design is allocating one third to treatment in the first period, an additional third in the second period, and the remaining third in the final period.

Our model describes unit-specific effects, time-specific effects, and time trends in the potential outcomes. Our inquiry is the average treatment effect among time periods *before* the last period, since in the stepped-wedge design, we don't obtain information about the control potential outcome in the final period. In the data strategy, we assign treatment by randomly assigning the wave in which each unit will receive treatment. We use cluster assignment at the unit level because the data is at the unit-period level. We then transform this treatment variable into a unit-period treatment indicator if the time period is at or after the treatment wave. The answer strategy also only uses the data from the first two periods (we probably would not collect outcome data after the last period for this reason). We fit a two-way fixed effects regression model by periods and units, with standard errors clustered at the unit level.

The stepped-wedge experimental design, described in Declaration 18.10, shares much in common with the observational difference-in-differences design. We show in Section 16.3 that the two-way fixed effects estimator is biased for the average treatment effect on the treated in the presence of treatment effect by time interactions. However, in the stepped-wedge design, we randomize treatment, so we do not need to make a parallel trends assumption. Our diagnosis below shows no bias when estimating the average treatment effect with the two-way fixed effects estimator in the stepped-wedge design even when treatment effects vary by period. A regression with only period effects would also return unbiased answers as would a design with inverse assignment probability weights described in Gerber and Green (2012, ch. 8), but if there are large unit differences the two-way design will be more efficient. Only including unit fixed effects, by contrast, without period effects, will yield biased answers, because the probabilities of assignment vary by round.

Declaration 18.10 Stepped-wedge design.

```
effect_size <- 0.35

declaration_18.10 <-
  declare_model(
    units = add_level(
      N = 100,
      U_unit = rnorm(N)
    ),
    periods = add_level(
      N = 3,
      time = 1:max(periods),
      U_time = rnorm(N),
      nest = FALSE
    ),
    unit_period = cross_levels(
      by = join_using(units, periods),
      U = rnorm(N),
      potential_outcomes(
        Y ~ scale(U_unit + U_time + time + U) + effect_size * Z
      )
    )
  ) +
  declare_assignment(
    wave = cluster_ra(clusters = units, conditions = 1:max(periods)),
    Z = if_else(time >= wave, 1, 0)
  ) +
  declare_inquiry(ATE = mean(Y_Z_1 - Y_Z_0), subset = time < max(time)) +
  declare_measurement(Y = reveal_outcomes(Y ~ Z)) +
  declare_estimator(Y ~ Z, fixed_effects = ~ periods + units,
                    clusters = units,
                    subset = time < max(time),
                    inquiry = "ATE", label = "TWFE")
```

18.8.1 When to use a stepped-wedge experiment

Compared to the equivalent two-arm randomized experiment, a stepped-wedge experiment involves the same number of units, but more treatment (all versus half) and more measurement (all units are measured at least twice). The decision of whether to adopt the stepped-wedge design, then, rides on budget, the relative costs of measurement and treatment, ethical and logistical constraints such as the imperative to treat all units, and beliefs about effect sizes and outcome variances.

Table 18.3: Design parameters in the comparison between stepped-wedge and two-arm experimental designs.

Design	N	m treated	n measurements
Stepped-wedge	100	100	200
Two-arm v1	100	50	100
Two-arm v2	200	100	200

We compare the stepped-wedge design to a two-arm randomized experiment with varying sample sizes to assess these trade-offs. First we compare designs with the same number of units, which would be the relevant comparison if the number of units is fixed. The second comparison is a two-arm experiment with double the number of units, which would be the right comparison if the number of units can be increased at some cost. We summarize each design in terms of the number of study units, the number that are treated, and the number of unit measurements taken.

We declare a comparable two-arm experimental design in Declaration 18.11, with the wrinkle being that the estimand is slightly different by necessity. In the stepped-wedge design, we target the average treatment effect averaging over all periods up to the penultimate one, because there is no information about the control group from the last period. In a single period design, by its nature, we cannot average over time. We would obtain a biased answer if we targeted an out-of-sample time period. The average treatment effect we target is the current-period ATE for the period that is chosen. We cannot extrapolate beyond that if treatment effects vary over time. If we expect time heterogeneity in effects, we may *not* want to use a stepped-wedge design but instead to design a new experiment that efficiently targets the conditional average treatment effects within each period. Then we could describe both the average effect and how effects vary over time.

Declaration 18.11 Comparison single-period two arm trial design.

```
declaration_18.11 <-
  declare_model(
    N = n_units,
    U_unit = rnorm(N),
    U = rnorm(N),
    effect_size = effect_size,
    potential_outcomes(Y ~ scale(U_unit + U) + effect_size * Z)
  ) +
  declare_assignment(Z = complete_ra(N, m = n_units / 2)) +
  declare_inquiry(ATE = mean(Y_Z_1 - Y_Z_0)) +
  declare_measurement(Y = reveal_outcomes(Y ~ Z)) +
  declare_estimator(Y ~ Z, inquiry = "ATE", label = "DIM")
```

18.8 Stepped-Wedge Experiments

Diagnosis 18.11 Diagnosis of stepped-wedge design compared to two single-period two-arm trial designs.

```
design_stepped_wedge <-
  declaration_18.11 |>
  redesign(n_units = 100, effect_size = seq(from = 0, to = 0.75, by = 0.05))

design_single_period_100 <-
  declaration_18.11 |>
  redesign(n_units = 100, effect_size = seq(from = 0, to = 0.75, by = 0.05))

design_single_period_200 <-
  declaration_18.11 |>
  redesign(n_units = 200, effect_size = seq(from = 0, to = 0.75, by = 0.05))

designs <- c(design_stepped_wedge,
             design_single_period_100,
             design_single_period_200)
attr(designs, "names") <- paste0("design_", 1:length(designs))

diagnosis_18.11 <- diagnose_design(designs)
```

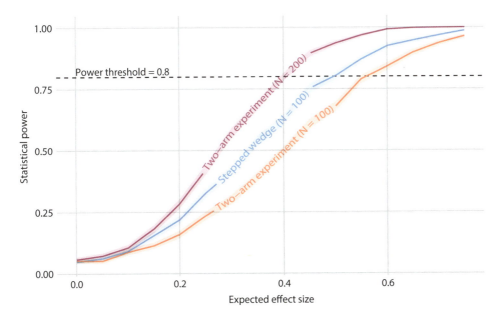

Figure 18.13: Power analysis of three designs: stepped wedge with 100 units and 1/3–1/3–1/3 allocation, two-arm experiment with 100 units, and two-arm experiment with 200 units.

We plot power curves for the three comparison designs in Figure 18.13. The top line (purple) is the 200-unit study, which is preferred in terms of power, and by a considerable margin. That design involves the same amount of measurement and treatment as the stepped-wedge design, so may have the same cost. However, if only 100 units are available for study, then the relevant comparison is between the stepped-wedge and the 100-unit two-arm study. Here, the stepped-wedge design is preferable in terms of power and may satisfy ethical requirements to eventually treat all subjects.

18.8.2 Design examples

- Gerber et al. (2011) use a stepped-wedge design to randomize the timing of political television ads in 18 media markets in Texas in advance of a primary election.

- Pennycook et al. (2021) conduct an online field experiment with Twitter users who had shared links to untrustworthy Web sites. The authors randomized the timing of direct messages to those users, asking them to rate the accuracy of a nonpolitical headline, then observed the quality of the news articles they subsequently shared.

18.9 Randomized Saturation Experiments

> We declare a multilevel design in which we randomize first the "saturation" or probability of assignment with clusters and then randomly assign within the clusters based on that saturation probability. The diagnosis highlights that the efficiency for estimating the causal effect of the saturation level is low, because assignment is clustered, and is higher for estimating the individual treatment effect within clusters of a given saturation.

We study most treatments at an isolated, atomized, individualistic level. We define potential outcomes with respect to a unit's own treatment status, ignoring the treatment status of all other units in the study. Accordingly, our inquiries tend to be averages of individual-level causal effects, and our data strategies tend to assign treatments at the individual level as well. All of the experimental designs we have considered to this point have been of this flavor.

However, when the potential outcome revealed by a unit depends on the treatment status of other units, then we have to make adjustments to every part of the design. We have to redefine the model M to specify what potential outcomes are possible. Under a no-spillover model, we might only have the treated and untreated potential outcomes, $Y_i(1)$ and $Y_i(0)$. But under spillover models, we have to expand the set of possibilities. For example, we might imagine that unit i's potential outcomes can be written as a function of their own treatment status and that of their housemate, unit j: $Y_i(Z_i, Z_j)$. We have to redefine our inquiry I with respect to those reimagined potential outcomes. The average treatment effect is typically defined as $\mathbb{E}[Y_i(1) - Y_i(0)]$, but if $Y_i(1)$ and $Y_i(0)$ are no longer well-defined, we need to choose a new inquiry, like the average direct effect of treatment when unit j is not treated: $\mathbb{E}[Y_i(1, 0) - Y_i(0, 0)]$. We have to alter our data strategy D so that the randomization procedure produces healthy samples of all of the potential outcomes involved in the inquiries, and we have to amend our answer strategy A to account for the important features of the new randomization protocol.

We divide up our investigation of experimental designs to learn about spillovers into two sets. This chapter addresses randomized saturation designs, which are appropriate when we can exploit a hierarchical clustering of subjects into groups within which spillover can occur but across which spillover can't occur. The next chapter addresses experiments over networks, which are appropriate when spillover occurs over geographic, temporal, or social networks.

The randomized saturation design (sometimes called the partial population design, as in Baird et al., 2018) is purpose-built for scenarios in which we have good reason to imagine that a unit's potential outcomes depend on the fraction of treated units within the same cluster. For example, we might want to consider the fraction of people within a neighborhood assigned to receive a vaccine: a person's health outcomes could easily depend on whether two thirds or one third of neighbors have been treated.

In the model, we now have to define potential outcomes with respect to both the individual level treatment and also the saturation level. We can imagine a variety of different kinds of potential outcomes functions. Consider the vaccine example, imagining a 100% effective vaccine against infection. Directly treated individuals never contract the illness, but the probability of infection for untreated units depends on the fraction who are treated nearby. If the treatment is a persuasive message to vote for a particular candidate, we might imagine that direct treatment is ineffective when only a few people around you hear the message, but becomes much more effective when many people hear the message at the same time. The main challenge in developing intuitions about complex interactions like this is articulating the discrete potential outcomes that each subject could express, then reasoning about the plausible values for each potential outcome.

The randomized saturation design is a factorial design of sorts, and like any factorial design can support a number of different inquiries. We can describe the average effect of direct treatment at low saturation, at high saturation, the average of the two, or the difference between the two. Similarly, we could describe the average effect of high versus low saturation among the untreated, among the treated, the average of the two, or the difference between the two. In some settings, all eight of these inquiries might be appropriate to report, in others just a subset.

The design employs a two-stage data strategy. First, predefined clusters of units are randomly assigned to treatment saturation levels, for example, 25% or 75%. Then, in each cluster, individual units are assigned to treatment or control with probabilities determined by their clusters' saturation level. The main answer strategy complication is that now there are two levels of randomization that must be respected. The saturation of treatment varies at the cluster level, so whenever we are estimating saturation effects, we have to cluster standard errors at the level saturation was assigned. The direct treatments are assigned at the individual level, so we do not need to cluster.

Declaration 18.12 describes 50 groups of 20 individuals each. We imagine one source of unobserved variation at the group level (the `group_shock`) and another at the individual level (the `individual_shock`). We build potential outcomes in which the individual and saturation treatment assignments each have additive (noninteracting) effects, though more complex potential outcomes functions are of course possible. We choose two inquiries in particular: the conditional average effect of saturation among the untreated and the conditional average effect of treatment when saturation is low.

We can learn about the effects of the dosage of indirect treatment by comparing units with the same individual treatment status across the levels of dosage. For example, we could compare untreated units across the 25% and 75% saturation clusters. We can also learn about the direct effects of treatment at either saturation level, e.g., the effect of treatment when saturation is low. We use difference-in-means estimators of both inquiries, subsetted and clustered appropriately.

Declaration 18.12 Randomized saturation design.

```
declaration_18.12 <-
  declare_model(
    group = add_level(N = 50, group_shock = rnorm(N)),
    individual = add_level(
      N = 20,
      individual_shock = rnorm(N),
      potential_outcomes(
        Y ~ 0.2 * Z + 0.1 * (S == "low") + 0.5 * (S == "high") +
          group_shock + individual_shock,
        conditions = list(Z = c(0, 1),
                          S = c("low", "high"))
      )
    )
  ) +
  declare_inquiry(
    CATE_S_Z_0 = mean(Y_Z_0_S_high - Y_Z_0_S_low),
    CATE_Z_S_low = mean(Y_Z_1_S_low - Y_Z_0_S_low)
  ) +
  declare_assignment(
    S = cluster_ra(clusters = group,
                   conditions = c("low", "high")),
    Z = block_ra(blocks = group,
                 prob_unit = if_else(S == "low", 0.25, 0.75))
  ) +
  declare_measurement(Y = reveal_outcomes(Y ~ Z + S)) +
  declare_estimator(
    Y ~ S,
    .method = difference_in_means,
    subset = Z == 0,
    term = "Shigh",
    clusters = group,
    inquiry = "CATE_S_Z_0",
    label = "Effect of high saturation among untreated"
  ) +
```

```
declare_estimator(
  Y ~ Z,
  .method = difference_in_means,
  .subset = S == "low",
  blocks = group,
  inquiry = "CATE_Z_S_low",
  label = "Effect of treatment at low saturation"
)
```

Diagnosis 18.12 Randomized saturation diagnosis.

```
diagnosis_18.12 <- diagnose_design(declaration_18.12)
```

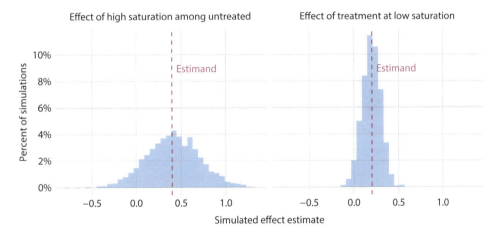

Figure 18.14: Sampling distributions of indirect and direct treatment effect estimators.

The diagnosis plot in Figure 18.14 shows the sampling distribution of the two estimators with the value of the relevant inquiry overlaid. Both estimators are unbiased for their targets, but the thing to notice from this plot is that the estimator of the saturation inquiry is far more variable than the estimator of the direct treatment inquiry. Saturation is by its nature a group-level treatment, so must be assigned at a group level. The clustered nature of the assignment to saturation level brings extra uncertainty. When designing randomized saturation experiments, researchers should be aware that we typically have much better precision for individually randomized treatments than cluster-randomized treatments, and should plan accordingly.

18.9.1 Design examples

- Cheema et al. (2022) used a randomized saturation design in their study of a get-out-the-vote campaign in Pakistan. Wards could be assigned to one of three treatment conditions or to a control condition; within treated wards, four of five study households received the assigned condition but the fifth was assigned to control. A comparison of untreated households in treated wards to untreated households in untreated wards generates an estimate of the spillover effect (small and nonsignificant in this case).

- Egger et al. (2019) study how a cash transfer program implemented in one locality may affect outcomes in neighboring localities. In Kenya, the authors grouped villages into "saturation groups" and randomized the saturation groups to have one third or two thirds of their constituent villages assigned to treatment. A comparison of the untreated villages in the one third and two thirds saturation groups yields an estimate of the spillover effect.

18.10   Experiments over Networks

> We declare a design for a randomized trial in which the researcher controls the assignment of direct treatment, but then assesses the effects of direct treatment *and* of being indirectly treated by being geographically proximate to a unit directly treated. The diagnosis demonstrates both can be estimated without bias if the probability of indirect treatment is estimated through simulation, but that common estimators differ greatly in efficiency.

When experimental subjects are embedded in a network, units' outcomes may depend on the treatment statuses of nearby units. In other words, treatments map spillover across the network. For example, in a geographic network, vote margin in one precinct may depend on outdoor advertisements in neighboring precincts. In a social network, information delivered to a treated subject might be shared with friends or followers. In a temporal network, treatments in the past might affect outcomes in the future.

This chapter describes the special challenges associated with experiments over networks. In the previous chapter, we discussed randomized saturation designs, which are appropriate when we can describe a hierarchy of units embedded in clusters, within which spillovers can occur but across which spillovers cannot occur. In other words, the randomized saturation design is appropriate when the network is composed of many disconnected network components (the clusters). But most networks are not disconnected. Instead, all or almost all units are typically connected in a vast web. This chapter describes how we need to modify the model, inquiry, data strategy, and answer strategy to learn from experiments over networks.

In the model, our main challenge is to define how far apart (in social, geographic, or temporal space) units have to be in order for unit i's potential outcomes not to depend on unit j. We might say units within 5 km matter, but units further away do not. We might say that units within two friendship links matter, but more distal connections do not. We might allow the treatment statuses of three, two, or one

Table 18.4: Example treatment conditions for an experiment over a network.

Condition	Potential outcomes
Pure control	$Y_i(\text{direct}=0, \text{indirect}=0)$
Direct only	$Y_i(\text{direct}=1, \text{indirect}=0)$
Indirect only	$Y_i(\text{direct}=0, \text{indirect}=1)$
Direct and indirect	$Y_i(\text{direct}=1, \text{indirect}=1)$

period ago to impact present outcomes differently from one another. For example, we might stipulate that each unit has only four potential outcomes that depend on whether a unit is directly treated or indirectly treated by virtue of being adjacent to a directly treated unit as in Table 18.4.

With potential outcomes defined, we can define inquiries. With four potential outcomes, there are six pairwise contrasts that we could contemplate. For example, the direct effect in the absence of indirect treatment is defined as $\mathbb{E}[Y_i(\text{direct}=1, \text{indirect}=0) - Y_i(\text{direct}=0, \text{indirect}=0)]$ and the direct effect in the presence of indirect treatment is $\mathbb{E}[Y_i(\text{direct}=1, \text{indirect}=1) - Y_i(\text{direct}=0, \text{indirect}=1)]$. We could similarly define indirect effects as $\mathbb{E}[Y_i(\text{direct}=0, \text{indirect}=1) - Y_i(\text{direct}=0, \text{indirect}=0)]$ or $\mathbb{E}[Y_i(\text{direct}=1, \text{indirect}=1) - Y_i(\text{direct}=1, \text{indirect}=0)]$. We may be interested in how direct and indirect treatments interact, which would require taking the difference between the two direct effect inquiries or taking the difference between the two indirect effect inquiries. Which inquiry is most appropriate will depend on the theoretical setting.

The data strategy for an experiment over networks still involves random assignment. Typically, however, experimenters are only in control of the direct treatment application, and exposure to indirect treatment results from the natural channels through which spillovers occur. The mapping from a direct treatment vector to the assumed set of treatment conditions is described by Aronow and Samii (2017) as an "exposure mapping." The exposure mapping defines how the randomized treatment results in the exposures that reveal each potential outcome. The probabilities of assignment to each of the four conditions are importantly *not constant* across units, for the main reason that units with more neighbors are more likely to receive indirect treatment. Furthermore, exposures are dependent across units: if one unit is directly treated, then all adjacent units must be indirectly treated.

We need to adjust our answer strategy to compensate for the differential probabilities generated by this complex data strategy. As usual, we need to weight units by the inverse of the probability of assignment to the condition that they are in. In the networked setting we have to further account for dependence in treatment assignment probabilities. This dependence tends to increase sampling variability.

For intuition, consider how clustering (an extreme form of across-unit dependence in treatment conditions) similarly tends to increase sampling variability. Aronow and Samii (2017) propose Hajek- and Horvitz-Thompson-style point and variance estimators that account for these complex joint probabilities of assignment, which are themselves estimated by simulating the exposures that would result from many thousands of possible random assignments.

To illustrate these ideas, we declare a hypothetical experimental design to estimate the effects of lawn signs (modeled after Green et al., 2016). The units are the lowest level at which we can observe vote margin, the voting precinct. In our model, we define four potential outcomes. Precincts can be both directly and indirectly treated, only directly treated, only indirectly treated, or neither. Indirect treatment occurs when a neighboring precinct is treated. This model could support many possible inquiries, but here we will focus on three: the direct effect of treatment when the precinct is not indirectly treated, the effect of indirect treatment when the precinct is not directly treated, and the total effect of direct and indirect treatment versus pure control. The data strategy will involve randomly assigning some units to direct treatment, which will in turn cause other units to be indirectly treated. We will need to learn via simulation the probabilities of assignments to conditions that this procedure produces. We'll make use of two answer strategies: the Horvitz-Thompson and Hajek estimators proposed by Aronow and Samii (2017), along with their associated variance estimators, as implemented in the `interference` package.

To do this, we load the Fairfax County, Virginia, voting precincts shapefile, and remove the state capital which is not part of the county. We plot the precincts in Figure 18.15.

To declare the full design, shown in Declaration 18.13, we first need to obtain the adjacency matrix of precincts in Fairfax. Second, we obtain a permutation matrix of possible random assignments, from which probabilities of assignment to each condition can be calculated. The `declare_model` call builds in a dependence of potential outcomes on the length of each precinct's perimeter to reflect the idea that outcomes are correlated with geography in some way. The `declare_inquiry` call describes the three inquiries in terms of potential outcomes. The `declare_assignment` call first conducts a random assignment according to the procedure described by `declare_ra` earlier in the code, then obtains the exposures that the assignment generates. Finally, all the relevant information is fed into the Aronow and Samii estimation functions via `estimator_AS` (the `get_exposure_AS` and `estimator_AS` helper functions are available in the `rdss` package).

Declaration 18.13 Experiments over spatial networks design.

```
library(rdss) # for helper functions
library(spdep)
library(interference)
```

18.10 Experiments over Networks   295

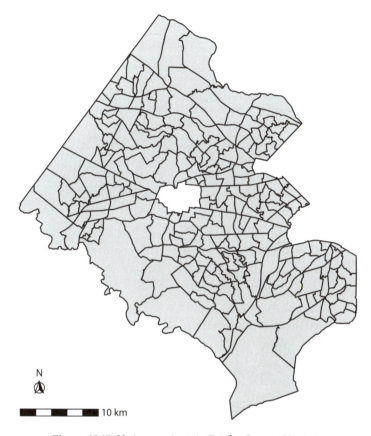

Figure 18.15: Voting precincts in Fairfax County, Virginia.

```
# Here we obtain the adjacency matrix
adj_matrix <-
  fairfax |>
  as("Spatial") |>
  poly2nb(queen = TRUE) |>
  nb2mat(style = "B", zero.policy = TRUE)

# Here we create a permutation matrix of possible random assignments
ra_declaration <- declare_ra(N = 238, prob = 0.1)

permutatation_matrix <-
  ra_declaration |>
  obtain_permutation_matrix(maximum_permutations = 10000) |>
  t()

declaration_18.13 <-
  declare_model(
    data = select(as_tibble(fairfax), -geometry),
    Y_0_0 = pnorm(scale(SHAPE_LEN), sd = 3),
    Y_1_0 = Y_0_0 + 0.02,
    Y_0_1 = Y_0_0 + 0.01,
    Y_1_1 = Y_0_0 + 0.03
  ) +
  declare_inquiry(
```

Chapter 18: Experimental : Causal

```
    total_ATE = mean(Y_1_1 - Y_0_0),
    direct_ATE = mean(Y_1_0 - Y_0_0),
    indirect_ATE = mean(Y_0_1 - Y_0_0)
  ) +
  declare_assignment(
    Z = conduct_ra(ra_declaration),
    exposure = get_exposure_AS(make_exposure_map_AS(adj_matrix, Z, hop = 1))
  ) +
  declare_measurement(
    Y = case_when(
      exposure == "dir_ind1" ~ Y_1_1,
      exposure == "isol_dir" ~ Y_1_0,
      exposure == "ind1" ~ Y_0_1,
      exposure == "no" ~ Y_0_0
    )
  ) +
  declare_estimator(handler = estimator_AS_tidy,
                    permutatation_matrix = permutatation_matrix,
                    adj_matrix = adj_matrix)
```

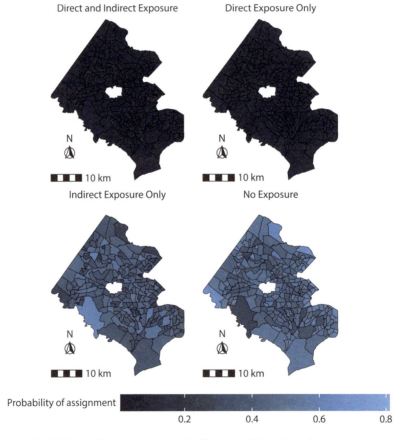

Figure 18.16: Probabilities of assignment to each of four conditions depend on position in geographic space.

The maps in Figure 18.16 show how this procedure generates differential probabilities of assignment to each exposure condition. Units that are in denser areas of the county are more likely to be in the Indirect Exposure Only and Direct and Indirect Exposure conditions than those in less dense areas.

Diagnosis 18.13 Experiments over spatial networks diagnosis.

Figure 18.17 compares the performance of the Hajek and Horvitz-Thompson estimators. Both are approximately unbiased for their targets, but the Horvitz-Thompson estimator exhibits much higher variance, suggesting that in many design settings, researchers will want to opt for the Hajek estimator.

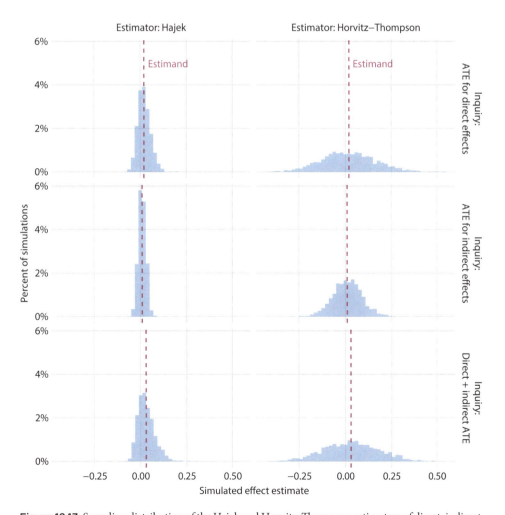

Figure 18.17: Sampling distribution of the Hajek and Horvitz-Thompson estimators of direct, indirect, and direct plus indirect effects. The vertical lines refer to the true values of the inquiries.

18.10.1 Design examples

- Zelizer (2019) conducts experiments within a legislative network defined by office-sharing. Legislators were randomly assigned briefings on a subset of bills and their decision to cosponsor the bill (or not) was recorded. The design was able to estimate spillover effects bill by comparing legislators whose office mates were and were not assigned to treatment on various bills.

- Green et al. (2016) conducts a randomized experiment within a geographic network of adjacent voting precincts. Treated units were assigned many lawn signs supporting a candidate. The design supported inference on the direct effects (treated units relative to untreated units surrounded by untreated units) and the indirect effects (untreated units adjacent to treated units relative to untreated units surrounded by untreated units). The answer strategy accounted for the different probabilities of assignment to each of these conditions depending on geographic network position.

CHAPTER 19

Complex Designs

In the designs we presented thus far, the aim was generally to learn about the level of some variable or some particular causal effect. In most cases, a single set of data was collected and an answer strategy was applied directly to the data to generate an answer to a causal or descriptive inquiry.

In practice, however, many published studies are more complicated than this and draw in complex ways on a series of research designs, each targeted to a different inquiry, that when brought together answer the deeper theoretical question at the heart of the research.

But studies can also be complex in other ways. For instance, although we have assumed researchers start with well-defined inquiries, some studies focus on first figuring out what question to ask and then proceed to ask and answer it. Such studies engage first in model building, then report the results of a follow-on research design targeted at questions posed by the new model.

Some studies seek not to learn about levels and effects but search explicitly for a model of a phenomenon, asking, for instance, "what causes Y?" or "what model, in some class, best accounts for observed data?" These studies have complex inquiries. Other studies have complex data and answer strategies, for instance, mixing qualitative and quantitative inference strategies or gathering together findings from multiple sub-studies in order to arrive at an overall conclusion.

19.1 Discovery Using Causal Forests

> We declare a design in which a researcher examines a large set of continuous covariates to discover (i) which covariate best explains heterogeneity in the effects of a treatment and (ii) which subjects experience the weakest or strongest effects. The design declaration clarifies the inquiries when the goal of the study is discovery and can be used to guide design decisions regarding how best to split data into training and testing sets.

In most designs that we have discussed, researchers have a clear idea what they are looking for when they begin the research. How big is some population? What is the size of some effect? But some research involves questions that are much more open in nature. We focus here on discovery research that has two types of more open inquiry. The first inquiry poses an open question of the form, "what matters?" (rather than the more common closed question of the form, "what is the effect of this on that?"). The second inquiry poses a question about an as-yet unspecified group—the people for whom effects are especially strong or weak.

We imagine a setting in which a researcher has access to a large group of covariates X and has conducted an experiment to assess the effects of Z on Y. The researcher is interested in the *heterogeneity* of effects of Z as a function of variables in X and poses two inquiries. First, which covariate in X best "explains" variation in the effect of Z? Second, what combination of values in X characterize individuals for whom effects are particularly weak?

Declaration 19.1 proceeds as follows.

Declaration 19.1 Random forests design.

```
library(rdss) # for helper functions
library(grf)

covariate_names <- paste0("X.", 1:10)

f_Y <- function(z, X.1, X.2, X.3, X.4, u)
  z * X.1 + z * X.2 ^ 2 + z * exp(X.3) + z * X.3 * X.4 + u

get_best_predictor <-
  function(data) select(data, estimate = var_imp) |> slice(1)

declaration_19.1 <-
  declare_model(
    N = 1000,
    X = matrix(rnorm(10 * N), N),
    U = rnorm(N),
    Z = simple_ra(N)) +
  declare_model(
    Y_Z_1 = f_Y(1, X.1, X.2, X.3, X.4, U),
    Y_Z_0 = f_Y(0, X.1, X.2, X.3, X.4, U),
    tau = Y_Z_1 - Y_Z_0) +
  declare_inquiry(handler = best_predictor,
                  covariate_names = covariate_names,
                  label = "best") +
  declare_measurement(Y = reveal_outcomes(Y ~ Z)) +
  declare_measurement(
    handler = causal_forest_handler,
    covariate_names = covariate_names,
    share_train = 0.5
  ) +
  declare_measurement(
    handler = fabricate,
    low_test = (test & (pred < quantile(pred[test], 0.2))),
    low_all = pred < quantile(pred, 0.2)
  ) +
```

19.1 Discovery Using Causal Forests

```
declare_inquiry(
    ate = mean(tau),
    worst_effects_all = mean(tau[tau <= quantile(tau, 0.2)]),
    worst_effects_test = mean(tau[test & tau <= quantile(tau[test], 0.2)]),
    weak_effects_all = mean(tau[low_all]),
    weak_effects_test = mean(tau[low_test])) +
declare_estimator(Y ~ Z, inquiry = "ate") +
declare_estimator(Y ~ Z, subset = low_test,
                  inquiry = c("weak_effects_test", "worst_effects_test"),
                  label = "lm_weak_test") +
declare_estimator(Y ~ Z, subset = low_all,
                  inquiry = c("weak_effects_all", "worst_effects_all"),
                  label = "lm_weak_all") +
declare_estimator(handler = label_estimator(get_best_predictor),
                  inquiry = "best_predictor", label = "cf")
```

For the model, we imagine a possibly complex function linking Z to Y in which the effect of Z depends nonlinearly on some but not all variables in X. As always, this model can and should be altered to help understand whether diagnosis depends on the particular type of structure assumed.

We declare two inquiries beyond the standard average treatment effect. For the first inquiry we need to be specific about what we mean by "best explains." We will imagine asking which covariate X produces the lowest conditional variance $\mathbb{E}(\mathbb{V}(Y_i(1) - Y_i(0)|X_i = x))$. Specifically, we partition each covariate into quantiles and take the average variance in treatment effect across each quantile. We will call this the `best_predictor` inquiry and calculate it using the R^2 from a fixed-effects model applied to the true treatment effects. The `best_predictor` function in `rdss` calculates this estimand, dividing covariates into 20 quantiles by default.

There is both a simple and a more complex understanding of the second inquiry. The simple understanding is that we are interested in the average effect among the units whose effects are in the bottom 20% (say) of all effects. We will call this the `worst_effects` inquiry. This is a natural notion of the worst affected, but it is a very difficult quantity to estimate.

The more complex understanding involves examining the realized data in order to identify a set of units (say of size 20%) that we think will have weak effects, and with this set identified return to M and ask what the average effect is for this set. We will call this the `weak_effects` inquiry, to acknowledge the fact that the effects for this group may not be the worst effects. This data-dependent inquiry is more complicated to articulate theoretically (it is, in fact, an answer strategy dependent inquiry), but it is more straightforward to estimate empirically.

We assume the data strategy is the same as for a simple two-arm trial (see Section 18.1).

This causal forests design gets its name from the answer strategy. The "causal forests" algorithm randomly partitions data into a training and a testing group. Within the training group it repeatedly generates "trees" by repartitioning the covariates (generating "branches") to identify subgroups ("leafs") with similar treatment effects. At each step, partitioning is implemented to yield estimated minimum variance in treatment effects. Unit level predictions of treatment effects (in both the training and the testing sets) are then generated by combining estimates of effects for units over different trees (see Wager and Athey, 2018, for full details of the approach). Our estimate of the `best_predictor` is based on the variable that is most frequently partitioned to reduce variance, though we note that this indicator was not designed to capture the variable that induces the greatest reduction in variance. Including it here allows us to illustrate the ability of diagnosis to assess the performance of an estimator for a task for which it was not designed.

To implement causal forests in `DeclareDesign`, we wrote a "handler" that calls a function from the `grf` (generalized random forests) package. This handler produces two types of quantities: estimates of unit level causal effects and the name of the variable that is most frequently partitioned to reduce variance (`var_imp`). Because the output includes a prediction for each unit, it is natural to add the output to the primary data frame. For that reason, the causal forests estimation is introduced as a data strategy step and not specifically in an answer strategy step. The estimates of the unit level causal effects are used in order to identify the weakly performing group (within the test set and within the full set), which is in turn used to calculate the two versions of the `weak_effects` estimands, one for the test set and one for the full sample. To accommodate these complexities, the final inquiry declaration takes place after the implementation of the causal forests algorithm.

Finally, we use regression to estimate the ATE as well as the weak effects and worst effects estimands, using both the identified low performing group in the test set data and the identified low performing group in the full data. We assess the performance of these against both the `weak_effects` inquiry and the `worst_effects` inquiry.

Before turning to diagnosis we can get a feel for the performance of the causal forest estimator by comparing the predicted effects for each unit generated by the estimator, with the actual unit level treatment effects generated by *M*, as shown in Figure 19.1.

We see that we get some traction—but we also get a lot wrong. Estimating unit level causal effects is hard. We see in particular that the *range* of the predictions is narrower than the range of the true effects, which will mean that the average effects in the groups with the best or worst predicted effects will generally not be the same as the effects for the groups with the best and worst actual effects.

To see how the design is choosing the best predictor, we illustrate the adjusted r-squared for a regression predicting the treatment effect with a partitioning of each variable, as well as the rank of predictors given the R-squared number in Figure 19.2. We see that the third covariate `X.3` has a very high adjusted R-squared, and is ranked first, and most of the covariates are bunched at a very low R-squared.

19.1 Discovery Using Causal Forests

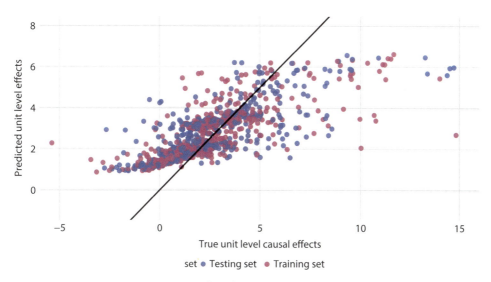

Figure 19.1: One draw from the causal forests design.

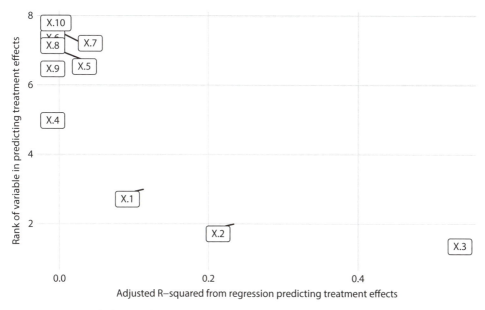

Figure 19.2: How the best predictor estimates are constructed, from ranking variables in terms of their prediction power of the individual treatment effects as measured by the R-squared in a regression.

Diagnosis 19.1 Causal forests diagnosis.

For the diagnosis we need to take account of the fact that the answers to one of the inquiries ("Which X accounts for the most variation in effects?") should be treated as categorical. For this reason, we report the modal estimate and estimand, rather than relying on the average estimate and average estimand. We calculate the probability

Chapter 19: Complex Designs

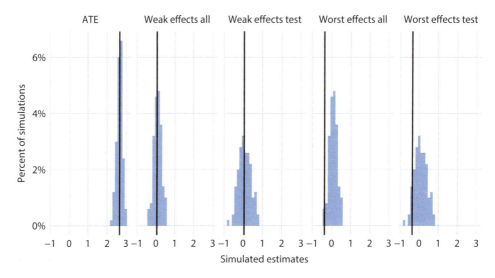

Figure 19.3: Sampling distributions of estimates of five estimands from the causal forest design.

that we get the correct answer, rather than relying on bias. We illustrate the diagnosis in Figure 19.3.

```
most_common <-
  function(x) {
    ux <- unique(x)
    ux[which.max(tabulate(match(x, ux)))]
  }
discovery_diagnosands  <-
  declare_diagnosands(
    correct = mean(estimate == estimand),
    bias = mean(estimate - estimand),
    rmse = sqrt(mean((estimate - estimand)^2)),
    mean_estimate = mean(estimate),
    modal_estimate = most_common(round(estimate, 1)),
    mean_estimand = mean(estimand),
    modal_estimand = most_common(round(estimand, 1))
  )

diagnosis_19.1 <-
  diagnose_design(declaration_19.1,
                  diagnosands = discovery_diagnosands)
```

We see that we do very well in identifying the most powerful predictor of heterogeneity, correct nearly all of the time. (We are never "correct" for the continuous estimands, but we would never expect to be.) Our estimator for the effects for the weak group within the testing set is unbiased. This follows from the fact that we are in essence estimating the causal effect within a subgroup that has been selected without knowledge of the potential outcomes. Substantively the effects for this group are indeed considerably lower than the average treatment effects, and so we have been successful in identifying units that experience weak effects on average and estimating the effects for these. Thus we have been successful for a version of both inquiries.

The other diagnoses sharpen our understanding of what questions cannot be so easily answered with this design. First we see that estimates of the effects for the weak performers do not do a good job of estimating effects for the *worst* performers. This highlights that the procedure can generate unbiased estimates for *a* group that does poorly but not for *the* group that does most poorly. We can further see from the diagnosis that while we recover effects for the test group well, we have some bias when trying to estimate the effects for the weak performing set in the combined training and test data. The reason for bias here is that training group units enter the worse performing set in part because of their realized outcomes (which helped define the set) and not just on the basis of pretreatment features. The bias is small, however—so small it is barely discernible in the histograms—and so the restriction of analysis to the training set only ultimately increases mean-squared error here.

Overall the approach fares well and through diagnosis we get clarity over which quantities are well estimated. Modifications of this design can help us assess how sensitive performance is to types of stipulated models and choices about train-test splits.

19.1.1 Design examples

- Bauer and Clemm von Hohenberg (2021) uses a causal forests algorithm to explore the heterogeneous effects of a manipulation of the source (real or fake) of political news. The average effect of a real (versus fake) source on belief in the facts reported in the article is positive, and it is more positive for those with greater trust in media and more political knowledge.

- Green et al. (2022) study the effects of messages designed to increase vaccine intentions with a survey experiment. They apply a causal forests algorithm to uncover the possibly heterogeneous effects of the treatment, depending on observed covariates like income, local disease burden, and political ideology, but find that responses to treatment are mostly homogeneous.

19.2 Structural Estimation

> We declare a design in which a researcher wants to use experimental data to estimate the parameters of a game-theoretic model. The premise of the approach is that, to the extent that the model is correct, in-sample parameter estimation allows the researcher to make interesting external inferences about effects in other settings. The risk is that bad models will produce bad inferences.

Structural estimation is used when researchers have in mind a model for how processes work and their goal is to estimate the parameters of that model. We referred to this type of a model as an "inquiry model" in Section 2.2.1 to distinguish it from the reference models that are required to provide a setting in which to assess the performance of a design. If only they knew the parameters of the model, they could draw inferences about levels of unobserved variables, treatment effects, or other quantities. They might even extrapolate to estimate counterfactual quantities, such as the effects of interventions that have not been implemented (Reiss and Wolak, 2007).

We illustrate this design with a bargaining game, drawing on an example used in Wilke and Humphreys (2020). We imagine a customer i makes payments from some endowment to a taxi driver. Bargaining proceeds as one player makes an offer that is accepted or rejected; if rejected the other player makes a counteroffer. The game continues for n rounds with zero payoffs if no deal is made. Our main interest is the share of the endowment retained by the customer.

In Declaration 19.2, we imagine two types of customers, strategic ($\theta_i = 0$) and nonstrategic ($\theta_i = 1$). If a customer is strategic, the equilibrium offer made by the first mover is the one predicted by the solution given in Rubinstein (1982). If, however, the player is nonstrategic, then they always (successfully) insist on invoking a payment norm that lets them retain a fixed share of their endowment, $\tilde{\pi}$. We let α denote the probability that a player is nonstrategic. A player's payoff then is given by:

$$\pi_i = (1 - \theta_i)(z_i \widehat{\pi} + (1 - z_i)(1 - \widehat{\pi})) + \theta_i \tilde{\pi},$$

where

$$\widehat{\pi} = \sum_{j=2}^{n} (-1^j) \delta^{j-1}$$

is the Rubinstein solution. The customer's payoff depends on whether they go first ($z_i = 1$) or second ($z_i = 0$) and on the common discount factor δ.

One complication with structural estimation is that it's hard to know what to infer when an action is taken that the model says shouldn't happen. A common way to address this challenge is to allow for the possibility that *implemented* actions are noisy reflections of *predicted* actions noisy either because of measurement error or because in fact players deviate randomly from optimal behavior. Here we will allow for a disturbance like this by assuming that *measured* payments, y, are a random draw from a Beta distribution with expectation given by the expected payment π and variance parameter κ.

In our data strategy, we randomly assign Z (who goes first) and measure payments y. We will also assume we know what norms nonstrategic players are following, specifically that $\tilde{\pi} = 0.75$. Our goal is to use observed payments along with treatment allocation to estimate the model parameters, α, δ, κ. These in turn can be used to estimate treatment effects and other counterfactual quantities (if we assume the model is true).

19.2 Structural Estimation

Our inquiries are the parameters kappa, delta, and alpha (corresponding to κ, δ, and α). We set up the design so that we can vary these features easily but also so that we can vary n (the total number of rounds in the bargaining game).

The answer strategy is implemented using maximum likelihood to identify which parameter values are most consistent with the data. More specifically, this approach takes the model as true and asks for what collection of parameter values the observed data is most likely. See King (1998) for an introduction to the method of maximum likelihood. One nice feature of the method is that the problem of maximizing the likelihood is (asymptotically) equivalent to finding the probability distribution that minimizes the Kullback–Leibler divergence to the true probability distribution (of course, all that within the class of distributions that can be specified under the model). For more, see White (1982).

The heart of the estimation strategy is the specification of the likelihood function. The likelihood function reports the probability of the data given particular stipulated values of the parameters. This value is different depending on n, so in fact we write down a function that writes a function given n. The likelihood function reflects the theoretical model described above, which means that in this declaration, the same event generating process is used in M and in the construction of the likelihood function in A. In other words, the "reference model" is the same as the "inquiry model." An optimistic assumption.

Declaration 19.2 Structural estimation declaration.

With the likelihood function defined, we can declare a design with an estimation step that uses the `bbmle` package

```r
library(bbmle)

# Equilibrium offers for a game of length n
offer <- function(n, d){
  sum(sapply(2:n[1], function(t) ((-1)^t)*(d^{t-1})))
}

# Likelihood function
likelihood  <- function(n){
  function(k, d, a) {
    m <- Z * offer(n, d) + (1 - Z) * (1 - offer(n, d))
    R <- a * dbeta(y, k * .75, k * .25) +
      (1 - a) * dbeta(y, k * m, k * (1 - m))
    return(-sum(log(R)))
  }
}

n <- 2         # Number of rounds bargaining (design choice)
delta <- 0.8   # True discount factor (unknown)
kappa <- 2     # Parameter to govern error in offers (unknown)
alpha <- 0.5   # Share of behavioral types in the population (unknown)

declaration_19.2 <-
  declare_model(
```

```
    # Define the population: indicator for behavioral type (norm = 1)
    N = 200,
    type = rbinom(N, 1, alpha),
    n = n) +
declare_inquiry(kappa = kappa,
                delta = delta,
                alpha = alpha) +
declare_assignment(Z = complete_ra(N)) +
declare_measurement(
    # Equilibrium payoff
    pi = type * .75 +
        (1 - type) * (Z * offer(n, delta) + (1 - Z) * (1 -offer(n, delta))),
    # Actual payoff (stochastic)
    y = rbeta(N, pi * kappa, (1 - pi) * kappa))+
    # Estimation via maximum likelihood
declare_estimator(.method = mle2,
                  minuslogl = likelihood(n),
                  start = list(k = 2, d = 0.50, a = 0.50),
                  lower = list(k = 0.10, d = 0.01, a = 0.01),
                  upper = list(k = 100, d = 0.99, a = 0.99),
                  method = "L-BFGS-B",
                  term = c("k", "d", "a"),
                  inquiry = c("kappa","delta", "alpha"),
                  label = "Structural model")
```

Diagnosis 19.2 Structural estimation diagnosis.

```
diagnosis_19.2 <- diagnose_design(declaration_19.2)
```

Table 19.1: Estimation of structural parameters from behavior in a bargaining game.

Inquiry	Mean Estimand	Bias	RMSE
alpha	0.50	−0.00	0.08
	(0.00)	(0.01)	(0.01)
delta	0.80	0.00	0.03
	(0.00)	(0.00)	(0.00)
kappa	2.00	0.07	0.26
	(0.00)	(0.03)	(0.02)

Turning to diagnosis we see first that we do a good job in recovering parameter values. All three parameters are estimated precisely. From these, we can calculate estimates of causal quantities such as the first mover advantage and assess the extent to which this depends on features such as the length of the game.

As always, diagnosis can be used to fine-tune designs. In figure 19.4, we compare design performance as we vary α and n. We see from the comparison of designs that estimates are less accurate when either longer games are used or when there are many nonstrategic players. Shorter games have an advantage here of producing

19.2 Structural Estimation

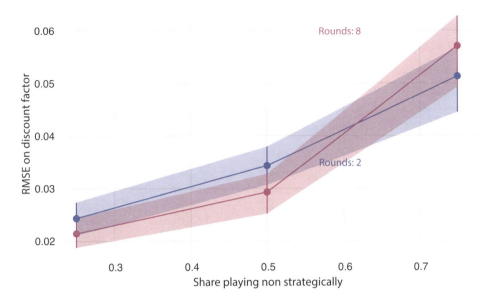

Figure 19.4: Performance of the structural estimation design depends on the number of rounds and the types of players.

a more pronounced difference in the payoffs of first and second movers. The gains from shorter games are especially pronounced in settings in which many nonstrategic players dampen the variation in payoffs. Though not shown here, we can also use design diagnosis to show that the design fails if we set n at 3 (for instance) as in this case δ is not identified (the same probability distribution is consistent with different values for δ).

The basic structure used here can be used for a wide range of structural models. The first step is to write down the theory well enough to specify the implied likelihood function. Doing so might require adding noise to the model so that the data that are seen in practice can be seen in theory. The next step is to estimate the model parameters that have the greatest likelihood of having produced the observed data. (The same fundamental approach can be used with estimation via Bayesian methods or methods of moments.)

The payoffs from structural estimation can be great: we can operationalize our theoretical models to make specific real-world predictions by disciplining them with real-world information. The risks are large, too. Because the inferences are necessarily model-dependent, model misspecification can lead to faulty conclusions. When doing structural estimation, apply Principle 3.2: *Design agnostically* liberally.

19.2.1 Design examples
- Samii (2016) enumerates some examples of structural estimation in economics and predicts future political scientists will take to structural estimation in earnest.

- Francois, Rainer, and Trebbi (2015) provides a structural model to explain how leaders allocate cabinet positions to bolseter coalitions; the analysis compares the performance of a preferred theory to rival theories.
- Frey, López-Moctezuma, and Montero (2022) estimates a structural model of party competition and coalitions on the basis of a regression discontinuity design. With the model parameters estimated, the authors simulate counterfactual scenarios without party coalitions.

19.3 Meta-analysis

> We declare a design for a meta-analytic study in which a researcher seeks to combine findings from a collection of existing studies to form an overall conclusion. Declaration helps clarify the estimand in such studies. Diagnosis highlights risks associated with a common estimator used in meta-analysis, the fixed effect estimator.

In a meta-analysis, inquiries are typically population-level quantities like the population average treatment effect (PATE). The relevant population might be the full set of units that happened to participate in past research studies or it might be a broader population, like all human adults since 1950. The data strategy for a meta-analysis involves collecting all (or a subset) of the estimates generated by past research studies on the topic and standardizing them so they can be meaningfully compared or combined. Meta-analyses are valuable because they can tell us about the empirical consensus on a particular inquiry. Because they typically aggregate a large amount of information, meta-analyses are usually more precise than individual studies. We can also learn what we *don't* know from a meta-analysis. After aggregating all the available evidence on a given inquiry, we may find that we don't know very much at all.

The PATE inquiry, however, might not be so interesting if the constituent inquiries—the site-level ATEs—vary greatly from context to context. The ATEs that make up the PATE might vary because of the contextual features that condition the effect. Galos and Coppock (2022), for example, reanalyze audit studies of gender-based employment discrimination to find that the ATE on callbacks of being a woman is strongly positive in women-dominated sectors and is strongly negative in men-dominated sections. For this reason, meta-analyses often include inquiries about the variance of effects across studies or the covariance of effects with groups.[1]

The largest choice in the data strategy for a meta-analysis is the set of study inclusion and exclusion criteria. These criteria should be guided by the inquiries of the meta-analysis and whether the designs of the constituent studies appropriately

---
[1] Not all variation in estimates across sites is due to differences in true effects. Different studies employ different data strategies, so some differences in the treatments and outcomes are inevitable. If the differences across studies grow too large, meta-analysis on the full set of studies becomes inappropriate.

inform the meta-analytic inquiry. If the inquiry is the population mean and standard deviation of the site-level ATEs of treatment Z on outcome Y, we want to include only studies that credibly estimate the effect of Z on Y. This requirement means checking that all included studies use similar-enough treatments and similar-enough measurements of the outcome. It also means excluding studies that are prone to bias. For example, Pettigrew and Tropp (2006) assemble 515 studies of the contact hypothesis, but Paluck, Green and Green (2019) exclude all but 5% of these studies in their updated meta-analysis for failing to randomize intergroup contact. Meta-analyses that include biased studies can compound biases, giving us falsely precise and incorrect answers. Finally, inclusion decisions should be made on the basis of the designs of the constituent studies and *not* their results. For example, we should not exclude studies that fail to reach statistical significance or yield unexpected answers.

The answer strategies for meta-analyses often amount to a weighted average of the individual study estimates. We take a weighted average instead of a simple average because we want to give different studies different amounts of pull in the overall estimate. In particular, we often want to give studies that are more precise more weight and studies that are less precise less weight. In fixed-effect estimation, for example, study weights are often proportional to the inverse of the estimated variance from the study. In random-effects estimation, by contrast, the weights are often proportional to the inverse of the estimated variance from the study, plus an estimate of the between-study variance in effects. With this adjustment, the study weights are less extreme in random effects relative to fixed effect (for more, see Borenstein et al., 2021, ch. 13). Fixed-effect meta-analysis may be appropriate in settings in which we have a strong theoretical reason to think the site-level inquiries are all equal to the PATE, but typically we think effects vary from site to site, so random effects is usually the meta-analytic answer strategy of choice.

In Declaration 19.3, we declare a meta-analytic research design for 100 studies with a true PATE (μ) of 0.2. We represent the standard deviation of the study-level ATEs with τ, which we vary between 0 and 1. When $\tau > 0$ the true effects vary across contexts. The studies each have different measurement precision, with standard errors between 0.025 and 0.6. The inquiries are μ and τ^2. In the answer strategy, we use both fixed effect and random effects meta-analysis.

Declaration 19.3 Meta-analysis design.

```
library(metafor)

mu <- 0.2 # true PATE
tau <- 0.0 # true SD of site-level ATEs

design <-
  declare_model(
```

```
    N = 200,
    site = 1:N,
    std.error = pmax(0.1, abs(rnorm(N, mean = 0.8, sd = 0.5))),
    theta = rnorm(N, mean = mu, sd = tau), # when tau = 0, theta = mu
    estimate = rnorm(N, mean = theta, sd = std.error)
  ) +
  declare_inquiry(mu = mu, tau_sq = tau^2) +
  declare_estimator(
    yi = estimate, sei = std.error, method = "REML",
    .method = rma_helper, .summary = rma_mu_tau,
    term = c("mu", "tau_sq"), inquiry = c("mu", "tau_sq"),
    label = "random-effects") +
  declare_estimator(
    yi = estimate, sei = std.error, method = "FE",
    .method = rma_helper, .summary = rma_mu_tau,
    term = c("mu", "tau_sq"), inquiry = c("mu", "tau_sq"),
    label = "fixed-effect")

declaration_19.3 <- redesign(design, tau = c(0, 1))
```

Diagnosis 19.3 Meta-analysis diagnosis.

Figure 19.5 explores the bias and coverage of the two estimators under each model both for the mean effects inquiry μ and for the variance of effects inquiry τ^2. We find that the random effects estimator, across both models of how effects are realized, performs best. Whether the variance of site-level ATEs is 1 or 0, random effects estimates both inquiries without bias and coverage is nominal. By contrast, the fixed effect estimator has two problems. When τ^2 is 1, the estimator gets the variance in estimates wrong, because it *assumes* it is 0. Second, the estimator is extremely overconfident, generating confidence intervals that are drastically too small, as reflected in the poor coverage. This overconfidence stems from the fixed effect assumption that the only reason study-to-study estimates differ is due to estimation noise, not true differences across sites.

```
diagnosis_19.3 <- diagnose_design(declaration_19.3)
```

19.3.1 Design examples

- Blair, Christensen, and Rudkin (2021) meta-analyze 46 difference-in-difference studies of the effects of commodity price shocks on conflict, excluding over 300 studies of the same effect that relied on weaker identification strategies.

- Schwarz and Coppock (2022) collect 67 candidate choice conjoint experiments that randomized candidate gender to estimate the average effect of gender on electoral support.

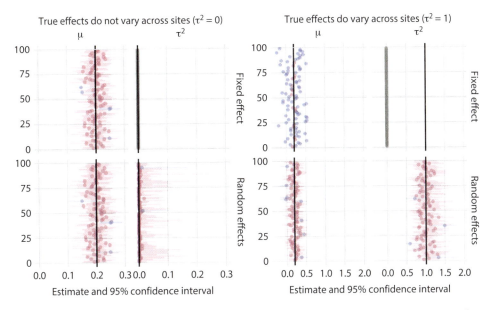

Figure 19.5: Coverage and bias of the fixed effect and random effects under two settings, effect homogeneity and effect heterogeneity.

19.4 Multi-site Studies

> We declare a design for a coordinated research project in which multiple research teams combine data gathering and analysis strategies to address a common inquiry. Diagnosis clarifies the benefits and risks of coordination versus tailoring of treatments to contexts.

Nearly all social science is produced atomistically: individual scientists identify a question and a research strategy for answering it, apply the research strategy, and try to publish the results of that one study. Increasingly, scholars have come to realize that, though the standard research process may promote discovery, it is not optimized for the accumulation of general insights. One reason is that scientists are opportunistic in the contexts and units they study. If inquiry values are idiosyncratic to the contexts and units that scientists choose to study, then our studies will not generalize.

Scholars have addressed themselves to the problem of generalizability in a variety of ways. One approach is the replication of past studies in new contexts or with new populations. A second has been the application of statistical methods for extrapolating from single studies, relying on variation within studies in unit characteristics and effect heterogeneity. Both of these approaches are important.

We explore a third approach here: coordinated multi-site studies. The idea here is to implement the same research design (or one as close as possible) across multiple contexts at the same time, each targeting the same inquiry with similar methods with the explicit intention of meta-analyzing the eventual results. In the previous chapter, we described *retrospective* meta-analysis in which a meta-analyst gathers together previous scholarship on a research question; harmonization of the studies is achieved ex post by including the studies that target the same theoretical quantity well and excluding those that do not. A coordinated multi-site study is a *prospective* meta-analysis; harmonization is achieved ex ante through the sometimes painstaking process of ensuring comparability of treatments, outcomes, and units across contexts.

How much we can learn about the generalizability of effects depends on how many sites we study, how we *select* the sites, our beliefs about effect heterogeneity, and the level of harmonization across studies. Of these, the harmonization level is most important. Without harmonization of research designs across sites, researchers risk answering different questions in different sites. If the goal is to understand a common inquiry and how values of the inquiry vary across contexts, then each site must provide answers to (essentially) the same inquiry. For this, researchers coordinate measurement strategies so as to collect the same outcome measures and coordinate the details of treatment procedures to ensure they are studying the effects of the same intervention. They may also wish to coordinate on details like sampling to ensure the same types of subjects are enrolled at each site and on the consent and enrollment procedures so as to avoid introducing selection or demand effects differentially across sites.

The disadvantage of harmonization is that researchers might end up answering a different question than the one they started out with. In the worst case, they end up answering one common question across all sites that is interesting for none. We explore these trade-offs by declaring a modified multi-site design in which different treatments have different effects in different sites.

Declaration 19.4 describes a multi-site study with five sites. A conceptual challenge with multi-site studies is that in practice a single design has to take account of various differences across sites, such as differences in sample sizes, assignment probabilities, or expectations. The design below shows how these multi-site features can be introduced in a simple way as part of a single "meta-design." The design allows for variation across sites, implements analysis separately using data from different sites, and then combines findings for an overall conclusion. Note that the inquiries here are defined by creating site-level inquiries and averaging over these. Implicitly each *site* is weighted equally in the inquiry, so you can see a clear similarity between *I* and *A*. You could alternatively use different weighting schemes if you wanted each unit in the sample to have equal weight or if you wanted each each unit in the population to have equal weight—and of course, adjust *A* accordingly.

We imagine two possible treatments that might be implemented in each site. One, with treatment effect `tau_1` (possibly different in each site), is the treatment that

19.4 Multi-site Studies

researchers are meant to coordinate on. The second, with treatment effect `tau_2`, is an alternative treatment that researchers could implement if they were not coordinating. We imagine that if there is no strong coordination, then researchers select which version of the treatment to implement (here, we imagine they implement the treatment they think will yield larger effects).

We specify two inquiries. The first is for the coordinated treatment, with a focus on the average effect across studies. The second is less easy to describe: it is the average effect, again across cases, of whatever treatment was implemented in those cases. Though unusual, this inquiry is still well defined.

Estimation proceeds in two steps: first we calculate site-level effects, just as we do for a meta-analysis, then we meta-analyze those site-level effects. We use here a random effects model, reflecting our expectation that true site effects differ (see Section 19.3 for a discussion of alternative answer strategies for meta analysis).

Declaration 19.4 Multi-site studies with and without coordination.

```r
library(metafor)

# Idiosyncratic features of studies
study_sizes <- c(500, 1000, 1500, 2000, 2500)
study_assignment_probabilities <- c(0.5, 0.5, 0.6, 0.7, 0.8)
study_intercepts <- 1:5
study_priors <- seq(from = 0, to = 0.3, length = 5)
study_coordination <- "high"

# helper function to estimate study level effects
declaration_19.4 <-
  
  declare_model(
    sites = add_level(
      N = 5,
      size = study_sizes,
      intercept = study_intercepts,
      tau_1 = rnorm(N, study_priors, 0.1),
      tau_2 = rnorm(N, 0.3, 0.2),
      coordination = study_coordination,
      # if coordinated, take tau_1, otherwise take the bigger of the two
      tau = if_else(coordination == "high",
                    tau_1,
                    pmax(tau_1, tau_2))
    ),
    subjects = add_level(
      N = size,
      U = rnorm(N)
    )
  ) +
  
  declare_model(
    potential_outcomes(
      Y ~ intercept + tau * Z_implemented + U,
      conditions = list(Z_implemented = c(0, 1))),
    potential_outcomes(
      Y ~ intercept + tau_1 * Z_common + U,
      conditions = list(Z_common = c(0, 1)))
  ) +
```

```r
  declare_inquiries(handler = function(data) {
    data |>
      group_by(sites) |>
      summarize(
        ATE_implemented_site = mean(Y_Z_implemented_1 - Y_Z_implemented_0),
        ATE_common_site = mean(Y_Z_common_1 - Y_Z_common_0)) |>
      ungroup() |>
      summarize(ATE_implemented = mean(ATE_implemented_site),
                ATE_common = mean(ATE_common_site)) |>
      pivot_longer(cols = everything(), names_to = "inquiry",
                   values_to = "estimand")
  }) +
  
  declare_assignment(
    Z_implemented = block_ra(
      blocks = sites,
      block_prob = study_assignment_probabilities)
  ) +
  
  declare_measurement(Y = reveal_outcomes(Y ~ Z_implemented)) +
  
  declare_step(function(data) {
    data |>
      group_by(sites) |>
      summarize(tidy(lm_robust(Y ~ Z_implemented))) |>
      ungroup() |>
      filter(term == "Z_implemented")
  }) +
  
  declare_estimator(
    yi = estimate,
    sei = std.error,
    method = "REML",
    .method = rma_helper,
    .summary = rma_mu_tau,
    term = "mu",
    inquiry = c("ATE_implemented", "ATE_common")
  )

design_high_coordination <-
  redesign(declaration_19.4, study_coordination = "high")
design_low_coordination <-
  redesign(declaration_19.4, study_coordination = "low")
```

Diagnosis 19.4 Multi-site studies diagnosis.

We now diagnose the two designs, with and without coordination, and assess the bias for the average common effect treatment and the average effect of the site-specific optimal treatment inquiries. Figure 19.6 displays the sampling distribution of the estimates from the two designs along with the estimands from the two inquiries in each case.

In the coordinated trial, of course, the common treatment and the implemented treatment are the same. Only the coordinated study produces unbiased estimates for the coordinated inquiry. However, the diagnosis shows that *both* approaches (strongly and weakly coordinated trials) are unbiased for the (more powerful) "selected treatment" inquiry. This inquiry then is well defined and can be estimated

19.4 Multi-site Studies

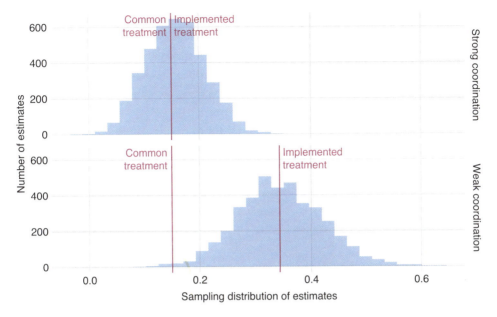

Figure 19.6: Sampling distribution of the meta-analytic estimates from a multi-site trial compared to the true average common treatment effect and the true average effect of the site-specific optimal treatment effect.

without bias, even when coordination fails. The difficulty with this inquiry though is that being able to make an out-of-sample prediction for it requires information you might not have: what version of a treatment is likely to be selected in that new context.

19.4.1 Design examples

- Dunning et al. (2019) present the results of a "Metaketa" study (a term for coordinated multi-site studies) of the effects of voter information campaigns on political accountability in five countries: Benin, Burkina Faso, Brazil, Uganda (two studies), and Mexico.

- Coordinated multi-site studies need not be enormously expensive undertakings. Frederiksen (2022) reports the results of the same conjoint survey experiment measuring the effects of undemocratic behavior on electoral support in five countries (the United States, the United Kingdom, the Czech Republic, Mexico, and South Korea).

PART IV

Research Design Lifecycle

CHAPTER 20

Research Design Lifecycle

A research design begins with a spark of inspiration or an opportunity, develops through a planning phase, comes to fruition in the stages of realization, and adds to knowledge and influences decisions as it is integrated into collective scientific understanding. At each step in the research design lifecycle, your specification of M, I, D, and A can shape your choices and how others will learn from your work.

This part of the book works through stages of the research design lifecycle. We describe in each entry how we can use the declaration, diagnosis, and redesign framework to make progress at each step. Of course, not every research project will feature each and every stage but Part IV should serve we hope as a useful checklist as you work through the major phases of your research.

We divide the research design lifecycle into three broad categories: planning, realization, and integration. Planning includes all of the activities you undertake before data collection starts: conducting ethical reviews, obtaining approvals, organizing partnerships, securing funding, running pilots, gathering criticism, and filing analysis plans. Realization begins with the execution of the data strategy as planned, and continues through the inevitable changes that come with analytic challenges and scientific surprises. We trace realization through implementation, pivoting in response to unexpected developments, writing up results, reconciling planned and implemented designs, and responding to peer reviewers. In the final phase of a research project, the results are integrated into the scientific literature. Integration includes how the study will inform theories and decisions and also how the study will later be reanalyzed, replicated, and, someday, meta-analyzed.

CHAPTER **21**

Planning

We list "design early" among our research design principles (Principle 3.4) to emphasize the gains from early planning. Research projects are very long journeys: going from the kernel of an idea to a published paper typically takes multiple years. Once the data strategy has been implemented, you're stuck with it, so mindful planning beforehand is important. "Measure twice, cut once."

The planning process changes designs. We work out designs that meet ethical as well as scientific standards, accommodate the needs of research partners, and operate within financial and logistical constraints. When we are insufficiently sure of key inputs to design declarations, we can run pilots, but we need to be careful about how we incorporate what we learn from them. Finally, when we write up a declaration or a PAP with a declaration, this can be a useful moment to get feedback from our peers to improve the design. We discuss each of these steps in this chapter.

21.1 Ethics

As research designers, we have ethical obligations beyond the requirements of national laws and the regulations of institutional review boards.

For a long time, thinking about research ethics has been guided by the ideas in the Belmont report, which emphasizes beneficence, respect for persons, and autonomy. Recently, more attention has been given to principles that extend beyond care for human subjects to include considerations for the well-being of collaborators and partners and the broader social impact of research. Social scientific professional associations have developed principles and guidelines to help think through these issues. Key references include:

- American Political Science Association ethics guidelines
- American Sociological Association Code of Ethics
- American Psychological Association Ethical Principles of Psychologists and Code of Conduct

The considerations at play vary across context and methods. For example, Teele (2021) describes ethical considerations in field experimentation, Humphreys (2015) focuses on development settings, Slough (2020) considers the ethics of field experimentation in the context of elections, and Wood (2006) and Baron and Young (2021) consider ethical challenges specific to field research in conflict settings.

However, a common meta-principle underlying many of these contributions is the injunction to consider the ethical dimensions of your work ex ante and to report on ethical implications ex post. Lyall (2022) specifically connects ethical reflection to ex ante design considerations.

We encourage you to engage with ethical considerations in this way, early in the research design lifecycle. Some design declarations and diagnoses elide ethical considerations. For instance, a declaration that is diagnosand-complete for statistical power may tell you little about the level of care and respect accorded to subjects. Many declarations are diagnosand-complete for bias, but obtaining an unbiased treatment effect estimate is not always the highest goal.

In principle, ethical diagnosands can be directly incorporated into the declare-diagnose-redesign framework. Diagnosands could include the total cost to participants, how many participants were harmed, the average level of informed consent measured by a survey about comprehension of study goals, or the risks of adverse events. More complex ethical diagnosands may be possible as well: Slough (2020) provides a formal analysis of the "aggregate electoral impact" diagnosand for experiments that take place in the context of elections. To illustrate, we describe two specific ethical diagnosands here, costs and potential harms, though many others may apply in particular research scenarios.

Costs. A common ethical concern is that measurement imposes a cost on subjects, if only by wasting their time. Subjects' time is a valuable resource they often donate willingly to the scientific enterprise by participating in a survey or other measurement. Although subjects' generosity is sometimes repaid with financial compensation, in many scenarios direct payments are not feasible. Regardless of whether subjects are paid, the costs to subjects should be top of mind when designing the study and can be explicitly specified as a diagnosand.

Potential harms. Different realizations of the data from the same data strategy may differ in their ethical implications. Ex post, a study may not have ended up harming subjects, but ex ante, there may have been a risk of harm (Baron and Young, 2021). The design's ethical status depends on judgments about *potential* harms and *potential* participants: not only what did happen, but what could have happened. The potential harm diagnosand might be formalized as the maximum harm that could eventuate under any realization of the data strategy. Researchers could then follow (for example) a minimax redesign procedure to find the design that minimizes this maximum potential harm.

When the design is diagnosed, we can characterize the ethical status of possible realizations of the design as well as the ethical status of the *distribution* of these realizations. Is the probability of harm minimal "enough"? Is the degree of informed consent sufficient? Given that these characteristics vary across designs and across realizations of the same design, writing down concretely both the measure of the ethical status and the ethical threshold can help structure thinking. These diagnoses and the considerations that inspire them can be shared in funding proposals, preanalysis plans, or other reports. Articulating them in a design may help clarify whether proper account was taken of risks ex ante, or, more usefully, remind researchers to be sure to take account of them.

21.1.1 Illustration: Estimating expected costs and expected learning

We illustrate how researchers can weigh the trade-offs between the value of research and its ethical costs with a hypothetical audit study of discrimination in government hiring. We imagine that three characteristics of applicants to a municipal government job are randomized and whether the applicant receives a callback is recorded. The three candidate characteristics are race (Black or White), area of residence (urban or suburban), or high school attended (East or West).

Suppose we could rank the scientific importance of measuring discrimination along all three dimensions and we judged race-based discrimination of high importance and discrimination on the basis of residence or high school to be of medium and low importance, respectively.

The value of the research then is a function of the importance of the inquiries, of course, but also of how much we learn about it. We proxy for the learning from the experiment by sample size: the higher the N, the more we learn, but with decreasing marginal returns (it's a lot better to have a sample of 100 compared to 10; it matters less if it is 1010 or 1100). Figure 12.1 shows the three expected learning curves labeled by the importance of the inquiry.

We turn now to the expected costs side of the calculation. Because the job applicants are fictitious but appear real, alongside concerns around deception, a primary ethical concern in audit experiments is how much time hiring managers waste reviewing fictitious applications. In the case of government hiring, it is public money spent on their review. Suppose the cost to participants is linear in the number of applications, since an application takes about ten minutes to review. We represent the cost to participants as the purple line in Figure 12.1.

We have placed the costs to participants on the same scale as the value of the research, by placing a value to society of the research and a value to society of the administrative time. Doing so requires taking positions that can be read off from the definition of the diagnosands. When benefit exceeds cost (upper blue region),

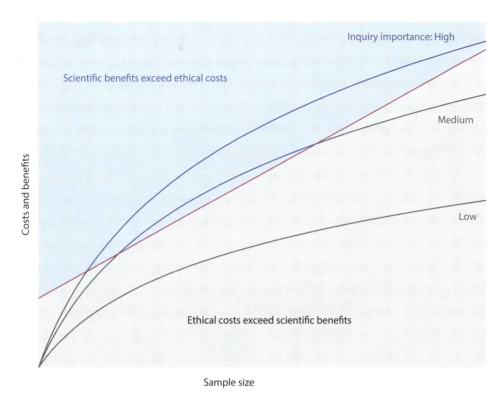

Figure 21.1: Trade-offs between ethical costs and scientific benefits. A design might have too *many* subjects but also too *few* subjects.

we decide to move forward with the research; if costs exceed benefits (lower gray region), we do not conduct the study.

The key takeaway from the graph is that there is a region at low sample sizes where the cost to participants exceeds the benefits from the research, because of the very imprecise answers we get from the research. We don't learn enough about the inquiry, despite its importance, to make it worth wasting the hiring managers' time. In the medium importance cases there is a "goldilocks" range: there is a region of the benefits curve (highlighted in blue) where it is worth doing the study, but there are two regions (highlighted in gray) above and below it where it is not worth it. The left region is where the sample is too small, so the value of the research is low both because of its medium importance and because we do not learn enough about it. The second gray region at right in the medium importance curve is where, though we learn a lot about the inquiry, the cost is too high from the many hours of hiring managers' time to justify what we learn because the inquiry is not important enough.

In short, in principle, ethical decisions can be informed by diagnosis both of how much we learn and of how much it costs participants (along with other ethical costs). The key benefit of this approach comes from getting a sharper understanding of the gains from design decisions on the research side; the problem of placing value on those gains is not addressed within the framework of course but using the framework makes it clearer what positions researchers are taking on these issues.

Calculations of this form, however, always open up risks that researchers overestimate the importance of their research or are blind to ethical costs (in this case, for instance, an additional cost might arise if, because of the study, subjects, or other officials, became more skeptical of future real applicants). In practice, strategies that maximize autonomy for implicated actors can make these choices easier. In this case, for instance, prior consultations with members of the subject population that assessed how *they* saw the benefits of the research relative to the costs, and how they assessed the costs from this type of deception, would go a long way to allay ethical concerns.

21.1.2   Institutional review boards

When researchers sit at universities in the United States, research must be approved by the university's institutional review board (IRB) under the federal regulation known as the "Common Rule." Similar research review bodies exist at universities worldwide and at many independent research organizations and think tanks. Though these boards are commonly thought to judge research ethics, they have a second function to protect their institution from liability for research gone awry (King and Sands, 2015, and Schrag, 2010). Insofar as institutional and ethical goals are aligned, IRBs help ensure responsible research practices, but as a general matter institutional approval is not a substitute for ethical engagement by researchers.

21.2   Partners

Partnering with third-party organizations in research entails cooperating to intervene in the world or to measure outcomes. Researchers seek to produce (and publish) scientific knowledge; they work with political parties, government agencies, nonprofit organizations, and businesses to learn more than they could if they worked independently. These groups join the collaborations to learn about how to achieve their own organizational goals. Governments may want to expand access to healthcare, corporations to improve their ad targeting, and nonprofits to demonstrate program impact to funding organizations.

In the best-case scenario, the goals of the researchers and partner organizations are aligned. When the scientific question to be answered is the same as the practical question the organization cares about, the gains from cooperation are clear. The research team gains access to the organization's financial and logistical capacity to act in the world, and the partner organization gains access to the researchers' scientific expertise. Finding the right research partner almost always amounts to finding an organization with a common—or at least not conflicting—goal. Selecting a research design amenable to both parties requires understanding each partners' private goals. Research design declaration and diagnosis can help with this problem by formalizing trade-offs between the two sets of goals.

One frequent divergence between partner and researcher goals is that partner organizations often want to learn, but they care most about their primary mission (Levine, 2021). This dynamic is sometimes referred to as the "learning versus doing" trade-off. (In business settings, this trade-off goes by names like "learning versus earning" or "exploration versus exploitation"). An aid organization cares about delivering their program to as many people as possible. Learning whether the program has the intended effects on the outcomes of interest is obviously also important, but resources spent on evaluation are resources *not* spent on program delivery.

Diagnosis 21.1 Learning versus doing diagnosis.

Research design diagnosis can help navigate the learning versus doing trade-off. One instance of the trade-off is that the proportion of units that receive a treatment represents the rate of "doing," but this rate also affects the amount of learning. In the extreme, if all units are treated, we can't measure the effect of the treatment. The trade-off here is represented in Figure 21.2, which shows the study's power versus the proportion treated (top facet) and the partner's utility (bottom facet). The researchers have a power cutoff at the standard 80% threshold. The partner also has a strict cutoff: they need to treat at least 2/3 of the sample to fulfill a donor requirement.

A researcher might use this graph together with the partner to jointly select the design that has the highest power that has a sufficiently high proportion treated to meet the partner's needs. This is represented in the "zone of agreement" in gray: in this region, the design has at least 80% power and at least two thirds of the sample are treated. Deciding within this region involves a trade-off between power (which is decreasing in the proportion treated here) and the partner's utility (which is increasing in the proportion treated). The diagnosis surfaces the zone of the agreement and clarifies the choice between designs in that region. Unfortunately, some partnerships simply will not work out if the zone of agreement is empty.

Choosing the proportion treated is one example of integrating partner constraints into research designs. A second common problem is that there are a set of units that must be treated or that must not be treated for ethical or political reasons (e.g., the home district of a government partner must receive the treatment). If these constraints are discovered after treatment assignment, they lead to noncompliance, which may substantially complicate the analysis of the experiment and even prevent providing an answer to the original inquiry. Gerber and Green (2012) recommend, before randomizing treatment, exploring possible treatment assignments with the

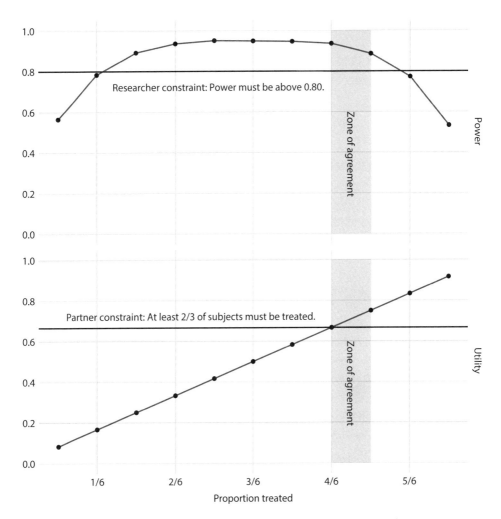

Figure 21.2: Finding the zone of agreement in a research partnership.

partner organization and using this exercise to elicit the set of units that must or cannot be treated. King et al. (2007) describe a "politically-robust" design, which uses pair-matched block randomization. In this design, when any unit is dropped due to political constraints, the whole pair is dropped from the study.[1]

A major benefit of working with partners is their deep knowledge of the substantive area. For this reason, we recommend involving them in the design declaration and diagnosis process. How can we develop intuitions about the means, variances, and covariances of the variables to be measured? Ask your partner for their best guesses, which may be far more educated than your own. For experimental studies, solicit your partner's beliefs about the magnitude of the treatment effect on each outcome variable, subgroup by subgroup if possible. Engaging partners in the declaration

---

[1] This procedure is prone to at risk of bias for the average treatment effect among the "politically feasible" units if within some pairs, one unit is treatable but the other is not.

process improves design—and it very quickly sharpens the discussion of key design details. Pro-tip: Share your design diagnoses and mock analyses *before* the study is launched to quickly build consensus around the study's goals.

21.3 Funding

Higher quality designs usually come with higher costs. Collecting original data is more expensive than analyzing existing data, but collecting new data may be more or less costly depending on the ease of contacting subjects or conducting measurements. As a result, including cost diagnosands in research design diagnosis can directly aid data strategy decision-making. These diagnosands may usefully include both average cost and maximum cost. Researchers may make different decisions about cost: in some cases, the researcher will select the "best" design in terms of research design quality subject to a budget constraint. Others will choose the cheapest among similar quality designs to save money for future research. Diagnosis can help identify each set and decide among them.

To relax the budget constraint, researchers apply for funding. Funding applications have to communicate important features of the proposed research design. Funders want to know why the study would be useful, important, or interesting to scholars, the public, or policymakers. They also want to ensure that the research design provides credible answers to the question and that the research team is capable of executing the design. Since it's their money on the line, funders also care that the design provides good value for money.

Researchers and funders have an information problem. Applicants wish to obtain as large a grant as possible for their design but have difficulty credibly communicating the quality of their design given the subjectivity of the exercise. On the flip side, funders wish to get the most value for money in the set of proposals they decide to fund and have difficulty assessing the quality of proposed research. Design declaration and diagnosis provide a partial solution to the information problem. A common language for communicating the proposed design and its properties can communicate the value of the research under design assumptions that can be understood and interrogated by funders.

Funding applications could usefully include a declaration and diagnosis of the proposed design. In addition to common diagnosands such as bias and efficiency, two special diagnosands may be valuable: cost and value for money. The cost can be included for each design variant as a function of design features such as sample size, the number of treated units, and the duration of survey interviews. Simulating the design across possible realizations of each variant explains how costs vary with choices the researcher makes. Value for money is a diagnosand that is a function of cost and the amount learned from the design.

In some cases, funders request applicants to provide multiple options and multiple price points or make clear how a design could be altered so that it could be funded at a lower level. Redesigning over differing sample sizes communicates how the researcher conceptualizes these options and provides the funder with an understanding of trade-offs between the amount of learning and cost in these design variants. Applicants could use the redesign process to justify the high cost of their request directly in terms of the amount learned.

Ex ante power analyses are required by an increasing number of funders. Current practice, however, illustrates the crux of the misaligned incentives between applicants and funders. Power calculators online have difficult-to-interrogate assumptions built in and cannot accommodate the specifics of many common designs (Blair et al., 2019). As a result, existing power analyses can demonstrate that almost any design is "sufficiently powered" by changing expected effect sizes and variances. Design declaration is a partial solution to this problem. By clarifying the assumptions encoded in the design declaration, applicants can more clearly link the assumptions of the power analysis to the specifics of the design setting.

Finally, design declarations can, in principle, help funders compare applications on standard scales: root-mean-squared error, bias, and power. Moving design considerations onto a common scale takes some of the guesswork out of the process and reduces reliance on researcher claims about properties of designs.

21.4 Piloting

Designing a research study always entails relying on a set of beliefs, what we've referred to as the set of possible models in M. Choices like how many subjects to sample, which covariates to measure, or which treatments to allocate all depend on beliefs about treatment effects, the correlations of the covariates with the outcome, and the variance of the outcome.

We may have reasonably educated guesses about these parameters from past studies or theory. Our understanding of the nodes and edges in the causal graph of M, expected effect sizes, the distribution of outcomes, feasible randomization schemes, and many other features are directly selected from past research or chosen based on a literature review of past studies.

Even so, we remain uncertain about these values. One reason for the uncertainty is that our research context and inquiries often differ subtly from previous work. Even when replicating an existing study as closely as possible, difficult-to-intuit features of the research setting may have serious consequences for the design. Moreover, our uncertainty about a design parameter is often the very reason for conducting a study. We run experiments *because* we are uncertain about the average treatment effect. Frustratingly, we always have to design under model uncertainty.

The main goal of pilot studies is to reduce this uncertainty. We would like to learn which models in *M* are more likely, so that the main study can be designed under beliefs that are closer to the truth. Pilots take many forms: focus groups, small-scale tests of measurement tools, even miniature versions of the main study. We want to learn things like the distribution of outcomes, how covariates and outcomes might be correlated, or how feasible the assignment, sampling, and measurement strategies are.

Almost by definition, pilot studies are inferentially weaker than main studies. We turn to them in response to constraints on our time, money, and capacity. If we were not constrained, we would run a first full-size study, learn what is wrong with our design, then run a corrected full-size study. Since running multiple full studies is too expensive or otherwise unfeasible, we run either smaller mini-studies or test out only a subset of the elements of our planned design. Accordingly, the diagnosands of a pilot design will not measure up to those of the main design. Pilots have much lower statistical power and may suffer from higher measurement error and less generalizability. Accordingly, the goal of pilot studies should not be to obtain a preliminary answer to the main inquiry, but instead to learn the information that will make the main study a success.

Like main studies, pilot studies can be declared and diagnosed—but importantly, the diagnosands for main and pilot studies need not be the same. Statistical power for an average treatment effect may be an essential diagnosand for the main study, but owing to their small size, power for pilot studies will typically be abysmal. Pilot studies should be diagnosed with respect to the decisions they imply for the main study.

Figure 21.3 shows the relationship between effect size and the sample size required to achieve 80% statistical power for a two-arm trial using simple random assignment. Uncertainty about the true effect size has enormous design consequences. If the effect size is 0.17, we need about 1,100 subjects to achieve 80% power. If it's 0.1, we need 3,200.

Suppose we have prior beliefs about the effect size that can be summarized as a normal distribution centered at 0.3 with a standard deviation of 0.1, as in the bottom panel of Figure 21.2. We could choose a design that corresponds to this best guess, the average of our prior belief distribution. If the true effect size is 0.3, then a study with 350 subjects will have 80% power.

However, redesigning the study to optimize for the "best guess" is risky because the true effect could be much smaller than 0.3. Suppose we adopt the redesign heuristic of powering the study for an effect size at the 10th percentile of our prior belief distribution, which works out here to be an effect size of 0.17. Following this rule, we would select a design with 1,100 subjects.

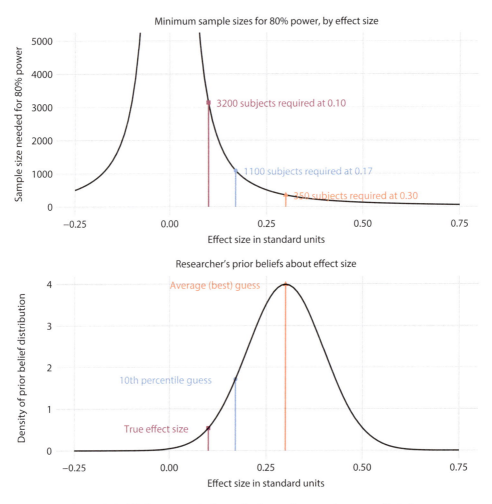

Figure 21.3: Minimum required sample sizes and uncertainty over effect size.

Now suppose the true effect size is, in actuality, only 0.1, so we would need to sample 3,200 subjects for 80% power. The power of our chosen 1,100-subject design is a mere 38%. Here we see the consequences of having incorrect prior beliefs: our ex ante guess of the effect size was too optimistic. Even taking what we thought of as a conservative choice—the 10th percentile redesign heuristic—we ended up with too small a study.

A pilot study can help researchers update their priors about important design parameters. If we do a small-scale pilot with 100 subjects, we'll get a noisy but unbiased estimate of the true effect size. We can update prior beliefs by taking a precision weighted average of our priors and the estimate from the pilot, where the weights are the inverse of the variance of each guess. Our posterior beliefs will be closer to the truth, and our posterior uncertainty will be smaller. If we then follow the heuristic of powering the 10th percentile of our (now posterior) beliefs about effect size, we will have come closer to correctly powering our study. Figure 21.4 shows how

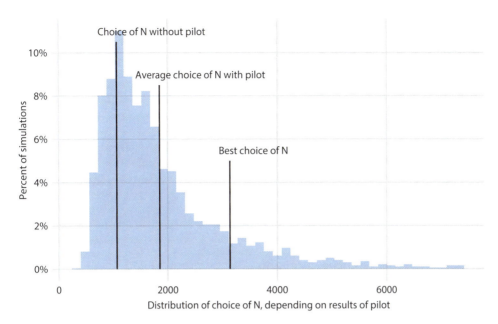

Figure 21.4: Distribution of post-pilot sample size choices.

large the studies would be, depending on how the pilot study came out if we were to follow the 10th percentile decision rule. On average, the pilot leads us to design the main study with 1,800 subjects, sometimes more and sometimes less.

This exercise reveals that a pilot study can be quite valuable. Without a pilot study, we would choose to sample 1,100 subjects, but since the true effect size is only 0.1 (not our best guess of 0.3), the experiment would be underpowered. The pilot study helps us correct our diffuse and incorrect prior beliefs. However, since the pilot is small, we don't update our priors all the way to the truth. We still end up with a main study that is on average too small (1,800), with a corresponding power of 56%. That said, a 56% chance of finding a statistically significant result is better than a 38% chance.

In summary, pilots are most useful when we are uncertain—or outright wrong—about important design parameters. This uncertainty can often be shrunk by quite a bit without running pilot studies by meta-analyzing past empirical studies. Some things are hard to learn by reading others' work; pilot studies are especially useful tools for learning about those things.

21.5   Criticism

A vital part of the research design process is gathering criticism and feedback from others. Timing is delicate here. Asking for comments on an underdeveloped project can sometimes lead to brainstorming sessions about what research questions one might look into. Such unstructured sessions can be quite useful but essentially restarts the research design lifecycle from the beginning. Sharing work only after a full draft has been produced is worse, since the data strategy will have already yielded the realized data. The investigators may have become attached to favored answer strategies and interpretations. While critics can always suggest changes to *I* and *A* post-data collection, an almost finished project is fundamentally constrained by the data strategy as it was implemented.

The best moments to seek advice come before registering preanalysis plans or, if not writing a PAP, before implementing major data strategy elements. The point is not to seek advice exclusively on sampling, assignment, or measurement procedures; the important thing is that there's still time to modify those design elements (Principle 3.4: *Design early*). Feedback about the design as a whole can inform changes to the data strategy before it is set in stone.

Feedback will come in many forms. Sometimes the comments are directly about diagnosands. The critic may think the design has too many arms and won't be well powered for many inquiries. Or they may be concerned about bias due to excludability violations or selection issues. These comments are especially useful because they can easily be incorporated in design diagnosis and redesign exercises.

Other comments are harder to pin down. A fruitful exercise in such cases is to understand how the criticism fits into *M, I, D,* and *A*. Comments like "I'm concerned about external validity here" might seem to be about the data strategy. If the units were not randomly sampled from some well-specified population, we can't generalize from the sample to the population. But if the inquiry is not actually a population quantity, then this inability to use sample data to estimate a population quantity is irrelevant. The question then becomes whether knowing the answer to your sample inquiry helps make theoretical progress or whether we need to generalize—to switch the inquiry to the population quantity to make headway. Critics will not usually be specific about how their criticism relates to each element of design, so it is up to the criticism-seeker to understand the implications for design.

Sometimes we seek feedback from smart people, but they do not immediately understand the design setting. If the critic hasn't absorbed or taken into account important features of the design, their recommendations and amendments may be off-base. For this reason, it's important to communicate the design features—the model, inquiry, data strategy, and answer strategy—at a high enough level of detail that the critic is up to speed before passing judgment.

21.6   Preanalysis Plan

In many research communities, it is becoming standard practice to publicly register a preanalysis plan (PAP) before implementing some or all of the data strategy (Casey, Glennerster and Miguel, 2012, Humphreys, de la Sierra and van der Windt,

2013, Miguel et al., 2014). PAPs serve many functions, but most importantly, they clarify which design choices were made before data collection and which were made after. Sometimes—perhaps every time!—we conduct a research study, and aspects of M, I, D, and A shift along the way. A concern is that they shift in ways that invalidate the apparent conclusions of the study. For example, "*p*-hacking" is the shady practice of trying out many regression specifications until the *p*-value associated with an important test attains statistical significance. PAPs protect researchers by communicating to skeptics *when* design decisions were made. If the regression specification were detailed in a PAP posted before any data were collected, the test could not have been the result of a *p*-hack.

PAPs are sometimes misinterpreted as a binding commitment to report all preregistered analyses and nothing but. This view is unrealistic and unnecessarily rigid. While we think that researchers should report all preregistered analyses *somewhere* (see Section 22.2 on "populated PAPs"), study write-ups inevitably deviate in some way from the PAP—and that's a good thing. Researchers learn more by conducting research. This learning can and should be reflected in the finalized answer strategy. One guardrail against extensive post-PAP design changes can be a set of standard operating procedures that lays out what to do when circumstances change (Green and Lin, 2016).

Our hunch is that the main consequence of actually writing PAPs is that research designs improve. Just like design declaration forces us to think through the details of our model, inquiry, data strategy, and answer strategy, describing those choices in a publicly posted document surely causes deeper reflection about the design. In this way, the main audience for a PAP is the study authors themselves.

What belongs in a PAP? Recommendations for the set of decisions that should be specified in a PAP remain remarkably unclear and inconsistent across research communities. PAP templates and checklists are proliferating, and the number of items they suggest ranges from nine to 60. PAPs themselves are becoming longer and more detailed. Some in the American Economic Association and Evidence in Governance and Politics (EGAP) study registries reach hundreds of pages as researchers seek to be ever more comprehensive. Some registries emphasize the registration of the hypotheses to be tested, while others emphasize the registration of the tests that will be used. In a review of many PAPs, Ofosu and Posner (2022) find considerable variation in how often analytically relevant pieces of information appear in posted plans.

In our view a PAP should center on a design declaration. Currently, most PAPs focus on the answer strategy A: what estimator to use, what covariates to condition on, and what subsets of the data to include. But of course, we also need to know the details of the data strategy D: how units will be sampled, how treatments will be assigned, and how the outcomes will be measured. We need these details to assess the properties of the design and gauge whether the principles of analysis respecting

Chapter 21: Planning

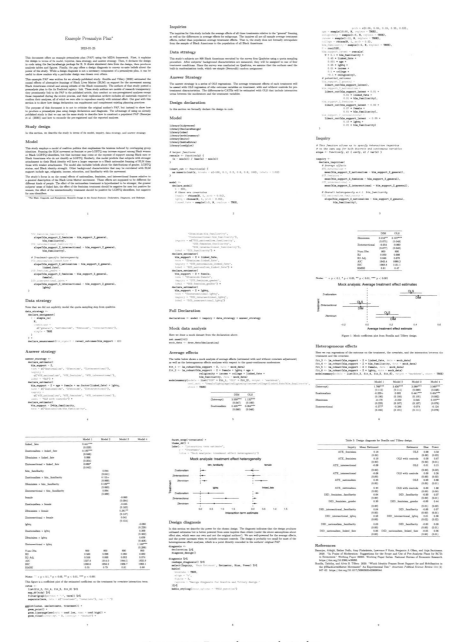

Figure 21.5: Example preanalysis plan.

sampling, treatment assignment, and measurement procedures are being followed. We need to know about the inquiry I because we need to know the target of inference. A significant concern is "outcome switching," wherein the eventual report focuses on different outcomes than initially intended. When we switch outcomes, we switch inquiries! We need enough of the model M in the plan to describe I in sufficient detail. In short, a design declaration is what belongs in a PAP because a design declaration specifies all of the analytically relevant design decisions.

In addition to a design declaration, a PAP can usefully include mock analyses conducted on simulated data. If the design declaration is made formally in code, creating simulated data that resemble the eventually realized data is straightforward. We think researchers should run their answer strategy on the mock data, creating mock figures and tables that will ultimately be made with real data. In our experience, *this* is the step that really causes researchers to think hard about all aspects of their design.

PAPs can, optionally, include design diagnoses in addition to declarations, since it can be informative to describe why a particular design was chosen. For this reason, a PAP might include estimates of diagnosands like power, root-mean-squared error, or bias. If a researcher writes in a PAP that the power to detect a very small effect is large, then if the study comes back null, the eventual write-up can much more credibly rule out "low precision" as an explanation for the null.

21.6.1 Example preanalysis plan

In Figure 21.5, we provide an example preanalysis plan (see the appendix for the document itself) for Bonilla and Tillery (2020), a study of the effects of alternative framings of Black Lives Matter on support for the movement. The authors of that study posted a preanalysis plan to the As Predicted registry. These study authors are models of research transparency: they prominently link to the PAP in the published article, they conduct no non-preregistered analyses except those requested during the review process, and their replication archive includes all materials required to confirm their analyses, all of which we were able to reproduce exactly with minimal effort. Our goal with this alternative PAP is to show how design declaration can supplement and complement existing planning practices.

We show in Section 22.2 how to "populate" this PAP once the data have been realized and collected.

CHAPTER 22

Realization

Realization is the implementation phase of a study. Implementing the data strategy means sampling the units as planned, allocating treatments according to the randomization procedure, and executing the measurement protocol. Implementing the answer strategy means applying the planned summary functions to the realized data. Of course, things never go so smoothly. Inevitably, some portion of the design fails to go according to plan: subjects do not comply with treatments, others cannot be located to answer survey questions, or governments interfere with the study as a whole. Sometimes, the answer strategies are discovered to be biased or imprecise or otherwise wanting. Declared designs can be adapted as the study changes, both to help make choices when you need to pivot and so that at the end there is a "realized design" to compare to the "planned design."

When implementation is complete, the design preregistered in an analysis plan can be "populated" to report on analyses as planned and the realized design reconciled with the planned design. In writing up the study, the design forms the center: why we should believe the answers we report. The declared design can be used in the write-up to convince reviewers of the study's quality, and also as a tool to assess the impact of reviewer suggestions on the design.

22.1 Pivoting

When something goes wrong or you learn things work differently from what you expected, you need to pivot. You face two decisions: go/no-go, and if go, should you alter your research design to account for the new realities? Redesigning the study and diagnosing the possible new designs can help you make these decisions.

We illustrate with three real choices we had to make, one in which criticism of a design by participants led to a simple improvement to the assignment mechanism (D) and two in which difficulties implementing assignments led to a change in inquiries (I) but for quite different reasons.

The first choice was for a research design one of us worked on in coordination with political parties in Uganda. Under the design, a set of MPs were to be randomly selected into a pilot political communications program. Shortly before implementation, however, the political parties complained that the randomization scheme was one that could produce inequalities between the parties, with some parties getting more benefits than others just because of the luck of the draw. They asked whether it would be possible to fix things so that each party would have the same share participating.

The answer of course was yes: a change in D to employ blocked random assignment addressed the fairness concerns of the party, but also led to a demonstrably better design. In the final design, members of each party pulled names out of a hat that contained names only of people from their own party. This is the rare pivot that both attends to an unanticipated complaint and improves the design in the offing.

The second study was one in which another one of us faced a serious noncompliance problem. We launched a cluster-randomized, placebo-controlled 2x2 factorial trial in Nigeria of a film treatment and a text message blast treatment. Treatment was to be rolled out in 200 communities. A few days after treatment delivery began, we noticed that the number of replies was extremely similar in treatment and placebo communities, counter to expectations. We discovered that our research partner, the cell phone company, had delivered the treatment message to both groups! By that time, treatments had been delivered to 106 communities (about half the sample).

We faced the choice to abandon the study or pivot and adapt. We quickly agreed that we could not continue research in the 106 communities, because they had received at least partial treatment. We were left with 109 from our original sample of 200 plus 15 alternates that were selected in the same random sampling process. We determined we could not retain all four treatment conditions and the pure control. We decided that at most we could have two conditions, with about 50 units in each. But which ones? We were reluctant to lose the text message or the film treatments, as both tested two distinct theoretical mechanisms for how to encourage prosocial behaviors. We decided to drop the pure control group, the fifth condition, as well as the placebo text message condition. In this way, we could learn about the effect of the film (compared to placebo) and about the effect of the text messages (compared to nothing).[1] Thus we had to reduce the size of our inquiry set. Essentially we ended up salvaging a subpart of our design without having to materially change any design elements *within* this subpart.

Finally, one of us was involved with a get-out-the-vote canvassing experiment gone wrong during the 2014 Senate race in New Hampshire. We randomly assigned 4,230

---

[1] We randomized half of the communities to receive the treatment film and half the placebo. We then used an over-time stepped-wedge design to study the effect of the text message, randomizing how many days after the film was distributed the text message was sent.

of 8,530 subjects to treatment. However, approximately two weeks before the election, canvassers had only attempted 746 subjects (17.6% of the treatment group) and delivered treatment to just 152 subjects (3.6%). In essence, the implementer had been overly optimistic about the number of subjects they would be able to contact in time for the election. In their revised assessment the organization estimated that they would only be able to attempt to contact 900 more voters. They also told us also that they believed that their efforts would be best spent on voters with above-median vote propensities.

We faced a choice: should we (1) stick to our design and continue trying to treat 900 of the remaining subjects that were allocated to treatment, knowing that we will have many non-compliers in this set or (2) alter D to conduct a whole new random assignment among above-median propensity voters only. A design diagnosis reveals a clear course of action. Even though it decreases the overall sample size, restricting the study to the above-median propensity voters substantially increases the precision of the design.[2] Opting for this modification to D required thinking through whether we were willing to accept a change in I since the set of compliers for which we could generate estimates is different under the two designs.

Pivoting is sometimes hard and sometimes easy but, very often, assessing whether or how to pivot requires thinking through the full design to see which parts have to change as others change. If you do this through redesign your design becomes a living document and becomes a tool to guide you along the research path, not just as a document to write at the beginning of the study and revisit when you are writing up.

22.2 Populated Preanalysis Plan

A preanalysis plan describes how study data will eventually be analyzed, but those plans may change during the process of producing a finished report, article, or book. Inevitably, authors of preanalysis plans fail to anticipate how the data generated by the study will eventually be analyzed. Some reasons for discrepancies were discussed in the previous section on pivoting, but others intervene as well. A common reason is that PAPs promise too many analyses. In writing a concise paper, some analyses are dropped, others are combined, and still others are added during the writing and revision process. In the next section, we'll describe how to reconcile analyses-as-planned with analyses-as-implemented, but this present section is about what to do with your analysis plan immediately after getting the data back.

We echo proposals made in Banerjee et al. (2020) and Alrababa'h et al. (2022) that researchers should produce short reports that fulfill the promises made in their PAPs. Banerjee et al. (2020) emphasize that writing PAPs is difficult and usually

---

[2]This conclusion follows the logic of the placebo-controlled design described in Section 18.7.

time-constrained, so it is natural that the final paper will reflect further thinking about the full set of empirical approaches. A "populated PAP" serves to communicate the results of the promised analyses. Alrababa'h et al. (2022) cite the tendency of researchers to abandon the publication of studies that return null results. To address the resulting publication bias, they recommend "null results reports" that share the results of the preregistered analyses. We think these reports (whether the results come back null or otherwise) can easily be added to the appendix of the final write-up or posted to a study registry.

We recommended in Section 21.6 that authors include mock analyses in their PAPs using simulated data. Doing so has the significant benefit of being specific about the details of the answer strategy. A further benefit comes when it is time to produce a populated PAP, since the realized data can quite straightforwardly be swapped in for the mock data. Given the time invested in building simulated analyses for the PAP, writing up a populated PAP takes only as much effort as is needed to clean the data (which will need to be done in any case).

22.2.1 Example

In Section 21, we declared the design for Bonilla and Tillery (2020) following their preanalysis plan. In doing so, we declared an answer strategy in code. In our populated PAP (shown in Figure 22.1 and available in the appendix), we can run that same answer strategy code, but swap out the simulated data for the real data collected during the study.

22.3 Reconciliation

Reconciliation is the process of comparing the final design to the planned design. Understanding the differences between the two and the justifications for the changes can help us understand what to learn from the final results.

Suppose the original design described a three-arm trial: one control and two treatments, but the design as implemented drops all subjects assigned to the second treatment. Sometimes, this is an entirely appropriate and reasonable design modification. Perhaps the second treatment was simply not delivered due to an implementation failure. Other times, these modifications are less benign. Perhaps the second treatment effect estimate did not achieve statistical significance, so the author omitted it from the analysis.

For this reason, we recommend that authors reconcile the design as planned with the design as implemented. A reconciliation can be a plain description of the deviations from the PAP, with justifications where appropriate. A more involved reconciliation would include a declaration of the planned design, a declaration of the implemented design, and a list of the differences. This "diff" of the designs can be automated

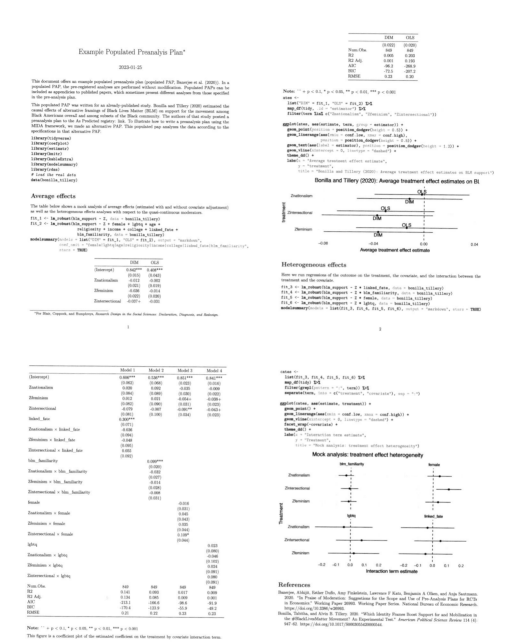

Figure 22.1: Example populated PAP.

through the declaration of both designs in computer code, then comparing the two design objects line by line (see the function `compare_designs()` in `DeclareDesign`).

In some cases, reconciliation will lead to additional learning beyond what can be inferred from the final design itself. When some units refuse to be included in the

Table 22.1: Illustration of an *Inquiry reconciliation* table.

Inquiry	In the preanalysis plan	In the paper	In the appendix
Gender effect	X	X	
Age effect			X

Table 22.2: Illustration of an *Answer strategy reconciliation* table.

Inquiry	*A* in PAP	*A* in paper	Notes
Gender effect	estimate = 0.6	estimate = 0.6	change in control variables
	s.e = 0.31	s.e = 0.25	[cross references to tables /code]

study sample or some units refuse measurement, we get important information about those units. Understanding sample exclusions, noncompliance, and attrition not only may inform future research design planning choices, but also contribute substantively to our understanding of the social setting.

There are no current standards for how to report reconciliation. We recommend, however, providing two types of tables, a qualitative *Inquiry reconciliation* table and a quantitative *Answer strategy reconciliation table*. In the latter case, especially, guiding readers to relevant discussions or sections of replication code can make the reconciliation tables easier to evaluate. Such answer strategy reconciliation tables could also usefully include output from diagnosis comparisons to provide motivation for change. In general they should also include brief explanations for decisions taken.

We provide illustrations for both of these in Table 22.1 and Table 22.2.

22.3.1 Example

In Section 21, we described the preanalysis plan registered by Bonilla and Tillery (2020). We reconcile the set of conditional average treatment effect (CATE) analyses planned in that PAP, the analyses reported in the paper, and those reported in the appendix at the request of reviewers in Table 22.3. In column two, we see that the authors planned four CATE estimations: effects by familiarity with Black Lives Matter; by gender; by LGBTQ status; and by linked fate. Only two of those are reported in the paper; the others may have been excluded for space reasons. Another way to handle these results would be to present them in a populated PAP posted on their Web site or in the paper's appendix.

In their appendix, the authors report on a set of analyses requested by reviewers. We see this as an excellent example of transparently presenting the set of planned analyses and highlighting the analyses that were added afterward and why they were

Table 22.3: *Inquiry reconciliation* table based on Bonilla and Tillery (2020) analysis and their preanalysis plan.

Covariate	In the preanalysis plan	In the paper	In the appendix (at the request of reviewers)
Familiarity with BLM	X		
Gender	X	X	
LGBTQ status	X	X	
Linked fate	X		
Religiosity			X
Region			X
Age			X
Education			X

added. They write: "We have been asked to consider other pertinent moderations beyond gender and LGBTQ+ status. They are contained in the four following sections."

This small Inquiry reconciliation table describes the heterogeneous effects analyses the researchers planned, those reported in the paper, and those reported in the appendix at the request of reviewers.

22.4 Writing

When writing up an empirical paper, authors have multiple goals. They want to convince reviewers and readers that the research question they are tackling is important and their research design provides useful answers to that question. They sometimes also want to influence decision-makers like policymakers, businesses, and journalists. Communicating the elements of MIDA and a diagnosis of the design in a study write-up serve both goals. The declaration in terms of MIDA in the paper enables readers to understand what research design was implemented, and the diagnosis the inferential properties of the design.

Elements of MIDA may appear throughout a paper. In Figure 22.2 below, we annotate Mousa (2020) by highlighting where in the article each design component is discussed. The study reports on the results of a randomized experiment in which Iraqi Christians were assigned either to an all-Christian soccer team or a team in which they would play alongside Muslims. The experiment tested whether being on a mixed team affected intergroup attitudes and behaviors, both among teammates and back at home after the games were over. We highlight in color areas discussing

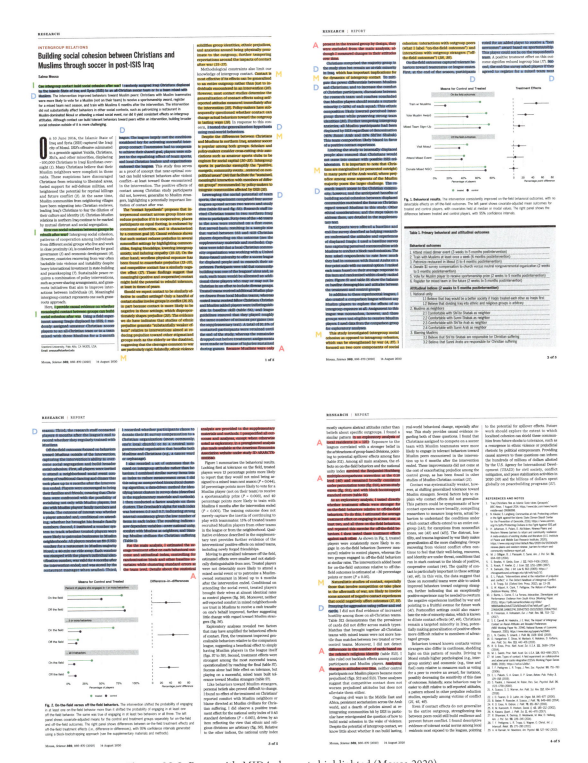

Figure 22.2: Paper with *MIDA* elements highlighted (Mousa 2020).

the model M in yellow, the inquiry I in green, the data strategy D in blue, and the answer strategy A in pink.

The model and the inquiry largely appear in the abstract and introductory portion of the paper, though aspects of the model are discussed later on. Much of the first three pages are devoted to the data strategy, while the answer strategy only appears briefly. This division makes sense: in this paper, the action is all in the experimental design whereas the answer strategy follows straightforwardly from it. The paper mostly describes M and D, with only a small amount of text devoted to I and A. Finally, it is notable that the data strategy is interspersed with aspects of the model. The reason is that the author is justifying choices about randomization and measurement using features of the model. In our experience, describing each of the four dimensions of MIDA separately can be a clarifying structure when communicating designs.

CHAPTER 23

Integration

After publication, research studies leave the hands of their authors and enter the public domain.[1]

Most immediately, authors share their findings with the public through the media and with decision-makers. Design information is useful for helping journalists to emphasize design quality rather than splashy findings. Decision-makers may act on evidence from studies, and researchers who want to influence policymaking and business decisions may wish to consider diagnosands about the decisions these actors make.

Researchers can prepare for the integration of their studies into scholarly debates through better archiving practices and better reporting of research designs in the published article. Future researchers may build on the results of a past study in three ways. First, they may *reanalyze* the original data. Reanalysts must be cognizant of the original data strategy D when working with the realized data d. Changes to the answer strategy A must respect D, regardless of whether the purpose of the reanalysis is to answer the original inquiry I or to answer a different inquiry I'. Second, future researchers may *replicate* the design. Typically, replicators provide a new answer to the same I with new data, possibly improving elements of D and A along the way. If the inquiry of the replication is too different from the inquiry of the original study, the fidelity of the replication study may be compromised. Lastly, future researchers may *meta-analyze* a study's answer with other past studies. Meta-analysis is most meaningful when all of the included studies target a similar enough inquiry and when all studies rely on credible design.

All three of these activities depend on an accurate understanding of the study design. Reanalysts, replicators, and meta-analysts all need access to the study data and materials, of course. They also need to be sure of the critical design information in M, I, D, and A. Later in this section, we outline how archiving procedures that preserve study data and study design can enable new scientific purposes and describe strategies for doing each of these three particular integration tasks.

---

[1] This section does not apply to private research, which unfortunately does not get "integrated."

23.1 Communicating

The findings from studies are communicated to other scholars through academic publications. But some of the most important audiences—policymakers, businesses, journalists, and the public at large—do not read academic journals. These audiences learn about the study in other in other ways, through op-eds, blog posts, and policy reports that translate research for nonspecialist audiences.

Too often, a casualty of translating the study from academic to other audiences is the design information. Emphasis gets placed on the study results, not on the reasons why the results of the study are to be believed. In sharing the research for nonspecialist audiences, we revert to saying *that* we think the findings are true and not *why* we think the findings are true. Explaining why requires explaining the research design, which in our view ought to be part of any public-facing communication about research.

Looking at recent studies published in *The New York Times* Well section on health and fitness, we found that two dimensions of design quality were commonly ignored. First, experimental studies on new fitness regimens with very small samples, sometimes fewer than 10 units, are commonly highlighted. When both academic journals and reporters promote tiny studies, the likely result is that the published (and public) record contains many statistical flukes results reflecting noise rather than new discoveries. Second, very large studies that draw observational comparisons between large samples of dieters and non-dieters with millions of observations receive outsize attention. These designs are prone to bias from confounding, but these concerns are too often not described or discussed.

How can we improve scientific communication so that we better communicate the credibility of findings? The market incentives for both journalists and authors reward striking and surprising findings, so any real solution to the problem likely requires addressing those incentives. Short of that, we recommend that authors who wish to communicate the high quality of their designs to the media do so by providing the design information in *M*, *I*, *D*, and *A* in lay terms. Science communicators can state the research question (*I*) and explain why applying the data and answer strategies is likely to yield a good answer to the question. The actual result is, of course, also important to communicate, but *why* it is a credible answer to the research question is just as important to share—specifically what has to be believed about *M* for the results to be on target (Principle 3.6: *Design to share*).

How can we as researchers communicate about other scholars' work? Citations can't covey the entirety of *MIDA* in one sentence, but they can give an inkling. Here's an example of how we could cite a (hypothetical) study in a way that conveys at least some design information. "Using a randomized experiment, the researchers (Authors, Year) found that donating to a campaign causes a large increase in the number of subsequent donation requests from other candidates, which is consistent with theories of party behavior that predict intra-party cooperation."

The citation explains that the data strategy included some kind of randomized experiment (we don't know how many treatment arms or subjects, among other details), and that the answer strategy probably compared the counts of donation requests from any campaign (email requests, or phone, we don't know) among the groups of subjects that were assigned to donate to a particular campaign. The citation mentions the models described in an unspecified area of the scientific literature on party politics, which all predict cooperation like the sharing of donor lists. We can reason that, if the inquiry, "Is the population average treatment effect of donating to one campaign on the number of donation requests from other campaigns positive?" were put to each of these theories, they would all respond "Yes." The citation serves as a useful shorthand for the reader of what the claim of the paper is and why they should think it's credible. By contrast, a citation like "The researchers found that party members cooperate (Author, Year)" doesn't communicate any design information at all.

23.2 Archiving

One of the biggest successes in the push for greater research transparency has been the changing norms surrounding data sharing and analysis code after studies have been published. Many journals now require authors to post these materials at publicly available repositories like the OSF or Dataverse. This development is undoubtedly a good thing. In older manuscripts, sometimes data or analyses are described as being "available upon request," but of course, such requests are sometimes ignored (93% were ignored in a recent attempt to request 1,792 such datasets according to Gabelica, Bojčić and Puljak, 2022). Furthermore, a century from now, study authors will no longer be with us even if they wanted to respond to such requests. Public repositories have a much better chance of preserving study information for the future, especially if they are actively maintained (Peer, Orr, and Coppock, 2021).

What belongs in a replication archive? Enough documentation, data, and design detail that those who wish to reanalyze, replicate, and meta-analyze results can do so without contacting the authors.

Data. First, the realized data d itself. Sometimes this is the raw data. Sometimes it is only the "cleaned" data that is actually used by analysis scripts. Where ethically possible, we think it is preferable to post as much of the raw data as possible after removing information like IP addresses and geographic locations that could be used to identify subjects. The output of cleaning scripts—the cleaned data—should also be included in the replication archive.

Reanalyses often reexamine and extend studies by exploring the use of alternative outcomes, by varying sets of control variables, and by considering new ways of grouping data. As a result, replication data ideally includes all data collected by the authors even if the variables are not used in the final published results. Sometimes authors exclude these to preserve their own ability to publish on these other variables or because they are worried alternative analyses will cast doubt on their results. We hope norms will change such that study authors instead want to enable future researchers to build on their research by being expansive in what information is shared.

Analysis code. Replication archives also include the answer strategy A, or the set of functions that produce results when applied to the data. We need the actual analysis code because the natural-language descriptions of A that are typically given in written reports are imprecise. As a small example, many articles describe their answer strategies as "ordinary least squares," but do not fully describe the set of covariates included or the particular approach to variance estimation. These choices can substantively affect the quality of the research design—and nothing makes these choices explicit like the actual analysis code. Analysis code is needed not only for reanalysis but also replication and meta-analysis. Replication practice today involves inferring most of these details from descriptions in text. Reanalyses may directly reuse or modify analysis code and replication projects need to know the exact details of analyses to ensure they can implement the same analyses on the data they collect. Meta-analysis authors may take the estimates from the past studies directly, so understanding the exact analysis procedure conducted is important. Other times, meta-analyses reanalyze data to ensure comparability in estimation. Conducting analyses with and without covariates, with clustering when it is appropriate, or with a single statistical model when they vary across studies all require having the exact analysis code.

To the extent possible we encourage you to think of analysis code as being a data-in data-out function: a function that takes in your dataset—or a future replication dataset—implements analysis, and reports a dataset containing answers: estimates and estimates of uncertainty.

Data strategy materials. Increasingly, replication archives include the materials needed to implement treatments and measurement strategies. Without the survey questionnaires in their original languages and formats, we cannot exactly replicate them in future studies, hindering our ability to build on and adapt them. The treatment stimuli used in the study should also be included. Data strategies are needed for reanalyses and meta-analyses too: answer strategies should respect data strategies, so understanding the details of sampling, treatment assignment, and measurement can shape reanalysts' decisions and meta-analysis authors' decisions about what studies to include and which estimates to synthesize.

To the extent possible we encourage you to describe data strategies also as a data-in data-out function. Functions that take in information about a known context, and use this, together with parameters that characterize your strategy, return a dataset similar in structure to the data you generated.

Design declaration. While typical replication archives include the data and code, we think that future replication archives should also have a design declaration that fully describes M, I, D, and A. This declaration should be done in code and words. A diagnosis can also be included, demonstrating the properties as understood by the author and indicating the diagnosands that the author considered in judging the quality of the design.

Design details help future scholars not only assess, but replicate, reanalyze, and extend the study. Reanalysts need to understand the answer strategy to modify or extend it and the data strategy to ensure that their new analysis respects the details of the sampling, treatment assignment, and measurement procedures. Data and analysis sharing enables reanalysts to adopt or adapt the analysis strategy, but a declaration of the data strategy would help more. The same is true of meta-analysis authors, who need to understand the designs' details to make good decisions about which studies to include and how to analyze them. Replicators who wish to exactly replicate or even just provide an answer to the same inquiry need to understand the inquiry, data strategy, and answer strategy.

Figure 23.1 below shows the file structure for an example replication. Our view on replication archives shares much in common with the TIER protocol and the proposals in Alvarez, Key and Núñez (2018). It includes raw data in a platform-independent format (.csv) and cleaned data in a language-specific format (.rds, a format for R data files). Data features like labels, attributes, and factor levels are preserved when imported by the analysis scripts. The analysis scripts are labeled by the outputs they create, such as figures and tables. A main script is included that runs the cleaning and analysis scripts in the correct order. The documents folder consists of the paper, the supplemental appendix, the preanalysis plan, the populated analysis plan, and codebooks that describe the data. A README file explains each part of the replication archive. We also suggest that authors include a script that consists of a design declaration and diagnosis. Bowers (2011) offers one reason above and beyond research transparency to go to all this effort: good archiving is like collaborating with your future self.

23.3 Reanalysis

A reanalysis of an existing study is a follow-up study that reuses the original realized data for some new purpose. The reanalysis is a study with a research design that can be described in terms of M, I, D, and A. Reanalyses are fundamentally constrained by the data strategy of the original study. The data strategy D and the resulting data are set in stone—but reanalysts can make changes to the answer strategy A and sometimes also to the model M or inquiry I.

We can learn from reanalyses in several ways. First, we can fix errors in the original answer strategy. Reanalyses fix simple mathematical errors, typos in data transcription, or failures to account for features of the data strategy when analyzing

Chapter 23: Integration

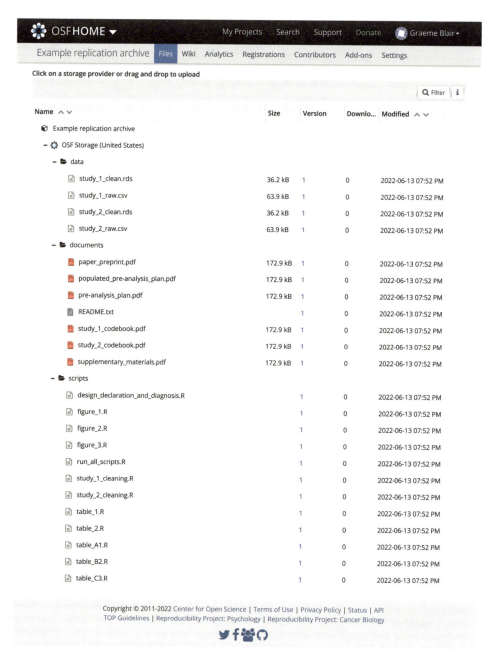

Figure 23.1: File structure for archiving.

the data. These reanalyses show whether the original results do or do not depend on these corrections. Second, we can reassess the study in light of new information about the world learned after the original study was published. That is, sometimes M changes in ways that color our interpretation of past results. Perhaps we learned about new confounders or alternative causal channels that undermine the original design's credibility. When reanalyzed, demonstrating the results do (or do not) change when new model features are incorporated improves our understanding of the inquiry. Third, reanalyses may also aim to answer new questions that were not considered by the original study but for which the realized data can provide useful answers.

Lastly, many reanalyses show that original findings are not "robust" to alternative answer strategies. These are better conceptualized as claims about robustness to alternative models: one model may imply one answer strategy, and a different model, with another confounder, suggest another. If both models are plausible, a good answer strategy should be robust to both and even help distinguish between them. A reanalysis could uncover robustness to these alternative models or lack thereof.

Reanalyses are themselves research designs. Just as with any design, whether a reanalysis is a strong research design depends on *possible* realizations of the data (as determined by the data strategy), not just on the realized data. Because the realized data is fixed in a reanalysis, analysts are often instead tempted to judge the reanalysis based on whether it overturns or confirms the original study's results. A successful reanalysis in this way of thinking demonstrates, by showing that the original results are changed under an alternative answer strategy, that the results are not robust to other plausible models.

This way of thinking can lead to incorrect assessments of reanalyses. Instead, we should consider what answers we would obtain under the original answer strategy A and the reanalysis strategy A' under many *possible* realizations of the data. A good reanalysis strategy reveals with high probability the set of models of the world under which we can make credible claims about the inquiry. Whether or not the results change under the answer strategies A and A' tells us little about this probability because the realized data is only one draw.

23.3.1 Example

In this section, we illustrate the flaw in assessing reanalyses based on changing significance of results alone. We demonstrate how to assess the properties of reanalysis plans, comparing the properties of original answer strategies to proposed reanalysis answer strategies.

The design we consider is an observational study with a binary treatment Z that may or may not be confounded by a covariate X. Suppose that the original researcher had in mind a model in which Z is not confounded by X:

```
# X is not a confounder and is measured pretreatment
model_1 <-
  declare_model(
    N = 100,
    U = rnorm(N),
```

```
      X = rnorm(N),
      Z = rbinom(N, 1, prob = plogis(0.5)),
      potential_outcomes(Y ~ 0.1 * Z + 0.25 * X + U),
      Y = reveal_outcomes(Y ~ Z)
  )
```

The reanalyst has in mind a different model. In this second model, X confounds the relationship between Z and Y:

```
# X is a confounder and is measured pretreatment
model_2 <-
  declare_model(
    N = 100,
    U = rnorm(N),
    X = rnorm(N),
    Z = rbinom(N, 1, prob = plogis(0.5 + X)),
    potential_outcomes(Y ~ 0.1 * Z + 0.25 * X + U),
    Y = reveal_outcomes(Y ~ Z)
  )
```

The original answer strategy `A` is a regression of the outcome Y on the treatment Z. The reanalyst collects the covariate X and proposes to control for it in a linear regression; call that strategy `A_prime`.

```
A <- declare_estimator(Y ~ Z, .method = lm_robust, label = "A")
A_prime <- declare_estimator(Y ~ Z + X, .method = lm_robust,
                              label = "A_prime")
```

Applying the two answer strategies, we get differing results. The treatment effect estimate is significant under `A` but not under `A_prime`. Commonly, reanalysts would infer from this that the answer strategy `A_prime` is preferred and that the original result was incorrect.

```
draw_estimates(model_2 + A + A_prime)
```

Table 23.1: Analysis and reanalysis estimates.

estimator	estimate	std.error	p.value
A	0.385	0.176	0.031
A_prime	0.219	0.188	0.246

As we show now, these claims depend on the validity of the model and should be assessed with design diagnosis. Consider a third model in which X is affected by Z and Y. (In many observational settings, which variables are causally prior or posterior to others can be difficult to know with certainty.) We now diagnose both answer strategies under all three models.

Declaration 23.1 Reanalysis declaration.

```
# X is not a confounder and is measured posttreatment
model_3 <-
  declare_model(
    N = 100,
    U = rnorm(N),
    Z = rbinom(N, 1, prob = plogis(0.5)),
    potential_outcomes(Y ~ 0.1 * Z + U),
    Y = reveal_outcomes(Y ~ Z),
    X = 0.1 * Z + 5 * Y + rnorm(N)
  )

I <- declare_inquiry(ATE = mean(Y_Z_1 - Y_Z_0))

design_1 <- model_1 + I + A + A_prime
design_2 <- model_2 + I + A + A_prime
design_3 <- model_3 + I + A + A_prime

declaration_23.1 <- list(design_1, design_2, design_3)
```

Diagnosis 23.1 Reanalysis diagnosis.

Table 23.2: Diagnosis of the reanalysis design under alternative models.

design	estimator	bias
design_1	A	−0.005
design_1	A_prime	−0.005
design_2	A	0.210
design_2	A_prime	0.003
design_3	A	0.001
design_3	A_prime	−0.114

What we see in the diagnosis below is that A_prime is only preferred if we know for sure that X is measured pretreatment. In design 3, where X is measured posttreatment, A is preferred, because controlling for X leads to posttreatment bias. This diagnosis indicates that the reanalyst needs to justify their beliefs about the causal ordering of X and Z to claim that A_prime is preferred to A. The reanalyst should not conclude on the basis of the realized estimates only that their answer strategy is preferred.

Three principles emerge from the idea that changing A to A' should be justified by diagnosis, not by the comparison of the realized results of the two answer strategies.

1. **Home ground dominance.** Holding the original M constant (i.e., the home ground of the original study), if you can show that a new answer strategy A' yields better diagnosands than the original A, then A' can be justified by home ground dominance. In the example above, model 1 is the "home ground," and the reanalyst's A' is preferred to A on this home ground.

2. **Robustness to alternative models.** A second justification for a change in answer strategy is that you can show that a new answer strategy is robust to both the original model M and a new, also plausible, M'. In observational studies, we are uncertain about many features of the model, such as the existence of unobserved confounders. In the example above, A' is robust to models 1 and 2 but is not robust to model 3. By contrast, A is robust to models 1 and 3 but not to model 2.

3. **Model plausibility.** If the diagnosands for a design with A' are worse than those with A under M but better under M', then the switch to A' can only be justified by a claim or demonstration that M' is more plausible than M. As we saw in the example, neither A nor A' was robust to all three alternative models. A claim about model plausibility would have to be invoked to justify controlling for X. Such a claim could be made on the basis of substantive knowledge or additional data. For example, the reanalyst could demonstrate that data collection of X took place before the treatment was realized in order to rule out model 3.

23.4 Replication

After your study is completed, it may one day be replicated. By replication we mean collecting new data to study the same inquiry. A new model, data strategy, or answer strategy may also be proposed.

So-called "exact" replications hold key features of I, D, and A fixed, but draw a new dataset from the data strategy and apply the same answer strategy A to the new data to produce a fresh answer. Replications are said to "succeed" when the new and old answer are similar and to "fail" when they are not. Dichotomizing replication attempts into successes and failures is usually not that helpful, and it would be better to simply characterize how similar the old and new answers are. Literally exact replication is impossible: at least some elements of m^* have changed between the first study and the replication. Specifying how they might have changed, e.g., how outcomes vary with time, will help judge differences observed between old and new answers.

Replication studies can benefit enormously from the knowledge gains produced by the original studies. For example, we learn a large amount to inform the construction of M and we learn the value of the inquiry from the original study. The M of the replication study can and should incorporate this new information. For example, if we learn from the original study that the estimand is positive, but it might be small, the replication study could respond by changing D to increase the sample size. Design diagnosis can help you learn about how to change the replication study's design in light of the original research.

When changes to the data strategy D or answer strategy A can be made to produce more informative answers about the same inquiry I, exact replication may not be preferred. Holding the treatment and outcomes the same may be required to provide an answer to the same I, but increasing the sample size or sampling individuals rather than villages or other changes may be preferable to exact replication. Replication designs can also take advantage of new best practices in research design.

So-called "conceptual" replications alter both M and D, but keep I and A as similar as possible. That is, a conceptual replication tries to ascertain whether a relationship in one context also holds in a new context. The trouble and promise of conceptual replications lie in the designer's success at holding I constant. Too often, a conceptual replication fails because in changing M, too much changes about I, muddying the "concept" under replication.

A summary function is needed to interpret the difference between the original answer and the replication answer. This function might take the new one and throw out the old if design was poor in the first. It might be taking the average. It might be a precision-weighted average. Specifying this function ex ante may be useful to avoid the choice of summary depending on the replication results. This summary function will be reflected in A and in the discussion section of the replication paper.

23.4.1   Example

Here we have an original study design of size 1,000. The original study design's true sample average treatment effect (SATE) is 0.2 because the original authors happened to study a very treatment-responsive population. We seek to replicate the original results, whatever they may be. We want to characterize the probability of concluding that we "failed" to replicate the original results. We have four alternative metrics for assessing replication failure.

1. Are the original and replication estimates statistically significantly different from each other? If the difference-in-SATEs is significant, we conclude that we failed to replicate the original results, and if not, we conclude that the study replicated.

2. Is the replication estimate within the original 95% confidence interval?

3. Is the original estimate within the replication 95% confidence interval?

4. Do we fail to affirm equivalence[2] between the replication and original estimates, using a tolerance of 0.2?

Figure 23.2 shows that no matter how big we make the replication, we find that the rate of concluding the difference-in-SATEs is nonzero only occurs about 10% of the time. Similarly, the replication estimate is rarely outside of the original confidence interval, because it's rare to be more extreme than a wide confidence interval. The relatively high variance of the original study means that it is so uncertain, it's tough to distinguish it from any number in particular.

Turning to the third metric (is the original outside the 95% confidence interval of the replication estimate), we find that we become more and more likely to conclude that the original study fails to replicate as the quality of the replication study goes up. At very large sample sizes, the replication confidence intervals become extremely small, so in the limit, it will always exclude the original study estimate.

The last metric, equivalence testing, has the nice property that, as the sample size grows, we get closer to the correct answer—the true SATEs are indeed within 0.2 standard units of each other. However, again because the original study is so noisy, it is difficult to affirm its equivalence with anything, even when the replication study is quite large.

The upshot of this exercise is that, curiously, when original studies are weak (in that they generate imprecise estimates), it becomes *harder* to conclusively affirm that they did not replicate. This set of incentives is somewhat perverse: designers of original studies benefit from a lack of precision if it means the studies can't "fail to replicate."

23.5 Meta-analysis

One of the last stages of the lifecycle of a research design is its eventual incorporation into our common scientific understanding of the world. Research findings are synthesized into our broader scientific understanding through systematic reviews and meta-analysis.

Research synthesis takes two basic forms. The first is meta-analysis, in which a series of estimates are analyzed together in order to better understand features of the distribution of answers obtained in the literature (see Section 19.3). Studies can be averaged together in ways that are better or worse. Sometimes the answers are averaged together according to their precision. A precision-weighted average gives more weight to precise estimates and less weight to studies that are noisy. Sometimes

---

[2] For an introduction to equivalence testing, see Hartman and Hidalgo (2018).

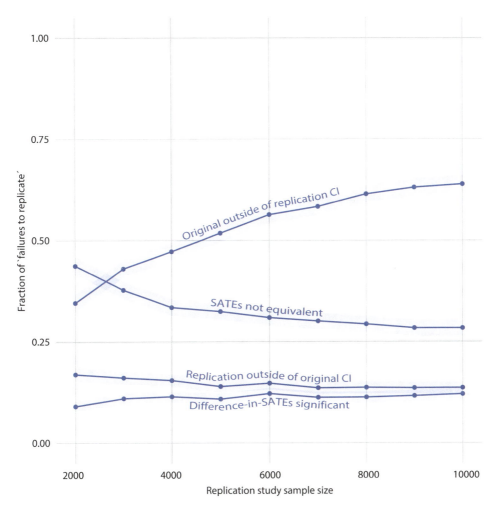

Figure 23.2: Rates of 'failure to replicate' according to four diagnosands. Original study N = 1000; true original SATE: 0.2; true replication SATE: 0.15.

studies are "averaged" by counting up how many of the estimates are positive and significant, how many are negative and significant, and how many are null. This is the typical approach taken in a literature review. Regardless of the averaging approach, the goal of this kind of synthesis is to learn as much as possible about a particular inquiry *I* by drawing on evidence from many studies.

A second kind of synthesis is an attempt to bring together the results of many designs, each of which targets a different inquiry about a common model. This is the kind of synthesis that takes place across an entire research literature. Different scholars focus on different nodes and edges of the common model, so a synthesis needs to incorporate the diverse sources of evidence. Such synthesis strategies include, for example, Bayesian model averaging approaches and stacking approaches (see, e.g., Yao et al., 2018).

How can you best anticipate how your research findings will be synthesized? For the first kind of synthesis—meta-analysis—you must be cognizant of keeping a commonly understood I in mind. You want to select inquiries not for their novelty, but because of their commonly understood importance. While the specifics of the model M might differ from study to study, the fact that the Is are all similar enough to be synthesized allows for a specific kind of knowledge accumulation.

For the second kind of synthesis—literature-wide progress on a full causal model—even greater care is required. Specific studies cannot make up bespoke models M but instead must understand how the specific M adopted in the study is a special case of some broader M that is in principle agreed to by a wider research community. Perhaps in this spirit, Samii (2016) sets the role of "causal empiricists" apart from the role of theorists. The nonstop, never-ending proliferation of study-specific theories is a threat to this kind of knowledge accumulation. In a telling piece, McPhetres et al. (2020) document that in a decade of research articles published in *Psychological Science*, 359 specific theories were named. Of these 70% were named just once and a further 12% were named just twice.

Design then with a view to integration. In the ideal case the meta-analytic design will already exist and your job will be to design a new study that can demonstrably add value to the collective design.

PART

V

Epilogue

CHAPTER 24

Epilogue

Social science is undergoing a period of structural change. The credibility of decades of research findings has been questioned and many studies have been found to be flawed.

The first prong of the response to the upheaval was the so-called "credibility revolution," which sought new research designs that could deliver credible evidence to answer social scientific questions. Randomized experiments rapidly rose in popularity in economics and political science. Observational causal inference methods such as regression discontinuities and difference-in-differences designs have become popular in sociology, political science, and economics. Sample sizes have increased and new populations outside university students have been explored in psychology and experimental economics.

The second prong was the so-called "open science movement." Open science practices are motivated by the idea that even when a credible *general* design for drawing inferences is adopted, myriad small design decisions may influence the validity of the results. Sharing the plans, computer code, and materials used to implement the research as well as the data that result allows peer reviewers and readers to assess the large and small decisions the authors made and come to their own judgment about what was learned. Preregistration of plans before implementing research provides additional clarity: which of these decisions were made before seeing data and results and which were made after.

The two prongs are closely related to each other. Open science practices are meant to reinforce the work on credible designs: transparency of research methods incentivizes researchers to select credible research designs in the first place. Common to both is the idea that research design matters.

Strikingly, however, these advances have been made without a clear common understanding of what a design is or how to evaluate one. In this book, we provided a flexible approach to defining a design and a procedure for assessing its qualities. We identified four generic elements of a research design: the Model, the Inquiry, the Data Strategy, and the Answer strategy. "Declaring" these four elements makes it easier to communicate the most important analytic features of a design, enabling "diagnosis" of the credibility of claims that depend on them.

We hope our effort adds two new steps to the workflow promoted by credibility and transparency revolutionaries. First, we want scholars to develop designs by declaring them—in code, when possible, diagnosing their properties in terms of scientific, logistical, and ethical goals, and redesigning across feasible designs to select the final design. Second, we want scholars to share their designs so they can be more easily understood, more easily interrogated, and more easily built upon.

We see these steps as deeply complementary to the credibility revolution and the open science movement.

Declaring and diagnosing designs can make designs stronger. Many design choices can be made on the basis of analytic results, and these should be used when possible. But oftentimes analytic results provide incomplete answers. Sampling and eligibility procedures can interact with treatment allocation schemes, so causal identification results can be insufficient to assess the unbiasedness of the design for a population average treatment effect. Moreover, many theoretical results about research design are conditional on certain sample sizes, correlations between variables, or the correctness of functional forms. Assessing how designs perform based on the specific research setting and its sample size and empirical correlations between variables augments the general theoretical guidance. Of course, theory guides how to set up the design itself: identifying what kinds of problems can emerge in a model is an exercise shaped by theory.

Sharing research designs in code complements common open science practices in use today. By providing the design in code, the study can be replicated exactly in a new setting or at a later time period, reanalyzed with the realized data but new estimators, and the diagnosands reassessed on the authors' original terms and under new conjectures about the model. Declarations also complement current practices in preregistration. Considerable debate surrounds what should be included in a preanalysis plan. Declarations in code provide an answer: you should declare sufficient information to enable someone to diagnose the design in terms of study-relevant diagnosands.

Better software tools will come along to declare, diagnose, and redesign studies in code. A body of domain-specific knowledge will develop about what models design must be assessed against to assure robustness. What we hope will remain is the idea that research designs can be thought of as objects that can be interrogated, defined by the specific steps in the procedures used to generate data and analyze it to provide answers to particular inquiries that are themselves well defined with respect to specified representations of the world. We hope that these ideas and tools will enable scholars to better respond to changed incentives in the social sciences to adopt credible research designs for the questions they are asking and to communicate that they have done so to reviewers and readers.

PART VI

References

Bibliography

Abadie, Alberto, Susan Athey, Guido W. Imbens and Jeffrey Wooldridge. 2017. "When should you adjust standard errors for clustering?"

Abell, Peter and Ofer Engel. 2021. "Subjective causality and counterfactuals in the social sciences: Toward an ethnographic causality?" *Sociological Methods & Research* 50(4):1842–1862.

Aguilar, Rosario, Saul Cunow and Scott Desposato. 2015. "Choice sets, gender, and candidate choice in Brazil." *Electoral Studies* 39:230–242.

Alrababa'h, Ala', Scott Williamson, Andrea Dillon, Jens Hainmueller, Dominik Hangartner, Michael Hotard, David Laitin, Duncan Lawrence and Jeremy Weinstein. 2022. "Learning from null effects: A bottom-up approach." *Political Analysis*.

Alvarez, R. Michael, Ellen M. Key and Lucas Núñez. 2018. "Research replication: Practical considerations." *PS: Political Science & Politics* 51(2):422–426.

Angrist, Joshua D. and Jörn-Steffen Pischke. 2008. *Mostly Harmless Econometrics: An Empiricist's Companion*. Princeton: Princeton University Press.

Angrist, Joshua D., Guido W. Imbens, and Donald B. Rubin. 1996. "Identification of causal effects using instrumental variables." *Journal of the American Statistical Association* 91, no. 434: 444–455.

Aronow, Peter M. and Benjamin T. Miller. 2019. *Foundations of Agnostic Statistics*. Cambridge, UK: Cambridge University Press.

Aronow, Peter M. and Cyrus Samii. 2017. "Estimating average causal effects under general interference, with application to a social network experiment." *The Annals of Applied Statistics* 11(4):1912–1947.

Aronow, Peter M., Donald P. Green and Donald K. K. Lee. 2014. "Sharp bounds on the variance in randomized experiments." *The Annals of Statistics* 42(3):850–871.

Aronow, Peter M., Jonathon Baron and Lauren Pinson. 2019. "A note on dropping experimental subjects who fail a manipulation check." *Political Analysis* 27(4):572–589.

Avdeenko, Alexandra and Michael J. Gilligan. 2015. "International interventions to build social capital: Evidence from a field experiment in Sudan." *American Political Science Review* 109(3):427–449.

Bai, Yuehao. 2021. "Why randomize? Minimax optimality under permutation invariance." *Journal of Econometrics* 232(2):565–575.

Baird, Sarah, J. Aislinn Bohren, Craig McIntosh and Berk Ozler. 2018. "Optimal design of experiments in the presence of interference." *Review of Economics & Statistics* 5(100):844–860.

Balcells, Laia, Valeria Palanza and Elsa Voytas. 2022. "Do transitional justice museums persuade visitors? Evidence from a field experiment." *The Journal of Politics* 84(1).

Banerjee, Abhijit, Esther Duflo, Amy Finkelstein, Lawrence F Katz, Benjamin A Olken and Anja Sautmann. 2020. "In praise of moderation: Suggestions for the scope and use of pre-analysis plans for RCTs in economics." Working Paper 26993 National Bureau of Economic Research.

Bansak, Kirk, Jens Hainmueller, Daniel J. Hopkins and Teppei Yamamoto. 2021. "Beyond the breaking point? Survey satisficing in conjoint experiments." *Political Science Research and Methods* 9(1):53–71.

Baron, Hannah and Lauren E. Young. 2021. "From principles to practice: Methods to increase the transparency of research ethics in violent contexts." *Political Science Research and Methods* pp. 1–8. Forthcoming.

Bateson, Regina. 2012. "Crime victimization and political participation." *American Political Science Review* 106(3):570–587.

Bauer, Paul C. and Bernhard Clemm von Hohenberg. 2021. "Believing and sharing information by fake sources: An experiment." *Political Communication* 38(6):647–671.

Benjamin, Daniel J., James O. Berger, Magnus Johannesson, Brian A. Nosek, E. J. Wagenmakers, Richard Berk, Kenneth A. Bollen, Björn Brembs, Lawrence Brown, Colin Camerer, David Cesarini, Christopher D. Chambers, Merlise Clyde, Thomas D. Cook, Paul De Boeck, Zoltan Dienes, Anna Dreber, Kenny Easwaran, Charles Efferson, Ernst Fehr, Fiona Fidler, Andy P. Field, Malcolm Forster, Edward I. George, Richard Gonzalez, Steven Goodman, Edwin Green, Donald P. Green, Anthony G. Greenwald, Jarrod D. Hadfield, Larry V. Hedges, Leonhard Held, Teck Hua Ho, Herbert Hoijtink, Daniel J. Hruschka, Kosuke Imai, Guido W. Imbens, John P. A. Ioannidis, Minjeong Jeon, James Holland Jones, Michael Kirchler, David Laibson, John List, Roderick Little, Arthur Lupia, Edouard Machery, Scott E. Maxwell, Michael McCarthy, Don A. Moore, Stephen L. Morgan, Marcus Munafó, Shinichi Nakagawa, Brendan Nyhan, Timothy H. Parker, Luis Pericchi, Marco Perugini, Jeff Rouder, Judith Rousseau, Victoria Savalei, Felix D. Schönbrodt, Thomas Sellke, Betsy Sinclair, Dustin Tingley, Trisha Van Zandt, Simine Vazire, Duncan J. Watts, Christopher Winship, Robert L. Wolpert, Yu Xie, Cristobal Young, Jonathan Zinman and Valen E. Johnson. 2018. "Redefine statistical significance." *Nature Human Behaviour* 2(1): 6–10.

Bennett, Andrew. 2015. Appendix. In *Process Tracing: From Metaphor to Analytic Tool*, ed. Andrew Bennett and Jeffrey Checkel. New York: Cambridge University Press.

Bennett, Andrew and Jeffrey Checkel. 2015. "Process tracing: From philosophical roots to best practices." In *Process Tracing: From Metaphor to Analytic Tool*, ed. Andrew Bennett and Jeffrey Checkel. New York: Cambridge University Press, pp. 3–37.

Birkelund, Gunn Elisabeth, Bram Lancee, Edvard Nergård Larsen, Javier G Polavieja, Jonas Radl and Ruta Yemane. 2022. "Gender discrimination in hiring: Evidence from a cross-national harmonized field experiment." *European Sociological Review* 38(3):337–354.

Bisbee, James. 2019. "BARP: Improving Mister P using Bayesian additive regression trees." *American Political Science Review* 113(4):1060–1065.

Blair, Graeme, Alexander Coppock and Margaret Moor. 2020. "When to worry about sensitivity bias: A social reference theory and evidence from 30 years of list experiments." *American Political Science Review* 114(4):1297–1315.

Blair, Graeme, Darin Christensen and Aaron Rudkin. 2021. "Do commodity price shocks cause armed conflict? A meta-analysis of natural experiments." *American Political Science Review* 115(2):709–716.

Blair, Graeme, Jasper Cooper, Alexander Coppock and Macartan Humphreys. 2019. "Declaring and diagnosing research designs." *American Political Science Review* 113(3):838–859.

Blair, Robert A., Manuel Moscoso-Rojas, Andres Vargas Castillo and Michael Weintraub. 2022. "Preventing rebel resurgence after civil war: A field experiment in security and justice provision in rural Colombia." *American Political Science Review* pp. 1–20. Forthcoming.

Bonilla, Tabitha and Alvin B. Tillery. 2020. "Which identity frames boost support for and mobilization in the #BlackLivesMatter movement? An experimental test." *American Political Science Review* 114(4):947–962.

Borenstein, Michael, Larry V Hedges, Julian PT Higgins and Hannah R Rothstein. 2021. *Introduction to Meta-analysis*. John Wiley & Sons.

Bowers, Jake. 2011. "Six steps to a better relationship with your future self." *The Political Methodologist* 18(2):2–8.

Bradley, Valerie C., Shiro Kuriwaki, Michael Isakov, Dino Sejdinovic, Xiao-Li Meng and Seth Flaxman. 2021. "Unrepresentative big surveys significantly overestimated US vaccine uptake." *Nature* 600(7890): 695–700.

Brady, Henry E. 2004. Data-set observations versus causal-process observations: The 2000 US presidential election. In *Rethinking Social Inquiry: Diverse Tools, Shared Standards*. Lanham: Rowman & Littlefield, pp. 267–272.

Broockman, David E., Joshua L. Kalla and Jasjeet S. Sekhon. 2017. "The design of field experiments with survey outcomes: A framework for selecting more efficient, robust, and ethical designs." *Political Analysis* 25(4):435–464.

Broockman, David and Joshua Kalla. 2016. "Durably reducing transphobia: A field experiment on door-to-door canvassing." *Science* 352(6282):220–224.

Butler, Daniel M. and Charles Crabtree. 2017. "Moving beyond measurement: Adapting audit studies to test bias-reducing interventions." *Journal of Experimental Political Science* 4(1):57–67.

Calonico, Sebastian, Matias D. Cattaneo and Rocio Titiunik. 2014. "Robust nonparametric confidence intervals for regression-discontinuity designs." *Econometrica* 82(6):2295–2326.

Carnegie, Allison and Cyrus Samii. 2019. "International institutions and political liberalization: Evidence from the World Bank loans program." *British Journal of Political Science* 49(4):1357–1379.

Carreri, Maria and Oeindrila Dube. 2017. "Do natural resources influence who comes to power, and how?" *The Journal of Politics* 79(2):502–518.

Casey, Katherine, Rachel Glennerster and Edward Miguel. 2012. "Reshaping institutions: Evidence on aid impacts using a pre-analysis plan." *The Quarterly Journal of Economics* 127(4):1755–1812.

Cheema, Ali, Sarah Khan, Asad Liaqat and Shandana Khan Mohmand. 2022. "Canvassing the gatekeepers: A field experiment to increase women voters' turnout in Pakistan." *American Political Science Review* pp. 1–21. Forthcoming.

Chopra, Felix, Ingar Haaland, Christopher Roth and Andreas Stegmann. 2022. "The null result penalty." Unpublished manuscript.

Clingingsmith, David, Asim Ijaz Khwaja and Michael Kremer. 2009. "Estimating the impact of the Hajj: Religion and tolerance in Islam's global gathering." *The Quarterly Journal of Economics* 124(3):1133–1170.

Collier, David, David A Freedman, James D Fearon, David D Laitin, John Gerring and Gary Goertz. 2008. "Symposium: Case selection, case studies, and causal inference." *Qualitative & Multimethod Research* 6(2):2–16.

Collins, Jonathan E. 2021. "Does the meeting style matter? The effects of exposure to participatory and deliberative school board meetings." *American Political Science Review* 115(3):790–804.

Coppock, Alexander. 2017. "Did shy Trump supporters bias the 2016 polls? Evidence from a nationally-representative list experiment." *Statistics, Politics and Policy* 8(1):29–40.

Coppock, Alexander. 2019. "Avoiding post-treatment bias in audit experiments." *Journal of Experimental Political Science* 6(1):1–4.

Coppock, Alexander, Alan S. Gerber, Donald P. Green and Holger L. Kern. 2017. "Combining double sampling and bounds to address nonignorable missing outcomes in randomized experiments." *Political Analysis* 25(2):188–206.

Coppock, Alexander and Dipin Kaur. 2022. "Qualitative imputation of missing potential outcomes." *American Journal of Political Science* 66(3):681–695.

Creighton, Mathew J. and Amaney Jamal. 2015. "Does Islam play a role in anti-immigrant sentiment? An experimental approach." *Social Science Research* 53:89–103.

Cruz, Cesi. 2019. "Social Networks and the targeting of vote buying." *Comparative Political Studies* 52(3):382–411.

Dawid, Philip, Macartan Humphreys and Monica Musio. 2022. "Bounding causes of effects with mediators." *Sociological Methods & Research* .

de Chaisemartin, Clément and Xavier d'Haultfoeuille. 2020. "Two-way fixed effects estimators with heterogeneous treatment effects." *American Economic Review* 110(9):2964–96.

Deaton, Angus S. 2010. "Instruments, randomization, and learning about development." *Journal of Economic Literature* 48(2):424–55.

Dunning, Thad. 2012. *Natural Experiments in the Social Sciences: A Design-Based Approach.* Cambridge, UK: Cambridge University Press.

Dunning, Thad, Guy Grossman, Macartan Humphreys, Susan D. Hyde, Craig McIntosh, Gareth Nellis, Claire L. Adida, Eric Arias, Clara Bicalho, Taylor C. Boas, Mark T. Buntaine, Simon Chauchard, Anirvan Chowdhury, Jessica Gottlieb, F. Daniel Hidalgo, Marcus Holmlund, Ryan Jablonski, Eric Kramon, Horacio Larreguy, Malte Lierl, John Marshall, Gwyneth McClendon, Marcus A. Melo, Daniel L. Nielson, Paula M. Pickering, Melina R. Platas, Pablo Querubín, Pia Raffler and Neelanjan Sircar. 2019. "Voter information campaigns and political accountability: Cumulative findings from a preregistered meta-analysis of coordinated trials." *Science Advances* 5(7):1–10.

Egami, Naoki and Erin Hartman. 2022. "Elements of external validity: Framework, design, and analysis." *American Political Science Review.* Forthcoming.

Egger, Dennis, Johannes Haushofer, Edward Miguel, Paul Niehaus and Michael W. Walker. 2019. "General equilibrium effects of cash transfers: Experimental evidence from Kenya." Working Paper 26600 National Bureau of Economic Research.

Fairfield, Tasha and Andrew E. Charman. 2017. "Explicit Bayesian analysis for process tracing: Guidelines, opportunities, and caveats." *Political Analysis* 25(3):363–380.

Fang, Albert H, Andrew M. Guess and Macartan Humphreys. 2019. "Can the government deter discrimination? Evidence from a randomized intervention in New York City." *The Journal of Politics* 81(1):127–141.

Fearon, James and David Laitin. 2008. Integrating qualitative and quantitative methods. In *Oxford Handbook of Political Methodology,* ed. Janet M. Box-Steffenmeier, David Collier and Henry E. Brady. London, England: Oxford University Press, pp. 756–776.

Fenno, Richard F. 1978. *Home Style: House Members in Their Districts.* New York: Longman.

Foos, Florian, Peter John, Christian Müller and Kevin Cunningham. 2021. "Social mobilization in partisan spaces." *The Journal of Politics* 83(3):1190–1197.

Francois, Patrick, Ilia Rainer and Francesco Trebbi. 2015. "How is power shared in Africa?" *Econometrica* 83(2):465–503.

Frangakis, Constantine E. and Donald B. Rubin. 2002. "Principal stratification in causal inference." *Biometrics* 58(1):21–29.

Frederiksen, Kristian Vrede Skaaning. 2022. "Does competence make citizens tolerate undemocratic behavior?" *American Political Science Review*, pp. 1–7. Forthcoming.

Freedman, David A. 2008. "On regression adjustments to experimental data." *Advances in Applied Mathematics* 40(2):180–193.

Frey, Anderson, Gabriel López-Moctezuma and Sergio Montero. 2022. "Sleeping with the enemy: Effective representation under dynamic electoral competition." *American Journal of Political Science.* Forthcoming.

Gabelica, Mirko, Ružica Bojčić and Livia Puljak. 2022. "Many researchers were not compliant with their published data sharing statement: Mixed-methods study." *Journal of Clinical Epidemiology.* Forthcoming.

Galos, Diana and Alexander Coppock. 2022. "Gender Composition Predicts Gender Bias: A Meta-reanalysis of Hiring Discrimination Audit Experiments." Unpublished manuscript.

Geddes, Barbara. 2003. *Paradigms and Sand Castles: Theory Building and Research Design in Comparative Politics.* Ann Arbor, Michigan: University of Michigan Press.

Gelman, Andrew and John Carlin. 2014. "Beyond power calculations assessing type S (Sign) and type M (Magnitude) errors." *Perspectives on Psychological Science* 9(6):641–651.

Gerber, Alan S. and Donald P. Green. 2012. *Field Experiments: Design, Analysis, and Interpretation.* New York: W.W. Norton.

Gerber, Alan S., James G. Gimpel, Donald P. Green and Daron R. Shaw. 2011. "How large and long-lasting are the persuasive effects of televised campaign ads? Results from a randomized field experiment." *American Political Science Review* 105(1):135–150.

Gerring, John and Lee Cojocaru. 2016. "Selecting cases for intensive analysis: A diversity of goals and methods." *Sociological Methods & Research* 45(3):392–423.

Goertz, Gary. 2008. "Choosing cases for case studies: A qualitative logic." *Newsletter of the APSA Section on Qualitative & Multi-Method Research* 6(2):11–4.

Goertz, Gary and James Mahoney. 2012. *A Tale of Two Cultures: Qualitative and Quantitative Research in the Social Sciences*. Princeton: Princeton University Press.

Green, Donald P. and Andrej Tusicisny. 2012. "Statistical analysis of results from laboratory studies in experimental economics: A critique of current practice." Available at SSRN 2181654.

Green, Donald P., Jonathan S. Krasno, Alexander Coppock, Benjamin D. Farrer, Brandon Lenoir and Joshua N. Zingher. 2016. "The effects of lawn signs on vote outcomes: Results from four randomized field experiments." *Electoral Studies* 41:143–150.

Green, Donald P. and Winston Lin. 2016. "Standard operating procedures: A Safety net for pre-analysis plans." *PS: Political Science & Politics* 49(3):495–499.

Green, Jon, James N. Druckman, Matthew A. Baum, David Lazer, Katherine Ognyanova, Matthew Simonson, Jennifer Lin, Mauricio Santillana and Roy H. Perlis. 2022. "Using general messages to persuade on a politicized scientific issue." *British Journal of Political Science*. Forthcoming.

Gulzar, Saad and Muhammad Yasir Khan. 2021. "'Good politicians:' Experimental evidence on motivations for political candidacy and government performance." Working paper.

Hainmueller, Jens, Daniel J. Hopkins and Teppei Yamamoto. 2014. "Causal inference in conjoint analysis: Understanding multidimensional choices via stated preference experiments." *Political Analysis* 22(1):1–30.

Halpern, Joseph Y. 2000. "Axiomatizing causal reasoning." *Journal of Artificial Intelligence Research* 12:317–337.

Hartman, Erin and F. Daniel Hidalgo. 2018. "An equivalence approach to balance and placebo tests." *American Journal of Political Science* 62(4):1000–1013.

Heckathorn, D. D., 1997. Respondent-driven sampling: a new approach to the study of hidden populations. Social problems, 44(2), pp. 174–199.

Hedayat, A. S., Hansheng Cheng and Jennifer Pajda-De La O. 2019. "Existence of unbiased estimation for the minimum, maximum, and median in finite population sampling." *Statistics & Probability Letters* 153:192–195.

Hellevik, Ottar. 2009. "Linear versus logistic regression when the dependent variable is a dichotomy." Quality and Quantity 43, 59–74.

Herron, Michael C. and Kevin M. Quinn. 2016. "A careful look at modern case selection methods." *Sociological Methods & Research* 45(3):458–492.

Humphreys, Macartan. 2015. "Reflections on the ethics of social experimentation." *Journal of Globalization and Development* 6(1):87–112.

Humphreys, Macartan and Alan Jacobs. Forthcoming. *Integrated Inferences*. Cambridge: Cambridge University Press.

Humphreys, Macartan and Alan M. Jacobs. 2015. "Mixing methods: A Bayesian approach." *American Political Science Review* 109(4):653–673.

Humphreys, Macartan, Raul de la Sierra and Peter van der Windt. 2013. "Fishing, commitment, and communication: A proposal for comprehensive nonbinding research registration." *Political Analysis* 21(1):1–20.

Imai, Kosuke. 2011. "Multivariate regression analysis for the item count technique." *Journal of the American Statistical Association* 106(494):407–416.

Imai, Kosuke, Gary King and Clayton Nall. 2009. "The essential role of pair matching in cluster-randomized experiments, with application to the Mexican universal health insurance evaluation." *Statistical Science* 24(1):29–53.

Imai, Kosuke, Gary King and Elizabeth A. Stuart. 2008. "Misunderstandings between experimentalists and observationalists about causal inference." *Journal of the Royal Statistical Society: Series A (Statistics in Society)* 171(2):481–502.

Imbens, Guido W. 2010. "Better LATE than nothing: Some comments on Deaton (2009) and Heckman and Urzua (2009)." *Journal of Economic Literature* 48(2):399–423.

Imbens, Guido W. and Donald B. Rubin. 2015. *Causal Inference in Statistics, Social, and Biomedical Sciences.* Cambridge: Cambridge University Press.

Iyengar, Shanto and Sean J. Westwood. 2015. "Fear and loathing across party lines: New evidence on group polarization." *American Journal of Political Science* 59(3):690–707.

Jamison, Julian C. 2019. "The entry of randomized assignment into the social sciences." *Journal of Causal Inference* 7(1):1–16.

Jefferson, Hakeem. 2022. "The Politics of Respectability and Black Americans' Punitive Attitudes." *American Political Science Review.* Forthcoming.

Johnson, Noel D. and Alexandra A Mislin. 2011. "Trust games: A meta-analysis." *Journal of Economic Psychology* 32(5):865–889.

Kalla, Joshua, Frances Rosenbluth and Dawn Langan Teele. 2018. "Are you my mentor? A field experiment on gender, ethnicity, and political self-starters." *The Journal of Politics* 80(1):337–341.

Kao, Kristen and Mara R. Revkin. 2022. "Retribution or reconciliation? Post-conflict attitudes toward enemy collaborators." *American Journal of Political Science.* Forthcoming.

Karpowitz, Christopher F., J. Quin Monson and Jessica Robinson Preece. 2017. "How to elect more women: Gender and candidate success in a field experiment." *American Journal of Political Science* 61(4):927–943.

Kasy, Maximilian. 2016. "Why experimenters might not always want to randomize, and what they could do instead." *Political Analysis* 24(3):324–338.

King, Gary. 1998. *Unifying Political Methodology: The Likelihood Theory of Statistical Inference.* Ann Arbor, Michigan: University of Michigan Press.

King, Gary, Emmanuela Gakidou, Nirmala Ravishankar, Ryan T. Moore, Jason Lakin, Manett Vargas, Martha María Téllez-Rojo, Juan Eugenio Hernández Ávila, Mauricio Hernández Ávila and Héctor Hernández Llamas. 2007. "A 'politically robust' experimental design for public policy evaluation, with application to the Mexican universal health insurance program." *Journal of Policy Analysis and Management* 26(3):479–506.

King, Gary and Melissa Sands. 2015. "How human subjects research rules mislead you and your university, and what to do about it." Unpublished manuscript.

Kirkland, Patricia A. 2021. "Business owners and executives as politicians: The effect on public policy." *The Journal of Politics* 83(4):1652–1668.

Klar, Samara and Thomas J Leeper. 2019. "Identities and intersectionality: A case for purposive sampling in survey-experimental research." *Experimental Methods in Survey Research: Techniques That Combine Random Sampling with Random Assignment*, pp. 419–433.

Kling, Jeffrey R., Jeffrey B. Liebman and Lawrence F. Katz. 2007. "Experimental analysis of neighborhood effects." *Econometrica* 75(1):83–119.

Lax, Jeffrey R. and Justin H. Phillips. 2009. "Gay rights in the states: Public opinion and policy responsiveness." *American Political Science Review* 103(3):367–386.

Levine, Adam Seth. 2021. "How to form organizational partnerships to run experiments." In *Advances in Experimental Political Science.* Cambridge, UK: Cambridge University Press, pp. 199–216.

Levy, Jack S. 2008. "Case studies: Types, designs, and logics of inference." *Conflict Management and Peace Science* 25(1):1–18.

Lieberman, Evan S. 2005. "Nested analysis as a mixed-method strategy for comparative research." *American Political Science Review* 99(3):435–452.

Lin, Winston. 2013. "Agnostic notes on regression adjustments to experimental data: Reexamining Freedman's critique." *Annals of Applied Statistics* 7(1):295–318.

Lyall, Jason. 2022. "Preregister your ethical redlines: Vulnerable populations, policy engagement, and the perils of e-hacking." Unpublished manuscript.

Lyall, Jason, Yang-Yang Zhou and Kosuke Imai. 2020. "Can economic assistance shape combatant support in wartime? Experimental evidence from Afghanistan." *American Political Science Review* 114(1):126–143.

Martin, Lisa. 1992. *Coercive Cooperation: Explaining Multilateral Economic Sanctions*. Princeton: Princeton University Press.

McPhetres, Jonathon, Nihan Albayrak-Aydemir, Ana Barbosa Mendes, Elvina C. Chow, Patricio Gonzalez-Marquez, Erin Loukras, Annika Maus, Aoife O'Mahony, Christina Pomareda, Maximilian Primbs, Shalaine L. Sackman, Conor J. R. Smithson and Kirill Volodko. 2020. "A decade of theory as reflected in psychological science (2009–2019)." PsyArXiv.

Mellon, Jonathan. 2021. "Rain, rain, go away: 176 potential exclusion-restriction violations for studies using weather as an instrumental variable." *Unpublished Manuscript* .

Merkley, Eric and Dominik A. Stecula. 2021. "Party cues in the news: Democratic elites, Republican backlash, and the dynamics of climate skepticism." *British Journal of Political Science* 51(4):1439–1456.

Middleton, Joel A. 2008. "Bias of the regression estimator for experiments using clustered random assignment." *Statistics & Probability Letters* 78(16):2654–2659.

Miguel, Edward, Colin Camerer, Katherine Casey, Joshua Cohen, Kevin M Esterling, Alan S. Gerber, Rachel Glennerster, Donald P. Green, Macartan Humphreys and Guido W. Imbens. 2014. "Promoting transparency in social science research." *Science* 343(6166):30.

Mill, John Stuart. 1869. *A System of Logic, Ratiocinative and Inductive: Being a Connected View of the Principles of Evidence and the Methods of Scientific Investigation*. New York: Harper & Brothers.

Miller, Judith Droitcour. 1984. "A new survey technique for studying deviant behavior." PhD thesis. George Washington University.

Montgomery, Jacob M. and Erin L. Rossiter. 2020. "So many questions, so little time: Integrating adaptive inventories into public opinion research." *Journal of Survey Statistics and Methodology* 8(4):667–690.

Morris, Tim P., Ian R. White and Michael J. Crowther. 2021. "Using simulation studies to evaluate statistical methods." *Statistics in Medicine* 38(11):2074–2102.

Mousa, Salma. 2020. "Building social cohesion between Christians and Muslims through soccer in post-ISIS Iraq." *Science* 369(6505):866–870.

Nellis, Gareth and Niloufer Siddiqui. 2018. "Secular party rule and religious violence in Pakistan." *American Political Science Review* 112(1):49–67.

Offer-Westort, Molly, Alexander Coppock and Donald P. Green. 2021. "Adaptive experimental design: Prospects and applications in political science." *American Journal of Political Science* 65:826–844.

Ofosu, George and Daniel Posner. 2022. "Pre-analysis plans: An early stocktaking." *Perspectives on Politics*. Forthcoming.

Paglayan, Agustina S. 2019. "Public-sector unions and the size of government." *American Journal of Political Science* 63(1):21–36.

Paler, Laura, Leslie Marshall and Sami Atallah. 2018. "The social costs of public political participation: Evidence from a petition experiment in lebanon." *The Journal of Politics* 80(4):1405–1410.

Paluck, Elizabeth Levy and Donald P. Green. 2009. "Deference, dissent, and dispute resolution: An experimental intervention using mass media to change norms and behavior in Rwanda." *American Political Science Review* 103(4):622–644.

Paluck, Elizabeth Levy, Seth A. Green and Donald P. Green. 2019. "The contact hypothesis re-evaluated." *Behavioural Public Policy* 3(2):129–158.

Pearl, Judea. 1999. "Probabilities of causation: Three counterfactual interpretations and their identification." *Synthese* 121(1-2):93–149.

Pearl, Judea. 2009. *Causality: Models, Reasoning and Inference*. Second edition ed. Cambridge: Cambridge University Press.

Pearl, Judea and Dana Mackenzie. 2018. *The Book of Why: The New Science of Cause and Effect*. New York: Basic Books.

Peer, Limor, Lilla Orr and Alexander Coppock. 2021. "Active maintenance: A proposal for the long-term computational reproducibility of scientific results." *PS: Political Science & Politics* 54(3):462–466.

Pennycook, Gordon, Ziv Epstein, Mohsen Mosleh, Antonio A. Arechar, Dean Eckles and David G. Rand. 2021. "Shifting attention to accuracy can reduce misinformation online." *Nature* 592(7855):590–595.

Pettigrew, Thomas F. and Linda R. Tropp. 2006. "A meta-analytic test of intergroup contact theory." *Journal of Personality and Social Psychology* 90(5):751–783.

Peyton, Kyle, Michael Sierra-Arévalo and David G. Rand. 2019. "A field experiment on community policing and police legitimacy." *Proceedings of the National Academy of Sciences* 116(40):19894–19898.

Plümper, Thomas, Vera E. Troeger and Eric Neumayer. 2019. "Case selection and causal inference in qualitative research." *PloS one* 14(7):1–18.

Porter, Ethan and Yamil Velez. 2021. "Placebo selection in survey experiments: An agnostic approach." *Political Analysis*, pp. 1–14. Forthcoming.

Prillaman, Soledad Artiz. 2022. "Strength in numbers: How women's groups close India's political gender gap." *American Journal of Political Science*. Forthcoming.

Reiss, Peter C and Frank A Wolak. 2007. "Structural econometric modeling: Rationales and examples from industrial organization." *Handbook of Econometrics* 6:4277–4415.

Revkin, Mara Redlich and Ariel I. Ahram. 2020. "Perspectives on the rebel social contract: Exit, voice, and loyalty in the Islamic State in Iraq and Syria." *World Development* 132:104981.

Rubin, Donald B. 1980. "Randomization analysis of experimental data: The Fisher randomization test comment." *Journal of the American Statistical Association* 75(371):591–593.

Rubinstein, Ariel. 1982. "Perfect equilibrium in a bargaining model." *Econometrica: Journal of the Econometric Society* pp. 97–109.

Samii, Cyrus. 2016. "Causal empiricism in quantitative research." *The Journal of Politics* 78(3):941–955.

Samii, Cyrus and Peter M. Aronow. 2012. "On equivalencies between design-based and regression-based variance estimators for randomized experiments." *Statistics & Probability Letters* 82(2):365–370.

Scacco, Alexandra and Shana S. Warren. 2018. "Can social contact reduce prejudice and discrimination? Evidence from a field experiment in Nigeria." *American Political Science Review* 112(3):654–677.

Schrag, Zachary M. 2010. *Ethical Imperialism: Institutional Review Boards and the Social Sciences, 1965–2009*. Johns Hopkins University Press.

Schwarz, Susanne and Alexander Coppock. 2022. "What have we learned about gender From candidate choice experiments? A meta-analysis of 67 factorial survey experiments." *Journal of Politics* 84(2): 655–668.

Seawright, Jason and John Gerring. 2008. "Case selection techniques in case study research: A menu of qualitative and quantitative options." *Political Research Quarterly* 61(2):294–308.

Shadish, William, Thomas D. Cook and Donald Thomas Campbell. 2002. *Experimental and Quasi-experimental Designs for Generalized Causal Inference*. Boston: Houghton Mifflin.

Sinclair, Betsy, Margaret McConnell and Donald P. Green. 2012. "Detecting spillover effects: Design and analysis of multilevel experiments." *American Journal of Political Science* 56(4):1055–1069.

Skocpol, Theda. 1979. *States and Social Revolutions: A Comparative Analysis of France, Russia and China*. Cambridge, UK: Cambridge University Press.

Slough, Tara. 2020. "The ethics of electoral experimentation: Design-based recommendations." Unpublished manuscript.

Snyder, Jack and Erica D. Borghard. 2011. "The cost of empty threats: A penny, not a pound." *American Political Science Review* 105(3):437–456.

Stokes, Leah C. 2016. "Electoral backlash against climate policy: A natural experiment on retrospective voting and local resistance to public policy." *American Journal of Political Science* 60(4):958–974.

Stokes, Susan C. 2005. "Perverse accountability: A formal model of machine politics with evidence from Argentina." *American Political Science Review* 99(3):315–325.

Swank, Duane. 2002. *Global Capital, Political Institutions, and Policy Change in Developed Welfare States*. New York: Cambridge University Press.

Swire, Briony, Adam J. Berinsky, Stephan Lewandowsky and Ullrich K. H. Ecker. 2017. "Processing political misinformation: Comprehending the Trump phenomenon." *Royal Society Open Science* 4(3):1–21.

Tausanovitch, Chris and Christopher Warshaw. 2013. "Measuring constituent policy preferences in Congress, state legislatures, and cities." *The Journal of Politics* 75(2):330–342.

Teele, Dawn. 2021. Virtual consent: A bronze standard for experimental ethics. In *Cambridge Handbook of Experimental Political Science*, ed. Donald P. Green and James N. Druckman. New York: Cambridge University Press.

Thistlethwaite, Donald L. and Donald T. Campbell. 1960. "Regression-discontinuity analysis: An alternative to the ex post facto experiment." *Journal of Educational Psychology* 51(6):309.

Van der Vaart, Aad W. 2000. *Asymptotic Statistics*. Vol. 3 Cambridge University Press.

Van Evera, Stephen. 1997. *Guide to Methods for Students of Political Science*. Ithaca: Cornell University Press.

Wager, Stefan and Susan Athey. 2018. "Estimation and inference of heterogeneous treatment effects using random forests." *Journal of the American Statistical Association* 113(523):1228–1242.

White, Ariel R., Noah L. Nathan and Julie K. Faller. 2015. "What do I need to vote? Bureaucratic discretion and discrimination by local election officials." *American Political Science Review* 109(1):129–142.

White, Halbert. 1982. "Maximum likelihood estimation of misspecified models." *Econometrica: Journal of the Econometric Society* 50(1):1–25.

Wickham, Hadley and Grolemund, Garrett. 2016. R for data science: import, tidy, transform, visualize, and model data. "O'Reilly Media, Inc."

Wilke, Anna M. 2021. "How does the state replace the community? Experimental evidence on crime control from South Africa." Unpublished manuscript.

Wilke, Anna M., Donald P. Green and Jasper Cooper. 2020. "A placebo design to detect spillovers from an education–entertainment experiment in Uganda." *Journal of the Royal Statistical Society: Series A (Statistics in Society)* 183(3):1075–1096.

Wilke, Anna M. and Macartan Humphreys. 2020. "Field experiments, theory, and external validity."

Wood, Elisabeth Jean. 2006. "The ethical challenges of field research in conflict zones." *Qualitative Sociology* 29(3):373–386.

Yamamoto, Teppei. 2012. "Understanding the past: Statistical analysis of causal attribution." *American Journal of Political Science* 56(1):237–256.

Yao, Yuling, Aki Vehtari, Daniel Simpson and Andrew Gelman. 2018. "Using stacking to average Bayesian predictive distributions (with discussion)." *Bayesian Analysis* 13(3):917–1007.

Zelizer, Adam. 2019. "Is position-taking contagious? Evidence of cue-taking from two field experiments in a state legislature." *American Political Science Review* 113(2):340–352.

Index

A

Abadie, A., 111
Aguilar, R., 242
Ahram, A., 207
answer strategy, 12–13, 36, 48, 92–115; Bayesian, 102; characterization, 93; examples, 13; procedure, 96
archiving, 349
Arechar, A. A., 288
assignment: block randomized, 78–80; cluster randomized, 78–80; complete randomized, 78–79, 186; multi-arm random, 80; nonrandomized, 83–84; saturation, 78–80, 288–291; simple randomized, 80; stepped-wedge random, 82, 283–288; response-adaptive strategies, 83
attrition, 88–89
audit experiments, 228–232; design examples, 231–232
Avdeenko, A., 248
Average Treatment Effect (ATE), 36, 53, 108, 148, 267, 288
Average Treatment Effect on the Treated (ATT), 53, 58, 59, 214
Average Treatment Effect on the Untreated (ATU), 54, 58

B

Baron, H., 323
Bateson, R., 211
Bauer, P. C., 305
Baum, M. A., 305
Bayesian learning, 123
behavioral games, 242–248; design examples, 248
Berinsky, A. J., 266
bias, 123, 129
bias-eliminated coverage, 123
bias-variance trade-off, 143; illustration, 145
Birkelund, G., 231
Bisbee, J., 194
Blair, G. 312
Blair, R. A., 278
block-randomized experiments, 257–260; design examples, 260
Bonilla, T., 337
Borghard E., 208
Bradley, V. C., 189
Broockman, D., 202, 282

C

Carnegie, A., 226
Carreri, M., 216
Castillo, A. V., 278
causal forest designs, 299–305; design examples, 305
Christensen, D., 312
Clemm von Hohenberg, B., 305
cluster-randomized experiment, 260–263; design examples, 263
cluster random sample, 190–193; design examples, 193
Collins, J. E., 266
communicating, 348–349
compliance types, 87–88, 218, 272–273, 276–282
Complier Average Causal Effect (CACE), 54, 57, 273–278, 282
Conditional Average Treatment Effect (CATE), 57, 165, 251, 267–270, 343
conjoint experiments, 236–242; design examples, 241–242
Cook, T., 53
Cooper, J., 283
Coppock, A., 231, 236, 298, 310, 312
Coverage, 118, 123, 129, 131
criticism, 333–234
crossover design, 82–83
Cruz, C., 236

D

data strategy, 11–12, 36, 65–91; challenges, 87–91; elements, 67–85; examples, 12; illustration, 88
deception, 242, 247
de Chaisemartin and d'Haultfoeuille estimator, 212, 214–215

Index

declaration, diagnosis, redesign workflow, 14–17; example, 17
design declaration, 14, 35–40; in code, 29; complete, 118
design diagnosis, 14–15, 116–136; analytic, 124–126; by simulation, 126–130; under model uncertainty, 133–135
DesignLibrary, 32
diagnosand, 15–16, 118; definition, 116, 118; diagnosand-completeness, 48, 118; estimation, 124; examples, 123; statistics, 118–119
diagnosis, 30
diagnostic statistics, 15; of competing models, 135; definition, 15, 118–119; examples, 122
difference-in-differences, 211–216; design examples, 215–216
Directed Acyclic Graphs (DAGs), 43–44
discovery, 299–305; design examples, 305
Druckman, J. N., 305
Dube, O., 216
Dunning, T., 317

E

Ecker, U.K.H., 266
Eckles, D., 288
Egger, D., 292
encouragement designs, 271–279; design examples, 278–279
Epstein, Z., 288
estimand, 10–11
ethics, 322–329
excludability assumption, 50, 89–90, 219, 274
exogeneity assumption, 219, 274
expected maximum cost, 123
experiments over networks, 292–298; design examples, 298

F

factorial designs. *See* factorial experiments
factorial experiments, 266–271; design examples, 270–271
Fang, A., 232
Farrer, B. D., 298
Fisher, R. A., 111
Flaxman, S., 189
Foos, F., 113
Francois, P., 310
Frederiksen, K.V.S., 317
Freedman, D., 255
Frey, A., 310
funding, 329

G

Gelman, A., 116
Gerber, A. S., 89, 113, 124–125, 285, 288, 327
Gilligan, M., 248
Green, D. P., 124–125, 263, 283, 298, 327
Green, J., 305

Gulzar, S., 148
Guess, A., 232

H

Haushofer, J., 292
Humphreys, M., 76, 103, 232, 306, 323
hypothesis tests, 99–102, 113–115, 120

I

Imai, K., 125, 233, 259
index creation, 198–202; design examples, 202
instrumental variables, 216–221; design examples, 221
inquiry, 10–11, 36, 52–64; causal, 53; causal attribution, 58–60; complex counterfactual, 60; with continuous causal variables, 60–61; data-dependent, 58; descriptive, 36, 53, 55–56, 185; examples, 11; outcomes, 9, 55; units, 9, 53–55; values, 9, 54 (*see also* estimand)
instrumental variables, 46, 203, 216–221; design examples, 221
Intention-to-treat (ITT), 218, 274–275
interference, 87, 90–91
interval estimators, 104–107
Intra-cluster Correlation (ICC), 158, 190, 260–263
Isakov, M., 189
Iyengar, S., 248

J

Jacobs, A., 76, 103, 204
Jefferson, H., 202

K

Kalla, J. 202, 259, 282
Kao, K., 241
Karpowitz, C. F., 270
Khan, M., 148
Kirkland, P., 226
Krasno, J. S., 298
Kuriwaki, S., 189

L

Lancee, B., 231
Larsen, E. N., 231
Lax, J. R., 198
Lazer, D., 305
Lenoir, B., 298
Lewandowsky, S., 266
Lin, J., 305
Lin, W., 255
Lin estimator, 255–257
list experiments, 232–236; design examples, 236
Local Average Treatment Effect (LATE), 54, 222, 273
López-Moctezuma, G., 310
Lyall, J., 259, 323

M

matching. *See* selection-on-observables
maximum proportion of subjects harmed, 123, 323
measurement, 84–86; data-adaptive, 86–87; multiple, 86; over-time, 86
measurement error, 85
Meng, X., 189
Merkley, E., 190
meta-analysis, 310–312; design examples, 312
MIDA: definition, 6–7; elements, 37; illustration, 7
Middleton, J. A., 125
Miguel, E., 292
Mills methods, 75–76
Minimum Detectable Effect (MDE), 15, 123, 134–135, 139–140
model, 41–42; causal models, 8, 35, 41–51; functional relations, 35, 43–45; how to specify, 48–51; inquiry models, 8, 65, 306, 307; in MIDA, 8, 35–36, 41–44, 48, 65, 306, 307; probability distribution over exogenous variables, 45–46; reference models, 8, 36, 41–44, 48, 65, 306, 307; as a set, 8; signature, 35, 42–43; statistical models, 8, 113, 169; variables in, 46–47
monotonicity assumption, 50, 204, 207, 219–220, 274
Monte Carlo simulation, 116; for qualitative research, 76; in simulation error, 130
Montero, S., 310
Moscoso-Rojas, M., 278
Mosleh, M., 288
Mousa, S., 263, 344–345
Multi-level Regression and Poststratification (MRP), 193–198; design examples, 198
multi-site studies, 313–317; design examples, 317

N

Nellis, G., 221
Neyman standard errors, 122, 251
Niehaus, P., 292
noncompliance. *See* compliance types
noninterference assumption, 219, 274
nonresponse, 88, 188
nonzero effect assumption, 220, 274–275
null risk, 123

O

Ognyanova, K., 305

P

Paglayan, A., 215
Paler, L., 193
Paluck, E., 263, 311
parallel trends assumption, 217
partners, 326–328,
Pennycook, G., 288
Perlis, R. H., 305
Phillips, J. H., 198
piloting, 330–333
pivoting, 338–340

placebo-controlled experiments, 279–283
point estimator, 97
Polavieja, J. G., 231
Population Average Treatment Effect (PATE), 310
potential outcomes framework, 44–45
power, 124–125, 127, 129, 132
preanalysis plans, 334–337; populated, 340–344
Prillaman, S., 374
principles: Analyze As You Randomize (AAYR), 107, 110–115; design agnostically, 22, 25, 50–51, 87, 112; design early, 23, 26; design for purpose, 22, 25; design holistically, 22, 24; design often, 23, 26; design to share, 23, 26–27; plug-in, 107–108, 110
process tracing, 203–208; design examples, 207–208; illustration, 205

Q

qualitative research, 73, 85, 99, 103, 107, 203–208

R

Radl, J., 231
Rainer, I., 310
Rand, D. G., 288
randomization, 249; inference, 63–64, 113–15; in sampling, 68–72. *See also* assignments; sampling
randomized experiments, 249–298
randomized saturation experiments, 288–291; design examples, 291–292
reality tracking, 48–49
reanalysis, 351–355
reconciliation, 341–344
redesign, 16–17, 137–147; over answer strategies, 143; over estimators, 145; over two data strategy parameters, 141; under model uncertainty, 139
regression discontinuity design, 221–226; design examples, 226; illustration, 223
replication, 356–358; archive, 349–351
Revkin, M., 207, 241
robustness, 113, 123, 356
Root-mean-squared Error (RMSE), 123, 131
Rubinstein, A., 306
Rudkin, A., 312

S

Samii, C., 122, 216, 226, 293–294, 309, 360
Sample Average Treatment Effect (SATE), 11, 251
sampling, 65–67, 67–68; bias, 123; cluster, 70; cluster randomized, 190–193; cluster randomized design examples, 193; complete randomized, 69; convenience, 72–73; multi-stage randomized, 70; nonrandomized, 72–73; purposive, 72–73; for qualitative research, 73–76; simple random, 69–70, 185–190; simple random design examples, 189–190; simple random illustration, 187; stratified, 69–70
Santillana, M., 305
Scacco, A., 278
Schwarz, S., 312

Sejdinovic, D., 189
selection-on-observables, 208–211; design examples, 211
Siddiqui, N., 221
Simonson, M., 305
simulation, 116–117, 125–126; error, 130–131; in MIDA, 117. *See also* Monte Carlo simulation
Slough, T., 323
Snyder, J., 208
Stable Unit Treatment Value Assumption (SUTVA), 251
statistical power. *See* power
Stecula, D., 190
stepped-wedge experiments, 283–288; design examples, 288
Stokes, L., 221
Stokes, S., 193
structural estimation, 305–310; design examples, 309–310
subgroup designs, 263–266; design examples, 266
success, 15,17,19,123,331
Swire, B., 266

T

Tausanovitch, C., 198
Teele, D., 323
treatment assignment. *See* assignment
Trebbi, F., 310
Tillery, A., 337
true standard error, 123, 129
trust game, 242–248; design examples, 248
two-arm randomized experiment, 250–257; DAG Illustration, 252; examples, 257
two-way fixed effects estimator, 214–215
Type I error, 102, 123
Type II error, 102, 120, 123
Type-S error rate, 116, 123

U

uncertainty, 94–95; Bayesian, 94; frequentist, 95
UTOS framework, 53

V

value for money, 124, 329
variable, latent, 198–202

W

Walker, M. W., 292
Warren, S. S., 278
Warshaw, C., 198
Weintraub, M., 278
Westwood, S., 248
Wilke, A. M., 271, 283, 306
Wood, E., 323
writing, 344–346

Y

Yemane, R., 231
Young, L., 323

Z

Zelizer, A., 298
Zingher, J. N., 298